UNCIVIL WAR

UNCIVIL WAR

Intellectuals and Identity Politics
during the
Decolonization of Algeria

SECOND EDITION

James D. Le Sueur
Foreword by Pierre Bourdieu

UNIVERSITY OF NEBRASKA PRESS
LINCOLN AND LONDON

A portion of chapter 8 previously
appeared as "Ghost Walking
in Algiers? Why Aleck Baylee Toumi
resurrected Sartre and de Beauvoir,"
in *Modern and Contemporary France*
10.4 (2002): 507–17.
www.tandf.co.uk/journals.
Reprinted with permission.
Manufactured in the United States of America
∞

Library of Congress
Cataloging-in-Publication Data
Le Sueur, James D.
Uncivil war: intellectuals
and identity politics during the
decolonization of Algeria /
James D. Le Sueur;
Foreword by Pierre Bourdieu.—2nd ed.
p.   cm.
Includes bibliographical references and index.
ISBN-13: 978-0-8032-8028-1 (pbk.: alk. paper)
ISBN-10: 0-8032-8028-9 (pbk.: alk. paper)
1. Intellectuals—Algeria—
Political activity.
2. Group identity—Political
aspects—Algeria.
3. Decolonization—Algeria.
I. Title.
DT295.L345   2005
965'.0461—dc22
2005023761
Set in Quadraat by Bob Reitz.
Designed by Ray Boeche.

In loving memory of
Vivian Le Sueur
and for
Keith Le Sueur

And dedicated to
the memory of
William B. Cohen

CONTENTS

FOREWORD

Pierre Bourdieu

To tell the role played by French and Algerian intellectuals in Algeria's war of liberation, one of the longest and most terrible in history, needed a historian who was both meticulous and rigorous, one not only capable of interpreting archives and questioning witnesses, but sensitive and understanding enough to deeply feel and communicate the tragic experiences of this *Uncivil War*. The best evidence of this understanding and sensitivity seems to me to be the place James Le Sueur gives in his book to the death of Mouloud Feraoun. The whole horror and absurdity of those years of violence and terror are somehow condensed in the savage execution of this writer and his friends from the Centres Sociaux by a group of OAS killers, one March morning in 1962, only a few days before the cease-fire that was to lead to the end of the war. I remember my immense sadness and revulsion of the time, as I revisit the last moments of this fair-minded, generous man (he had read and annotated, with benevolent indulgence, my first writings on Kabylia) suddenly confronted with the violence and hatred of mindless killers, who had turned not only on the man of truth and peace that he was, but on everything he might have been once peace returned. Besides the personal loss of a very dear friend, whose fond but realistic evocations of Kabyle society, imparted to me over the many days spent together in his house in El Biar, still echoed in my memory, I wept for the universal loss of one of those rare men who, at the height of terror, managed to keep his head and even to control the violence aroused by the horror of violence.

Without claiming to offer an exhaustive picture of all the positions taken by intellectuals during the war of liberation, James Le Sueur proceeds by a series of still shots, striving to restore those aspects of the struggle against the contempt and violence of racism that, due to their obscurity and relative inefficacy, are least known and perhaps most tragically admirable. Here he spotlights the dogged actions of the founders and leaders of the Centres Sociaux, dedicated to transmitting precious knowledge and skills to the men and women of Algeria, in the absence of any desire to indoctrinate or proselytize. There the initiative of Albert Camus, who, with his "Call for a Civil Truce," sent out from Algiers on 22 January 1956, violated a taboo with just as much heroic courage as did the signatories of the famous "Manifesto of the 121" in defense of torture resistance. And there again, the unseen and, one may say, virtually futile resistance of those who, in Algiers, were dubbed "liberals": those French men and women, and those Algerians, born in Algeria for the most part, but also in France, students, teachers, railway and office workers, and others, who continually risked their lives in the struggle against racist violence. (I am thinking, for example, of the Comité Étudiant d'Action Laïque et Démocratique, in which I had many friends, and which, in addition to its everyday activities, managed to marshal enough energy and courage to confront the henchmen of fascism in various peace demonstrations.)

If I summon up all these defenders of lost causes who, without historians like James Le Sueur, would be readily forgotten by history after so many failures and abortive attempts, it is because the Algeria of today may be able to find, in the memory of their sacrifices and their devotion to a desperate ideal, a means to break the obsessive circle of past violences.

Translated by James Le Sueur

ACKNOWLEDGMENTS

Throughout the writing of this book, I had the good fortune to work with the most remarkable and kind people. In fact, this work truly would not have been possible without the guidance, generosity, and good will of countless scholars, intellectuals, and friends. The project was first conceived at the University of Chicago with the thoughtful aid of Colin Lucas, Rashid Khalidi, Jan Goldstein, and John MacAloon. When I migrated to France during the summer of 1993, I had the honor and privilege to work with Pierre Bourdieu at the École des Hautes Études en Sciences Sociales. Professor Bourdieu's comments and suggestions regarding my project before and after I arrived in France were pivotal. I shall never forget Professor Bourdieu's encouragement and grace as he and I worked on the translation of the preface and on the parts of the interviews that I used for the book—all the while keeping from me the fact that he was dying. The news of his death several months later came as a complete shock and with a profound sense of loss, and I will always regret that he would never receive the bottles of fine California wine I had readied for him for my visit to Paris a few months too late. Frequent visits with Pierre Vidal-Naquet (and access to his private papers) also played a key role in helping me think through what the French-Algerian War meant and means for French intellectuals. Professor Vidal-Naquet is, in my opinion, the best model of intellectual commitment to ideals and justice that France has to offer. The late François Furet—who was my research director in France—provided invaluable assistance. Professor Furet often shared with me his views on the importance of the history of the decolonization of Algeria for France, and I am grateful for many hours I spent with him. Professors Bourdieu, Vidal-Naquet, and Furet each facilitated many professional contacts without which this project would have remained two-dimensional.

The next group is of special relevance to my project because the interviews they granted helped me come to terms with the tremendously diverse nature of intellectual action during the French-Algerian War. I therefore wish to thank the following for allowing me to conduct interviews with them: Henri Alleg, Etienne Balibar, the late Jacques Berque, Robert Bonnaud, Pierre Bourdieu, Robert Chérmany, Jean Daniel, Issabelle Deblé, Marcel Gast, Mohammed Harbi, Francis Jeanson, Jean Leca, Marcel Lesne, the late Claude Lévi-Strauss, André Mandouze, the late Dionys Mascolo, Gilles Martinet, Albert Memmi, Edgar Morin, the late Madeleine Rebérioux,

Paul Ricoeur, the late Jules Roy, Benjamin Stora, Robert Silman, Germaine Tillion, Joseph Tubiana, Alek Toumi, Jacques Vergès, and Pierre Vidal-Naquet. Without these interviews, I would never have been in a position to draw many important connections.

Without doubt, I owe a substantial debt to many French archivists. In particular, I wish to thank Madame Bonazzi at the Archives Nationales in Paris for helping me locate the papers and archives that otherwise would have been lost to me. I must also thank Odile Gaultier-Voituriez at the Archives d'Histoire Contemporaine for directing me through archival holdings of the Fondation Nationale des Sciences Politiques. At the Center des Archives d'Outre-Mer in Aix-en-Provence, I extend gratitude to Elizabeth Rabut, and at the archives of the Rectorat de Paris (the Sorbonne), I would like to acknowledge David Peycené for helping me track down many hard-to-find documents. In addition, I also wish to express my gratitude to the staff at the Archives Nationales, the Services Historiques de l'Armée de Terre, the Bibliothèque Nationale, the Bibliothèque Musée de l'Homme, the Bibliothèque Littéraire Jacques Doucet, the Bibliothèque Documentation Internationale Contemporaine, the Institut d'Histoire du Temps Présent, the Archives du Ministre de l'Éducation Nationale, and especially the Institut Mémoire de l'Édition Contemporaine. Without the constant aid of these staffs, my project would not have become a reality.

I also want to thank several other archives and individuals. At the Centre de Recherche Politique Raymond Aron, Elizabeth Dutartre kindly helped me discover many new and significant facets of Raymond Aron's career. Special thanks here go to Dominique Schnapper for granting me unrestricted use of her father Raymond Aron's papers. And here I must again acknowledge François Furet for his much-needed help in locating and facilitating the use of Aron's papers. At the Institut Pierre Mendès France, Véronique René, Alain Ménil, and Marie-Claire Mendès France were instrumental in helping me work through the daunting but fascinating papers of Pierre Mendès France. The archival collections at the Centre de Recherche Politique Raymond Aron and Institut Pierre Mendès France proved invaluable to my research and allowed me to gain even greater insight into the milieu of French intellectuals and politicians.

I have many people to thank for letting me come into their homes and offices to view their private papers. To begin, I wish to mention Germaine Tillion for indulging me on many rainy afternoons with café noir as I looked over her papers and documents. I am very much indebted to her and I will always cherish the many conversations and afternoons spent in her company. I also appreciate Isabelle Deblé and Marcel Lesne for trusting me to be the first scholar to use the papers from the Centres Sociaux. My gratitude on this count cannot be properly expressed here. Moreover, although I cannot mention her by name, I would like to recognize the support of the "Frenchwoman," whose private papers, interview, and many friendly conversations were extremely important in the chapter on the Centres Sociaux. Daniel Massignon deserves special mention for allowing me to read over the private papers of his father, Louis Massignon. The late Dionys Mascolo's open invitation to the papers of the Comité d'Action contre la Poursuite de la Guerre en Afrique du Nord was critical for arriving at an accurate understanding of the role of intellectuals in the first years of the Algerian war. Jean Daniel took time out of his schedule at Le Nouvel observateur to meet with me and let me sift through his private correspondence in the comfort of his office. Additionally, I would like to thank Eve Paret and Henri Blachère for giving me the opportunity to look through the correspondence of Régis Blachère. And finally, I give special thanks to Robert Silman and Madame de la Croix for allowing me to use the documents relating to the career of Jacques Soustelle.

I also thank the families of Albert Camus, François Mauriac, and André Malraux for granting me permission to use the papers I requested. Further thanks go to Susanne Merleau-Ponty for allowing me to review the papers of her late husband, Maurice Merleau-Ponty.

I am especially thankful to the Georges Lurcy Charitable Trust for the 1993–94 Lurcy Fellowship, which allowed me to live in France and complete most of my archival research. I am thankful for the experience of living with the Deforges family over the course of several years in Paris. The very generous financial support of the Andrew W. Mellon Foundation gave me the freedom to write without interruption. The University of La Verne provided me with critical financial assistance and moral support as I wrote the first edition of Uncivil War, and I am profoundly grateful for this—in particular I would like to thank William A. Cook.

At the University of La Verne, I would also like to thank the superb reference and Inter-Library Loan department at Wilson Library, whose assistance was critical throughout the preparation of this book: Donna Bentley, Marlin Heckman, Elisabeth Anghel, Irene Morris, Diana Quevedo, Mary L. Peters, and Betty Caldwell. Similarly, I appreciate the many hours that Maria L. Muñoz and Zoila Garcia gave to complete this project.

At the University of Nebraska, Lincoln, I would like to thank my colleagues in the Department of History and in the College of Arts and Sciences. I would also like to acknowledge my three brilliant research assistants, Justin Sheets, David Thomas, and April Kirkendall, whose help proved invaluable in preparing the second edition, and I must say thanks here to Laura Damuth for working with me on the UCARE grants at UNL that make research assistance possible.

As for the writing process of this book, I want to express my most sincere appreciation to several people who read the various drafts, pointed out many changes to be made, and challenged me to come to terms with the material and various arguments. To begin, I thank Georgia Sarroub and Abdelkader Sarroub for allowing me to impose my drafts on them over the life of this project. Abdelkader's many conversations (and disagreements) on Algeria proved invaluable. Dorena Wright read and commented on the manuscript. Above all, I thank the colleagues in my field who have truly shown a generosity of spirit and professionalism that cannot be repaid: the late William B. Cohen, David L. Schalk, Philip Dine, John Ruedy, Patricia M. E. Lorcin, and Warren Breckman. It has been an unquestionable privilege to have been graced with their unflinching and irreplaceable attention throughout the writing process. These six are model scholars—friends who represent the best this profession has to offer, and David Schalk's suggestions were crucial for the completion of the revised edition. But, as a close personal friend and a most trusted colleague, words cannot express the immeasurable sense of loss that I have felt after William Cohen's premature death in 2002. In many ways, the final chapter of this edition was written with William in mind. With William, the profession of history lost its best citizen and an unwavering humanist.

The person who really endured the whole process of research and writing with me is my wife, Loukia K. Sarroub. It is truly difficult to express how much her support and patience made this book a reality.

At the University of Nebraska Press, I would like to thank Elizabeth Demers—whose commitment and talent remains unrivaled in the publishing world—and Heather Lundine, who made vital suggestions throughout the writing of the final chapter and who keep asking for the new text. I would also like to thank Karen Brown for her fine copyediting work.

Finally, I wish to thank my parents, Keith and Vivian Le Sueur, for their inspiration, and my son Sef Sarroub-Le Sueur for his smiles.

ABBREVIATIONS

AIS	Armée Islamique
ALN	Armée de Libération Nationale
AML	Les Amis du Manifeste et de la Liberté
BDIC	Bibliothèque de Documentation Internationale Contemporaine
CAOM	Centre des Archives d'Outre-Mer, Aix-en-Provence
CNR	Conseil National de la Résistance
CNRA	Conseil National de la Révolution Algérienne
CRPRA	Centre de Recherche Politique Raymond Aron, Paris
CRUA	Comité Révolutionnaire d'Unité et d'Action
CSP	Comité du Salut Public
DST	Direction de la Surveillance du Territoire
FFS	Front des Forces Socialistes
FIS	Front Islamique du Salut
FLN	Front de Libération Nationale
GIA	Group Islamique Armée
GPRA	Gouvernement Provisoire de la République Algérienne
IFHS	Institut Français d'Histoire Sociale, Paris
IHTP	Institut d'Histoire du Temps Present, Paris
IMEC	Institut Mémoire de l'Édition Contemporaine, Paris
IPMF, DPMF	Institut Pierre Mendes France, Paris, Documents Pierre Mendes France
MNA	Mouvement National Algérien
MTLD	Mouvement pour la Triomphe des Libertés Démocratiques
MRP	Mouvement Républicain Populaire
OAS	Organisation de l'Armée Secrète
OS	Organisation Spécial
PCA	Parti Communiste Algérien
PCF	Parti Communiste Français
PPA	Parti du Peuple Algérien
RCD	Rassemblement pour la Culture et la Démocratie
SAS	Sections Administrative Specialisés
SFIO	Section Française de l'Internationale Ouvrière
SHAT	Service Historique de l'Armée de Terre, Paris
UDMA	Union Démocratique du Manifeste Algérien

UNCIVIL WAR

INTRODUCTION

Intellectuals and Identity

Intelligence stinks. But not more than stupidity. There are odors for every taste. Stupidity smells of animals; intelligence, of men.

JEAN-PAUL SARTRE, 1958

From 1954 to 1962, the French military and Algerian nationalists fought one of the bloodiest wars of independence of the twentieth century. Even observers accustomed to the stormy climate of French politics acknowledge that the French-Algerian War unleashed a torrent of events with an astonishing and disturbing legacy.[1] By the war's end, France's infant Fourth Republic had collapsed under the weight of lassitude and mismanagement, Algeria's infrastructure lay in complete ruins, an estimated four hundred thousand people had perished (a major demographic catastrophe for Algeria, akin to what France suffered during World War I), Charles de Gaulle's fledgling Fifth Republic faced the Organisation Armée Secrète's (OAS) fascist terrorism in metropolitan France (including several assassination attempts on him), and Algeria was sliding into what would regrettably become the firm thirty-year grip of the Front de Libération Nationale's (FLN) authoritarian leadership. In brief, it would be sheer folly for today's historians to deny or downplay the significance of the war in modern and contemporary French and Algerian cultural, political, social, and intellectual history, especially the effect of its unprecedented violence—torture, terrorism, and military actions—on the French and Algerian national communities.

The war's importance is moreover manifold. It occupies a seminal place in the history of European decolonization; and, perhaps more important, it either forged new notions of identity and nationalism in Europe and North Africa or forced a reconsideration of old ones. Furthermore, the war gave rise to an identity politics that continues to influence debates in France and Algeria as well as academic discussions about identity around the world. Because the war continues to have lasting significance for intellectual history and discussion of Otherness, the primary focus of this work is on the relationship of intellectual communities in France and Algeria to the war and on the identity politics generated by decolonization.[2]

However, one might legitimately ask, why another work on intellectuals? The simplest answer is that intellectuals during decolonization, es-

I

Figure 1. "This week—ground leftist intellectuals 6 francs a kilo. Crouïa 7.90 francs, bicot 6.80 francs." One of eight cartoon postcards created between 1958 and 1961 by Siné (Maurice Sinet), published by François Maspéro in Paris. Courtesy of Maurice Sinet.

pecially the decolonization of Algeria, make a fascinating and captivating story, and key elements of this tale have yet to be told. In fact, most of the archival materials in this work come from private and personal records or recently opened (and declassified) public archives. Much of the material here is thus presented for the first time. Without question, the French state, with its excessively restrictive laws affecting the use of public state-controlled archives, has impeded historical inquiry into the French-Algerian War. This renders the private and personal collections all the more important because, through these holdings, historians can begin to work through this complex and fascinating history without the heavy hand of state censorship of historical documents.

Perhaps more satisfying answers might be that the French-Algerian War was a crucible for intellectuals, that it remains a critical dimension of on-going debates in France and Algeria, and that it has wider implications for discussions of identity—particularly the legacy of violence and concept of the Other. The process of decolonization was, for intellectuals, pivotal for emerging conceptions of identity. Intellectuals were quick to realize that changing colonial relations would alter French and Algerian life forever, and they understood that decolonization—like it or not—would also inevitably affect claims to intellectual legitimacy and conceptions of French and Algerian identity.

Although the French have no claim on originating the concept of the Other, many historians have pointed out that the very word "intellectual" is a French construct, invented during the Dreyfus affair at the end of the nineteenth century. Of course there were intellectuals long before the Dreyfus affair, but from that time on there was general consensus that the category defined individuals who not only occupied the status of thinker but who also intervened, often at personal risk, in public debates.[3] Henceforth intellectuals continued to define themselves as such in the public sphere with pragmatic objectives in mind.

The issue of self-definition has remained crucial for French and other intellectuals, certainly during the four great wars in the French twentieth century: World War I, World War II, Indochina, and the French-Algerian War. The French-Algerian War compelled intellectuals to return to the workshop of identity to refashion their self-definitions of intellectual legitimacy. Some went to this workshop eagerly; a few wandered in reluctantly; others—knowing full well that they were being asked to downsize their conceptions of national identity to correspond to the realities of the postcolonial, super-

3

power era—refused to cross the threshold. For this reason alone (though there are many others), decolonization (especially of Algeria) remains a critical feature of France. This claim alone puts much of the present research at odds with Tony Judt's assessment of French intellectual life during the era of decolonization. Although I do agree with Judt (and François Furet) that many intellectuals fell far short of the expectations (and illusions) created by and for them in the postwar epoch, I do not agree with Judt's attempts to diminish the importance of the French-Algerian War for intellectual life. [4] Put simply, in opposition to Judt's claim in Past Imperfect: French Intellectuals, 1944–1956 that to see the Algerian conflict "as a major turning point is to concede rather too much" (286), this work demonstrates why, precisely, the war must be understood as a major turning point for French and Algerian intellectuals. The injunction to take the war seriously is not to suggest that World War I, World War II, the Vichy regime, and the war in Indochina were not prominent aspects of French history, only to suggest that the French-Algerian War cannot be seen as less important than the rest; and that because it was metropolitan France's most important war of decolonization, it affected many aspects of intellectual and social life in ways these other wars did not. To overlook its unique place in French history and memory would render much of contemporary French and Algerian thought, politics, and culture incomprehensible. [5]

Inquiries into the war are particularly vital today because—with a few very important exceptions—academic historians of France (especially on the west side of the Atlantic) have until recently shied away from the French-Algerian War in particular and French colonial history in general. The fact that France had the second largest empire in modern European history, and that its overseas empire was an integral aspect of French national identity and interests, makes the gap in historiography all the more peculiar. The conspicuous absence of colonialism in the historiography of modern France (again, with notable exceptions) could itself be the subject of an important study. Furthermore, intellectual history remains one of the richest fields of inquiry in colonial history, all the more true because intellectuals (especially republican and leftist ones) set the tone for French colonialism.

If intellectuals were a potent force during colonialism, they were perhaps more active during decolonization. For example, during the French-Algerian War intellectuals (on right and left) intervened in the public debates over decolonization, and they were frequently targeted by the state, military, police, other intellectuals, vigilante groups, and even the fascistic terrorism of the OAS for their real or perceived roles as intellectuals. They were therefore extraordinarily conscious of their sometimes perilous status and the relationship of that status to French colonialism and decolonization. Not surprisingly, some intellectuals, supremely aware of the importance of the term, naturally played off the overlapping symbolism of the Dreyfus affair as a means of endowing the anticolonialist movement with symbolic capital.[6] They tended to see themselves as protectors of the ideals of justice, truth, equality, and liberty. Other intellectuals—especially those working for the Centres Sociaux in Algeria (see chapter 3)—attempted to stay out of the public eye for fear (unfortunately correct) that they would be harassed, tortured, or murdered by French extremists if they were too public about intellectual and moral obligations to fight against the abuses of the colonial system.

As for most categories, however, the more the category "intellectual" was used during the French-Algerian War, the more fluid its meaning became. There were heated debates over just how fluid the category could be and frequent attempts to reach or even force public consensus. The most obvious efforts concerned whether an intellectual, French or Algerian, should advocate French colonialism in Algeria or express admiration for the so-called advantages Western colonialism/progress had brought to Algeria and Africa. This issue alone—especially given the tendency during the 1950s and 1960s to see things through Cold War Manichaean eyes—had volcanic potential to devastate even the strongest intellectual alliances and forced to the surface many preexisting antagonisms. It was as if the heat radiating off the colonial conflict melted the glue that held the postwar intellectual community's wings together. Perhaps the glue was always superficial and would not have withstood the test of time, but it did melt and send many intellectuals tumbling like Icarus into stormy national and political seas. The heat of the war and the flames of the identity politics to which it gave rise forced intellectuals to take stock of their own sense of personal and national identity and, in many ways, either brought them down to earth or left them suspended in lofty utopianism. But just as heat contains the power to separate, it also possesses the power to mold new alliances. Indeed, at key moments throughout the conflict awkward but effective alliances were cast between conservative Christian groups and radical leftist groups. A major force behind new alliances was the French army's scandalous use of torture or violence against Algerian and French men and women.

There were, of course, intellectuals who did not attack the French state

5

for its decision to maintain the colonial status quo in Algeria. One of the most controversial of the French intellectuals whose ideas ran against dominant notions was Jacques Soustelle.[7] This established and respected French professor at the École Pratique des Hautes Études and ethnologist of pre-Columbian societies, last governor general of Algeria, and former Free French minister so desired the preservation of French colonial interests that he was eventually forced to self-imposed exile in 1961 to avoid arrest by de Gaulle's police. Soustelle eventually even advocated overthrowing de Gaulle and condoned OAS actions because "the General" had initiated plans for the final decolonization of Algeria. Mocking de Gaulle all the way home, Soustelle returned to France only in 1968. Ironically, this return came only after Prime Minister Georges Pompidou made a deal with Jean-Louis Tixier-Vignancour (the right-wing challenger in the 1965 presidential elections) that the OAS members would be released from prison or allowed to return to France in return for Tixier-Vignancour's support for the Gaullist candidates in the June 1968 parliamentary elections. As a result, de Gaulle reluctantly granted Soustelle and other fugitives amnesty.

Albert Camus, like Soustelle, posed a serious problem for the anticolonialist movement after his very private decision to abstain from speaking publicly about Algeria out of fear that his position would only provoke more violence against French settlers such as his mother, who lived in Oran (see chapter 4). Soustelle, Camus, and others forced the important issue of whether there could be a nuanced definition of a legitimate intellectual. In an age of extremes, this was no simple question.

To make matters more complex, debates raged within the Algerian intellectual and nationalist communities because many intellectuals from French colonial territories such as Jean Amrouche, Mouloud Feraoun, Albert Memmi, and Frantz Fanon maintained divergent notions of how a so-called colonized intellectual ought to relate to the culture and politics of the "colonizing" nation. French intellectuals and their colonial counterparts were forging new conceptions of intellectual and cultural identity in response to decolonization.

Unquestionably, for intellectuals one of the largest issues related to the status of French culture. According to the French philosopher Paul Ricoeur the reconsideration and reconstruction of French identity ushered in by decolonization required, perhaps for the first time since the Enlightenment, honestly coming to terms with the fact that French culture was not universal.[8] The French-Algerian War and the process of decolonization that

effected this profound break necessitated a fundamental reconceptualiza-
tion of French (and Algerian) national identity in a changing world, a world
without European empires and colonies. So, while French and Algerian intellectuals coped with the loss of French universalism and tried to understand the significance of the demise of French power overseas, they also
had a unique opportunity to create new theories of identity and reevaluate
France's place in the world. The war erupted at the precise moment French
intellectuals, especially the French left, realized that they were entering a
period of crisis.[9] A sudden decline in adherence to French universalism is
understandable given that many intellectuals protesting against the brutality and inhumanity of the colonialism in Algeria realized that the notion
had been a dominant factor in the oppression of Muslims there since the
conquest of Algeria in 1830. Intellectuals (French and Algerian alike) were
forced to move beyond the privileged and omnipresent belief that the universal ideals of truth, justice, and liberty were a priori wedded to the French
Republic. Needless to say, the effects of this realization triggered a profound
questioning of national identity in Algeria and in France.

On a theoretical level sociologists, philosophers, ethnographers, historians, anthropologists, and other social scientists attempted to forge new
and better conceptual models and systems to express the problems and
complexities of identity; these academics were also at work on the practical
level, but journalists, writers, lawyers, and politicians tended to dominate
the attempts to represent colonial identity. The division between academic
attempts to represent Algerian identity (which made identity a theoretical concern) and practical or pragmatic efforts (which had real legal, nor-
mative, and empirical consequences) remains fundamental to the study of
intellectuals and decolonization. There were heated contests among participants: journalists criticized academics and theoreticians for their abstractions; academics criticized journalists for their crude, stereotypical over-
simplifications; revolutionaries criticized academics and journalists; and
academics criticized revolutionaries and journalists. Through these debates
we get a better glimpse at patterns and the politics of identity.

In this way, the French-Algerian War presented intellectuals with perhaps the first and certainly the most complex intersection between a critical
rethinking of their own intellectual identity and the crumbling of an empire.
It soon became clear to many that intellectual legitimacy was going to become more allied with anticolonialism, and many intellectuals consciously
or unconsciously linked their careers to the anticolonialist movement.[10]

Very few (Soustelle and Camus are the important exceptions) opted to attach their careers to an empire in peril. Contextually, therefore, the connections between intellectuals confronting the beleaguered empire and the struggles for intellectual legitimacy were framed by a host of national and personal considerations.

Because the French-Algerian War erupted in the middle of the Cold War, the relationship of Communism to anticolonialism turned out to be a framing motif. Many intellectuals in favor of decolonization frequently moved into the sphere sympathetic to Communism, which was, according to participants such as Madeleine Rebérioux, the sole means of expressing anticolonialism.[11] There were, of course, equally important Catholic and other clusters of anticolonialist intellectuals who kept a marked distance from Communism because they understood that it could hamper the anticolonialist movement. Moreover, many French Communists were put on the spot and forced to agree with anticolonialism in toto (which meant that they would also have to condemn the Soviet Union's imperialistic actions in Hungary and the Eastern Bloc).

The long-standing history of the organization of intellectual life and right-left polarities further illustrated French intellectuals' need for constant self-differentiation and self-definition. One of the most important aspects of self-definition during the French-Algerian War was the development of the notion of autocritique (self-criticism). Autocritique was defined as the intellectuals' methodological attempt to step away from themselves through a process of self-objectification. Many French intellectuals strove to work out theories of praxis (especially in the context of de-Stalinization), and it was mostly among or in response to these efforts that the notion of autocritique was advanced in the French intellectual community. Intellectuals were often forced to define their positions to a skeptical French public and to their peers; autocritique offered them general guidelines for the "public" role of the intellectual and a point of reference when taking up the struggle for the oppressed. Autocritique also served as the means of expressing Cold War soul-searching. In 1959 Edgar Morin wrote in his Autocritique: "In returning to myself—how have I become an Other without even changing?—I want to interrogate myself on a faith, yesterday the source of all assurances, today a stranger and an enemy. I am trying to excavate the subsoil where the beliefs of a generation elaborated themselves. I ask myself anew the problem of thought and revolutionary action."[12]

Nikita Khrushchev's revelations in February 1956 of the violence and crimes committed by Stalin's regime, coupled with the revolutionary and military violence of the French-Algerian War and the voting of special powers by the Parti Communiste Français (PCF) in 1956, increased the stakes for leftist intellectuals engaged in *autocritique*. Coping with the problem of Soviet violence, the civil-war quality of decolonization in Algeria, the paralysis of the PCF, the nauseating violence and torture of Algerians and Europeans by the French military, and the incomprehensible and misunderstood violence of intra-Algerian rivalries required new theories of violence and identity. For many intellectuals, defining violence theoretically implied a (re)definition of the state (and republican ideologies) and, by default, of the intellectual's relationship to the state (and the republic).[13] Furthermore, these definitions increased the tension between those who were willing to fight against the state *for* the state and those who supported it wholesale. To chart a way through the political minefield of the French-Algerian War, intellectuals had to have a methodologically precise definition of politics and the category of the intellectual, especially as more and more intellectuals entered the public arena with their self-definitions in hand.

The penchant for self-reflection and self-criticism became so prevalent that one of France's leading sociologists, Raymond Aron, wrote in 1960 that self-criticism in France had become "a national sport, if not an endemic disease."[14] This was encouraged by ongoing (and often unwanted) contact with Algerian nationalists and intellectuals. Hence, with an interesting twist of irony, Algerian intellectuals and nationalists became increasingly important elements in the struggles among French intellectuals seeking to define themselves and their society. This dialogical interaction became even more important as Algerians offered resistance to the French penchant for speaking *for* the Algerians.

Tracing the political and methodological tensions resulting from intellectuals' *autocritiques* brings me to the introspective turn embedded in questioning the relationship between the French and Algerian Muslim communities. Comprehending how this turn came about during, and as a result of, decolonization is essential to analysis of the relationship between the question of identity and the process of intellectual (self-)legitimation. The French-Algerian War is an incredibly rich area for the study of identity because it represents a point of convergence of so many diverse yet related concerns: violence, politics, morality, intellectual life, Franco-Muslim reconciliation, and nationalism.

One of the most effective ways to understand the complexities of intellec-

9

tuals' relationships with the world is to look at their own groupings and efforts to situate themselves within debates over their role. During the French-Algerian War not even the professionally independent Jean-Paul Sartre tried to separate himself completely from others. There was a striking development of organizations, committees, and other means for intellectuals to assemble. And as they became organized they increasingly found themselves at odds with the values and policies of their nation. According to Gilles Martinet, a former journalist at *France observateur*, one of the most important aspects of the war was the French government's unintended role in strengthening the opposition between intellectuals and the state.[15]

Not only were intellectual unity and identity strengthened by the French government's declarations and actions during the war but intellectuals seldom offered political opposition to the state without having the formation of this unity and creation and protection of intellectual identity as their motive. Hence, intellectuals on the political left and right approached the problems of the war and reconciliation not only as detractors or advocates of colonialism. As the war progressed and Algerian terrorism seemed to culminate with the Mélouza massacre in 1957 (see chapters 5 and 6), the French left was placed in the precarious position of defending Algerian nationalism (but not necessarily independence) and trying, at the same time, to determine the future of the French nation. The extreme violence of both French and Algerian actors in the war eventually forced intellectuals to rethink how their sympathy or antipathy toward Algerian nationalists and the French state fit in with their personal, political, and ideological objectives.

Not all these concerns arose simultaneously, but most intellectuals understood how each issue fed into the next. Those more overtly involved in the politics of the day began to challenge the colonial regime with rigorously formulated conceptions of French and Algerian identity. Finally, the unsuccessful attempt to achieve reconciliation between the French and Algerian people encouraged French intellectuals such as Sartre to use the most radical notion of identity, the concept of the Other, as both an analytical tool and a political ploy.[16]

The fall of reconciliation during the French-Algerian War occurred as Othering was on its way in. Perhaps the most powerful and lasting example of the polarization of concepts during the war is the politics surrounding the construction of the concept of the Other. As it was employed throughout the war, and perhaps not unlike its current popular use, the concept underscores a concern for the relationship between intellectuals' political preoccupations and theoretical attempts to understand identity; it also illuminates how the question of violence relates to attempts to represent identity. However, it is extremely important to recognize that the concept does not enter seriously into the debate until the middle phases of the war—after intellectuals had had sufficient time to digest the war's complexities and after the high-stakes efforts to achieve Franco-Muslim reconciliation had failed.

This is not to argue that the concept simply and magically emerged during the French-Algerian War. Yet, it was on French soil during the 1930s and 1940s that intellectuals planted the philosophically imported seeds, eventually bringing the concept to full fruition. In their attempts to steer clear of the French neo-Kantian epistemological tradition, French intellectuals looked once again to the other side of the Rhine, to Hegel, Husserl, and Heidegger. [17] With the aid of Hegelian phenomenology and German existentialism, they attempted to bridge the gap between interior lived experiences and the rigors of epistemology. According to Michael Roth, the 1929 publication of Jean Wahl's *Le Malheur de la conscience dans la philosophie de Hegel* marked an important moment in French intellectual history because it began the Hegelian renaissance in France. [18] Jean Hyppolite translated Hegel's *Phänomenologie des Geistes* into French, in 1939, and helped retool Hegelian phenomenology with an interpretation of Hegel's dialectic, *Genèse et structure de la phénoménologie de l'esprit de Hegel* (1946), which became an important driving force in French philosophy. Finally, Alexandre Kojève's lectures on Hegel from 1933 to 1939 from his courses at l'École Pratique des Hautes Études—published in 1947 as *Introduction à la lecture de Hegel: Leçons sur la phénoménologie de l'esprit*—profoundly influenced French intellectuals' conceptualizations of the Other. In part, this shift toward Hegel (and by implication the centering of the Other in social theory) in the 1930s and 1940s represented the intellectuals' concern with history itself and with the centrality of struggle (24). Marx's 1844 manuscripts were available to French readers by 1937; the complete works of Marx were available by 1940. With the increasing influence of the left in France and on philosophy, it is not coincidental that the employment of the concept of the Other, with notable exceptions, was initiated by leftist thinkers. [19]

As mentioned above, debates over the construction and appropriation of the Algerians as Other by the French intellectuals in the French-Algerian War were preceded by an initial phase that emphasized Franco-Muslim reconciliation. In fact, some intellectuals used the concept to foster reconciliation. However, the war's later phases placed the question of violence in a theoretical framework—generally a dialectical one, since philosophers like Sartre rooted violence in problems arising from existential phenomenology and the dialectics of the Self-Other distinction.

The decolonization of Algeria involved a war of liberation as well as a civil war in which three main types of violence were propagated: state or military violence (French), the revolutionary or so-called terrorist violence of the Mouvement National Algérien (MNA) and FLN, and the reactionary, fascistic violence of the OAS. The combination of civil, revolutionary, and fascistic war placed French intellectuals, from the right to the left, in the precarious position of trying to eliminate what they perceived as pressing social problems while trying to preserve their own ideas of democracy and justice. Few French intellectuals were able to think outside the hexagonal realm, meaning that their perception of violence was colored by the history of French (Western) revolutionary violence. Another important consideration, according to Paul Ricoeur, is that French intellectuals, with the notable exception of Jacques Berque and a few others, were almost completely ignorant of the Algerian and Islamic dimensions of the war.[20] (The same can be said for FLN writers such as Frantz Fanon.) Gilles Martinet has suggested that part of this ignorance can be attributed to the fact that many French intellectuals sympathetic with Algerian nationalism sided with the FLN (as opposed to the rival Algerian leader, Messali Hadj), in part because the FLN's members were younger than Messali, lacked his Islamic image (beard and religious dress), and looked, dressed, and spoke more like the French.[21] This helps us understand Algerian historian Mohammed Harbi's claims that French intellectuals (and I would add Fanon) fundamentally misunderstood the causes and communal specificity of the violence during the war. For Harbi, the violence—especially the internal violence of Algerians fighting other Algerians—was misunderstood as purely political and therefore senseless. But the internal dynamism of Algerian society, Harbi argued, required adherence to communal rules. Punishments inflicted on those who broke these communal ties were often very harsh, including throats cut, noses chopped off, or lips cut off for smoking cigarettes.[22] In short, Harbi says, most French intellectuals did not understand this violence, because it could not be universalized and placed into a Western revolutionary framework.[23] When referred to by the French left in journals and newspapers, it was called Algerian "Jacobinism," illustrating how most French intellectuals tried to place the culturally specific violence of the Algerians into a Western revolutionary and often Marxist grid.

Violence, identity politics, intellectual and political legitimacy, the problem of reconciliation, and the concept of the Other all merged during the French-Algerian War to form one of the most contested periods in modern French and world history. As nationalist violence escalated and as the French government increased its propaganda efforts, Algerian Muslims—who were made French citizens during the war—became (for many moderate and right-wing French intellectuals) less and less "French," less and less "Western," and more and more "Islamic," more and more "Muslim," or simply more and more "Other." Algerians were literally Othered by French intellectuals out of or into (via quasi-Marxist ideologies) French society (and universal history).

However, in using the Other to stand for Algerian nationalists, the so-called avant-garde Marxist left did little to address the specific, local dimensions of Algerian identity and nationalism and were quite willing to condone the violence of Algerian nationalists because this violence could be interpreted (and therefore justified) as a legitimate response to the capitalist West. Many, such as Sartre, attempted to co-opt Algerian nationalism by spinning it into the vortex of the popular metanarrative, the myth of the Third World proletariat. [24] According to Pierre Bourdieu and Jean Daniel, this ultimately meant that some intellectuals—especially Sartre and the Martiniquais psychiatrist Frantz Fanon—neglected the specificity of Algerian nationalism and Algerian culture. [25] Sartre's and Fanon's efforts had severe, long-standing, and devastating repercussions on the identity debates in contemporary Algeria. It is tragic and doubly ironic that many of the dimensions of today's Manichaean debates in Algeria over authenticity, identity, and language were dangerously conditioned during decolonization by non-Algerian intellectuals inspired more by fantasies of revolutionary mythology than by realities (and problems) of hybrid colonial identity. [26]

Part 1 of this work focuses on the attempts of French intellectuals to achieve Franco-Muslim/Franco-Algerian reconciliation. It concentrates on the practical representation of Algerian identity in colonial theory, newspapers, journals, books, public education, and politics. I also present the corresponding attempts, by both intellectuals and other forces, to sabotage these reconciliation efforts, which depended on specific representations of Algerians.

Part 2 illustrates how the shift from the idea of reconciliation merged with French intellectuals' political concerns to form the full-scale and politically charged concept of the Other. The connection between the abstract representations of Algerians in philosophy, sociology, ethnography, and history was a product of the radicalization of the politics of decolonization. In moving from part 1 to part 2, I illuminate how the representation of Algerian identity was linked to the reconciliation efforts, revealing the interdependence of the questions of identity, intellectual legitimacy, violence, and the failure of Franco-Muslim reconciliation. Finally, in the new concluding chapter I examine the legacy of decolonization in both France and Algeria.

PART ONE

Decolonization and
Visions of Reconciliation

1. HISTORY AND
FRANCO-MUSLIM RECONCILIATION
French Colonialism in Algeria

Westerners do not seem to have understood that, for us, the problem of blocs and zones of influence is, for the moment, secondary. Because we are debating and struggling to resolve the problem par excellence: that of our existence.

AHMED TALEB from prison in Algeria,
December 10, 1957

On June 22, 1957, a teacher in an Algiers primary school asked his class of thirty-two Muslim children to respond to the following question: "What would you do if you were invisible?" [1] In nearly every case, the students responded like this ten-year-old:

> If I were invisible, the first thing I would do would be to go and take revenge on the paratroopers ["paras"] who have brought plenty of misery to my brothers. I would take a rope, I would strangle the last of the paratroopers who patrols the corridors in our area, and I would take his weapons from him, and then I would run up behind the other paratroopers and kill them. And if they dared to do what they usually do, I will torture them twice before I kill them. And it's not all, I would sabotage all their plans; I would put bombs in the French areas, I would go all the way to Mollet and Robert Lacoste, I would kill them, I would go to Djebel-Aures, I would give courage to my brothers the GLORIOUS FIGHTERS [GLORIEUX MOUDJAHIDINNES] who I would find there, I would throw grenades at the paratroopers who come from there, in that sacred place, and until we win Independence, I will carry the flag myself, and, if I die, that's nothing, for I will have finished the mission that Allah charged me with. (Response 1)

Another student wrote that, in addition to stealing "apricots" and "oranges," he would steal jewelry and "kill all the French and the soldiers" (Response 2). One student wrote that he too would steal "apples," "figs," "bananas," but that he would also put twenty-three bombs in the "rue bab azoune," and "rip up his school notebook" (Response 3). Without exception, these children's responses target French civilians, the French police, and the French military in Algeria. These attacks from the "invisible" young fighters illustrate that even children were traumatized by the violence of the French paratroopers. When these thirty-two responses were written, it was already well known that the French military and police had used torture liberally throughout Algeria to end the conflict. Responses such as these from Algerian children help us to understand how deeply rooted the divisions were between Algerian Muslims and the French and to see why Franco-Muslim reconciliation was already doomed.

Franco-Muslim reconciliation had not always been a futile idea, at least for the vast majority of French intellectuals and politicians, and it had powerful proponents. One of the best-known and most respected supporters was the French sociologist and ethnographer Germaine Tillion. When the "What would you do if you were invisible?" responses were penned, Tillion was part of an international commission charged with investigating the violation of human rights in Algeria. As it happened, the children's teacher (a Muslim) gave Tillion the class work assignments of his young students and asked her to take the responses to the French politicians as proof of the war's irreparable damage to the future of Franco-Algerian relations. When Tillion received these letters, her immediate reaction was disbelief. An exemplary advocate of peace, she had worked long and hard in Algeria and in France to ensure the peaceful coexistence of the two communities. However, considerations of how violence had affected the Muslim and French populations had forced her to reevaluate the possibility of reconciliation. After looking over these letters, she took them to the socialist prime minister, Guy Mollet, in order to show him what his policies had accomplished in Algeria and "to show him his future Algerian electorate."[2] Mollet, too, read the letters in shock and acknowledged he had no appropriate response.

After members of the French press found out about these letters, Tillion states, both Jean-Jacques Servan-Schreiber and Jean Daniel (two of the most important journalists in France) wanted to publish them in L'Express. Aware of the reprisals that would surely await the Algerian teacher, Tillion refused to allow the letters' publication. She admits that she herself was nearly devastated by the letters because it was now clear that Franco-Muslim reconciliation had been overrun by the brutality of military and police action (repression, pacification, and torture) in Algeria. Tillion did not finally relinquish all hope for Franco-Muslim reconciliation until the end of the war, though after reading the letters her thoughts were couched in cautionary, if not openly pessimistic, language.[3] The children's letters were all the more shocking because, when the war began on November 1, 1954, very few, if any, intellectuals advocated a complete divorce between France and Algeria. Yet, from the French-Algerian War's beginning until its conclusion with the signing of the Evian Accords on March 18, 1962, reconciliation remained an extremely powerful narcotic and the dominant peace paradigm for moderate left- and right-wing intellectuals; few intellectuals who worked for this reconciliation could accept the idea that the Algerians did not aspire (culturally and politically) to remain French. The French army's repression increased, as the French vigilantes and the fascistic Organisation de l'Armée Secrète (OAS) began to murder indiscriminately, and as revolutionary violence against France escalated, pro-reconciliation intellectuals acquiesced to the idea of an independent Algeria, but grudgingly and only after hurling many caveats at the Algerian nationalists and the French ultras.[4]

Reconciliation did not suddenly appear ex nihilo in the debates over the decolonization of French Algeria. In fact, the idea grew out of French colonial history, was a theoretical cousin of the mid-nineteenth- and twentieth-century debates over "assimilation" and "association," and fed directly into the mid-twentieth-century identity debates and the French government's policy of "integration."[5] By the time the war was over, the idea of Franco-Muslim reconciliation had been relegated to the dustbin of history, and it had lost support on both sides of the Mediterranean.

Since the conquest of Algeria in 1830—when the French monarch Charles X attacked the Ottoman Hussein Dey and overthrew his government—France had maintained an ambivalent relationship with the Muslim population. Algeria first became a military colony; by April 1845, it was divided into three provinces. In the 1860s and 1870s it began to experience a new wave of European colonists who expropriated most of the best lands, leaving the Arabs and the Kabyles with the leftovers. After conquering Algeria, France never fully opened its cultural and political arms to Algeria's indigenous population, at least not without attaching unacceptable strings to the idea of rapprochement.

But just where did the idea of reconciliation come from, and how was it used during the war? According to theorist and historian Tzvetan Todorov in his seminal work On Human Diversity, two dominant themes about human identity emerged in French thought just prior to and during the Enlightenment: monogenesis, which presented identity as universalist, and polygenesis, based on particularistic representations of identity.[6] According to Todorov, the universalism of monogenesis gave way to ethnocentrism, which he maintains had "two facets: the claim to universality on the one hand, and a particular content (most often national) on the other" (2). Some thinkers (La Bruyère, for example) were universalistic in their approach to identity but were not truly ethnocentric; others (such as Pascal) embraced universalistic and ethnocentric views of French cultural superiority because Western values and beliefs claimed to be universal and therefore superior. During the Enlightenment, Diderot, Condorcet, and others put unity above plurality and consequently moved French thought toward a universal absolutism that encouraged ethnocentrism. Todorov argues that Diderot's syllogism, for example, began with his general idea of the unity of nature and ended by making particular claims about human diversity.

Todorov locates this syllogism not in the Enlightenment project itself (since other leading figures did not share Diderot's deductions) but in Diderot's science-based desire to dissolve human variation. Montesquieu and Rousseau (to take two alternative thinkers) moved French thought in a different direction and offered formidable critiques of ethnocentric doctrines during the Enlightenment. Whereas Diderot began with science, which led to an ethics based on science, Rousseau and Montesquieu based ethics on human freedom and saw the perils inherent in scientific ethics.

If Diderot's scientism was dangerous for human diversity, Condorcet's was even more so. As the "last of the Encyclopedists," Condorcet wanted to eradicate divisions between different peoples through the "transformation of the world from an agglomeration of countries into a single State." Ignoring the historical and cultural conditions of each country, Todorov argues, Condorcet's scientism rested on a totalizing universalism: "since the principles of justice are everywhere the same, laws must be the same as well" (24). After Condorcet's death in prison during the French Revolution, his project was adopted by the ideologue Destutt de Tracy, was carried still further by Henri de Saint-Simon, and eventually went on to affect the writings of Auguste Comte.

What is important here, Todorov stresses, is that Comte, the father of positivism, called for a return to Condorcet's scientism. This scientism would, of course, displace diversity and replace it with homogeneity. "Comte believes it is possible to establish—with the help of science—the one and only 'correct' constitution, which will rapidly impose itself on all peoples transcending national differences" (27). Conveniently, in Comte's theory, France would be the epicenter and would export its cultural and intellectual goods to other countries (29). Furthermore, white Frenchmen alone would be able to export their cultural and intellectual goods. In this new "universal state," Comte made important divisions between the "white," "yellow," and "black" races. "Whites are most intelligent, yellows work the hardest, blacks are the champions of feeling" (31). Comte's positivist theories eventually affected other major French thinkers such as Émile Durkheim and Gustave Le Bon.

Most specialists of French colonial theory would agree with Todorov's assessment of the connection between universalism and ethnocentrism within French thought. Most would also concur with his distinction between "racialism" and "racism," a distinction central to the theoretical foundations and justifications for French colonialism.[7] Todorov locates the "flowering" of racialist ideology in the period between the mid-eighteenth and mid-twentieth centuries. During this time there were many active racialist theorists, the best known of whom were Ernst Renan, Joseph-Arthur de Gobineau, Gustave Le Bon, and Hippolyte Taine. According to Todorov, the idea of polygenesis united these four theorists. Understandably, Todorov has few kind words for them because in their own way they each privileged white Europeans over other, non-Europeans. He says that for Renan "The white race alone is endowed with the dignity of the human subject" (111); that Le Bon in the spirit of scientism constructed hierarchies of race that combined with hierarchies of class and gender (113); that Taine's racialist determinism created hierarchies that rejected the notions of a unified human race and equality; that Gobineau, like the others, remained at odds with the humanistic aspirations of the Enlightenment and, like Taine, subscribed to the idea that "men's behavior [was] entirely determined by the race to which they belong" (123).[8] De Gobineau's work, Todorov continues, is particularly disturbing because he proposes a theory of social history that "postulates that a society's quality must be judged by its capacity to assimilate other societies, to subjugate by absorption" (135). The consequences of scientism are there to be drawn: "for Hitler, as for Gobineau, civilization was identified with military superiority" (160).[9]

Raymond Betts offers a similar criticism of scientism as he traces the genesis of the two seminal doctrines of colonial theory, assimilation and association, in his landmark *Assimilation and Association in French Colonial Theory, 1890–1914*. Like Todorov, Betts underscores the importance of the idea of universalism in French intellectual history and colonial theory. Furthermore, Betts demonstrates that the French imperial drive toward assimilation was based on the idea that the French could bring other civilizations into their universalistic credo. This drive toward French or European universalism was felt in both ideological and political arenas. Before the French Revolution France's relations with indigenous populations (in North America, for example) were based on religious assimilation, but afterward the "idea of religious conversion evident during the *ancien régime* was now translated into political assimilation."[10] What made this transition possible, according to Betts, was the belief first in human reason and second in the notion of "universal man" (14), or, as Todorov would have it, monogenesis.

This particular Enlightenment conception of reason and universal humankind led the French to posit that it is not only possible but also better for the natives to assimilate into French civilization because it alone was capable of ensuring human progress. Betts argues that Condorcet gave the idea of French superiority and universalism form in his "expression that 'a good law is good for all men,' " which in turn came to form the bedrock for French colonial policy. By 1848 France was clearly moving toward assimilation without much resistance by intellectuals. In 1863, Emperor Napoleon III wrote to the governor general of Algeria, Peissier, that he wished to see the idea of an "Arab Kingdom" act as proof for the Arabs that the French "have not come to Algeria to impress and exploit them, but to bring them the benefits of civilization" (10).[11] Two years later, Napoleon issued the *senatus consulte*, which essentially granted Algerian Muslims French citizenship on the condition that they relinquish their civil status under Islamic law, a measure tantamount to rejecting Islam, which by 1936 fewer than three thousand Muslims agreed to do.[12] Nevertheless, by the time the Third Republic was in full swing during the 1880s and 1890s, the notion of assimilation had become part and parcel of France's imperial (and national) identity, not only in Algeria, but throughout its colonial possessions.

The idea of assimilation reached its zenith during the Third Republic, precisely when French sociologists and psychologists were beginning to sketch the characteristics of the French psyche. As Betts shows, men like Alfred Fouillé, the author of *Psychologie de l'esprit français*, spearheaded the move away from assimilation. Fouillé was instrumental in helping formulate the notion that the French people were rational, logical, and universal-oriented. Not surprisingly, he argued that France had reached this stage of development through a gradual evolution passed down from the Romans and mutated into the Christian notion of universalism.[13]

In fact, it is possible to argue that the notion of the innate superiority of French society had become commonplace among most *fin-de-siècle* French intellectuals. For example, Émile Sedeyn in his preface to Edgard Denancy's 1902 *Philosophie de la colonisation* celebrated the notion of colonialism and went on to describe the French psyche in positivistic terms. "Two particularities dominate all definitions of the French psyche: intelligence and impressibility."[14]

According to Alice Conklin, in her brilliant study *A Mission to Civilize*, the urge to civilize the world was unique to the French Third Republic and thus rendered a unique form of European imperialism. From about 1870, when France began to enlarge its holdings in Africa and Indochina, French publicists, and subsequently politicians, declared that their government alone among the Western states had a special mission to civilize the indigenous peoples now coming under its control—what the French called their mission civilisatrice.[15]

The civilizing mission, then, generally defined France's relations with its colonies and always left France in the paternalistic position of the educator. After all, France could impress itself on others with its intelligence. Most Third Republican theorists were convinced that the people in the colonies could learn from the more advanced, rational, and modern French civilization. Moreover, because republicanism had been victorious at the beginning of France's modern colonial ventures, French theorists had no difficulty in reconciling republicanism with the civilizing mission. In fact, according to Betts, "The vocabulary relating to the doctrine of assimilation and that relating to these republican ideals were the same."[16]

While republican rhetoric seemed to justify the French notion of superiority over indigenous populations, new theories tying back to the idea of polygenesis were beginning to erode support for the doctrine of assimilation and giving way to the idea of association. De Gobineau's idea of the inequality of races was resuscitated to give credence to the idea that there were elements of civilization that could not simply transmigrate into the psyches of the so-called less advanced civilizations. Ernst Renan's linguistic analyses echoed de Gobineau's racialist distinctions, and Le Bon weighed in on de Gobineau's racialism by arguing that not all races were the same. In his most significant work, *Les Lois psychologiques de l'évolution des peuples*, Le Bon claims that "each people possesses a constitution as fixed as its anatomical characteristics." From this, Betts notes, Le Bon went on to draw up his typology of races: "primitive," "inferior," "intermediate," and "superior" (67).

Other theorists began to follow Le Bon's lead, and the French scientific community grew antagonistic toward the idea of assimilation. Perhaps the most notable skeptic of assimilation as it relates to Algeria was Paul Leroy-Beaulieu, who in his *De la Colonisation chez les peuples modernes* attempted to set the record straight with regard to Franco-Algerian relations. While insisting that some type of "fusion" was still needed between the two peoples, he "used 'fusion' interchangeably with 'rapprochement' and emphasized that what he meant was not a physical union of Europeans and Arabs, but a specific progress of cultural change."[17] Further, he suggested that various remnants of the so-called Arab aristocracy must be destroyed. This destruction could be accomplished by importing European institutions (schools and government offices) and everyday conditions (hygiene, agricultural reforms, and infrastructure).

According to Conklin and Betts, Leroy-Beaulieu can be seen as one of the most important representatives for the French impulse to civilize through ideology. As he phrased it in the preface to the second edition of his work, "Colonization is for France a question of life or death: either France will become a great African power, or, in a century or two, it will be a second-rate European power."[18] Moreover, echoing Le Bon's positivism, Leroy-Beaulieu described the French psyche and its relationship to colonialism in the following manner: "That which has been missing from French politics until now is uniformity [l'esprit de suite] in colonial thought. Colonialism has been relegated to the back seat of the national conscience; today it should be moved to the front seat" (xxiii). Although he argued that France should continue to exercise "intellectual and moral influence on the indigenous youth" in Algeria (513), he also suggested that Arabic should be taught in the colony's lycées (514).

Associative civilizing (my term for the phenomenon as it applied to Algeria) was a nice compromise for colonial theorists because it allowed the French to maintain the idea of their racial and cultural superiority and encouraged them to expand on the notion of an evolutionary and permanent separation between the European and Muslim populations. Imperialism was simply the natural expression of the Europeans' superiority over the indigenous populations under their control. Precisely this qualitative distinction between those who were lowest on the evolutionary and positivist's scale (indigenous) and those who were highest (French) allowed for a practical shift from assimilation to association.

Association, according to its proponents, allowed for a separate form of evolution for the indigenous population because it allowed for the types of variation de Gobineau, Le Bon, and Leroy-Beaulieu advocated. It also allowed theoreticians to mark out another key concept in the identity puzzle: time.

According to Raoul Girardet, the most important aspect of the French colonial idea was the French insistence that they were indeed the bearers of a new category of time for the indigenous populations. With the advent of the French empire, the French argued that they were responsible for bringing progress, technology, education, and order to an otherwise chaotic world. In Girardet's words:

> The Empire is celebrated only to the degree in which it permits France to rest true to its historical vocation, to not diminish in its stature, to maintain security, independence and grandeur. It is celebrated to the degree to which it can assure to the people placed under the protection of the tricolor flag the immense benefits of peace and progress, which allows them to educate themselves, to overcome sickness, to triumph over ignorance, to traverse as quickly as possible the stages of human history, and finally to attain the supreme values of dignity and liberty. There is nothing as constant in the colonial literature between the two world wars, official or unofficial, as the opposition of "before" and "after." "Before" means the time preceding the establishment of French sovereignty, which for Africa and Asia translates into the oppression of man by man, the subjection of the weak to the strong, slavery, the despotic and bloody reigns of the black kinglets or the greedy domination of the mandarins. . . . "After" means after the establishment of French sovereignty, which translates in Africa and Asia into the possibility that everyone can liberate themselves from the old terrors and subjugation, the ideal of profound fraternity substituted for an archaic past and degradation, oppression replaced by protection, newfound security, hospitals for the sick, and schools for the children.[19]

This notion that historical time miraculously began after the European conquest of Africa was not new to the history of imperialism. In fact, it related directly back to the old Roman notion of colonialism and assimilation; remnants of this notion of time can be found in Hegel's depiction of history. What is important is the degree to which the French believed they would be able to change indigenous cultures for the better simply by bringing them into European, progressive time.

By the 1940s and 1950s, a new understanding of history and time was beginning to capture the imagination of French intellectuals and politicians concerned with colonialism. It was possible to separate a progressive notion of time into indigenous time and European time. These times or histories would operate in parallel universes where the force field of European time would eventually pull indigenous time into its vortex. As a result, association gradually came to dominate colonial policy in Algeria. Considered a unique colonial acquisition by France, Algeria was divided into three French departments: Oran, Constantine, and Algiers. The French (especially the colonists) continued to believe that French culture divided time in the colony into before and after, but there was also a growing recognition that the colonial status quo was being challenged because most of the Muslim population (Arabs and Kabyles) were never truly considered French citizens.

Because association was also soon found to be unpalatable in Algeria, another paradigm—integration—was almost immediately offered by the French after the war began in 1954. This is when the problem of Franco-Muslim reconciliation took center stage. It is certainly no accident that the last governor general of Algeria, Jacques Soustelle, who articulated the transition away from association to integration, was also one of France's preeminent anthropologists. As an intellectual, Soustelle unquestionably privileged the French nation as a bearer of progress and civilization. He also believed that French technology, progress, science, and rationality were superior to Algerian indigenous culture. His idea of integration represents a mixture of the universalist overtones of assimilation and the racialist undercurrent of association. Integration, in fact, is a compromise: the child of the marriage of monogenesis and polygenesis. The collision of these two segments of human identity is precisely what gave rise to the idea of Franco-Muslim reconciliation.

According to Soustelle, integration recognized the essential cultural and ethnic differences of the populations in Algeria, whereas assimilation did not. Furthermore, distinct patterns of cultural evolution prevented advocating assimilation. In other words, because of their beliefs and practices, Muslims were evolving more slowly in Algeria than European civilization. Soustelle distrusted Islam and believed it was a backward, regressive religion that had delayed historical progress and the development of reason in Algeria. For this reason, he argues, "Integration takes Algeria as it is, the Algerians as they are—as history made them—in order to bring this province into equal footing with the rest of the French Republic."[20] Accordingly, integration would not mean "administrative uniformity" because the local administrative apparatus would respect distinctions; it would not mean "a colonial system" because all Algerians would be considered French, and therefore equal without distinction; it would not mean "succession" because Algeria would not have the structure of an independent state.

Integration, according to Soustelle, would mean the acceptance of the "Algerian fact." Here his definition is quite specific. Soustelle as a professional academic anthropologist endorsed the cultural differences in Algeria and realized that each ethnicity—Arab, Berber, and French—needed to be recognized as a separate ethnic group. However, regardless of the groups' individual characteristics they were each to be considered French first, which essentially meant that they were not only to coexist but also to come under the rubric of the French Republic. Essentially, this translated into a "separate but equal" doctrine for the Algerian "province" and all those in it. The French national budget would finance the administration in Algeria, linguistic and cultural differences would be respected, and all Algerians would be considered the provincial neighbors (if not brothers) of the metropolitan French (18–19).

At its heart Soustelle's policy of integration was undeniably paternalistic. Consider for a moment a "declaration" he delivered on Radio-Algérie on January, 12, 1956:

LADIES AND GENTLEMEN OF ALGERIA,
For Algeria's own good, she must stay French. Algeria without France would mean poverty in countless ways. Who else in the world would replace what France gives to Algeria? Who else would replace the millions of francs that Algerian workers send from metropolitan France? Foreigners who encourage the rebellion or who give advice to France are interested in Algeria only because they want to drill oil wells and dig mines there, but they are not interested in building roads or constructing schools. I say that the separation of Algeria and France would be for Algeria, and especially for its Muslim people, the worst of all catastrophes. Secession is ruin. . . .

Neither directly nor indirectly, through whatever form it may be, will I allow secession. As long as I am responsible here, as long as I am in charge of Algeria, everyone, friends and adversaries alike, should know that I will not consent to anything which will distance Algeria from France. . . .

27

The unleashing of violence will not bring an impossible victory to the rebellion; it can only increase the number of Algerians who will be condemned to death or who will face destruction every day. There is not a solution outside of France and without France. I only have one goal, one care, that is to clear the way and to prevail. I will attain it if you help me, if you give me your support and your confidence in the task I am undertaking. Thus, and only thus, will we be able to re-establish peace in dignity and union.[21]

Soustelle believed that France and Algeria could never be separated; there was no solution for Algeria outside France; the Algerians would be happier, and in a sense better off, if they remained connected to France. In other words, French colonial philosophies had taken two steps forward and three steps back since Condorcet's universalism, de Gobineau's racialism, and Soustelle's integration. Two steps forward, assimilation to association; three steps back, association, assimilation, integration.

Unfortunately for Soustelle, his dreams of a peaceful union between the benevolent French motherland and her obedient overseas territory could not be realized; very few Algerians could be tricked by his linguistic legerdemain. France had simply waited too long and had missed the opportunity to deal peacefully with the Algerian people. As a result, many Algerians ceased to identify with France, and there was a growing sense of division between the French and non-French populations in Algeria.

This is not to suggest, however, that the Algerians themselves had a clear sense of identity. Many, such as the leading Algerian intellectual Mouloud Feraoun, saw themselves as colonial hybrids. He wrote in his journal of the war: "What am I, dear God? Is it possible that as long as there are labels, there is not one for me? Which is mine? Can somebody tell me what I am! Of course, they want me to pretend that I am wearing a label because they pretend to believe in it. I am very sorry, but this is not enough."[22] A few months later he wrote: "The French, the Kabyle, the soldier, and the *fellagha* [the rebels] scare me. I am scared of myself. The French are inside me and the Kabyle are inside me. I feel disgust for those who kill, not because they want to kill me but because they have the courage to kill" (90).

Feraoun was not alone in his personal struggle to depict the effects of colonialism and the lived anxieties of colonial hybridity. In the words of another prominent Kabyle intellectual, Jean Amrouche, "The colonized lives in hell, isolated and introverted, without communication with the Other, uprooted from his history and his myths, cursed."[23] Not surprisingly, the "hell" in which the colonized lived was precisely Soustelle's earthly paradise. In January 1956, at a meeting of the Comité d'Action des Intellectuels contre la Poursuite de la Guerre en Afrique du Nord (see chapter 2), Amrouche called himself an "integrated native." Yet a few months later, in the March–April issue of *Économie et humanisme*, he wrote that he "represented, to a high degree of perfection, the *assimilated native*" but that he was certainly "no partisan of assimilation."[24]

The reasons for Amrouche's rejection of assimilation were clear: it provoked an identity crisis for the natives. "The Algerian tragedy," therefore, was not an exterior event. "The battlefield is in me: no parts of my mind and soul belong *at the same time* to the two camps that are killing themselves. I am Algerian, I believe myself to be fully French. France is the spirit of my soul, but Algeria is the soul of my spirit." Ironically, Feraoun and Amrouche had somewhat sympathetic views concerning French culture because they were elite intellectuals whose careers were made in the French-speaking publishing world.[25] Nevertheless, they both exhibited profoundly nuanced senses of personal, ethnic identity.

Although French intellectuals were often sympathetic to anticolonial critiques offered by Algerian intellectuals, they were much more at a loss when dealing with the anticolonialism of the subaltern, the non-intellectuals in the colonies. In part, this ambivalence arose from the fact that no one knew the degree to which other Algerians would want to preserve relations with France should independence occur. It took words from Algerians like Djamila Boupacha—a young Algerian Muslim woman accused of being a "terrorist" who was catapulted into French public opinion when Simone de Beauvoir, Gisèle Halimi, Germaine Tillion, and other prominent French intellectuals came to her defense—to make the French understand that Algerians wanted complete political independence. Boupacha phrased it in the following manner: "[A]ll of you in France must get it into your heads that what we feel isn't hatred. We just want to be like you, like the other African nations, like any other normal person—we want to be free."[26] Boupacha's words were all the more powerful after she had become (like many others) a "symbol" of French injustice and inhumanity when it was revealed that she had been raped with a bottle and tortured by the French army in March 1960 (see chapter 5).[27]

Many other instances illustrated Algerians' desire to distance themselves from France and Franco-Muslim reconciliation. "L'Affaire Guerroudj" involved two teachers in Algeria, Jacqueline and Abdelkader Guerroudj, a husband and wife. They were sentenced to death for being accomplices of Fernand Yveton, the first French citizen to receive the death penalty for his failed attempt to plant explosives in an electrical and gas building in Algeria in November 1956. Jacqueline, of French origin, and Abdelkader, of Algerian origin, were condemned but later freed. In Abdelkader Guerroudj's trial declaration in December 1957, he stated the problem plainly:

> No one can force the Algerians to feel French. But if Algeria does not want it, does not want to be French, if it seeks independence, is that to say that this independence should be made against France?
> No! And it is not because of the commodities of language; I am sure that we will need material, technicians, engineers, doctors, and professors to construct our country; it is to France which we address ourselves [for this] first. I believe that would be in the true interest of both of our countries.
> It is not in the interest of France to have valets ready at every moment here to run to the call of the most powerful master, but friends who have freely consented to this friendship. [28]

Hence, by his and many other Algerians' admissions, there was, at least until the final years of the war, a sense that the Algerians wanted to continue some of their former relations with France. Most Algerian nationalists who argued this were very well aware of the growing importance of technology and desired to modernize Algeria after independence.

However, an awareness of the fact that a post-independence Algeria would require technical assistance from France did not imply that Algerians would automatically wish to retain French identity or pursue Franco-Muslim reconciliation. Neither can we conclude that all Algerians rejected every aspect of French culture. And for all concerned it became increasingly clear that violence would play a large role in separating French and Algerians. Yet, contrary to what many claimed after independence, few Algerians immediately advocated absolute separation from France when the war broke out because most agreed that, like it or not, to some degree Algeria would need French support after liberation. The problem for French and Algerian intellectuals confronting violence and reconciliation was that intellectual and citizen responsibilities were often seen by intellectuals and state alike to be in conflict.

Although there was tremendous ambiguity concerning the identity of

Algerians and even the French during the war, various forms of colonial policy proved to be incompatible with the Algerian fact. Assimilation, association, and integration had failed, and, returning to the letters of the "invisible" children, cited at the beginning of this chapter, it became evident that reconciliation would never work. While adults struggled with problems such as colonial hybridity, children seem to have had a clearer sense that the French violence against them and their families had rendered it impossible for them to identify with France. Whereas for many Algerians (such as Feraoun and Amrouche) the "enemy" was both within and without, the children viewed the enemy as external and as other than their Algerian selves: the enemy were the French "paras," as purely and simply as only children can see. Extreme violence, especially that of the military's pacification, had destroyed the credibility of reconciliation. Consequently reconciliation, despite the best efforts of well-intentioned intellectuals such as Germaine Tillion, was truly doomed to failure.

2. IMBROGLIOS AND INTELLECTUAL LEGITIMACY

Anticolonialism and the Comité d'Action

I do not bury myself in a narrow particularism. But I do not want to lose myself in a limitless universalism. There are two ways to lose oneself: through a segregation walled in by particularism or through a dilution in the "universal."

AIMÉ CÉSAIRE, October 24, 1956

Even before the outbreak of the French-Algerian War on November 1, 1954, many French intellectuals had condemned their government's attempt to maintain its colonial regime in North Africa and elsewhere. Some, such as Jean-Paul Sartre, went further by urging French workers and colonized peoples to unite as an international force in order to cast off the yoke of bourgeois capitalist oppression.[1] Yet at the outset of the war very few French intellectuals (including Sartre) were able to think of Algeria as being completely independent from France. In fact the word *independence*, according to *pied noir* writer and journalist Jean Daniel, was heard by many French for the first time when the colonists in Algeria began to use the term in voicing their dissatisfaction with the French metropolitan government.[2]

If French intellectuals had a difficult time conceiving of full-scale independence, the French government was far more intransigent. The reaction of the minister of the interior, François Mitterrand, to the 1954 uprising of Algerian nationalists was simple: "Algeria is France. And France will recognize no authority in Algeria other than her own."[3] Initially, protests against the government's position emanated from the left-wing intelligentsia. Three months after the Algerian revolution commenced, French politicians turned to a well-respected liberal intellectual to help bring the situation under control and quiet intellectual protests. When Jacques Soustelle was nominated to the post of governor general of Algeria on January 25, 1955, by Prime Minister Pierre Mendès France, later confirmed by Edgar Faure, few could have predicted that the political appointment would have had such a tremendous influence on the debates over postwar intellectual legitimacy.[4]

By the end of his term in February 1956, Soustelle had done more than any other intellectual to shape the debates over the proper role of intellectuals during the war; he was the first major voice to challenge the burgeoning, post–1945 notion of intellectual engagement that linked intellectual legitimacy to the anticolonialist movement. Just as antifascism had from before World War II, anticolonialism emerged from the highly politicized battles of independence as the endorsed position of French intellectuals. This endorsement would go mostly unchallenged until the advent of Algeria's bloody civil war in the 1990s.

The encounter between Soustelle and the anticolonialist intellectuals during the first two years of the French-Algerian War illustrates the degree to which competition for the reconstruction of postwar French intellectual identity was submerged within the debates over Algerian nationalism and French anticolonialism. Soustelle was a first-rate academic anthropologist, and his effort to maintain French sovereignty in Algeria was important to address. [5] However, the real provocation in the debates over intellectual legitimacy resulted from Soustelle's highly publicized appropriation of the title "intellectual" to legitimize his political career.

Intellectually, Soustelle's credentials were extraordinary. Born a French Huguenot in 1912, Soustelle entered the École Normale Supérieure (ENS) in 1928 at the top of his class. By 1932 he had passed his *agrégation*, graduating with the highest grade in philosophy and breaking the ENS record; by 1935 he had reoriented his interest toward ethnology, in which he obtained his doctorate at the Sorbonne. From 1932 to 1935 he traveled on scientific missions to explore the little known regions of Mexico; in 1937 he was named assistant director of the Musée de l'Homme in Paris. Just before the outbreak of World War II, he gave courses on his ethnographic research at the École Coloniale. An expert on Aztec civilization, Soustelle charted the effects of the Spanish conquests on South American Indians and was quite aware of both the positive and negative transformative effects of Western European civilization on non-Western societies.

Soustelle was equally successful as a politician. His early reputation was that of a radical republican and, although he never joined, he was close to the PCF. [6] Because he had a reputation as a left-wing antifascist, he seemed a logical choice for the post in Mendès France's socialist government. Ironically, the right-wing French community in Algeria, which would grow to adore Soustelle, protested vehemently against his appointment because of his earlier radicalism. Aside from his unflinching antifascism, Soustelle had one specific qualification the right-wing *colons* distrusted: he was an intellectual, an ethnologist.

Soustelle entered Algeria as a reformist. He attempted to win support for France among Algerians by instituting economic and political programs that would clear the path for continued cooperation between French and Algerians. Concentrating on the implementation of the Organic Law of 1947, which recognized Algeria's civic personality and financial autonomy, he sought Algerians' eventual political enfranchisement. He called this program "integration"; it would recognize the distinct character of Algeria but keep it French. Soustelle was immediately handicapped, however, by two factors: he had been nominated by Mendès France but put in place by Edgar Faure, who was much more conservative, and he faced open hostility to his political reforms from a French-dominated Algerian Assembly.

Soustelle's policy of gradual reform met with another monumental obstacle, the escalation of terror and violence, which proved to be the bête noire of his tenure as governor general. The massacres in the beautiful coastal city of Philippeville on August 20, 1955, one of the bloodiest days of the revolution, highlighted the problem violence posed to Soustelle's reforms. On August 20, the FLN Wilaya Two section of Algeria, led by Youssef Zighout and his second in command, Lakhdar Ben Tobbal, decided to bring the revolution to the civilians. According to John Ruedy, the FLN's decision to massacre French and Muslims was largely an effort to create mass support for the nationalist movement by creating an atmosphere of deadly intercommunal tension.[7] The FLN killed 123 people in and around Philippeville, 71 of them Europeans; among the Muslims were several Algerian politicians.

The French reaction was swift and severe. The day after Philippeville, Soustelle went to inspect the city. He was horrified by the sight of children with slit throats and evidence of other indiscriminate attacks on women and children, and ordered massive reprisals against the "rebels" responsible.[8] As a result, the FLN claimed that twelve thousand Muslims were killed.[9] Soustelle swiftly labeled the nationalist violence racist and barbaric. November 1 and August 20 fueled Soustelle's claim that the "aggression was always the action of our adversaries."[10] But who, exactly, were France's adversaries in Algeria, according to Soustelle?

Before Philippeville, on June 1, 1955, Soustelle had written a nineteen-page quasi-anthropological "confidential" description of the Algerian situation that drew up a typology of the so-called Muslim personality exemplified by six possible groups: (1) pseudo-elected Muslims who were "installed in their chairs due to fraudulent elections"; (2) traditionalists who represented the old Arab families firmly connected to France; (3) Muslims tied to French republicanism and desiring integration into France as soon as possible; (4) "federalists" who, like Ferhat Abbas, wanted an Algerian state tied to France; (5) nationalists like Messali Hadj who were unwilling to allow Algeria to remain French but who were also far from accepting terrorist violence; and (6) the Comité Révolutionnaire d'Unité et d'Action (CRUA), the real leadership of the FLN, who conceived France as the ultimate enemy and decolonization as a "holy war." [11] For Soustelle the politician, one of the most important aspects of the war was to protect Algerians from the terrorism of those in the sixth category. Yet, important as terrorism was, the real problem lay "elsewhere": "it consist[ed] in not allowing the masses and the Muslim elites to slide toward dissidence today and tomorrow, in any case, for the short term" (18). [12]

On November 22, 1955, an administrative circular was written for civil and military authorities titled "The Proper Idea to Have of the Muslims in the Struggle Against Terrorism." Soustelle, more sensitive to revolutionary violence, defined the nationalists as "[t]he implacable rebels [who] are only a small minority of sectarians, fanatics, and criminals of common law to which are added the young, abused by deceitful talk, and sometimes the jobless driven to desperate solutions." [13] Having depicted Algerian nationalists as "criminals" and "fanatics" with a negative influence on the youth, Soustelle interpreted his actions as governor general to be "defensive," for the protection of both France and Algeria. For Soustelle, the Muslims' offensive aggression and what he considered to be the politics of Cairo and the CRUA (controlled, he argued, by Gamal Abdel Nasser, the exterior head of the Algerian nationalist movement) constituted something very similar to the Hitlerian threat.

In reality, the overzealous French military reactions to Philippeville destroyed the last chances of political moderation, forcing many of the remaining Algerian Muslims who had formally supported continued cooperation between France and Algeria to part company with Soustelle. For example, and much to Soustelle's chagrin, on September 26, the Algerian Muslims elected to the Second College (the Muslim and/or non-European representative body in the Algerian Assembly) formally rejected further collaboration with the French in their Declaration of 61, which condemned the "blind repression that strikes a considerable number of innocents." [14] The declaration effectively ended the policy of integration, now considered "dépassée"; it represented a tremendous change in the attitudes of the Muslim politicians, led by Dr. Mohammed Saleh Bendjelloul, who had previously been willing to follow Soustelle's reforms. With its affirmation of the "idea of the Algerian nation," it jeopardized Soustelle's reformist, political agenda.[15]

The Founding of the Comité d'Action

Another menacing challenge to Soustelle's politics came from intellectuals inside France. On November 5, 1955, in the Salle Wagram in Paris, the Comité d'Action des Intellectuels contre la Poursuite de la Guerre en Afrique du Nord was founded by Dionys Mascolo and Louis-René des Forêts (both writers and editors at Gallimard), Robert Antelme (a writer), and Edgar Morin (a sociologist and researcher at the Centre National de la Recherche Scientifique since 1950), who declared: "In addressing ourselves against this war [in Algeria], we defend our own proper principles and liberties. The war in North Africa, in fact, puts the Republic in danger."[16] The four initiators of the Comité wanted to assemble a federation of intellectuals who would fight against the colonial regime and emphasize its independence from political parties.[17] Their success was astonishing. In a very short time they collected the signatures of hundreds of writers, artists, professors, and journalists on their first manifesto, which called for all like-minded intellectuals and writers to join the struggle against repression, racism, and blocked negotiations, and for liberation of the African continent.

Despite a handful of intellectuals unwilling to support the manifesto, many of Soustelle's close friends had signed against his policies, rendering him painfully aware of the full implications of a committee of intellectuals gathering in opposition to the government he was commissioned to protect.[18] This left Soustelle, as both intellectual and politician, in an awkward position. In response to the Comité, on November 7, he began a polemic concerning the self-representation of the intellectual that would have repercussions throughout the French-Algerian War and beyond. In his press conference that day, Soustelle challenged the right of the newly founded Comité d'Action to speak for the Algerian nationalists' cause and address the public as intellectuals.

A few weeks later on November 26, Soustelle published his "A Letter of an Intellectual to a Few Others" in *Combat*. The title hints at the internal contours of the debate; it was not a response to the Comité per se but rather a letter addressed to "a few" intellectuals, those men Soustelle considered his peers. With a macho zing, Soustelle dismissed the women who signed this manifesto with the contemptuous term "demoiselles."[19] He began by acknowledging the presence on the Comité of some of his male friends and respected colleagues and continued by emphasizing that even his political career had caused him to abandon his academic posts. [20] He expressed his firm belief in the value of thought and research. The intellectual, according to Soustelle, had an important role to play in public life, but this role could not consist of substituting "vague passionate images" for the rigors worthy of the profession.

Soustelle did not dispute the notion of political engagement but rather attacked the Comité for what he considered its carelessness and dishonesty. If intellectuals were to engage in politics with organs like the Comité they are "only justified if they behave in this instance and more than ever as intellectuals, that is to say with concern for honesty and clarity which are in some respects our mark." [21] Likewise, if public opinion attached high importance to the words of a professor at the Sorbonne, it was because the public trusted a professor to maintain "strict impartiality." Whether or not Soustelle actually believed in the mythical notion of intellectual objectivity is not entirely clear; nevertheless, he insisted that the intellectual's special social status depended on objectivity, and this so-called impartiality could not be compromised by participation in trends such as anticolonialism.

In the spirit of impartiality, Soustelle also announced that he would use his academic skills to "analyze" the manifesto, to illustrate the "weakness" of the Comité's arguments, and to point out its "demagogic slogans." He insisted that the Comité was incorrect to use the term *war* to describe the events in Algeria. Today, Soustelle's taking issue with the term *war* seems peculiar, especially since the French military had deployed eighty thousand soldiers in Algeria in 1954. By autumn 1956 France had increased its forces to over four hundred thousand troops. Yet, to Soustelle and those officially in control of the French state, Algeria was France and France could not be at war with itself. This went beyond mere semantics for Soustelle because, if France was not at war, Algerian nationalists could be deemed "terrorists" and "outlaws" (les hors-la-loi). [22] Under French jurisdiction and subject to French laws, Algerian nationalists acted in civil disobedience but were not fighting a war. Soustelle argued that the very use of the term *war* was inappropriate for the Algerian situation and was used by the Comité only to provoke a "guilt complex" in the French. The current crisis was a "very particular state of things"—but not a "war."

During this "very particular state of things," Soustelle's view of the Algerian "rebels" solidified into loathing. His partiality for France's colonial adventure led to a willful, politicized sleight of hand by substituting the word *rebels* for *terrorists* to denote Algerian nationalists. This stratagem corresponded to his desire to legitimate his own intellectual and political identity vis-à-vis the conflict. As a colonial administrator, Soustelle blamed the violence on the indigenous population that repudiated France. As an anthropologist, his views were more curious. He remained devoted to the universalism of French grandeur, which meant that he refused to fault France for years of colonial oppression and denial of basic democratic rights to the Muslim majority. Indeed he wanted both reforms and repression, and he believed that only by striking a proper balance between these two issues would he be able to save French Algeria.

Soustelle's blatant neglect of France's historical role in the oppression of Algerian Muslims and his political decisions to intensify repression can be explained by his suspicion of Islam. In his "Letter of an Intellectual to a Few Others," he argued that Algerian leaders like Ahmed Ben Bella demanded the destruction of all that was European in North Africa, making an analogy between Hitler's final solution and the Algerian Muslims' rejection of the French empire. In the end, Soustelle argued, the Muslims would demand conversion to Islam of the remaining Algerians and create a "theocratic state" that would be "a racist member of the Arab League."[23] The outcome would be a united Arab front that would threaten Western democracies. Hence, according to him, the true racists were the Arabs, not the French. If France ceded to the threat of terrorism it would condemn Algeria forever to this totalitarian, Arab-based racism.

Soustelle's desire to represent Algerians and Arabs as racists and dangerous in his open "Letter" was not aberrant or written in haste. For example, along with a personal letter written on March 30, 1956, to Paul Rivet, Soustelle enclosed a copy of a speech he had just delivered at a conference designed to create a "large union" to "clarify public opinion on Algeria."[24] Besides restating his claim that the leaders of the Algerian revolution were "assassins without mercy" and "pitiful hostages of terror," he repeated his diatribe against the "pan-Arab" threat. All the while, his depiction of the French role in Algeria remained benign, if not heroic. France, according to him, had never abandoned its democratic principles in Algeria, nor had it systematically tried to exterminate a population, nor was it guilty of forced religious conversion—to which Islam aspired. The logic of his argument, as he himself concluded, was that French military and civil forces currently attempting to "pacify" Algeria merely sought the end of terror for both French and Muslims. The "pacification of hearts" in tandem with systematic economic and social reform would, he argued, have ended the current drama and transformed Algeria into an advanced society on the scale of metropolitan France.

The following week, on December 3, the Comité published its "Response to the Governor General of Algeria," which focused on self-representation of the legitimate intellectual and the representation of the Algerian nationalists. The Comité characterized intellectuals as those who can use "scientific rigor" to analyze a situation as complicated as Algeria.[25] The Comité attacked Soustelle for intellectually failing to see the French role in the conflict, misrepresenting the historical dimensions of colonialism, and escalating violence through his policy of repression. Understanding Algeria required knowledge of Algerians, which in turn meant discerning the real origin of the revolution. Breaking with Soustelle's naive view of history, the Comité argued that violence did not "date from the day" that Algerians "respond[ed] with arms" (3). Soustelle's silence on the sources of nationalist violence, the Comité claimed, deformed authentic intellectual identity, and with his objectivity eroded by the bravado of office, Soustelle had become intellectually and indefensibly myopic. In fact, the Comité asked, "Who rapes, pillages, kills, massacres, and tortures, in effect, in Algeria? The French authorities, isn't it?" (2).

Accepting Soustelle's claims as true, the Comité continued, would mean misreading the history of the French colonization of Algeria. In protecting its image of the legitimate intellectual from the image Soustelle projected, the Comité argued that his responses were not those of an intellectual but of a Machiavellian representative of a state, whose colonial oppression protected the status quo (4). Any hope of impartiality and intellectual credibility was annulled because Soustelle had betrayed his intellectual obligations by becoming a governmental mouthpiece.

The Comité continued its defense of Algerians and anticolonialism by distancing itself from French colonial practices. Driving a legitimacy wedge between colonialists and anticolonialists, it linked colonialism with French torture and terrorism. France had, the Comité claimed, developed into a "régime concentrationnaire" in Algeria, which reached all levels of the French bureaucracy, police, and administration.[26] In order to know better the intensity of repression and severity of the crimes, the Comité asked Soustelle to commission an inquiry into the reports of French abuses and the violation of human rights. This was needed, the letter concluded, because violence was systematic; concentration camps and police-sponsored torture remained undeniable. Hence the Comité insisted that the French military and civilians were guilty of collective assassinations.[27]

If the Comité distanced itself from the French state, for whom did it claim to speak and who authorized it? It claimed to draw its authority from three main sources: the names of its members (self-representation of intellectuals who have researched the truth), the French in France who manifested their distaste of the war, and the "engaged" nationalist Algerians (4). Backed by these forces, the Comité asked for the establishment of democratic principles, most notably freedom of the press and speech, concerning Algeria. As soon became clear, however, its desire to represent all three aspects forced the Comité into contradictory positions. Moreover, if these were the sources of legitimation the Comité claimed for itself, what did it hope to achieve?

Above all, it also asked for the destruction of illusions. To begin, the Algerian Muslims, according to the Comité, no longer wanted the Statute of 1947. The Comité asked for, among other things, the disbanding of the Algerian Assembly, the recalling of the military contingent, and the restoration of France's image now defaced by war. The day of progressive politics had passed and it was now the moment to offer Algerians real, democratic change. Nevertheless, in issuing these demands the Comité did not call for the complete separation of Algeria and France: "The path we want to see our country take is neither abandonment nor war: it is that of cooperation in friendship and confidence between two peoples equal in responsibilities and dignity" (4).

From Algiers on December 23, 1955, Soustelle continued the debate with the Comité in his attempts to maintain his dual politico-intellectual career. With another letter he attacked the Comité for not waiting for him to respond before it embarked on a program denouncing his silence. Again he evidenced his disdain for having to mix company with the "anonymous" intellectuals on the Comité and not just those he considered peers.[28] Furthermore, he argued that there had already been a commission created to investigate the situation in Algeria. He then fired: "You will permit me in response to raise doubts over the quality and the right of your Comité to substitute itself for the public powers. In the name of whom or what do you arrogate to yourselves this privilege? Who elected or mandated you? Why would I recognize the validity of a mission for which no one else but you is

40

fitted and for which you have already had the imprudence to establish in the total absence of objectivity?"

This direct epistolary polemic continued on January 10, 1956, when the Comité issued its second "Response of the Committee" to Soustelle. This letter displayed the Comité's complete skepticism concerning mixing intellectual and governmental authority. The heart of this response concluded that Soustelle was willing to engage the truth only insofar as it could be completely distanced from the reality of colonialism. The Comité then turned personal, stating that Soustelle must have been content with his "Letter of an Intellectual to a Few Others" because he had it immediately reprinted and distributed with his photograph and curriculum vitae attached to it. It was "sadly comical," the Comité stated, to engage in a polemic with a governor general masked in an intellectual's uniform; it was "comical" because Soustelle had tried to preserve the respect of an intellectual while simultaneously upholding the intellectually and morally dubious policies of the French government—especially the practice of concentration camps in Algeria. Furthermore, it was "sad" because this cost lives and paralleled attempts by the Gestapo to cover its systematic tortures with propaganda.[29] Becoming a vehicle of the state, Soustelle, according to the Comité, had been stripped of his privileged stature of intellectual: "You have not known how to remain an intellectual, according to the intellectuals." Soustelle had transgressed the Comité's imaginary line between intellectuals and the state.

The Salle Wagram

On January 27, 1956, the Comité ceased its epistolary confrontation and raised its public profile. Combating the policies of the French government and nurturing its identity, which aligned intellectuals with anticolonialism, the Comité held its first major public meeting in Paris's Salle Wagram. However, as the meeting and subsequent developments would demonstrate, the Comité found it increasingly difficult to maintain a coherent anticolonialist movement in the face of heterogeneous interpretations of anticolonialism, especially as widespread dissension resulting from internecine struggles between rival Algerian groups became more severe. Those giving speeches on January 27 reflected the diversity of anticolonial philosophies. Among those scheduled to speak were Jean Amrouche, Robert Barrat, Aimé Césaire, Alioune Diop, Michel Doo Kingue, Jean Dresch, Daniel Guérin, Michel Leiris, André Mandouze, Dionys Mascolo, Jean-Jacques Mayoux, Joseph

Raseta, Jean Rous, Jean-Paul Sartre, and Pierre Stibbe. Each spoke about a different aspect of the war and, with a few exceptions, the effects of the battle with Soustelle could easily be traced to their remarks concerning intellectual legitimacy. The Salle Wagram speeches also demonstrate the difficulty of balancing a desire to maintain Franco-Muslim fraternity, and, at the same, to articulate a coherent, anticolonialist philosophy.

More important, the speakers betrayed an internal struggle within the Comité concerning the identity of the anticolonialist intellectual. One of the most telling and complex efforts to address self-representation and the constitution of intellectual legitimacy was that of Jean Amrouche, the poet and renowned Algerian intellectual. "I am not mandated by anyone," he said. "I do not belong to any political party. I only represent myself: an intellectual and a citizen."[30] As what he described as an "integrated native" (a Kabylian Catholic), he was proudly aware of his cultural hybridity, the riches of his native land, and the intricate connections between French and Algerian cultures. At once Algerian and French, Amrouche offered personal testimony of this melding: "I am born Algerian, I believe myself to be French."

For Amrouche there existed two Frances: the continental or metropolitan France of European culture, the true France, and the bastardized version of France, the colonial France that "negated" the real France; this was the "anti-France" (23).[31] In this light, Algerians engaged in the conflict were not what Soustelle termed "common-law bandits" but men fighting for identity and dignity, and their struggle was an expression of faith in the universal principles (Rights of Man) that were the true France's raison d'être. Because the central problem facing intellectuals was to illuminate the real reasons for war, the intellectual had to counteract the lies and official French propaganda. The largest of these lies was integration (Soustelle's well-known project), which Amrouche argued was a failed policy that sought only to "disarm" the rebels. Integration was a worn-out colonial ideology.

According to Amrouche, his hybridity as an integrated native intellectual gave him the unique ability to assess the most important reasons for the conflict: the psychological and moral effects of the anti-France on the colonized. Because justice and dignity were most important here, the economic considerations at the heart of Soustelle's plans for reform and integration, he argued, were subsidiary concerns. The "native" has been beaten and forced to live in subjection in the territory of the anti-France, the undemocratic France of lies and misplaced confidences. The most lasting psychological effect was the dogma of "natural inferiority," and it remained more "rigid and more impenetrable than the most absolute religious dogmas" (26). This demoralization provoked a situation in which there remained no alternative left for the natives other than to rebel; in other words, the violence in Algeria was imminent in the contradiction between the two visions of France. Algerians, as displaced hybrids, stood in this no man's land between two contradictory French frontiers. Spinning his analysis into a phenomenological framework, Amrouche argued that the Other had not received due respect. The only option left was to "impose" this respect himself because at this point in history, in order to retrieve one's dignity, it "suffices to proclaim oneself free" (27). (Amrouche was one of the first Algerians to employ the concept of the Other in this regard.)

Paradoxically, even Amrouche, the French Amrouche, believer in the France of enlightened humanism, did not at this stage advocate the complete destruction of ties between France and Algeria. He argued that the very application of the liberal ideas that gave France its majestic place in the world would solve the psychological dimensions of the Algerian problem. Extended cooperation and the recognition of Algerian rights by France could ensure peaceful coexistence between the two peoples. A plan, in short, to abolish the reign of the anti-France was necessary and could only be realized when "free friendship, free fraternity, succeed[ed] the false friendship of the master and the slave" (28). The final reconciliation between French and Algerians was possible because both descended from the same religious ancestry, both had Abraham as their father (29).

Different in his conclusion but not completely in his orientation Aimé Césaire also qualified his authority to speak on behalf of Algerians by his unique identity as a politician (mandataire) of a people that had suffered colonial oppression, hence expressing a parallel between French and Martiniqais culture. Like Soustelle, Césaire's intellectual credentials were beyond reproach. Educated at the Lycée Louis-le-Grand in Paris, then at the École Normale Supérieure, Césaire was a professor at the Lycée of Fort-de-France in 1940–45. He entered politics as deputy of Martinique in 1946 and was reelected in 1951, enrolling in the Communist group of the National Assembly.

Césaire did not buttress his authority by addressing the audience as a "specialist of North Africa," but rather as a politician who fought for the oppressed.[32] For him, France was Janus-faced, divided between colonialists and anticolonialists. For progress to be made during the French-Algerian War, the anticolonialists had to unite and provide information to stand against the oppressive and tyrannical regime. Emphasizing its historical dimension, he isolated the Algerian revolution as one specific manifestation of colonialism's demise, placing Algeria into the problem of global decolonization. History, moreover, could be divided between two "historical epochs." The epoch of betrayed confidence was superseded by the epoch that produced the Bandung Conference, for which many countries had united to "proclaim that Europe no longer could unilaterally direct the world" (51).[33]

Despite Césaire's rejection of Eurocentrism, it would be wrong to see him as an intellectual who rejected Europe in toto. For him, Europe had played a fundamental part in the history and progress of civilization. However, history had gone as far as it could within the context of colonialism and demanded a new route. Pivotal in the transition of history from the past to the future was the liberation of the oppressed. This would mean that those who struggled in this transition period (the Algerians) could not be seen as "Algerian bandits" or practicing a "regression to the Middle Ages." History would certainly have its day with Soustelle, who was no doubt "a very civilized man," because he would be remembered not as an enlightened intellectual who understood the unstoppable currents of historical change but as the last "defender of an illegitimate and barbaric order" (52).

Exiting the historical impasse of colonialism, however, did not require the comprehensive destruction of the connections between France and Algeria. Like his fellow Comité member Amrouche, Césaire invited reconciliation based on a spirit of cooperation. Recognition of the Algerian national identity, not Soustelle's bogus project of integration, would foster this reconciliation.

Like Amrouche and Césaire, Jean-Jacques Mayoux, a professor in the Faculty of Letters in Paris, spoke of the self-representation of intellectual identity and aligned this identity squarely on the side of anticolonialism. "Intellectuals," he said, "are those who attempt to understand without limiting themselves to the immediate."[34] This opposition put intellectuals at odds with the established powers, the military, and sometimes the government. In relating his definition of intellectuals to his vision of anticolonialism, Mayoux asked "French patriots" to join forces with "Algerian patriots" in the struggle against the "tyranny that has usurped the name of France" (6). Colonialism was merely a nefarious quid pro quo in the sense that control of democratic institutions in France was compromised by the lack of democracy in Algeria.

Mayoux was not alone in his concern for the internal and external threats to democracy that the war in Algeria posed. Dionys Mascolo, one of the Comité's founders, argued that Algeria represented one aspect of the struggle against universal colonialism. In order to combat colonialism, Mascolo insisted, the French had to become cognizant of their collective responsibility in the war. Just as Germany had once denied the existence of mass concentration camps, he claimed, so did the French. Fulfilling the intellectual's role by exposing this atrocity, intellectuals would help create a "universally humane society."[35]

Although a universally humane society was the goal, it would have to be realized by a combined Franco-Algerian effort. Algerians needed to rethink their national identity by searching for their cultural roots; the French could assist by denouncing the "practical" and "theoretical" applications of colonialism. The French could then appropriate the Algerians and place them within society that transcended the limits of a culturally specific and historical situation. "We asked them for their aid, and they have very generously responded to our call. The support that they provide is of an immeasurable price" (10).

Following the same theme of the internalization of the conflict, Alioune Diop, director of *Présence africaine*, insisted that intellectuals ought to concentrate on the oppressor and not just the oppressed. In his words, intellectuals were compelled to condemn the "harmfulness of colonialism *for the colonizer*," and the Comité was an empirical manifestation of this responsibility.[36] Even Diop suggested that fraternity could be reestablished through a universal struggle against capitalism. Exploitation in the colonies was not fundamentally different from that in Europe—a collective identity was forged by an ontological sameness derived from capitalist exploitation, as it were, and this bound peoples in ways cultural sameness did not. In order for advances to be made, the workers in colonies and Europe had to realize that war in Algeria embodied not a conflict between civilizations but a battle against collective, capitalist oppression.

Sartre's Salle Wagram speech echoed Diop's, especially the effort to universalize the Algerian situation and underscore the relationship between colonialism and capitalism. In theorizing colonialism's systematic effects, Sartre argued that Algeria represented "the most readable" model of the colonial system at work.[37] Hence the Algerian revolution was at once an expression of a global trend toward nationalism and a revolt against capitalistic exploitation. The connection, for Sartre, was obvious because colonialism's antidemocratic exploitation was founded on racism, supported by military force, and characterized by economic, social, and psychological aspects. Colonialism created an economy in which Algerians could be controlled; it amplified educational and institutional differences between Algerians and European settlers (colons), and it fabricated psychological subhumans (sous-homme), convinced of their own inferiority. In order to combat colonialism these three nefarious components of systemic oppression had to be "tranquilized." Yet, somewhat ironically, while advocating this tranquilization, for the moment not even Sartre incited Algerians to destroy all existing connections between France and Algeria: "if they feed their hunger, if they work, and if they know how to read, there will no longer be the shame of being sub-human and we will find again the old Franco-Muslim fraternity" (26).

But the system was inherently doomed. In Hegelian fashion, Sartre argued that the three-tiered separation of Algerians from colons had kept Algerians outside the system and allowed them, forced them in fact, to become conscious of their own separate identity. Economic, social, and psychological segregation, therefore, had inadvertently contributed to the Algerians' becoming cognizant of their national identity. Similarly, Sartre believed that the fascist need of the European colons in Algeria to resort to force (the military and the police) had created a systemic dependence on the military. These contradictions were deeply implanted and could only be escaped through the demise of the system.

It was the role of the French intellectual, Sartre argued, to slay colonialism. The French intellectual's own identity mandated this final act because metropolitan French political and social institutions had been infected by the mockery of fascist racism radiating from Algeria. As a result, Soustelle's "neocolonialism" had to be stopped. Only by removing the impediments to justice and real social reform, by cutting the colons' resources of force, could "a free France and liberated Algeria" be achieved (47). In this sense, the struggle for a liberated Algeria was "at once" a struggle for France and for Algeria against "colonial tyranny" (48).

Is There an Orthodox Anticolonialism?

During the January 27 meeting there were two unscheduled speeches. Different reactions within the Comité to the speakers, André Mandouze and Moulay Merbah, reveal a great deal about the tensions that emerged from the desire to merge the identity of the anticolonialist intellectual with a coherent representation of Algerian nationalism. The first real fissures surfaced in response to the FLN's systematic use of violence to eradicate Algerian opposition. The FLN's main Algerian political rival, the MNA, was formed in December 1954 by longtime Algerian nationalist Messali Hadj. Moulay Merbah, a principal supporter of Messali Hadj, acted as the MNA's representative in Europe and at the United Nations and had come to the meeting to discuss the Algerian situation.

André Mandouze, the other unscheduled speaker at the Salle Wagram meeting, delivered a blistering speech titled "Admit the Facts." A professor in the Faculty of Letters at the University of Algiers, Mandouze had long been engaged in the Algerian struggle.[38] His sympathies for the FLN and antipathy for the MNA were well known, as was his characteristic briskness. At the time of his speech, Mandouze was perhaps the French intellectual most directly engaged in the daily combat of the Algerians. Delivering his speech, he did not miss the opportunity to refer to his last visit to Salle Wagram during Liberation. A decade later he pointed to the ironic parallels with the unlearned Nazi lessons of the past, which were a cause for shame for the French people. Just as the French Resistance had once fought against the Nazi oppression, the FLN's military branch, the Armée de Libération Nationale (ALN), now struggled bitterly against a similar fascist occupation.

Mandouze's self-declared position as direct FLN spokesman lent his speech an air of bitter superiority. In his words, he had nothing but disdain for "mere talking" and "holding colloquia" on the Algerian situation. He had come to bring a message of support from the FLN and to urge the Comité to respond by using all its influence to force immediate political negotiations between France and Algeria. Moreover, noticeably distanced from French interests, Mandouze represented the FLN cause directly, and from this position he criticized the Eurocentric appropriation of the Algerian struggles against colonialism by the very French intellectuals to whom he spoke. "You have to do more, my dear friends, than gather and applaud those who speak the truth. Tomorrow you have to demand from those whom you have given power that they recognize and understand the fact of Algeria and the opening of negotiations."[39] This must be done, he continued, without the slightest hint of paternalism and with the knowledge that in the battle for liberation, only the combatants (the Algerians) will have won.

Mandouze's optimism concerning negotiations did not appear entirely misplaced.[40] At first sight, his open support for the FLN might not seem very provocative, but reactions within the Comité were passionate. Perhaps the fact that Salle Wagram had been filled largely with an Algerian audience that sided with Messali Hadj, the MNA leader and principal Algerian opponent of the FLN, influenced matters.

More important, Mandouze had touched a nerve in the Comité. Daniel Guérin, a writer and longtime opponent of colonialism, a friend of Messali Hadj, and a Trotskyite (anti-PCF) member of the Comité, wrote an open letter protesting the Comité's decision to give a second hearing to a French representative of the FLN. Addressed to his "Dear Colleagues" on January 29, he published it in Libertaire on February 2. While commending the founders of the Comité, notably Edgar Morin, for their excellent work and "biting" response to Soustelle, Guérin's letter highlighted the undercurrent of discord among the Comité members concerning the politics of representing Algerian nationalists and defining the proper anticolonialist policy for French intellectuals. For example, in a Comité meeting just before the January 27 gathering, despite the objection of Edgar Morin and the absence of Sartre, the Central Bureau had decided not to mention Messali Hadj's name during the Wagram meeting. [41] Guérin, who also delivered a speech on January 27, had submitted his text to the bureau in advance and was urged not to comment on the history of Algerian nationalism (which would have placed heavy emphasis on Messali), but rather to describe the way Algerians have been made to feel as "strangers in their own country." [42] Guérin refused to participate in this political maneuver that would have benefited the FLN by excluding Messali, insisting that it was not possible to treat the history of Algerian nationalism without situating him in this history. At Wagram, Dionys Mascolo attempted to stop Guérin from taking the stand, and Guérin delivered only part of his speech. According to Guérin, this intentional distortion of the history of nationalism, which he rightly termed the "absence of impartiality," led to the direct attempt by some Comité members to support the FLN in its struggles against the MNA. In Guérin's eyes this distortion of history and Algerian politics and abuse of the very argument about objectivity that anti-colonialist intellectuals had used against Soustelle would destroy the Comité's public authority.

Guérin was not alone in his criticism of Comité actions. For example, in 1959 Edgar Morin admitted in Autocritique that when the Comité was founded most members were "profoundly ignorant of all Algerian political realities and incapable of discerning the meaning of the labels CRUA, FLN, MNA." [43] According to Morin, Mascolo, Antelme, and the Sartrians on the

Comité believed that Messali was under Soustelle's control; Morin claimed that he, Robert Chérmany, and Guérin were the only ones who defended the historical veracity of Messali's role in the development of Algerian nationalism. Because of the pro-Messali show of force at the Wagram meeting, some Comité members actually discussed expelling Chérmany for having plotted against the Comité by recruiting a considerable anti-FLN Algerian audience.[44] This was, according to Morin, the beginning of the rupture within the Comité (192).[45] This problem came with the realization that the Comité's desire to lead a clean anticolonial campaign was being debased by a naive and dangerous effort by some members to use it as a means for giving the FLN more standing as the only legitimate nationalist movement in Algeria. More recently, in 1998, Morin admitted that the tendency among the French left was to equate the FLN with the "avant-garde of the worldwide Revolution."[46]

In many ways, Guérin alerted intellectuals to the potential danger of mixing the politics of internationalism with anticolonialism. To drive home his point, he cited Jean Dresch's "deplorable" speech (also given at the Salle Wagram meeting), which presented the "poor European colons of Algeria!" as the real victims of colonialism.[47] With the large number of Algerians in the audience, this duplicitous effort to substitute Algerian nationalists' concerns for so-called proletariat concerns eroded the confidence of Algerians in French intellectuals' ability to swing the public's support behind the Algerian cause. It was clear to any audience member, Guérin argued, that Dresch (and other Communist intellectuals) denied the cultural specificity of the Algerian revolution by merging the Algerians and the colons into the same fraudulent Marxist interpretative grid of universal exploitation. Guérin therefore urged the Comité to distance itself from this manner of interpreting Algeria, otherwise its prestige would be severely tarnished.

According to Guérin, the final and perhaps most disturbing event of the gathering related to the attempt to deny Moulay Merbah—the only Algerian Muslim speaker—the right to take the microphone in the name of the MNA. What was particularly insulting for Algerians, Guérin pointed out, was that the effort to block Merbah came after affording André Mandouze—a Frenchman representing the FLN—the same privilege. After protests by the Comité, Merbah did deliver his speech, but it was the only one censored out of the Comité's publication. The Comité's paternalism and hypocrisy vis-à-vis Algerian nationalists, according to Guérin, became transparent when the members who had opposed Merbah's unforeseen speech refused to applaud and even gave the impression of "sickly laughter [rire jaune]" (2).[48]

This disgusting behavior compromised the Comité's ability to launch a legitimate crusade against colonialism and even endangered its right to speak about decolonization. To restore its image, the Comité would have to show more respect for Algerians, who, after all, were the victims of colonial oppression. And the Comité could not side with one nationalist faction against another. As Guérin stated, "Some of us, my dear colleagues, are not prepared for a committee of intellectuals, founded on a noble goal, to become a camp of disloyal intrigues at the end of which liberal thought is incarcerated. And we hope . . . that the bureau will observe strict impartiality towards all of the different tendencies of the Algerian resistance, all victims of the same repression" (2).

Guérin's challenge would not go unanswered, but it was not clear whether the Comité could overcome its disunity. Fractures in the united anticolonial front began to appear soon thereafter. Four days after the publication of Guérin's letter, Régis Blachère, a professor at the Collège de France, widely respected Islamic scholar, translator of the Qur'an, and member of the Comité, wrote a brief letter to Guérin denouncing his Salle Wagram speech. [49] He said Guérin replaced a "blind hatred" of colonialism with pan-Islamism: "Pan-Arabism is a monster as redoubtable as colonialism. Between the two, why choose? They both are at odds in North Africa, and Algeria will die from them. Permit me to not follow you because I do not want to have to ask myself each night: how much spilled blood am I responsible for today." [50] Blachère's criticisms of pan-Arabism were not new and had already put him at odds with Guérin and others. On December 13, 1954, Guérin had written to François Mauriac of his fear that Blachère's anti-Arab stance was becoming the "focus" of a different group, the Comité France-Maghreb. [51] Hence, in the quarrel between Guérin and the Comité, Blachère interpreted Guérin's desire for "impartiality" as playing into a pan-Arabism that would be far more oppressive than French colonial rule.

On February 10 Guérin widened his campaign against the Comité's interpretation of Algerian nationalism by writing to the Tunisian leader Habib Bourguiba. Guérin asked him to have courage to "take a position against the calumniators of Messali" and explained that he had already protested the Comité's effort to keep Messali from receiving just representation. [52] The attack against Messali, according to Guérin, was derived from three sources: the Communists, who had never "annexed" Messali; Abdel Nasser, who had no use for Messali's tactics; and the Muslims, who had not joined the FLN and disliked the "proletarian composition" of the Messalists.

The Comité responded to Guérin's public criticisms in its February 18 bulletin. Chastising him for bringing an internal conflict into the open, the Comité again insisted on impartiality and reiterated that it did not wish to enter the Algerians' internal political struggles. It then averred that Merbah had been wrong to come as Messali Hadj's representative without its consent.[53] Such patronage, the Comité wrote, was inappropriate because it was not created to cater to the "representations of one tendency more than another in the heart of the Algerian resistance." To better serve the Algerian cause, the Comité had to be above the fray, outside the immediate political manifestations of Algerian nationalism.

Members of the Comité also offered private criticism of Guérin. In an unsigned letter, one member wrote of Guérin's self-righteousness:

> I deplore this war of little papers among comrades united for the defense of a just cause; I deplore that these questions of personal *amour-propre* can lead to these deformed facts and men; I deplore that Mr. Guérin, due to his egocentrism, has come to denounce, despite of how he thinks of his qualifications . . . the intervention of one of our colleagues on the Comité [Mandouze]. . . . Mr. Guérin seems to be a "Messalist," yet he serves neither that tendency, nor the cause of a free Algeria, nor that of the French conscience.[54]

In a more personal exchange, Mascolo wrote Guérin explaining that an attitude of strict impartiality had indeed been observed. "If certain members of the Bureau have already individually taken a position in favor of Messalism, there will not be found any who have already taken positions in favor of the FLN."[55] Then, in an attempt to define the nature and the goals of anticolonialism again, Mascolo wrote:

> Where you see the maneuvers, there is nothing but care, very firm, it is true, care to be clean, not to dupe anyone and not to be duped by anyone—not to have sentimental preferences or to be partisan. Can you not conceive of this? To abandon such an attitude would be to play the game, certainly defensible, which would not suit us but would suit a political party. We are not a party. This is why we are able to do something that a party cannot. Otherwise, we would be reduced to feebleness. . . . Again, you are not with those who have

worked during these last months to ensure the Comité's success
or to give it direction. Your censor-like attitude is really facile, very
unjust, and completely out of place. . . .

It is misery, dear Sir, misery which forces us to be on the lookout
for every good intention. And it's a waste of time, even a waste of
time to have to write you like this. Everything is destined to end in
sadness, pure and simple, where nothing will make sense.

Metropolitan France's anticolonialist movement had been imperiled by
the temptation of taking sides in the FLN-MNA fratricide, but there were
other challenges to a united anticolonialism on the horizon. These came
into view in Guérin's critique of Francis and Colette Jeanson's important
discussion of the Algerian crisis, L'Algérie hors la loi, in France observateur in the
interest of "public opinion." [56] Guérin commenced his review by praising
his fellow Comité members' courageous and overdue book on Algeria and
ended with criticisms similar to those he had made concerning the Salle
Wagram meeting. In particular, he lambasted the book for demonstrating
a bias against Messali Hadj and preference for the FLN "without any attempt at impartiality." Moreover, Guérin criticized the Jeansons for mis-
quoting a private conversation between Islamic scholar Louis Massignon
and Soustelle in which Massignon said that Messali was the "last card"
for the French to play in Algeria. (Massignon later publicly disavowed this
claim.) While defending Messali against the Jeansons' siding with the FLN,
Guérin urged fellow anticolonialists to stay out of the Algerians' internal
battles.

Guérin was not flying solo in his attack on the Jeansons' book. Jean
Daniel, who would arguably become the most important journalist in
France, joined the chorus of intellectual discord. Daniel's French-Algerian
Jewish origin no doubt figured critically in his understanding of Algeria
and his decision to join the Comité, and he published "Between Sorrow
and Shrugged Shoulders" in L'Express because he was infuriated that Francis
Jeanson, like Soustelle, "believed himself to incarnate Algeria." [57] This self-
arrogation of the role of the "anticolonialist" intellectual, Daniel insisted,
illustrated a larger problem: "There is now an orthodox anticolonialism just
as there is an orthodox Communism. The dogma of this orthodoxy is not
the well-being of the colonized but the mortification of the colonizers."
Daniel claimed that Jeanson believed himself more capable of judging the
revolution than its leaders. In this sense, Jeanson's obvious solidarity with

the FLN evidenced bad faith because Jeanson thought himself "qualified to give out certificates of Algerian patriotism to the Algerians of his choice."

In response, Francis Jeanson wrote a semi-open letter to Daniel. Knowing that L'Express would not publish it, Jeanson had copies printed and sent to approximately one hundred "well-chosen" Parisian intellectuals. Jeanson wanted to offer a response to Daniel that would not be public enough to turn the already skeptical public opinion against intellectuals and the higher causes of Algerian nationalism and anticolonialism. [58] Jeanson referred to their mutual membership in the Comité and argued that this should produce reciprocal respect that would override intellectuals' individual differences. [59] Wholly enmeshed himself in the FLN-MNA conflict, Jeanson chastised Daniel for pretending that there existed a real political force inside Algeria other than the FLN. Moreover, Jeanson attacked Daniel's charge that he was attempting to divide the French left through his discussions of anticolonialism in France. What Daniel really feared, he argued, was the exposure of the new forms of neocolonialism in France, particularly at L'Express.

But what about the revolutionary violence of the FLN? Jeanson reminded Daniel that L'Express had been reluctant to discuss the violence of the "rebels," but that when it did it misrepresented violence, especially when arguing that " 'nothing excuses the massacres [of the French], and their authors will not escape judgment' " (6). Jeanson also contended that the "sensational facts," the news of the massacres that Daniel and his colleagues reported, led to the wrong conclusions. "A Frenchman," Jeanson wrote, "does not have the right to say, in relation to adverse violence: 'Nothing excuses these massacres . . .' because if this were the case, the chapter would have been long closed" (7). The time had come, Jeanson argued, to choose between the various aspects of the Algerian resistance, even for the French because there were only two forces left in Algeria: the army and the resistance (maquisards). Not involving oneself, Jeanson concluded, would ultimately play into the hands of the neocolonialism disguised as current anticolonialism.

As debates raged in the Comité over the proper role of anticolonial intellectuals, Soustelle's term as governor general of Algeria ended in February 1956, and his integration policies were now largely considered impossible. Extremism among both Algerian nationalists and French in Algeria increased. In February the new prime minister of France, Guy Mollet, was forced to withdraw the nomination of seventy-nine-year-old General Georges Catroux (Vichy governor general in Indochina) as Soustelle's replacement after the *ultras* mounted open opposition.[60] This capitulation to extremists who considered Catroux too liberal and too old eroded the government's authority and hindered promises of reform. Soustelle's eventual successor, Robert Lacoste, held his newly created post as resident minister for slightly over two years; during his tenure the French military presence grew to nearly half a million troops.[61]

Finally, on March 12, 1956, the French National Assembly voted for the Special Powers Act, which gave the French military authorities unrestricted power to resolve the conflict in Algeria and would weigh heavily on France in the upcoming years. Even the PCF ceded with very little resistance to the demands of the new Socialist government. Three weeks later Claude Bourdet, *France observateur* journalist and member of the Comité, was arrested for his article "Demoralization of the Army," signaling the government's impatience with intellectual criticism.

As if things were not already going badly enough for the Comité, on April 24 a group of right-wing civilians assaulted members during a reunion in Salle Wagram presided over by Jean-Jacques Mayoux. When Yves Dechezelles pronounced the names of Claude Bourdet and the *France observateur* at the meeting, the group of militants shouted "Treason!" and began an assault that lasted about half an hour. The real scandal, according to Mayoux, was the collusion between the police and these "fascists" because the French authorities did nothing to prevent the attack on the Comité.

By May 1956, and despite its internal intellectual fragmentation, the executive head of the Comité resolved to step up its crusade against the war. In the grandest of intellectual traditions, the Comité would use publications to "demystify" the war and provide "positive information."[62] Information would also be disseminated in the spirit of absolute impartiality, and the FLN's and MNA's own words would be used to combat the lies and misinformation of the "official" French press and the government.[63]

In its May bulletin, the Comité reprinted an FLN communiqué that stated the FLN's goals and objections to the slanderous portrayal of the Algerian resistance by the French government and press. Furthermore, the Comité attacked the French government's use of epithets such as "bandits" and "assassins" applied to legitimate Algerian nationalists as ignorant attempts to mislead French public opinion. Giving equal weight to the MNA, the Comité allowed Messali Hadj to respond to a series of questions ranging from the MNA's aspirations to the problem of citizenship for the European minority.

Then the Comité qualified its right to speak about Algeria. It addressed the French colons' claim that only those actually in Algeria or familiar with the realities of Algeria could legitimately speak about the colonial regime. The Comité asked whether the identity acquired from being on the soil gave one more authority, in fact ultimate authority, to speak about the events of Algeria. Intellectuals, the Comité responded, could not accept this specious argument because doing so would accord the French in Algeria a monopoly on French interests and give them moral and political authority vis-à-vis the metropolitan French (16). Moreover, to combat "seigneurs of colonization" (the men who ran the French colon press in Algeria), the Comité acknowledged that it would have to do more.

As a result, one of the central tasks of the Comité's intellectuals was to collect and diffuse information concerning Algeria. Information concerning terrorism was perhaps most important, and rather than deny the existence of Algerian terrorism, the Comité insisted that terrorism now remained the sole means for the Algerians to fight against colonial oppression. The Comité's members did not unanimously condone terror, though they did agree that terrorism was a product of French colonialism and not the cause of the current crisis.

This, of course, magnified the polemic already underway between intellectuals and the government. On May 12, 1956, a splinter group of the Comité wrote an open letter to Mollet's government. [64] Its title, "The Ethnologists' Letter," underlined their intellectual authority. The text (which received little press attention) was republished with a brief introduction stating in the authors' own words the letter's importance. The text was even more unusual because most of its signers had rarely taken open political positions. It invoked the names of Claude Lévi-Strauss, Gaston Wiet, and Charles-André Julien, all eminent in their fields, to dispel any doubts about intellectual credibility. Assembling more intellectual capital in the prologue, the letter went on to state that one professor from the Collège de France, two professors from the Sorbonne, five directors of study at the École des Hautes Études, and so on signed together as intellectual elites against France's attempts to maintain its colonial empire.

They argued that their titles endowed them with double obligations: as citizens they had the responsibility to acknowledge the truth concerning the French crimes in Algeria, and as ethnologists they were charged with defending other civilizations. They asked Mollet and his administration to recognize the revolution as the "expression of an authentic sentiment" among the Algerian people and not just an isolated case of a few "rebels" leading a rebellion (2). The Muslims' violence was a response to the French attempts to stamp out a misunderstood revolution. Violence was also the only means at the Muslims' disposal to express their self-determination. The French government simply had to acknowledge that, like other former colonized peoples (India, Indochina, Egypt), Algerians could no longer tolerate inequality by Europeans and that the first right of equality was self-determination (3). Following Guérin's lead of impartiality, the ethnologists asked for a cease-fire and direct negotiations with the leaders of all Algerian factions. They hoped for continued relations between France and Algeria that would extend the universal humanism and principles of the Rights of Man.

In June 1956 another important subgroup of the Comité's intellectuals offered "The Opinion of the University's Arab Specialists."[65] As "qualified specialists in Arabic and Islamic problems," they attacked the current usage of the term "pan-Arabism," which made it appear that there was no possible compromise to be reached in North Africa. It was "undeniable" the Arabs would be proud of their past and find solidarity in it, the group argued, but that did not mean that they would make Algeria into a uniquely Arab state. "We do not misunderstand," the group continued, "the difficulty of the problem posed by the co-existence of the two ethnic and religious communities. But from our experience with the Muslim world we estimate that the sole viable solution will be obtained from the negotiations with the partner who truly expresses the aspirations of the Algerian Muslims."

Suez and Budapest

By the end of 1956 the struggle against colonialism had changed completely. In March, Tunisia and Morocco obtained independence, thus opening up two important strategic sources of support for the Algerian revolutionaries. In August and September, a group of about fifty internal Algerian leaders gathered at the Soumma Valley Congress to reorient Algeria's struggle for independence. At this meeting, the FLN emerged as the dominant political representative of the Algerian people, and a political tract outlining the goals of the revolution created overarching political institutions, most notably, the Conseil Nationale de la Révolution Algérienne (CNRA). Perhaps the most important resolution of the conference was the reiteration that a cease-fire would not be discussed until the French authorities ceded independence. The French government then closed the Algerian Assembly on April 11, killing the last hopes of political resolution within Algeria's existing parliamentary system. After a long period of hesitancy, the Parti Communiste Algérien (PCA) finally attempted a rapprochement with the FLN. The FLN wanted their support as individuals, though not as a party, and the PCA voted to dissolve itself on July 1.

Other world events also began to impinge on the nature of French anti-colonialism. On July 26, 1956, Gamal Abdel Nasser, did the inconceivable by nationalizing the Suez Canal. Four days later Guy Mollet described him as "an apprentice dictator" analogous to Hitler. In August the British commenced diplomatic negotiations on the canal by inviting representatives of twenty-three countries to London. On October 23, Israel used the opportunity to start Operation Kadesky, with which it captured nearly the entire Sinai Peninsula. On October 30, the Anglo-French coalition sent an ultimatum for the withdrawal of all troops from within ten miles of the canal. The ultimatum going unheeded, the Anglo-French forces landed in Port Said, and on November 6 a cease-fire was called. The UN General Assembly asked Great Britain and France to withdraw their forces, accusing Israel, France, and Great Britain of colluding. By December 22, under U.S. pressure, all British and French forces withdrew from the canal.

On October 23, of much more significance for the anticolonialist movement in France, students at Budapest University set off a national uprising by advocating independence from the Soviets. Within five days, the country was almost completely liberated. Imre Nagy, who had become prime minister on October 24, called for the full and immediate withdrawal of Soviet troops from Hungary. On November 1, Nagy went even further by declaring Hungary a neutral country and asked the United Nations to recognize this status. Three days later Soviet tanks entered the capital, and Nagy, who sought refuge in the Yugoslav embassy, was captured and deported to Romania. Within a short time the Soviets regained control of the country and smashed the democratic uprising. The Soviet repression of Hungary sent shock waves throughout the world. Europeans were deeply disturbed, and Communist or Communist-sympathizing French intellectuals faced a nagging question: would they criticize or even break with the Soviet Communists and how would this affect the anticolonialist movement?[66]

Communist intellectuals in the Comité had been forced to address these issues earlier in the year when Khrushchev's February 25 report revealed Stalin's crimes. In his letter to PCF secretary general Maurice Thorez, written on the same day as the Hungarian uprising, Aimé Césaire testified that

Khrushchev's revelations were both positive and negative: they revealed the horrible crimes committed by Stalin but offered optimism concerning the possibilities of de-Stalinization. But Césaire unleashed harsh criticisms of PCF chauvinism and deceitfulness regarding the colonial question. The PCF, he claimed, was merely using the oppressed to benefit the party. [67] Moreover, Césaire stated that there would never be an African, West Indian, or Madagascan Communism because "the Parti Communiste Français thinks of the colonial peoples in terms of ruling and demanding and because the anticolonialism, even of the French Communists, still carries the stigmas of the colonialism it combats" (470). Speaking specifically for blacks, Césaire realized that the time to terminate his cohabitation with the PCF had come. Resigning, he insisted that the party had failed him (and colonized peoples) because its universalism annihilated the particular, and colonialism had to be understood as a local phenomenon.

Hence, even before the weight of Soviet suppression of Hungary had sunk in, Césaire sensed there was something unpardonable in the French left's appropriation of the oppressed. This tension in the French left and the Comité exploded after Hungary. On November 8, the *France observateur* published its text "Against Soviet Intervention." Those who signed the text agreed that "socialism" could not be "introduced with bayonets." [68] On November 9, in *L'Express*, Sartre denounced the crimes of Budapest. Although it may be true, as Tony Judt points out, that Sartre never publicly denounced the Soviet labor camps or Soviet anti-Semitism, [69] Sartre did state, "I entirely and without any reservations condemn the Soviet aggression. Without making the Soviet people responsible, I repeat that its current government has committed a crime . . . which today goes beyond the Stalinism that has already been denounced." [70]

The effect of Budapest on the Comité was devastating. The Comité's executive met on November 21, to discuss Hungary. It decided to distribute a circular to all Comité members asking them to choose among three possible responses to Budapest: (1) to concentrate on fighting against the war in Algeria, despite the similarities between the Soviet suppression of Hungary and French pacification of Algeria; (2) to condemn, with equal force, the war in Algeria and the repression of Budapest; and (3) not only to condemn without reserve the force used in Hungary, but to demand that all members of the Comité announce publicly their condemnation of the Soviet Union. [71] A general meeting was called for November 23. Reactions were diverse but nevertheless destroyed the Comité.

How did the Soviet intervention in Hungary effectively decapitate the first and only substantially unified intellectual anticolonialist movement in France during the war? The comments of Jean-Marie Domenach, editor of the moderate-left Christian journal L'Esprit and a member of the Comité, help us understand the connection. While the Comité's principal aim was to bring peace to Algeria, Domenach admitted, Budapest posed inescapable questions "of logic, of coherence, and of morality." [72] Knowing that the success of his journal depended on public opinion, Domenach admitted that it was not possible for him to continue collaborating with a Comité that did not publicly condemn the Soviet intervention in Hungary.

Characteristically, not everyone agreed. For example, in the general meeting Daniel Guérin stated that the Comité should not denounce the Soviets because it was a "bad idea" that could destroy the Comité whose "unique mission was to continue to struggle against the war in Algeria." [73] Others, like Sartre, went so far as to start their own petitions opposing the Soviet actions in Budapest. [74] For most of the members of the Comité, Budapest had rendered it impossible to maintain a coherent anticolonialist identity because it forced existing divisions between left, moderate, and extreme left-oriented intellectuals onto an embarrassing world stage where it was impossible to keep Soviet imperialism and French colonialism separated. [75] Edgar Morin recounted its paralyzing effect. "It was not possible to denounce French imperialism in Algeria, without denouncing something analogous to what the Soviet Union was doing in Hungary." [76] In his private notes just after Budapest, and in reference to the attempt to call for a meeting to denounce Budapest, Dionys Mascolo asked himself ironically whether members such as Jean Dresch would today participate in a "meeting for the right of people to act by themselves" against a Communist regime as he had done for Algeria in January? "Sinister joke. . . . Now the Comité is paralyzed by the smallest possibility of talking tomorrow of the people's right to dispose of themselves." [77]

Mascolo's response to this crisis, as a founder of the Comité, was to ask the Communists to leave the Comité in order for it to continue its assault on colonialism. [78] But even that was not enough to salvage the Comité so, on November 11, 1956, he wrote his own letter of resignation:

> It is not only odious, it is also ridiculous for a company of men to protest against the arrest of a few militant anticolonialists and then elect to treat the workers, soldiers, and intellectuals in the Hun-

garian insurrection as fascists—just as Soustelle and the traitors
of the socialist government of official France call the Algerian militants and terrorists bandits. I am not sectarian, but anticolonialism
should be total: it is a principle. . . .

I know that legally—by the statutes—those of whom I speak
cannot be chased from the Comité. I regret this. I invite them personally to leave it themselves.[79]

The Dissolution of the Comité

Budapest, although not an isolated incident of discord among intellectuals,
was the weight that sank the first and only unified anticolonialist movement
during the war. The problems the Comité faced regarding the MNA, the
FLN, and the violence would no doubt destroy the Comité as well. But because the Comité's might came from its independence from political parties
in general and the PCF specifically, adherence of both Communists and non-
Communists both blessed and cursed it. The Comité was skating on the thin
ice of unified anticolonialism that simply gave way to the crushing force of
the Soviet tanks in Budapest.

The cohesion among the members of the Comité and its eventual rupture
provide us with a good point of entry into the complexities of identity at
the beginning of the French-Algerian War. The initial phase of the Comité's
life illustrates the ability of a large body of French intellectuals to unite
against colonialism. The Comité's ability to unify against this common enemy served two separate but related functions for French intellectuals: it
provided them with a means to engage in France's internal politics and
it symbolized a genuine concern for the oppressed. However, as was the
case through the entire war, struggles against colonialism were continually
compromised by a host of interrelated concerns stemming from a twofold
problem: the politics of both representing the anticolonialist's identity and
representing and appropriating the colonized's identity.

Unquestionably, the representation of Algerian identity and Algerian
politics remained a constant source of friction for French intellectuals.
Guérin and Daniel were perhaps the first to point out that siding with the
FLN or the MNA would compromise the "objective" nature of the anticolonialists' mission. The criticisms Guérin leveled at some Comité members
for their attempts to appropriate the Algerians' struggle for Communist
purposes, thus misrepresenting the unique cultural and historical aspects
of Algeria's revolution, announced a central question that would have a last-

ing epistemological and political impact on the anticolonialist movement.

Ironically, the final blow to the Comité did not come from Soustelle's attacks; his criticisms actually benefited the anticolonialists' campaign. Rather, the cancer consuming the Comité became malignant when the unity of the anticolonialist identity came under scrutiny. Since most anticolonialists were members of the ideological left but were by no means Communists, it became imperative to define and redefine, present and represent, legitimize and "relegitimize" their anticolonialist identity. Nonetheless, by late 1956 it had become impossible to orient intellectual identity and public opinion as a unified intellectual front.

3. FRENCH EDUCATIONAL REFORM AND THE PROBLEM OF RECONCILIATION

The Service des Centres Sociaux

Sure, now they recognize their mistakes. Is that really the case? We cannot be sure. You do not recognize anything, you do not regret anything. It is still bad faith to speak about mistakes. From the very beginning, they knew what had to be done in order to be on good terms with the natives. They also knew what was required in order to be the only ones to benefit from colonization, much to the detriment of the native. They had to exploit him, make him sweat, beat him, and keep him ignorant. In the beginning, there was a choice to be made, and they made it. Why talk about mistakes at this point?

MOULOUD FERAOUN, November–December 1955

Mid-morning on March 15, 1962, in the Algiers suburb of El Biar, two OAS death squads interrupted what would be the final planning session of an ill-fated French educational institution known as the Centres Sociaux Éducatifs en Algérie. With weapons in hand, Gabriel Anglade and Joseph Rizza led their fascist comrades in the DELTA5 and DELTA9 OAS squads respectively into a tranquil administrative planning session and ordered seven men—Marcel Basset, Marcel Aimard, Ali Hammoutene, Mouloud Feraoun, Maxime Marchand, Salah Ould Aoudia, and Jean Petitbon—to follow them immediately.[1] Fortunately, for him, Petitbon was absent. The other six unfortunate and confused men were quickly ushered outside into the warm Mediterranean sunshine in the courtyard of the Château-Royal, the building that housed the administrative offices of the Centres Sociaux. Within seconds, as some of the victims' own children looked on, the six men were forced to line up against the wall. The fascists took aim. The six educators were riddled by machine guns. Three were French; three were Algerian. All were intellectuals. In one awful morning, just three days before the Evian Accords ended the war, this desperate fascist orgy of violence simultaneously liquidated the leadership of the Centres Sociaux and definitively ended hopes for lasting Franco-Muslim solidarity.[2]

This massacre was certainly not just another random act of savagery by the OAS. According to Alexander Harrison, the Centres leadership was scheduled to meet on that day with one of the "chiefs of staff of the barbouzes, Jean Petitbon, to discuss future strategy."[3] Aware that peace was in the air, the OAS troops, which had been menacing Algeria for the past year, immediately shifted their tactics in a last-ditch effort to disrupt the peaceful transition. The OAS death squads meant to institute a policy of absolute terror against Algerian Muslims and against officials of the French state. Nevertheless, and despite the senseless and grotesque massacre at El Biar on March 19, 1962, an official cease-fire went into effect.

But why were intellectuals and educators working for the Centres Sociaux targeted by one of the most notorious fascist organizations in French history, and why would a paramilitary group such as the OAS deliberately decapitate the intellectuals and the leadership of the only institution dedicated to the promotion of Franco-Muslim solidarity in Algeria? To answer these and other questions, we must consider the role of intellectuals during decolonization from yet another angle. The Centres Sociaux stands at the interstices between intellectual, cultural, social history, and military history, thus raising the question of when, if ever, this kind of intellectual engagement can have a positive social effect. The Centres Sociaux was a relatively small program, but it is emblematic of larger cultural, intellectual, and social problems that arose during the last years of French colonialism in Algeria.

Origins and Goals of the Centres Sociaux

About a year after the outbreak of the Algerian war and for the first time since the conquest of Algeria in 1830, the French government formally initiated a plan for global educational reform in Algeria.[4] This reform emphasized two principal objectives: combating the poverty of Algeria's underdeveloped population and fostering a viable Franco-Muslim community.[5] The metropolitan government hoped that in instituting these reforms the Muslim community would be able to overcome its overwhelming poverty and that independence would be prevented by integrating Muslims fully into modern French society. Attainment of these goals, the government argued, required rapid, large-scale social and moral modernization of Algeria's non-European majority. The means of achieving this modernization was basic education; the vehicle for it was the Service des Centres Sociaux en Algérie. The story of the Centres Sociaux is thus historically significant because it represents the last institutional attempt by the French government to preserve Franco-Muslim solidarity in Algeria.

Yet, even before the Service des Centres Sociaux was officially created in 1955, Algerian and French intellectuals (including Mouloud Feraoun) in Algeria were concerned with the problems of basic education. In Jan-

63

uary 1951 the Comité Algérien pour l'Éducation de Base, in existence since the end of World War II (and of which Feraoun was a member), issued an "appel" to sensitize the public to the need for educational reform. "In the middle of the twentieth century," the committee declared, "three quarters of the Algerian population lives practically on the margin of social progress. No honest man can accept or excuse the maintenance of a situation which compromises, unquestionably, the future and the unity of the country." [6] Besides advocating educational reform, which would touch all Algerians, the committee argued that combating "ignorance" entailed general social reforms ranging from hygiene to the "extension of democratic methods to administration."

When the war broke out in Algeria, the French metropolitan government understood immediately the role educational reform could play in appeasing the Algerian population. But the Centres Sociaux was really the brainchild of Jacques Soustelle. After all, the newly appointed governor general had things on his mind other than sparring with French intellectuals over the right to call himself an intellectual. Soustelle had two primary objectives when he arrived in Algiers in February 1955: pacifying the Algerian rebels and reforming the socio-political administration. Believing that these two goals were mutually dependent, Soustelle realized that he needed the support of Algeria's French and, perhaps more crucial, that of the Muslims—especially Muslim youth. Winning the Algerian masses' patronage required a mechanism capable of ensuring cooperation between the two populations. The most powerful mechanism available to Soustelle—other than the military, which he was deploying—was education.

Soustelle explained before the Algerian Assembly on February 23, 1955, why educating Algeria's Muslims was so important. [7] Because Algeria represented the "door" to Africa, he stated, "the time has passed when we can hope to make the happiness of a population paternally without its undertaking the task itself. That is to say, that there is immense educational effort necessary for us in order to get rid of ignorance and indifference, sisters of poverty and inspirations of despair" (3). Above all, the youth represented the hope of Algeria: "Think above all of the youth. Algeria is one of the youngest countries in the world. It would be unpardonable to let this youth slip far away from us. It is for the youth that we must first work and open the doors of hope" (4). This hope would be the expression of a "common culture" and find its application in Soustelle's policy of "integration."

In order to tap the richness of the Algerian youth and ensure this common culture, France had to combat the principal obstacle to progress in Algeria: terrorism.[8] If existence precedes essence in the existentialist credo, then pacification preceded progress in the Soustellian one. The terrorists, he argued, were those following the command of the exterior, and in order to counter terrorism the French had to take the next step, which was to pacify Algeria: "pacification must be the first duty" of the French.[9] Attacking "foreign agents" who "only work for themselves and for their masters and not for Algeria" required a sense of unity among the two Algerian populations.[10] Creating a sense of unity within Algeria capable of fending off the foreign threat necessitated isolating all attacks against the French state and French civilians, as well as against Muslims, Kabyles, and other non-European groups. Isolating, unifying, and pacifying the Algerian population meant confronting the "human" and not merely the "political" problems in Algeria. "Aspiring to human dignity is a powerful force; it is in the very heart of all democracies. Social solidarity, mutual respect, letting go of quarrels and discriminations, these are the principles that should guide our action."[11]

Although Soustelle had been envisaging a program of systemic reform in Algeria, his inspiration for a specific plan of educational reform did not take concrete form until the arrival of a former colleague, Germaine Tillion. Soustelle's turning to Tillion for help was no coincidence.[12] In early 1955, as a professor of sociology at the École Pratique des Hautes Études, Tillion had been sent by the French government to Algeria as part of a "scientific mission" to investigate reports of French abuses relating to the war.[13] Immediately struck by the level of poverty and the seriousness of the demographic problem, she asked herself what were the best means of struggling against Algeria's overwhelming poverty. This poverty, she reported, was "worse than it was fifteen years ago."[14] And combating it required an overarching attempt to modernize Algeria's rural economy through general education and modern agricultural techniques. It also required educating the female population in order to avoid the "brutal techniques" of demographic control known to China.[15] But the Centres Sociaux made it clear that Islam was not responsible for the demographic situation.[16]

During a stop in Algiers, Tillion met with Soustelle. Attentive to her concerns and agreeing that monumental reforms were necessary, he asked Tillion to join his cabinet and work on a plan for an immense educational reform that would stabilize cooperation between the French and non-European populations. In a letter to her friend Louis Massignon, she stated that she believed in the "efficacy and the complete good faith of the governor."[17] Soon after, Tillion agreed to help Soustelle create an educational reform team in Algeria.

Despite Soustelle's good faith, Tillion was already aware of the resistance reform would encounter from the local French administration and that the French police routinely tortured Muslims in Algeria.[18] She was rightly afraid of how this would affect the employees of the Centres Sociaux. Moreover, she sensed that the divisions among the local existing powers, the police, and the French national administration might grow larger as the war continued, and that the Centres Sociaux could become a serious trouble spot where these competing powers overlapped.

Tillion chose Charles Aguesse to lead the campaign of "modernization." Aguesse, an *agrégé* in history, was a liberal and a profound humanist; he had since 1945 been director (principal inspector) for the Centers of Popular Education and for the Youth Movements and Popular Education in Algeria's three departments.[19] Aguesse's principal aide, Isabelle Deblé, had also arrived in Algeria as an educator after liberation and had been a prime mover in the development of women's organizations. According to Deblé, Aguesse had long been interested in engaging elite French and Algerian intellectuals such as Albert Camus, Emmanuel Roblès, Mohammed Dib, and others in a project that would foster a fraternal spirit in Algeria.[20]

On October 27, 1955, with a staff chosen and a structure in place, Soustelle issued the administrative decree officially recognizing the Centres Sociaux.[21] The decree announced that Charles Aguesse would act as the director of the Service des Centres Sociaux and formally connected the Centres Sociaux to the Ministry of National Education in Paris. This was politically important because it meant that the Centres would be under metropolitan control; it was fiscally important because the finances came directly from the budget for French national education. However, the rector of the University of Algiers would be in control of the Centres' administrative supervision. According to Tillion—who returned to Paris at the end of 1955—it was necessary to connect the Service des Centres Sociaux to the Ministry of National Education in Paris because this offered the smallest chance of being overtly caught up in the politics of decolonization. From the Third Republic on, the ministry had been inspired by a liberal philosophy at the center of which was the respect for the individual.[22]

Structure and Strategies of the Centres Sociaux

The Service des Centres Sociaux was controlled by the director (Aguesse), the adjunct inspector (Deblé), and several assistants. It was further divided into the Planning Office, which dealt with construction, recruitment, and equipment; the Center of Basic Education, which concentrated on the teaching of personnel, documentation, and pedagogical research; the Administrative Office, which controlled budgets, courses, and mailing; and the Regional Inspection Office, which was charged with public relations, regional statistics, and administrative inspections. The general director of national education in Algeria and the representatives of the Service des Centres Sociaux met to discuss general educational and pedagogical problems.

The Service defined "humility," "useful character," and "concern with self-education" as the three principal characteristics of a Centre Social.[23] These were reflected in the ideal attributes of modern Algerians: "reading (a little), writing (a little)"—enough to help Algerians regulate their private affairs, dress themselves, and "defend themselves in everyday life." The Service's utilitarian character attempted to assure the "adaptation" of the Algerians to the administrative place occupied by "today's man," a place from which one could hope to ameliorate one's condition through "access to work." Self-education quite simply signaled the desire to help Algerians "help themselves" through the evolution inherent in education. The Centres Sociaux's tasks were divided into four areas: elementary education (for boys and girls who were not in primary school), basic education (for men and women), economic services (meant to increase individual and family resources), and finally, medical attention (intended to provide medical and pharmaceutical supplies to those in need).[24]

Despite their official capacity as an organization funded by the French state, from the very beginning the Centres Sociaux claimed specifically to be outside wartime politics and propaganda: "*It situates its action on the human plane, without being tied to the political preoccupations of the day and refuses to play the game of propaganda.*"[25] Regardless of its desire to eschew the politics of "propaganda," the Service did have its own liberal, humanitarian agenda that guided its social and educational philosophy. Above all, the Service's primary task was to affect the consciousness of Algerians. In a Cartesian manner, the Centre was supposed to act as a "human intermediary" between the collectivity and the institution and serve as a "living example of a social solidarity without divisions."[26] It would "regroup the individuals who have been separated by social life before being given the means to assure the qualities that make them human" (25). In order to help Algerians become conscious of their own value as humans, society would have to cease to view the isolated individuals merely in terms of economic functions: as workers, "planters," and so on. Struggling against illiteracy was more than teaching the student how to read the phrase " 'Ali goes to school.' " To really fulfill his or her functions, the basic education instructor had to help the Algerian "become conscious of his own human condition, to help him 'play his role and to assume his responsibilities in the heart of the group recognized by him and with which he feels himself solidarity.' Human dignity is founded on becoming conscious [la prise de conscience]" (25). The Centres Sociaux were to be the principal agents in the individual's self-recognition of his or her individual worth, and the leadership naively believed that this Cartesian call to consciousness would not be seen as political during the era of decolonization.

Concerns for decolonization aside, this method of education stressed the necessity of working closely with the preexisting system of French primary education. It was hoped that this could help overcome the "gulf" separating the privileged few who had benefited from primary education and the "masses" who had not.[27] But to work, the Centres Sociaux would have to identify the most gifted young students and assure that they continued their education in the tradition of the French primary schools. Thus the Service desired to avoid replicating in Algerian society the divisions existing between French and Algerians. To this end, the Service needed to work at "creating the elite without separating them from their milieu of origin, without creating, by consequence, that rupture which generates the psychological and social conflicts that already exist among the diverse elements of Algerian society" (7). In this sense, the Service's efforts to create a Gramscian organic elite resorted to an educational philosophy targeted specifically at Algerian culture, which underlined the connection between the collective and the individual.

Pursuing this course of action, the Service was less concerned with spreading republicanism than with the modernization of everyday life in Algeria. Hence, the metropolitan government's interest in integrating Muslims into French political life was slightly out of line with the Service's primary interests in Algeria. This was not very perceptible as long as the French government's central concern was to educate Algeria's underprivileged sector. In other words, while self-sufficiency was the objective of both the metropolitan government and the Service, there was little friction between the government and the educators in Algeria. Most Service educators remained in accord here because they believed that self-sufficiency implied in the "struggle against illiteracy" should be the central concern for the Centres Sociaux. [28] But there was a difference when it came to the apolitical spirit of the Service. Its members warned of the subtle political manipulation involved in the fight against illiteracy: "The basic education teacher should not see in the teaching of reading a means to form the intellect and to cultivate the mind—a shameful synonym of instruction" (9). In contrast to the Third Republic's use of education as a cover for civic lessons, the Centres Sociaux emphasized a nonpolitical struggle against illiteracy. Reading was reading, and there was no room for reading between the lines when a people's future was at stake.

Ironically, the militant but apolitical engagement that stressed the virtues of organic solidarity placed Aguesse and his coeducators in the center of the Algerian drama. As an "internal" agent of change in Algerian society, Centres Sociaux members were to take a phenomenological leap into the Algerians' world. Placing oneself within the drama would allow the misery and ailments of society to become part of one's own identity. This identity found expression in efforts to escape poverty. It also united everyone into a single society, and through this, it created a common identity. As a result, those working in the Centres Sociaux were asked to place themselves in a dangerous no man's land in the battle for Algeria.

Let the Politics Begin

While the Centres Sociaux attempted to wage social war against the common poverty of Algeria's underprivileged, the real war between the French nation and the Algerian rebels intensified. Just over one month after Robert Lacoste was named resident minister of Algeria, thus replacing Jacques Soustelle as governor general, the National Assembly, on March 12, 1956, voted for the Special Powers Act. As a result, the French government and military in Algeria would have greater flexibility to quash the rebellion. On January 7, 1957, General Jacques Massu was given full police power by Lacoste to destroy the terrorist networks in Algeria. The infamous Battle of Algiers ensued. By this time, the gap separating the French and Algerian communities had become as formidable as the pressures placed on the Centres to mend divisions. As one of the few institutions capable of demonstrating an ongoing cooperation between the French and Algerians, the Service des Centres Sociaux and its staff continued its attempts to instill a spirit of trust among those it sought to aid. Because of their intense and close relationship with the Algerian population, especially in a climate where existing paths of mutual comprehension between the two communities had been polarized by violence, the Centres Sociaux became suspect. In short, although committed to reform, they were gradually seen by extremists more as mechanisms enhancing the revolutionary move to independence than as a means to solidify France's presence in Algeria.

From October 1955 to 1957, with the exception of one incident where a woman of Swiss origin working for the Service was arrested for allegedly helping Algerian "rebels," personnel had few problems with the French police and military in Algeria. The first major scandal occurred in the heat of the Battle of Algiers in 1957. The Centres Sociaux, and consequently the last official attempts by the French government to breathe life into the utopian ideal of a Franco-Muslim community, would never fully recover.

On March 22, 1957, just after Lacoste announced that Larbi Ben M'hidi— one of the nine original FLN leaders who had been arrested on February 25—had supposedly "hanged" himself in his Algiers jail cell (though he had been fastened to his bed so he could not escape), the ultra-backed Algeria daily L'Écho d'Alger published an article alleging that members of the Centres Sociaux could be connected to anti-French acts of terrorism. Specifically, two people were accused of aiding in the flight of a bombing suspect and one of distributing the FLN publication El Moudjahid. The fugitive the two Centres employees helped to escape was Raymonde Peschard, a suspect in the infamous bombing of the Milk Bar at Place d'Isly in September 1957 and the bombing of a bus in the working class city of Diar-es-Saada. Three Centres Sociaux employees were captured in another dragnet effort by the police. Through a series of unrelated arrests, there were increasing accusations that a significant number of French and Algerian civilians posed threats to French national security. Thirty-five French and Algerians (several of them employees in the Centres Sociaux) were grouped together and accused of conspiring with the FLN. Because of their national and religious origins, the group of thirty-five were dubbed "progressivists" and/or "liberals" by the press. In all, two priests, members of two religious communities, and several civil servants and members of the Centres Sociaux were charged with various crimes against the French state. The accused were not acting in a unified manner, but the French-Algerian press opined about the danger they posed.[29]

Even the metropolitan press decried these dangers. On March 26, *Le*

Figaro ran the headline "By Friendship, Imprudence, or Passion: The Progressive Christians came to aid and hide terrorists." [30] According to Serge Bromberger, a correspondent for *Le Figaro* in Algeria, it appeared clear that the "progressivists" had acted on their own behalf and were effectively toys of the FLN. As a result of their exceptionally close contact with the Algerians, their crimes had been inspired by misdirected and overzealous sympathy. Their contact was based on the directives of a superior authority such as the PCF. Yet if the progressivists acted out of personal motivation derived from naive friendships with the rebels, as the press claimed, the same could not be said for those working for the FLN. Among the accused were several notable cases where friendship between French and Algerian nationalists had left the French deceived and betrayed.

Once the Service des Centres Sociaux was dragged into the political arena of decolonization against its will, it was never able to extricate itself from the infernal logic of wartime politics. Seen as a source of anti-French activity by the *ultras*, but conscious that they alone could help prepare Algerians for a better life through economic and social modernization, the members of the Centres Sociaux waged an unsuccessful campaign in Algeria. One of the most damning indictments of the French settlers (especially the *ultras*) was their resistance to the French educational campaigns of the Centres Sociaux. Perhaps the *ultras* feared the Centres' goals of helping the Algerians to become aware of their individual worth. Regardless of the reasons, instead of seeing the Centres as a social instrument for continued cooperation between the French and Muslim populations in Algeria, the *ultras*' paranoia prevented them from understanding how the Algerians would become more open to the French if they were given real economic and social opportunities.

The Progressivist Trial

It is difficult to prove that one act of violence was the culmination of years of fear and distrust. However, it is important to understand why the *ultras* represented the Centres Sociaux—an organization intended to preserve French interests and connected to the French national education system— as a threat to the future of French Algeria. For this, we must give close attention to several cases that led the French *ultras* to believe that the Centres Sociaux members were being coerced by the Algerian rebels. The friendship between a Frenchwoman, an assistant at the Centre Social of Maison-Carrée, and Chafika Meslem, a Muslim Centre director, exemplified the *ultras*' argument. [31] The Frenchwoman and Meslem were arrested for helping a suspected "Communist" terrorist, Raymonde Peschard (known to the press as "Mlle Louise"), flee from Algiers police. The two had helped Peschard avoid arrest by hiding her in the convent of the Soeurs Blanches in Algiers.

The case of the Frenchwoman and Meslem presented the ultras with a perfect occasion to exploit the supposedly diabolical character of Muslims engaged in the revolution. The ultras were able to attack efforts at dialogue between the two communities on the grounds that the French educators (and consequently France) were betrayed through their friendships with Muslims. Also, according to Bromberger, Meslem, a Muslim, had deliberately acted as a "liaison between the progressive Christians in order to get the maximum amount of 'efficacious' complicity" from them. "Those friendships," the Figaro correspondent continued, "made at the desk and in intellectual circles, were meant to yield results." It was thus the totalitarian nature of the FLN that "coldly exploited this unexpected seam where the emotional connections have created in them [the French] the very French instinct to take a priori the side of the fugitive against the police." Naturally, Bromberger continued, "[t]his instinct also 'disappears' after seeing the results of the fugitives' bomb at the exit of a Prisunic."[32]

For the progressivists accused of collusion with the enemy, there were severe consequences. For example, on April 11, 1957, the Frenchwoman working for the Centres Sociaux wrote a formal testimony to "The Prosecutor for the Republic and the General Prosecutor." Arrested on the night of February 26, she was immediately tortured by the French military. No one asked her identity until March 13, and she was not taken before a judge until April 3. Of the events of the night of her arrest she wrote:

> In the torture room, they stripped off all my clothes. They tied my feet to my hands, slapped me, acted as if they were going to strangle me to death; after these preliminaries, they laid me out on something like a ladder placed horizontally on a little water basin where my hands were soaking. Then they put a water pipe in my mouth and, as they pinched my nose, they forced me to drink until my body was completely distended. They "helped" me vomit the water by pressing on my stomach. Then they attached the electrodes to the different parts of my body, concentrating on my breast, my abdomen, and my mouth. They then started again with the water until I began to black out.[33]

After these tortures, she was tossed in a cell and left without food or water for three days. But, as she indicates in the letter, her treatment was not nearly as bad as that of the other women she saw who were "disfigured."

From behind the bars of Barbarouse in the next few months, until the progressivists' trial began on July 23, the Frenchwoman and her attorney gathered character witnesses for her defense. One witness wrote, "I have been a witness of profound human qualities of which she is proof. For a long time, she has given herself the goal of relieving the misery of the Other."[34] Another former colleague wrote:

> She ardently desired social justice, without ever becoming a fanatic. She certainly felt a real vocation for social work. . . . I know that she has made lots of friends in Algiers, French and Muslims, and above all among those working for a Franco-Muslim rapprochement. . . . [S]he worked with all her heart and intelligence to ameliorate the living conditions of the poorest sections of the population and to create the connections of friendship between the French and Muslim populations.[35]

On July 17, 1957, just a week before the trial started in Algiers, Charles Aguesse sent a letter attesting to his colleague's character. After recounting how she had been recruited by the Centres Sociaux on November 15, 1955, Aguesse stated that she was a "colleague of the first order in a service whose mission it was to come to the aid of the most disinherited populations. [She] sacrificed without complaint, brought and represented here the highest qualities that make France loved and nourishes the hope of seeing a true Franco-Muslim community built."[36]

As the debates surrounding the trial showed, not everyone shared Aguesse's sense of grace for those who had committed judgment errors regarding the Franco-Muslim community in Algeria. In the pretrial controversy, *Témoignage chrétien* published a highly provocative text concerning the progressivists and the Muslim community by an anonymous French priest.[37] The editors at *Témoignage chrétien* introduced the text by saying that they had waited two months, deciding to publish the text only after it first appeared in *D'Alger Université*, a European student newspaper at the University of Algiers. In the text, the priest argued that the Muslim fighters, the *fellagha*, as he called them, attempted to disguise their horrible crimes under the pretense of being "authentic fighters for liberty and justice." According to the priest, the rebels were nothing other than a "gang" that "killed, mutilated, terrorized women, the aged, and children, whether they were

European or Muslim" and which could only be dealt with by eradicating them completely.

The error the French government was making with this trial, the priest continued, was to treat the "gang" within the framework of the judicial system. Since they employed inhuman tactics, they did not deserve to be treated according to the rule of civil society. In his words, "For civilized people, the Penal Code; for the uncivilized people [*peuples primitifs*], the Penal Code of the uncivilized." The priest admitted that the so-called Catholic progressivists would find his comments harsh, but insisted that he was merely following God's rules for dealing with the uncivilized. "Exodus 21:12," he wrote, said all that was necessary here: "When someone strikes another and causes his death, let him be put to death," and 21:1, "If someone assassinates the neighbor, you bring him to my chair so he will be put to death." For the Christians who hid the guilty in Algeria, the priest argued, it was necessary to reflect on these passages to distinguish between "charity" and "complicity."

It was within this mind frame that the progressivists went to trial in the summer of 1957. The metropolitan and Algerian presses covered the event with great care. The trial merits consideration here not only because of the Centres members' involvement, but also because the thirty-five progressivists were tried together, despite the fact that many of their crimes were unrelated. Furthermore, it was a sensational trial because, for the first time during the war, a large cluster of Muslims and Europeans went to the stand together as alleged criminals. In covering the trial, even *Le Monde*'s reporter Bertrand Poirot-Delpech, remarked on the uncanny "Frenchness" of the accused Muslims. He wrote that in "remarkable French" they expressed their belief in the "political action" of the FLN but " 'deplored all violence wherever it [led].' " According to this portrait, the accused progressivists did not celebrate violence. " 'I deplore all innocent victims,' declared Chafika," *Le Monde* reported. The reporter went on to write that Meslem was "very Europeanized" and that her personality, "dominated the trial."[38]

On July 25 Poirot-Delpech reported the results and noted the predictions of Mercier (the lawyer for Meslem and the Frenchwoman) that the "Franco-Muslim" friendship forged by them would have lasting, positive effects in Algeria: "*When the fire has gone out, the work of these two friends will stay. It is our luck to see them together. Do not separate them. The rebellion is atrocious. Repression is atrocious. We cannot humanize evil. Refuse to see a crime in the trust born in the middle of an infernal cycle.*"[39] They were separated. Meslem, regarded by the press as the important contact point for the FLN, was sentenced to five years in prison with the possibility of parole. The Frenchwoman working for the Centres was acquitted and soon after returned to France.

The rest of the verdicts were reported without ceremony, though Poirot-Delpech did acknowledge that the "Muslims were much harder hit than the Europeans." Only one European, Pierre Coudre, a former Resistance hero and a Centre Social director, had been condemned without the possibility of parole. This was because he "affirmed his approval of the political goals of his Muslim friends."

Ironically, in February 1957, Coudre had been congratulated for his efforts in the Centres Sociaux by Mollet's minister of social affairs. Coudre's punishment was more severe because his was not merely a case of manipulation by the FLN. He and Denise Walbert, a former leader of the Muslim Scouts and a social assistant in juvenile delinquency education, had also been in contact with Meslem. According to the press, because of their relation with Meslem—who had encouraged their sympathies for the rebellion—they had decided to distribute copies of El Moudjahid. Walbert received a five-year term with parole, and Coudre—despite former minister Edmond Michelet's testimony on his behalf—a two-year term.[40]

As reported in the French metropolitan press, the most insidious aspect of the trial was the revelation of how Muslims could manipulate good, honest Christian sentiments to further terrorism. It was understandable, then, that in concluding coverage of the trial Le Monde also noted that the events of the trials had sparked heated debates within the Christian community in Algeria. Le Monde was not alone its assessment of the trial's effects. For example, Le Figaro's Serge Bromberger reported his concern for the "duping" of the Christian community by the Muslim-backed FLN: "It is possible for the mind to conceive that in Algeria Muslims are nationalists. It can even conceive, with difficulty, that a European can have sympathies for an Algerian nationalist movement, even directed against his own country. But that which the mind refuses is that a European can be a Muslim nationalist and belong to the FLN. Now, this is what springs from the behavior of Madame Walbert and from Pierre Coudre."[41] The other Europeans involved in the trial, according to the reporter, were "dupes" whose "noble sentiments" were "exploited" by fanatical Muslims.

Besides the problems confronting the Centres' members, there were more salient cases of the "exploitation of the feelings of Christian charity" by Algerians. Abbé Barthez from the Mission of France was the most notable example among the progressivists. Found guilty of hiding a printing press in his church hall, he stated that he had been "struck" by the "existing gap" between the French and the Muslims. Thus he had decided to work for a "Franco-Muslim rapprochement" by harboring a printing press for Algerians. He was sentenced to five months in prison with possibility of parole.

Not surprisingly, the collective trial—aided by hysterical media coverage—permeated French society in Algeria and called into question the patriotism of those who worked most closely with the Muslims, especially the educators working for the Centres Sociaux. The trial also gave all sides the first real glimpse of how costly the politics of rapprochement could be. Were the Centres Sociaux working in the interest of the French in Algeria or were they too easily coerced by the rebellion, as the ultras claimed? One Algerian daily, Dernière heure, responded thus: "[P]rogressivists" are "partisans of a materialist doctrine, naturalists, and rationalists, consequently directed toward communism. . . . The liberals are a creation which corresponds to the logical Cartesian need—which one attributes—often wrongly—to the French. They are situated between the 'ultras' and the leftist extremists."[42]

On July 30, in response to these and other like-minded newspapers, the archbishop of Algiers, Léon-Etienne Duval, released a declaration published in Témoignage chrétien and L'Écho d'Alger, claiming that to connect the so-called Christian progressivists with the Communist materialist doctrine was foolish.[43] Because the current period in Algeria was troubled, wrote the archbishop, one should, despite the imprudence committed by those tried, respect the "conscience of the accused."[44] According to Duval, this respect for individual conscience was fundamental to a sincere cooperation between "Algeria's two spiritual families." On August 2, L'Écho d'Alger took a more critical approach when it published an editorial comment on the trial, saying that a foundation of respect was necessary for the coexistence of the two spiritual communities, but that it would have been "good politics" for the accused to have tried to develop this respect with people other than "Muslim killers and executioners."[45] "More than ever," the editorial continued, "collaboration" was necessary but this time with "clear-seeing people."

Edmond Michelet, who had come to the defense of his friend Pierre Coudre, published his account of the significance of the progressivist trial in an article for Témoignage chrétien titled "The Trial of the Christians in Algeria."[46] He applauded the fact that "despite differences in race, language, and religions" there were individuals committed to the "establishment of a fraternal human community" in Algeria. And even before the trial began in July, Jean Gonnet, director of *L'Espoir-Algérie*, published an article in *Le Monde* defending members of the Centres Sociaux.[47] One could not deny, he wrote, that because of their direct contacts with "little Muslim people," those accused, the social workers, "the functionaries in the Centres Sociaux, teachers, and little supervisors" knew "better than anyone . . . the sufferings of the inhabitants . . . caught between the crossfire of repression and pacification." Gonnet went on to claim that the so-called liberals were those who took great risks in order to keep the dialogue open and "refused to betray their friendships." "Tossing in jail" those who tried to keep the friendships and the Franco-Muslim community alive, "those who *really believe in them*, is to avow to oneself that one no longer believes [in friendships or the Franco-Muslim community]."

It is clear from the trials that the Service des Centres Sociaux had been pulled into the antagonistic climate that, with the escalation of terrorism and torture in Algeria, rendered everyday cooperation between the two communities nearly impossible and at best suspect. But in 1957 this was not unique to the Centres; it was especially true for the Muslim population at large. One of the Centres' victims at El Biar, Mouloud Feraoun, commented on the junglelike atmosphere in Algiers in August 1957:

> You get the impression that you are living in an organized society. There are two clans: the police and the suspects. The military police station themselves at every intersection to check on suspects. They walk along the major roads to keep an eye on suspects. They position themselves at entrances of buildings and in front of public transport in order to frisk suspects. Armed and powerful, the police inspire great fear in the suspects.[48]

Unquestionably, given these clanlike conditions, where every Muslim was a suspect in the eyes of the French authorities, intellectuals and educators working for the Centres Sociaux faced an incredible dilemma. They could retreat from the Algerian Muslim population in order to protect themselves against the radicalizing *colons* in Algeria, or they could move forward with the Franco-Muslim reconciliation and thereby risk being seen by Algerian nationalists as working for French colonial and settler interests. Regardless of the new blemishes on the body of the Centres, Charles Aguesse continued his policy of rapprochement.[49] In an editorial in the January-

February 1958 edition of their publication, Aguesse praised the Centres for building twenty-five functioning centers, with eleven newly opened and another nine scheduled to open by the end of 1958. [50] Rather than stepping away from the local population or trying to move too fast to gain the confidence of the Algerians, he argued that they needed to continue their laborious efforts of making contact. "Everywhere, but particularly in Algeria, confidence demands time (often years) and preliminary and frequent contact. Does the team of the Centres Sociaux not respond better to this criteria since its goal is, above all, to establish contact, to create confidence?" [51]

While Aguesse had argued that more time was necessary to win the confidence of the local population, Paris wanted immediate results. New pressures fell on the Centres Sociaux. Faced with an explosive anticolonial war, the French Ministry of National Education decided to quicken the growth of the Centres Sociaux. But there were conflicting opinions on just how fast educational reform should proceed. For example, the French government did not understand that trust between educator and educated would have to be built before reforms could be implemented. " 'There is nothing urgent,' " Aguesse wrote, humorlessly recounting an old man's conversation with him, " 'there are only things done too late.' That is too true; but urgent or late, we cannot toss up programs in a few days, we cannot invent qualified personnel in a few weeks." [52] The ultimate danger in creating "superficial" members who lacked the true vocation of helping the Algerians would be that they could not be counted on to stay. If educators left after raising the Algerians' hopes, they would essentially betray the spirit of cooperation.

The Centres were also under heavy pressure to cooperate with the police. On March 19, 1958, Aguesse sent a "note" to the inspectors and directors of the Centres outlining a new academic status. This status required that all future nominations of instructors receive approval from the rector and that the director of each Centre be required to give descriptions of the Centre's activities to both the local authorities (police and military) and the rector.

May 1958 and Its Impact on the Centres Sociaux

As further reforms were being envisaged for the Centres, the largest governmental crisis of the war emerged. The Gaillard government fell on April 15. On May 6, Pierre Pflimlin was mentioned as a possible successor, but his nomination rested on the Independents, and they were too undecided. On May 13, three French prisoners of the FLN were killed in retaliation for the guillotining of two Algerians convicted of terrorism. In response, an enormous crowd of French civilians descended on the government headquarters in Algiers to stage a coup d'état. For the first time since the outbreak of the war, the French government in Paris faced total anarchy as the *ultras* began to cut contact between France and Algiers. As Simone de Beauvoir put it: "Algeria was cutting itself off from France to remain French." [53] Lacoste, understanding that his administration was in trouble, had already headed quietly out of Algiers and back to Paris. With the Communists abstaining, Pflimlin was quickly voted in by the Chamber of Deputies. Pflimlin, seeing that he would have to act quickly if he wanted to counter the subversive movement, ordered the arrest of several extreme right-wing leaders in Algeria and placed Jacques Soustelle under police surveillance in Paris. [54] In order to get a better hold of leadership in Algiers, the French military and *ultras* created a Committee of Public Safety. Generals Jacques Massu and Raoul Salan assured Paris that the committee was necessary only to keep the situation in Algiers from becoming a civil war. Finally, on May 13, Salan and Massu lent the army's support to the Committee of Public Safety.

With Paris directly threatened by the military in Algeria, de Gaulle answered the call and agreed to take power, despite the massive protests of the Communists, Socialists, and radicals against the military's attack on the Fourth Republic. On June 1, the helpless Parliament—facing an attack by its own military that had just landed in Corsica and was threatening to take over Paris—accepted de Gaulle as the new French president. Given the power to rule by decree for the first months, de Gaulle offered a new constitution for the Fifth Republic in September. It is generally accepted among historians that the transition to a military order was initiated by Socialist Robert Lacoste, when he signed over full police powers to the military in January 1957. [55]

When the Committee of Public Safety arranged its coup, the Service des Centres Sociaux was again suspected of potential subversion. The committee wrote a form letter on May 30 to Centres personnel, indicating the adoption of the following motion:

> As for what concerns the Centres Sociaux, created by JACQUES SOUSTELLE in order to aid in the evolution of the Muslim population in Algeria and to ameliorate the quality of life through elementary education, collective and global, the Committee of Public Safety of National Education recognizes in these elements the most

pressing task that, in the spirit of May 13, takes the figure of a veritable national obligation.

Considering that millions of beings for whom we should accelerate evolution are the sons that France gathered at her breasts, it follows that the Centres Sociaux should resolutely orient their action in the sense of a rapid and total integration of all the Algerian populations into the French nation.

We would be happy that you make known this position expressed by the C.S.P. of National Education concerning the role of these elements. . . . It is evident that the future of the Centres Sociaux will depend on the personnel's awareness of the mission that it must fulfill in the framework of French Algeria; that is to say that your response is important (which is asked of you in confidentiality). For the same reason, we will interpret your silence as disapproval. [56]

On June 1, 1958, the day of de Gaulle's investiture, the National Education branch of the Committee of Public Safety wrote another letter, addressed "Cher amis," to the sectional divisions in Algeria. Signed by the same Centres Sociaux inspector, Mr. Fourestier, the letter demonstrates that some of Aguesse's own employees opposed his apolitical stance. According to the committee, if the Centres had a bad reputation it was due to the presence of "anti-French elements" within. To find out who was subversive, members were asked to sign a political statement attesting their allegiance to the new regime. In the "interest even of the population who benefits from the Centres," the committee wrote, members must pronounce their views on "their mission in the new Algeria, [the one] born of the national turnaround of May 13." [57]

Disgusted by this intrusion in its educational affairs, the Service des Centres Sociaux sent a letter to the rector of the University of Algiers. What disturbed them most was that the need for a public commitment to the mission in the new Algeria "was presented . . . under the organic activity of their [own] service." [58] Rebuffing the demands of allegiance to May 13, they informed the rector that the educators within the Centres had always struggled for the "evolution of the Muslim population and the amelioration of the quality of life." They reemphasized the apolitical nature of the Service des Centres Sociaux and consequently did "not see how the politics of integration [could] modify their action, their educational techniques, or their means of action." Equally important, they regretted that the Committee of

Public Safety was threatening them by claiming that the Centres' "future" depended on the responses.[59]

After the chaos of May 1958, it took a few months before the real educational issues of the Centres Sociaux could be addressed. On August 18, 1958, the rector issued a statement that changed the orientation of the Centres by tightening their relations with other local authorities (the military and the police). The Service was to continue building a "bridge" between itself and the Muslim population.[60] But the Centres' plan for creating this bridge needed to be incorporated within a larger framework of all the different aspects of civil and military administration, including the SAS. In clarifying the relationship between the Centres and other branches of the administration, the rector congratulated the Centres for their work and for their "spirit of political and religious neutrality" (3).

In August 1958 de Gaulle's newly formed government began to consider the issue of public education in Algeria. On August 20 de Gaulle signed into effect an ordinance that announced the dramatic acceleration of "schooling" (scolarisation) in Algeria with an eight-year plan to increase the pace and numbers of those to be educated. This was supposed to be a clear sign to Muslims and Europeans in Algeria that de Gaulle's government intended to stay there. The schooling program, like the Centres, was something new to French education in Algeria, and it meant something specific within the Algerian context. Since the non-European population historically had been neglected—"untouched" as the French said—by French education, it was necessary to prepare the students before they could receive formal training in the normal French primary school system.

The schooling plan essentially changed the scope of the Centres. The educators were now to focus on scholastic performance and no longer on social issues. The goal of preparing an estimated 1,200,000 Algerian students for the normal French education system called for an ambitious construction of a total of 705 Centres by 1966.[61] There was a projected additional need of 1,800 new positions for educators to deal with the enormous increase in the number of students. The Centres, under this new ordinance, were to be redesigned to identify and upgrade talented Algerian students as quickly as possible with the aim of placing them in the normal French educational system, beginning with primary school.

Two motives become apparent when one looks at the change for the Centres. The most obvious is that the French government, at least publicly, was investing in long-term reform and planning its future in Algeria. It is clear, from this perspective, that the French state intended to remain in Algeria and that it considered the production of more traditional and nontraditional educational centers a key element in this equation. The second but less obvious motive relates to what type of society the French authorities hoped to create in this dramatic reform. This is best highlighted by the commentary on the plan by Jean Berthoin, de Gaulle's minister of national education:

> One can say without forcing the words that the present ordinance marks a decisive date, an historic date for the future of Algeria, from an economic point of view, as well as from a social and cultural one. But our Algeria merits such an effort from metropolitan France— it merits it by the intelligence of its sons, so avid to learn, so apt to instruct themselves from the moment that means are given to them. It needs them in order to release all the elements of activity and training necessary for its development on the human level. Thus, its original role, born of the meeting on her soil of two civilizations, will be affirmed and confirmed and will finally make them one within the French ensemble. [62]

The French were investing in the education of Algerian Muslims not only to improve Algerians' living standards, but also to ensure that French and Algeria would remain "one." In a word, education would do to the Algerians what it had done to the French: mediate cultural differences and foster loyalty to the French national community. Education from this perspective could retard or stop decolonization in Algeria and generate political loyalty among the Algerian masses.

It had been clear from the beginning that the French placed a premium on modernization and that modernization efforts revealed both respect for and fear of local Muslim customs. Following the August 20 ordinance, the rector, Laurent Capdecomme, wrote a brief study in which he claimed that "In respecting the customs and religions [in Algeria], France is charged with furnishing the entire population its language and its culture in order to permit access to the knowledge necessary for modern life."[63] Moreover, especially concerning the ordinance, the rector wrote that the reforms would be "socially" important but would also give Algeria "a framework indispensable to economic and social promotion, which is the integral guarantee of stability and peace" (6). In other words, if these reforms worked, Algerians could hope for a brighter future because in accepting them they would be accepting an unquestionably French modernity.[64]

The Service des Centres Sociaux
Éducatifs: A New Leader and a New Name

On July 7, 1959, Charles Aguesse stepped down as director of the Service des Centres Sociaux. The French officials had asked for his resignation for several reasons. Perhaps the most important relates to the change of emphasis for the Centres Sociaux. The social and adult educational aspects (such as domestic, hygienic, and technical education) were increasingly being replaced with standard academic programs. In the French republican system, academic schooling had everything to do with politics, for it implied creating an allegiance between students and republican values. Aguesse criticized this shift because it diverted energy away from the more pressing social needs of preparing Algerians, both young and old, for immediate social and economic modernization. It was clear that on this basis alone Aguesse would have to go. But there were equally pressing reasons for his dismissal. The French metropolitan government was particularly dissatisfied with his handling of the Centres' political affairs. As the progressivist trials had shown, Aguesse did not have the political acuity (if anyone could have) to deflect the overwhelming political hostility of the ultras in Algeria. Despite his good intentions and his liberal, humanitarian efforts, he had proved unable to keep his organization from being touched by scandal. If the Centres were to function well on Algerian soil, they would have to distance themselves from any actions that could be seen as subversive, and Aguesse had done just the opposite as director.

Aguesse's sudden departure, however, could do nothing to protect the Service des Centres Sociaux from an impending political crisis. Just days after Aguesse resigned and while the directorship of the Centres Sociaux was temporarily transferred to the rector of the University of Algiers, a new scandal riveted the Centres. The principal antagonists, the ultra press, headlined another outbreak of sedition and conspiracy in the Centres. On the day Aguesse flew from Algiers to Paris, L'Écho d'Alger started a series of articles connecting the Centres Sociaux to the FLN. [65] Although arrests of Centres members had started in May 1959, the press did not print the information until after Aguesse's resignation. On July 11 the Algerian newspaper Dépêche quotidienne claimed that the decision to relieve Aguesse and appoint General Dunoyer de Segonzac (whose appointment had been retracted within days) as director came after the police discovered a metropolitan-directed FLN network within the Centres. According to the newspaper, the arrests were the real cause of Aguesse's resignation.

83

The new scandal caused more problems for the Centre. The Service counted the apprehension of nineteen of its members on July 27, 1959. This time most were Muslim educators. Only one European figured among the two Centre directors, three adjuncts to the director, thirteen monitors, and one monitor aide arrested. Moreover, despite the de Gaulle government's claims that torture by police in Algeria had ceased, a handful of the nineteen arrested claimed to have been tortured. By July 2, six had been released, six indicted, and seven remained undetermined.[66] The principal charge against the members was that they had been aiding the rebels by illegally providing them with pharmaceutical supplies and medical equipment from the Centres.[67]

In late July another *ultra* paper, *Sud-Ouest*, ran a damaging story against the Centres Sociaux, "The Centres Sociaux of Algiers were infiltrated by the FLN."[68] The two years since the 1957 arrests, the article claimed, had shown "how much Aguesse was 'maneuvered' by the element of the FLN." With a dozen of these members found guilty, *Sud-Ouest* continued that the police had found the Centres Sociaux was a "real organization aiding the rebellion. . . . The importance of the Centres Sociaux, their dispersion, their materials, the medication at their disposition, their contacts with the population constitute an important stake for the rebellion. The problem is now to put [them] in order because [their] direction lacks surveillance."

While the press was engaged in its attacks on the Centres Sociaux, another effort was made by Aguesse's staff to reinstate him as director. Mr. Lepetre, a representative of the Centres Sociaux, went to Paris to meet with Bernard Tricot, de Gaulle's attaché and principal adviser on Algeria.[69] In this meeting, he was presented by the attaché with one dossier compiled by the police, who accused Aguesse of "treason," and another citing Aguesse's administrative incapacity.[70] Lepetre defended Aguesse, and in response Tricot attacked his administration for not being aware of the events leading up to the recent arrest of the Centres' members and showed his outrage that the police had discovered these incidents before Aguesse's own staff had. Lepetre acknowledged that Aguesse had always "ignored these facts," but argued that after the trial of the progressivists, Aguesse had attempted to take the necessary measures against these types of activities. Lepetre confirmed that medication and medical attention had been given to wounded rebels, an admission that demonstrated that the Centres had not remained entirely apolitical. Lepetre asked Tricot whether the French government had changed its stance on Algeria and insisted that the Centres Sociaux had always been the "third way between the two extremes becoming more and more excessive." Outraged at the question, Tricot reaffirmed that de Gaulle "desired" the continuation of the "third way."

In reality, two simultaneous factors were moving against the "third way" philosophy of the Centres Sociaux. The first was the change in academic structure and orientation, which strove to accelerate the pace of "scolarisation" for Algerian children in the Centres. This program, which had come with de Gaulle's August 20, 1958, ordinance, aligned the Centres Sociaux with the republic's educational aspirations and downplayed the Algerians' perceived social needs. The second force acting against Aguesse was the growing and unmitigated hostility of the French ultras, the police, and the military to an organization whose central concern was to make depoliticized contact with the Muslim population. In letters to his second in charge, Isabelle Deblé, Aguesse had long complained of the army's excessive campaign to control the Centres, and he understood that if the army took such control Algerians would lose what little faith they had left in France.

The Algérie française press wasted no time in attacking Aguesse's successor, Marcel Lesne. Lesne, who had spent the previous thirteen years as an educator in Morocco, was chosen directly by the rector of the University of Algiers, Capdecomme. After Lesne assumed his position in October 1959, the French newspaper 6 aux Écoutes wrote that the change had not at all "modified the unfortunate tendencies manifested by certain parts" of the Centres Sociaux.[71] Other ultra papers could not resist the opportunity to renew their attacks on the Centres. On November 2, L'Écho d'Alger republished the entire 6 aux Écoutes article, which cited a recent case of a Muslim, pro-FLN, "anti-French" member getting advancement within the Centres.[72]

In part, these attacks arose from the political chaos of de Gaulle's administration. Just over one year in power, de Gaulle permanently altered the contours of the Algerian debate with his September 16, 1959, "self-determination" speech, which indicated that he was moving cautiously toward independence. Not surprisingly, there appear to have been important connections between the politics of self-determination and the increased aid for schooling. By increasing education efforts in Algeria (which implied republican ideals and teachings), the French government may have been trying to secure a future in Algeria, regardless of the outcome of a free election. Just two months before the "self-determination" speech, the minister of national education changed the status and title of the Service des Centres Sociaux d'Algérie to Service des Centres Sociaux Éducatifs en Algérie in his efforts to draw closer parallels between the new goals.

With the change of leadership and name came an expressed belief in democratic values. On October 20, Lesne's administration published a circular that outlined the tasks confronted by the new leadership. As was the case with Aguesse's administration, Lesne was charged with accelerating the modernization of the Algerian population. This was no small task because a large part of it lacked "contact, not only with the schools and their discipline, but also with the modes of Western life." This statement was an unmistakable indication that education in Algeria was taking on increasing political significance and that the Service was to become an agent in preparing Algerian Muslims for the democratic responsibilities of citizenship in the French republican system. Unfortunately, Lesne argued, Aguesse had not understood all his tasks as director:

> Without a doubt, and as much as he [Aguesse] had already exercised his functions of Headmaster, he was by nature more prone to the games of ideas than to the ungrateful servitude of organization. He should have realized this himself and asked for an administrative assistant who could have guided him and could have served as his guide and his mentor. To the contrary, he took care to keep his academic administration as independent as possible and encircled himself with imaginative people of his kind, impatient with every reasonable constraint.[73]

The most damning part of this current tallying of the administrative disorder facing the new Centres Sociaux Éducatifs, however, came at the level of politics:

> Political consequences—It was inevitable, given the period in which we live [decolonization] and thanks to the permanent disorder, that the Service des Centres Sociaux finished by serving as a refuge to some of the rebellion's accomplices. Employing a large proportion of Muslim personnel, acting uniquely on the Muslim population, practicing in principle more "fraternization" than "paternalization," the Service des Centres Sociaux should have shown discretion in what concerns the secrets of the heart, which it has as its task to win and not to violate. It does not seem impossible, if the Service succeeded in its mission, that there would be Muslims among its agents with nationalist tendencies who would unknowingly change their mind as they collaborated with French people of

a different origin and as they tried to ameliorate the conditions of their brothers. Once again, this is all delicate, difficult, and should be followed very closely by a seasoned manager. It does not have to be that a sympathizing "ameliorator" turns into an accomplice of our enemies. It does not have to be the case that they [our enemies] use the means of the Service for their benefit. It does not have to be the case that, in such a troubled atmosphere, one can assume that they [Centres] are guilty. . . . It is clear that the project undertaken by the Centres Sociaux has its detractors of different stripes, avid to expose the errors and the mistakes of an organization whose interest they do not understand and to whom it (i.e., the organization) appears dangerous at different levels.[74]

According to Lesne, Aguesse's departure had been warranted on the basis of managerial malpractice. From an administrative point of view, Aguesse's error had been poor control of his own staff and failure to keep abreast of the very real possibilities that his employees could become partisans and not just mere sympathizers of the rebellion. More important, though, were Lesne's perceptions of the Service and its members becoming active in projecting the virtues of French culture. As Lesne wrote, even the Muslims working for the Centres could be unknowingly converted to the French cause through the process of helping their "brothers" as they collaborated with the French. The project of reform through education, given Lesne's considerations, would have a doubling effect whereby Muslims working with the French and from within a French system in order to help Algeria's underprivileged would unconsciously be converted to French values. As a result, educational reform would not lead the Centres into sedition; rather, it could serve as a silent proselytizing structure.

If this was the opinion of the leadership of the Centres, it seems appropriate to ask what the Muslims working for the Centres thought about the role of the Centres in Algeria, especially during decolonization. Perhaps there are no better sources than Ali Hammoutene and Mouloud Feraoun, two of the six men murdered by the OAS at El Biar. Both Feraoun and Hammoutene were educated at the prestigious École Normale d'Alger-Bouzaréah; both were respected educators who came to work for the Centres toward the end of the war in 1960. They left important records of their experiences as educators in Algeria. In particular, Hammoutene's *Réflexions sur la guerre d'Algérie* and Feraoun's *Journal, 1955–1962: Reflections on the French-Algerian War* and letters collected under the title *Lettres à ses amis* offer insight into how the Algerians viewed the possibility of a living Franco-Muslim community. Ironically, after Hammoutene (also a Kabyle) was deemed dangerous to French security and ordered to leave Tizi-Ouzou, he moved with his family to the Fougeroux school in Algiers. In 1960 he had great success on his Contours d'Inspecteur exams and was recruited as adjunct director of the Centres Sociaux Éducatifs. Feraoun and Hammoutene, along with the four others assassinated, perhaps best symbolized the last existing bridge for the Franco-Muslim communities. "The Franco-Muslim community cannot have hate and blood as its foundation," wrote Hammoutene in 1956.[75] As for most of the members in the Centres Sociaux, devotion to education inspired these six until the end of the war.

Feraoun understood that the French needed him and others like him to work for the French educational apparatus in Algeria, but he feared that French confidence in him rendered him suspect to his fellow Algerians: "I am maintaining my balance on a very tight, thin rope. This week, for example, I have most likely given the maquis the impression that I am leaning toward the French side."[76] And if he was ambivalent about working for the French in general, he was even more so about the Centres Sociaux in particular. In a letter to Emmanuel Roblès dated April 8, 1961, Feraoun wrote:

> At the Centres Sociaux, I do boring work for which I do not give a
> damn and which will not interest anyone. It is the most sterile bla-
> bla-bla, but I also realize that every Academy is bla-bla-bla. The only
> true work is that of the teacher. All the others, who call themselves
> the patrons, are in reality only parasites who exist because of him
> [the teacher] and spend their time pressing him like a lemon.
>
> If there were ever a good book to be written, it would certainly
> be that; to render justice to the teacher.[77]

In an August 1961 letter to his friend Paul Flamand, Feraoun further questioned his own role in the Centres Sociaux:

> Where am I? I have left the school in order to become an Inspector
> in the Service des Centres Sociaux Éducatifs which is an institution
> for basic education charged with bringing a comprehensive assis-
> tance which allows the rural masses access to the modern world:
> literacy for adolescents and adults, men and women, sanitary edu-
> cation, rural development, professional, social and civic education.
> In principle, a very grand program, very interesting: the old job as a
> teacher in the village systematized, codified, officially encouraged,

supported. . . . Three times over, alas! It should have been done in 1950 and now no one believes in it: neither the administration, nor the educators, nor the users. Maybe we should come back to it when the killing and self-deception has stopped. In itself, it is great, even a *coup*. But all is divided by the incertitude that fogs the street, and fills it with the most general agony and the most narrow-minded hatred. No one wants to do good any more.[78]

Like Feraoun, Hammoutene argued that France should have made efforts to improve relations between the French and Algerians long before the war began. In 1956 he wrote that "after a century" of "waste and errors" it was ironic that France finally attempted to "build a just and fraternal Franco-Muslim community."[79] However, now that the war had started, France's true self was revealed. The outdated value of colonialism could be legitimately questioned: "The role of France is not to oppress, but to help the Algerian people liberate themselves. In the ascension of the North African people toward the light, the role of France should consist in breaking the limits of a feudal administration founded on arbitrary inequality and social injustice" (62–63).

But to move to this next step France, and especially its liberals, would have to recognize the fundamental hypocrisy of the West. In this sense, both Feraoun and Hammoutene remained extremely critical of the Janus-faced West vis-à-vis Algeria. In the extraordinary international confusion at the end of 1956—the events of Hungary, the nationalization of the Suez Canal, Israel's attack on Egypt, the British and French attack on Port Said—both men criticized the West's covert racism as evidenced in the duplicitous outrage against the Soviet suppression of Budapest and the failure to react against France's war on the Algerian people. Feraoun, in showing his distaste for this split personality, asked why the scandal of Hungary could not equally apply to the scandalous colonial war France waged against Algeria. "Is it because the world that sees us suffer is not convinced that we are humans? It is true that we are only Muslims. That may be our unforgivable crime. That is a question I would like to discuss with Sartre or Camus or Mauriac. Why? Yes, why?"[80]

Hammoutene added that the willingness of the West to turn its back on the domination of the Arab people had been the cause of the Algerian peasants' misery, contrary to what Soustelle had argued during his tenure as governor general. However, in the face of the end of "Western imperialism,"

Hammoutene continued, "the profound error of the West is to believe that its authority would rest uncontested."[81]

At the Barricades and on Trial, Again?

As Algerian intellectuals such as Feraoun and Hammoutene assessed the role of France and the West during the war, the French government found itself on the brink of another military coup in Algiers. Again, a government crisis merged with indictments against the Centres. Colonel Jean Gardes, a committed Algérie française advocate and head of the army's Fifth Bureau (the "psychological warfare" division) was found to be working with the angry mob of ultras that again laid siege to the government headquarters and other public buildings in Algiers on January 23, 1960. On January 24, Gardes was ordered out of Algiers by General Challe, in charge of the French military in Algiers. Despite the government's attempts to calm the uprising of the Algérie française forces, a civil war started in Algiers, and for the first time since 1871 the French army was forced to fire on violent civilian protestors behind the barricades.

On January 26 Colonel Argoud, considered by many to be the best mind in the army, suggested to Prime Minister Debré, who had just arrived in the city, that de Gaulle would either have to renounce his self-determination policy or be replaced.[82] The army, which wanted to keep Algeria French, had displayed an ambivalent if not openly hostile attitude toward the policy and could not be counted on to put down the rebellion. Three days later, unclear as to the allegiance of military personnel in Algeria, de Gaulle made one of his most important national radio and television appearances, addressing the nation as "General de Gaulle."[83] The speech won over the possible military converts to the barricade rebellion. By February 1 the infamous rebellion was destroyed and those who had taken part in it either escaped or went to prison.

When the trial of those responsible for the barricade revolt began in November 1960, part of the defense strategy was to attack traitorous activities of the French administration itself. The Centres Sociaux Éducatifs again came into question. On December 12, Colonel Gardes, the only serving officer on trial, accused Aguesse and Lesne, the representatives of French national education in Algeria, of working for the FLN's benefit. Because of them, Colonel Gardes claimed, the Muslims were calling for independence in the streets and chanting FLN slogans.

Colonel Gardes and others testified that the Centres had initiated subversive activities. During his own defense, Gardes accused the Centres of being in the service of the FLN. After Lesne's arrival, Gardes claimed, "we [the army] saw the Service des Centres Sociaux peppered with agents whom we knew perfectly well to be men from the FLN, and among them important leaders of the FLN."[84] Gardes then recounted that, with the aid of the military, the secret police placed an undercover agent inside the Centres to investigate treasonous activity. Eventually, Gardes claimed, even the man who directed this secret intelligence operation, Colonel Ruyssen, quit out of disgust because although the "infiltration" of the Centres by the FLN was "known by all intelligence officers," the French authorities refused to take it seriously. Gardes went on to report that of the last eighty members recruited by the Centres Sociaux, twenty-seven had recently left internment camps, "that's to say, [they were] more or less important members of the FLN." According to Gardes, because the military knew the internment camps to be true "breeding grounds for the FLN," it was inexcusable that the Service recruit from them, especially considering that the Service was supposed to coordinate its recruiting efforts with the local administration and police. Gardes, whose ultimate defense of the military had been the accusations against those who had really "betrayed" France, closed his testimony by connecting the betrayal of France to de Gaulle's self-determination policy:

> I did not have the intention, your honor, to say all of this to you because these are affairs that are horrible for France. . . . But today there are new deaths, and many people are surprised. The surprise is that Muslims enter the streets, like some hoped, chanting "Vive l'Algérie Algérienne," "Vive de Gaulle." And a great number cry: "Vive l'Algérie Algérienne," "Vive l'indépendance." They have ransacked, and they have killed.

Immediately after Gardes's testimony, the new rector of the Academy of Algiers, Gilbert Meyer, criticized Gardes's attempt to free himself by smearing the Centres Sociaux Éducatifs. In a letter to the minister of national education on December 14, 1960, Meyer wrote: "It is convenient that, in his irresponsible attempt to relieve himself of guilt, he [Gardes] incriminates a service that has been almost completely ignored and attempts to tarnish the reputation of others when he is led to defend his own."[85] Then, on December 27, Meyer publicly defended the Centres in the Algiers court on the same day that he issued a communiqué to the press. "It is not wrong," he said, "that a certain number of errors and administrative irregularities were committed and obliged my predecessor [Capdecomme] to distance himself from the [former] Director of the Service [Aguesse] who assumed responsibility in 1955."[86] Since the time Lesne had taken over as director, he continued, "no contractual employee has been recruited without strictly observing the precautionary rules. . . . It is more deplorable that one could, in absolute irresponsibility, bring with such a lightness the false judgments on a service which functions regularly within the bosom of National Education and under the control of its leaders." Therefore the accusations against the educational system in Algiers went beyond the "personal attacks" against the Centres Sociaux; they were meant as a challenge to the legitimacy of de Gaulle's government.

In January Laurent Capdecomme, who had resigned as rector of the Academy of Algiers to become director of French higher education, appeared before the Algiers court. In his defense of the defamed director of the Centres, Capdecomme claimed that, "of all the functionaries" he knew, Lesne was "one of the most loyal and most devoted. His action [had] above all honored France as much as the Centres Sociaux."[87] In February Colonel Ruyssen counterattacked on the witness stand. With a staff composed of about "70 percent pro-FLN," he argued, it "well seemed that the Centres were infiltrated by the FLN."[88] Nevertheless, as a result of the testimonies, Gardes was eventually acquitted.

Unofficially, Lesne acknowledged the effect of Gardes's testimony about the Centres Sociaux Éducatifs. In a confidential letter dated February 20, 1961, Lesne wrote to the delegate general of Algeria that the "functioning of the Centres has suffered a great deal from this state of things, at all levels of the hierarchy. The personnel has clearly perceived the bad effect of the malevolent publicity derived from the declarations of the accused. Although I am personally brought into question, I nevertheless do not give any more importance to the declarations of Colonel GARDES than they merit."[89] More important, Lesne noted with concern that a police chief had recently erroneously stated to a colleague of the rector that certain members of the Centres Sociaux Éducatifs had in fact, since October 1959, recruited educators without asking beforehand for the approval of the police. "I consider this accusation very bad," Lesne wrote, affirming that he had made all dossiers of future employees open to police and military investigators.

Assassination at El Biar: The Murder of Franco-Muslim Rapprochement
On August 21, 1961, Lesne decided to leave the Centres Sociaux Éducatifs

and accept a professorship in ethnology and sociology at the University of Algiers. Directorship passed to Maxime Marchand, a French writer of distinction, a doctor of letters, and a veteran French educator in Algeria. By this time, violence had escalated to an uncontrollable level. Peace talks and the possibility of a settlement were underway. Both the OAS and the FLN were engaged in a high-pitched battle of terrorism and counterterrorism.

Now working for the Centres, Feraoun and Hammoutene were disturbed by the violence. But toward the end of the war the two men diverged in their interpretations of Algeria's future. Feraoun, though still an undeniable humanist, began to despair regarding the possibility of future Franco-Muslim solidarity. By September 1961, according to Feraoun, solidarity had been destroyed by the war's violence: "Even if France is successful in removing itself and its soldiers, the game is underway between the indigenous people and the Europeans, and it will terminate to the advantage of one or the other of the protagonists."[90]

As discouraged as he was by the increasing violence, Hammoutene responded differently to his calling by the Centres Sociaux Éducatifs, which he described as the "vast field of psychological observation where I will learn to know man in the ordinary sense of the word, man as life's actor."[91] Hammoutene seemed to find in the Centres a personal means to achieve leadership. In reference to perception by his colleagues he wrote: "I am not an Arab with a [personality] complex; my dignity will be protected whatever the price. It is a matter of showing that a Muslim has the responsibility to show himself equal to the importance of the position confided to him, that he can assume the responsibilities as leader of the Service." A month later he wrote that an important part of this responsibility was the "protection of the love of Man." Rooted within the love of man, for which Hammoutene expressed unflinching belief, he was certainly aware of the impact of politics on the Centres.[92] Moreover, like Feraoun, he realized that the antagonism between the two communities and between the OAS and the FLN did directly affect the Centres, but Hammoutene hoped one would realize that there was more to do than to "tear each other up" (139). Ultimately, directly in line with the liberal individualist philosophy expressed by Aguesse, Hammoutene wrote that the Centres could eventually play an important role in this realization by helping men and women "become conscious of their dignity" and in this way overcome their misery (144).

Perhaps the Algerian intellectuals realized too well that getting to this new stage would be difficult. For example, on February 17, 1962, in the letter to his lifelong friend Emmanuel Roblès, less than a month before he was assassinated, Feraoun seemed to foreshadow the tragic events of March 15.[93] "I am well set up at Clos-Salembier," he wrote, "but everything is poisoned, all seems to be resting on a volcano. We wait, like everyone else, that is all."[94] The last lines in his seven-year journal need no comment:

> Terror reigns in Algiers. . . . No, of course, we no longer distinguish between the courageous and the cowardly. Unless after living in fear for so long, we have all become insensitive and unaware. Of course, I do not want to die, and I certainly do not want my children to die. But I am not taking any special precautions, aside from those that have become habits for the past couple of weeks: limiting reasons to go out, stocking up for several days, cutting out visits to friends. Just the same, every time that anyone goes out, he comes back to describe a murder or report a victim.[95]

The next day Feraoun was shot twelve times with a machine gun, along with his five Centres Sociaux colleagues. Feraoun's son Ali wrote in a letter to Emmanuel Roblès directly after the murder: "I saw him at the morgue. Twelve bullets, but not one on his face. My father was beautiful, but completely frozen as though he did not want to look at anybody. There were fifty, maybe a hundred, like him, on tables, on benches, on the floor, everywhere. They had laid my father down on a table, in the center" (315).

There was a nationwide protest against the massacre of the six men working for the Centres Sociaux. French and Algerian commentators unanimously deplored it. Denis Forestier interpreted the crimes of El Biar in an article titled "Crime against Culture." The OAS, he wrote, was the "organization born of the criminal action of felon officers, of civilians without scruples, supported by the 'desperados' of youth, which has attained the highest level of nihilism."[96] The crime was against "culture" because these educators were attacked for their devotion to ameliorating the conditions of the Muslim masses. The persecution of the Centres was begun by those seeking to destroy the true promotion of peace. Despite being endangered by the activities of the fascists, Fourestier claimed, the educators continued to work for the expression of peace. It was Colonel Gardes, that "Machiavelli of the OAS," who had accused the Centres of being a holdout for the FLN. "How could that criminal felon have not set his killers against these educators, his fundamental adversaries?"

In Le Monde Germaine Tillion, the original architect of the Centres Sociaux, published an eloquent and furious article condemning the OAS for its fascist massacre of these innocent men. Like other commentators, she recounted her profound admiration for Mouloud Feraoun: "This honest man, this good man, this man who never did wrong to anyone, and who devoted his life to the public good, and who was one of the greatest writers in Algeria, has been assassinated. . . . Not by accident, not by mistake, but called by his name and killed with preference. This man who believed in humanity moaned and agonized four hours,[97] not by the fault of a microbe, of car brakes that did not work, of a thousand accidents which are on the lookout for our lives, but because it [his assassination] entered into the imbecilic calculations of murdering monkeys who make the law in Algeria."[98] What made this crime against Feraoun and his five colleagues particularly heinous was that the fascists in the OAS had murdered several men who, regardless of their religions and national background, were unified in the common and sublime goal of protecting the children in Algeria. In fact, this care for Algeria's youth is what probably mandated their execution in the minds of the OAS.[99] It is one of the most tragic ironies of the French-Algerian War that on March 18, 1962, the day the Evian Accords were signed, the lives of the six men massacred at El Biar were celebrated at the cemetery of El Alia, a town on the outskirts of Algiers. It was a day of peace, mourning, and bitter ironies. At the sides of the families of the slain were the rector of the University of Algiers (Gilbert Meyer), the French delegate general (Jean Morin), the French minister of public works (Pierre Guillaumat), and the French minister of national education (Lucien Paye). Paye celebrated the lives and heroism of the six men and confessed his public shame that French people could be in any way associated with the death of these noble men: "That such a crime can have been inspired, decided, and committed by men who claim to be part of France seemed not so long ago impossible."[100]

Yet, despite the public honor rendered to the victims of the "imbecilic" killing, the time had not come for reconciliation between the two communities. The French of Algeria faced a questionable future. While schools were temporarily suspended and while people were observing silence out of respect for those assassinated by the OAS, the General Association of the Students of Algeria, a right-wing student organization, issued a communiqué in Algiers on March 21 in which it claimed that the murder of the Centres Sociaux employees was being exploited by the French government— whereas, so the pied noir students complained, the murder of the European students by the FLN was being overlooked.

By the time the French fled Algeria after the Evian Accords, all realistic hopes of lasting Franco-Muslim solidarity had been abandoned. In France and Algeria, roaming OAS squads continued to seek out victims, and it was not until 1963 that most leaders were captured. Ironically Jacques Soustelle, the man responsible for the creation of the Centres Sociaux, was then living in exile from France because he had become one of four leaders of the Conseil National de la Résistance, widely considered the political wing of the OAS. When 90 percent of the French population left, the OAS feverishly destroyed hospitals, schools, agricultural resources, communications, and administrative fabrics. If they could no longer enjoy their former lifestyle, they would assure that the new Algerian nation also could not. For the next few years, under Ahmed Ben Bella and then Houari Boumediene, Algeria was faced with reconstructing its distorted economy and identity.

In retrospect, it is possible to see that the educational attempts of the Centres Sociaux represented the last noble but impossible effort to build a bridge of fraternity between the French and Algerians. Faced as they were with Algeria's turbulence, their labors of keeping fraternity alive were simply unequal to the violence and to the politics of decolonization. Had such an effort to "modernize" the Algerian population been activated before the war began, Feraoun and Hammoutene freely acknowledged, the situation might indeed have turned out differently. However, as evidenced in the trials of its members in 1957 and 1959, as well as in the continued accusations of police and military authorities, an apolitical educational philosophy simply did not conform to the pressures of the wartime hysteria. Consequently, the "third way" efforts of its original leader, Charles Aguesse, appeared hopelessly anachronistic.

This is not to argue that there was no utility in the programs instituted by the Service. The very fact that the Service was not victimized by the FLN, as it had been by the OAS, testified, according to former members, that the Service was seen as helpful to Algeria's postwar future.[101] It was widely acknowledged that after liberation the Algerian leaders realized the need for an elite and a mass capable of making the transition to a modern economy. Hence the need to provide the population with basic literacy, agricultural education, medical attention, and light industrial experience was seldom, if ever, challenged by the rebellion's leadership.

The Service was truly the final attempt to bridge the gap between the metropolitan French government and the Muslim community in Algeria. Unfortunately, the bridge of reform was constructed over a dangerous abyss of extremism and the bridge itself was engulfed in a chilling fog of uncertainty. When the *ultras* looked at the bridge from below, all they saw was a wobbly structure that allowed their "enemies" to cross to revolution. From above—from the far-removed safety of metropolitan France—the French government in Paris continually tinkered with a design it knew it had constructed on a major twentieth-century fault line. Those on the bridge, those trying to offer both sides of the Franco-Muslim community safe passage, felt only the fog's cold bite closing in on them and the tremors racing through the suspended structure. All they eventually heard were the shouts of hostility rising from the depths of the abyss—until, finally, six innocent and noble intellectuals were gunned down on a hot, March morning at El Biar in 1962. On that fateful day, French extremists pulled the only surviving bridge of Franco-Muslim solidarity into the abyss.

4. THE UNBEARABLE SOLITUDE OF BEING
The Question of Albert Camus

> *To tell the truth, it is not easy, and I can understand why artists regret their former comfort. The change is somewhat cruel. Indeed, history's amphitheater has always contained the martyr and the lion. The former relied on eternal consolation and the latter on raw historical meat. But until now the artist was on the sidelines. He used to sing purposely, for his own sake, or at best to encourage the martyr and make the lion forget his appetite. But now the artist is in the amphitheater. Of necessity, his voice is not quite the same; it is not nearly so firm.*
>
> ALBERT CAMUS, December 14, 1957

In the present chapter we return to metropolitan France and the debates over intellectual legitimacy by focusing on the question of Albert Camus. [1] Perhaps even more than Jacques Soustelle, Camus challenged the dominant paradigm of intellectual commitment and fought tooth and nail against the idea that being an intellectual meant being a full-fledged anticolonialist. Without doubt, by his death in 1960, his position on Algeria had become an unassailable wall between himself and a vast majority of French and Algerian intellectuals. In this respect, Camus's (non)participation in the Algerian drama became so central to the identity debates and issues of intellectual legitimacy that a comprehensive study of the French-Algerian War neglecting the question of Camus would be suspicious. Unpacking Camus's place in the history of the war also allows us to test the limitations of traditional distinctions between committed and apolitical intellectuals. As will become apparent, Camus's paradox was that he was both strikingly aware and unaware that, with time, his vision for Algeria became ever more outdated. He remained opposed to Algerian independence because he simply refused to acknowledge the existence of two irreconcilable "personalities" in Algeria and he believed that France (and the French) belonged there.

If being out of step with his own time was a curse for Camus during the French-Algerian War, this curse has proved to be his posthumous blessing. As is discussed near the end of the present chapter, many of Camus's former Algerian and French critics have been forced to make an abrupt about-face in light of recent political and moral catastrophes in contemporary Algeria. What critics now acknowledge is that Camus cannot be viewed just as an apologist for colonialism or for his mother—as many claimed during the war—because many of his disagreeable predictions about Algeria's future came true. He was especially adept in predicting how the FLN's penchant for authoritarianism would threaten Algerian society. Whether his ability to predict the future excuses or explains his refusal to acknowledge Algeria's right to become a fully autonomous nation is a very difficult question because it hinges on our ability to rethink and reassess Camus both with and without the benefit of hindsight. This is especially true vis-à-vis the issue of identity.

There was a unique relationship between Camus's view on the identity question and his politics, but for the majority of right-wing and left-wing intellectuals it remained enigmatic. In defying their logic, he also defied their definitions of intellectual legitimacy. In an epoch when "political correctness" required that both right-wing and left-wing intellectuals legitimate themselves by putting their beliefs on the public's table, his self-imposed silence on the Algerian question (which distinguished his position from Soustelle's) was no insignificant detail. [2] And Camus's "politics of clean hands," as one critic called it, won him few friends. [3] The idea of having clean hands in a dirty war simply discredited the notion of intellectual engagement. As a result, the French left, the French ultras, and even his Algerian intellectual comrades never forgave him for the unpopular and imprudent comments arising from his desire to keep his hands clean. Simone de Beauvoir offered one of the best examples of a peer's disdain for his politics:

> The use of torture was by now such a well-established fact that even the Church had been forced to make a pronouncement on its legality. Many priests rejected it, both in word and deed, but there were also chaplains on hand to encourage the corps d'élite; as for the bishops, most of them carried tolerance pretty far, and not one risked raising his voice in reprobation. Among the laity, what a deafening silence of consent! I was revolted by Camus' refusal to speak. He could no longer argue, as he had done during the war in Indochina, that he did not want to play the Communists' game; so he just mumbled something about the problem not being understood in France. When he went to Stockholm to receive his Nobel Prize, he betrayed himself even further. He boasted of the freedom of the press in France: that week, L'Express, L'Observateur, and France-Nouvelle were all seized. In front of an enormous audience, he declared: "I love Justice; but I will fight for my mother before Justice,"

which amounted to saying that he was on the side of the *pieds noirs*. The fraud lay in the fact that he posed at the same time as a man above the battle, thus providing a warning for those who wanted to reconcile this war and its methods with bourgeois humanism. [4]

What de Beauvoir neglected to mention was that Camus's decision to remain silent came only after he participated in public debates, and the public (French and Algerian Muslims alike) found his stance favoring Franco-Arab reconciliation not only unacceptable but also anachronistic. [5] But Camus had his reasons, for he believed that he could salvage Algeria's Franco-Arab community only through silence. Nevertheless, his contradictory transition from outspoken commentator on questions of violence and liberty during his Resistance days to quintessential reticent intellectual concerning the Algerian question raised eyebrows and exacted heavy personal and professional costs. Simone de Beauvoir was only one of hundreds of intellectuals who condemned Camus as a hypocrite. However, part of Camus's importance as an intellectual was his resiliency to criticism and his unequivocal belief that his silence was worth the price, especially if by it he could somehow calm the FLN's terrorism and the equally reprehensible violence of the French *colons*. Nonviolence, he insisted (especially since he refused to acknowledge that the French and the Arabs constituted two separate and antagonistic identities), clearly transcended the demands of Parisian intellectual legitimacy and Algerian or French nationalism.

But even his closest friends could not completely forgive (although many said they understood) him for holding a position that placed him on a par with the nefarious Jacques Soustelle. [6] Camus's insistence on the French settlers' rights to stay in Algeria and his denial of Algerian demands for independence, for many, made further hypocrisy of the principles for which he had come to be a major guardian in post–World War II France. Some, like Jean Daniel and Jules Roy, realized that criticizing Camus's silence would be no use, but (as French Algerians themselves) they recognized his personal motivations for not wanting to add to the chaotic Algerian violence. [7] Decolonization, they all agreed to some extent, engendered a specific type of violence that could be aggravated by inflammatory intellectual pronouncements.

Yet, because he was a cultural and intellectual icon, Camus's handling of the East-West question disheartened many intellectuals, especially Algerians, and was an unhealthy reminder of the chauvinism implicit in French representations of Algerians. Throughout the conflict, one of the principal reasons for Camus's opacity was his vision of Algerians ("Arabs") as being impregnated with French culture. A Frenchman from Algeria, Camus never seemed to hear the paternalism in his voice when he spoke of the "Orient," "Arabs," and Algerians. Important Francophone Algerian intellectuals such as Mouloud Feraoun and Kateb Yacine tried in vain to convince him that the Algerians' demands for national sovereignty overrode their identification with the French nation and the hypocritical French republic, but Camus refused to listen.

Eventually even his most loyal friends were forced to admit that Camus's dilemma was incredibly simple: he did not believe in Algerian independence. Dialogue would not change his mind. Strangely, after he died, Camus seemed to take on additional value in the debates, to live, as it were, a second life in the heart of the French intelligentsia. Although deeply saddened by his death, some felt liberated by their loss because Camus's intellectual afterlife gave them the sudden opportunity to set the record straight for him. His ghost thus became part of an intellectual tug-of-war between those who sought to resurrect him in order to claim him for French humanism and those who desired to see him forgotten in a shallow grave of chauvinistic hypocrisy.

Camus's private and public confrontations provide us with unique details of the agonizing contradictions of his personal identity and the Franco-Arab identity, which he believed to exist in Algeria. In this sense, we shall see how the drama of decolonization in Algeria gave rise to Camus's paradox and how the personal contradictions of a major French intellectual eventually affected other intellectuals. It will become clear that the politicization of intellectual legitimacy during the French-Algerian War overran Camus's liberalism, leaving it practically defenseless in the face of other intellectuals who deemed his notion of liberal humanism ideologically and politically outdated. In order to appreciate the full extent of his paradox and of the war's impact on his later politics, it is necessary first to understand how Camus emerged from his youth as a champion of Algerian political rights.

The Early Camus and His Commitment to Arab Equality

A pied noir, Camus was born on November 7, 1913 to French parents in the Algerian port city of Bône, now Annaba. Camus's father, Lucien Auguste Camus, had been a soldier in the military forces that invaded Morocco in 1907. His father later returned to North Africa, this time to Algeria, as an employee in the wine industry. In 1914, Lucien Camus was again called for military service and died in October of that year on a battlefield in northern France. Along with his mother Catherine and his brother Lucien, Albert Camus continued to live in Algeria. Until he was seventeen he stayed with his grandmother and mother in Belcourt, the working-class section of Algiers. Growing to adulthood in this city where the "Arabs" mixed unequally with the French profoundly marked Camus's writings, especially his concern for Arab equality.

As a journalist in his twenties, Camus was one of the first *pieds noirs* to write about the poverty of the non-European population and advocate political and social change for disinherited Algerians. As a result, he later claimed, he was also the first *pied noir* to be expelled from Algeria for taking up the Algerian cause. Both events—writing about Algerian poverty and being persecuted for doing so—served as constant points of reference throughout his life.

From his earliest writings, Camus never denied the existence of separate communities in Algeria. However, he usually divided these communities roughly into *colons* and "Arabs." He distinguished between the minority of *colons* who exploited and the majority who did not.[8] He separated "Arabs" loosely into the "Kabyles" and the "Muslims"—an inconsistent distinction because the Kabyles are Berber by ethnicity and Muslim by religion. The interaction of these divisions can be found in almost all Camus's writings on Algeria.

Throughout his personal and private life, he held to the idea that equality between *colons* and Arabs would be reached though the expansion of full French democratic rights and the assimilation of all Algerians into the French economy. From his earliest writings until his death in early 1960, he expressed his belief that a French-Arab community could survive in Algeria only through the assimilation of Algerians. Separating Arabs from the French in Algeria would destroy the Algerian community and cause the expulsion of the French.

As early as 1939 Camus wrote a series of articles in a socialist and radical newspaper, *Alger républicain*, titled "The Poverty of the Kabyles."[9] At age twenty-five he traveled through the Kabyle region, describing the "physical misery" (malnutrition) he believed was caused by overpopulation. In some areas, Camus wrote, 80 percent of the population was poor; in others 35 of 110 schoolchildren ate only one meal a day. To confront this extreme poverty, it was necessary to offer the Kabyles a "politics of social constructiveness"

(912). This meant fighting against prejudices, especially the current notion of "Kabyle mentality" (which argued that their poverty resulted from their mental character). According to Camus, the French used this notion to avoid responsibility for the Kabyles' social and economic conditions.

Addressing the Kabyles' misery, though, also meant that France had to educate them. According to Camus, the Kabyles were quick to realize "what an instrument of emancipation the schools could be" (919). But the chronic shortage of schools was tied to political and social inequality. "The Kabyles," Camus wrote, "will have more schools the day when we will have suppressed the artificial barrier which separates European teaching from indigenous teaching, the day, finally, when, on the chairs of the same school, two peoples made to understand each other will commence to know each other" (923).

Writing in 1939, Camus was well aware that the French in Algeria did not want Algerians fully assimilated into French society. Camus also understood that metropolitan France was not without sin, but he believed that one of the principal ways of rectifying past mistakes would be to offer schools to the Kabyles (and other Algerian ethnic groups). Through the social instrument of the schools, the two communities would move closer together. Camus's optimism met continual resistance, not from Algerians, but from Algeria's powerful French population.

Settler opposition to ameliorating indigenous Algerians' social and economic conditions was frustrating for Camus, but he argued earlier than many French intellectuals that real assimilation of Algerians into French society could be guaranteed only by granting full political rights under the French Republic. "In any case," he claimed, "if they [the French] really want assimilation and if they want these proud people to be French, we cannot start by separating them from the French" (923). In the end, according to Camus, by joining the two peoples equally, by providing the Kabyles with education, "mutual comprehension [would] start" (923).[10]

Since the French treatment of Algerians called into question French justice and humanity, Camus's diagnosis led him to question the essence of French identity: "I should say that it is difficult today to know how to be a good Frenchman." One prescription, Camus claimed, was to know how to "repair injustice" (937). And for Camus French democracy and responsibility from 1939 on would become inextricably bound up with the Algerian question. An essential part of Camus's *autocritique* was not only to question France's initial occupation of Algeria but also to acknowledge that a continued French presence in Algeria could be justified solely if France aided Algerians. According to Camus:

> If the colonial conquest can ever find an excuse, it is in the extent to which it aids those who are conquered to keep their personality. And if we have an obligation in that country, it is to permit one of the proudest and most human populations in the world stay true to itself and its destiny.
>
> The destiny of this people, I do not think I am wrong in saying, is to simultaneously work and think, and through these actions to give lessons of wisdom to the troubled conquerors that we are. Let us know, at least, how to pardon ourselves for this fever and need of power, so natural for mediocre people, in taking it upon ourselves to care for the needs of a wiser people, in order to deliver them, in their entirety, to their profound grandeur. (938)

Camus remained faithful to the argument that the original sin of the colonial conquest could be atoned for by delivering the "conquered" to their "profound grandeur," but he stopped short of bringing the proposition to its proper conclusion. If the French continually refused to bring out Algerians' grandeur, could Algerians reject French rights of occupation? This issue would go to the heart of the debate over the question of Camus, but in 1939 his decision to speak out in favor of a more just politics in Algeria was momentous.[11]

A few years later, during the Nazi occupation of France, Camus forged a well-established literary career and a reputation as a defender of the right to resist oppression. One of the most striking pieces he wrote during this period was "Letters to a German Friend." Written in 1943 about the Nazis' defeat of the French, Camus claimed that in attacking France, Germany had attacked the vanguard of justice:

> It taught us that, contrary to what we sometimes used to think, the spirit is of no avail against the sword, but that the spirit together with the sword will always win out over the sword alone. That is why we have now accepted the sword, after making sure that the spirit was on our side. . . . We have paid dearly, and we have not finished paying. But we have our certainties, our justifications, our justice; your defeat is inevitable.[12]

While Camus wrote about the injustice of the Nazi occupation, Algerian nationalists lodged similar complaints against the French "occupation" of

Algeria. In 1943, Ferhat Abbas drafted the "Manifesto of the Algerian People" with the approval of the banned Parti du Peuple Algérien (PPA) and other important Algerian leaders. The manifesto was given by Abbas to Governor General Peyrouton, who accepted it as the start of dialogue. [13] Among other things, the manifesto called for the "condemnation and abolition of colonialism," and specifically for an Algerian constitution, the right of all people to "determine their own fate," and the "release of all political prisoners and detainees regardless of party." [14] In response, the French government promised a program of reform known as the Ordinance of March 7, 1944, which did nothing to rid Algeria of the bicultural distinction or significantly alter the status quo. Consequently, it was rejected by Abbas, the Messalists, and the reformist 'ulama (Islamic leaders). Abbas then created a movement called Les Amis du Manifeste et de la Liberté (AML).

On May Day 1945, a demonstration led by the AML displayed the Algerian nationalist flag and called for the release of Messali Hadj from prison and for Algerian independence. Violence broke out in Algiers, Oran, and other places. A few days later, on May 8, the French and Algerians celebrated V-E Day. In Sétif and Guelma the Muslims did not collaborate with police orders not to display nationalist flags. Police charged the demonstrating Muslims, and the Muslims countered, triggering a larger insurrection. After more than a week of French military reprisals, an estimated one hundred Europeans were killed. Official French sources claimed that only 1,500 Muslims were killed by the French; other sources claimed between 7,000 and 40,000 (149). Abbas was arrested, along with 5,560 other Muslims; many other arrests were expected, and the AML was dissolved by the French government.

After the liberation of France, while directing the powerful newspaper Combat, Camus decided to report on Algeria again. In Paris he anxiously received information about the brutalities of May 1945. In the first article on the May crisis, Camus cautioned against hasty reprisals aimed at the Arab community. Since Algeria could not be seen by the French only as three departments belonging to France, the French would have to remember that the "Arab people exist. I mean that it is not an anonymous and miserable crowd, where the West sees nothing to respect or defend." [15] The Algerian people, he wrote, are proud and rooted in strong traditions. Violently reacting to the Algerian crisis would only damage future relations with Arabs. To understand the events of May, therefore, observers would have to see the crisis as the Algerians' thirst for justice. "Instead of responding with condemnations," Camus wrote, "let us try to understand the reasons and allow the democratic principles we claim for ourselves help us in understanding" (943).

In much the same vein as his earlier articles, Camus's perspective on May 1945 presented poverty and famine as the principal motivators in the uprising, The inequality in food distribution, for example, led to conflict. Just as important, political inequality had become unbearable for Algeria's Arabs. France, as the vanguard of democracy and justice, had created contradictions for itself because it had simultaneously claimed to incarnate the universalism of democracy and denied the application of democratic principles to colonial populations under its control. [16] The Arabs, according to Camus, had been deceived too often by the unfulfilled promises. Maintained in a position of constant inferiority, the Arabs "seem to have lost faith in democracy" (952). As a result, by 1945 assimilation had become a difficult proposition to uphold. Why?

Camus answered this question in an article in which he claimed that Ferhat Abbas was a product of French culture. As the animator of the AML, Abbas had once been an important advocate of assimilation. Abbas and others like him, however, had lost faith in the French and the assimilation movement because France failed to support democratic enfranchisement of Arabs. France had helped the separatist movements gain power because it had responded with imprisonment and repression. This policy of responding to nationalists with repression was "pure and simple stupidity." [17]

In the conclusion to these articles, Camus claimed that, despite the violence and repression, hope still existed. "If we want to save North Africa, we have to show our resolve before the world to make France known through its best laws and with the most just of men" (959). Hence in the earlier Camus writings we find a profound faith that the West could triumph in Algeria if it applied democratic reform. In his words, it is only the "infinite force of justice, and that alone, which should help us reconquer Algeria and its inhabitants" (959).

Until the outbreak of the French-Algerian War on November 1, 1954, Camus continued to exert his growing reputation in favor of justice for North Africa. For example, along with many influential intellectuals, Camus participated in the Comité pour l'Amnestie aux Condamnés Politiques d'Outre-Mer. [18] Under the presidency of Louis Massignon, this committee attempted to secure pardons for a significant number of condemned North Africans.

North Africa, however, was not Camus's only political preoccupation before the outbreak of the war. In 1947 he broke with the PCF because of his disenchantment with Soviet totalitarianism. In 1950 he clarified his position on political violence and revolutionary mythology with the publication of his play Les Justes.[19] With his two characters, Stepan and Kaliayev, Camus asked the audience whether justice could be done with assassination if innocent blood (in this case, children's) was spilled. Kaliayev exclaims to Stepan:

> I shall not strike my brothers in the face for the sake of some far-off city, which for all I know, may not exist. I refuse to add to the living injustice all around me for the sake of dead justice. . . . Killing children is crime against man's honor. And if one day the revolution thinks fit to break with honor, well, I'm through. . . .
>
> STEPAN: Honor is a luxury reserved for people who have carriages-and-pairs.
>
> KALIAYEV: No. It's the one wealth left to a poor man.[20]

Without a doubt, Camus challenged the dominant postwar orthodoxy, but it was really in 1951 that he struck hardest into the heart of contemporary Communist mythology with the publication of L'Homme révolté (The Rebel). After a review of Camus's work by Francis Jeanson for Les Temps modernes, Camus and Sartre engaged in a widely publicized epistolary exchange.[21] By most accounts, Camus came out wounded. History, at least its Marxist version, was on Sartre's side for the moment.

A few months before the publication of The Rebel, Camus began to get his first sense of the Algerian intellectuals' criticism of his work with regard to Algeria. On October 18, 1951, he received a letter from Mouloud Feraoun. Having recently sent Camus a copy of his own novel, Le Fils du pauvre: Menrad, l'instituer kabyle (1950), Feraoun praised Camus's La Peste (The Plague) and writings in Alger républicain, which Feraoun said he understood "better than he has ever understood any other [writer's work]."[22] However, as a Kabyle and a Muslim, Feraoun also noted his belief that Camus's work had fallen short because Camus had not made sufficient effort to incorporate Algerians into his writing:

> [It is regrettable that] among all your characters there was not one indigenous person and that Oran was in your eyes nothing but a banal police headquarters. Oh! This is not a reproach. I simply thought that, if there were not this gulf between us, you would have known us better, you would have sensed yourself capable to speak of us with the same generosity that benefits everyone else. I will always regret, with all my heart, that you do not know us

sufficiently and that we have no one who understands us, to make us understood, and who helps us understand ourselves. (203)

Feraoun conceded that Camus was successful in making the universal human character come out in all, whereas Feraoun had only rendered the Kabyles understandable to other Algerians. "I have the intention to write, to speak of our compatriots such as I see them, but I do not have illusions. My view would be too short and my means are too small" (203).

Camus and the French-Algerian War

As a leading *pied noir* intellectual, Camus worked hard during the first years of the French-Algerian War to make the crisis understandable to the people in metropolitan France. He did so, in part, by continually emphasizing his personal relationship to Algeria and to the French and Arabs there. As Feraoun suggested he should, he used his tremendous status as a French-Algerian intellectual to influence public opinion and to introduce the Algerian people to a distrustful and biased French audience. Camus was working in the interest of Franco-Arab reconciliation, however, so his vision of Algerians emphasized their basic resemblance to the French, not their differences.

One of Camus's principal vehicles for bringing his opinions to bear on the Algerian drama was his short-lived involvement with *L'Express*. Jean-Jacques Servan-Schreiber, *L'Express* director, had been trying to recruit Camus for some time. Jean Daniel (Camus's close friend, fellow French-Algerian, and *L'Express* editor) convinced him to contribute to *L'Express*. [23]

After a frustrating beginning in May 1955, Camus's articles concentrated on the problem of violence. [24] In "Terrorism and Repression," which appeared on July 9, 1955, Camus focused on the dialectics of violence and tried to restore confidence in reconciliation; he warned of a defeatism that consigned the Algerian drama to premature violence:

> Metropolitan France, indifferent that the colony is exasperated, seems to admit that a Franco-Arab community is impossible and that resorting to force is more or less necessary. In the name of progress or reaction here, by terror or repression over there, everyone seems to accept the worst in advance: the definitive separation of the French and the Arabs on the ground of blood and prisons.
>
> I am among those who cannot yet resign himself to see this great country break in two forever. The Franco-Arab community . . . exists already for me, as it does for many French Algerians. [25]

Refusing to accept the politics of expulsion for *colons*, Camus saw that the solution could not be as simple as "kill or flee" for the French. In order to overcome this tragic dilemma, Camus argued, one had to acknowledge the French role in fostering Algerian terrorism.

Unlike Soustelle, Camus argued that responsibility for terrorism lay in the miscarriage of French reforms and in the *colons'* unwillingness to make even limited concessions to Algeria's Arabs. The Arab people had been forced to "live without a future and in humiliation," as a result of the *colons'* blindness to Arab demands for political equality. Camus backed up this claim by pointing out how the *colons* had blocked the Blum-Viollette project in 1936, which would have allowed twenty to thirty thousand Algerian Muslims (*évolués*) to receive full political enfranchisement without having to relinquish their personal or religious status. He added that the Sétif massacre in 1945 along with the failure of the 1948 elections had clarified the fact that *colons* had continued to reject even partial assimilation of Algeria's Arabs into mainstream French society. These failures, Camus argued, were French and had given rise to the dialectic of violence.

Interestingly, however, Camus added that this dialectic was not immanent in the French-Arab community; rather, it was a historical phenomenon activated by the failure of French reforms. It could have been otherwise. In other words, terrorism was contingent, and the increase in repression fed the increase in terrorism. "Every repression, measured or demented, each police torture like every legal judgment, has accentuated the despair and the violence of the stricken militants. To finish, the police have hatched terrorists who have given birth themselves to a multiplied police force." Yet, regardless of French violence, Camus asked, Could the Arabs justifiably use terrorism to advance their cause?

The answer was no. Algerian terrorism and French repression each militated against the Franco-Arab community, and because they were both "negative actions" they could not solve the Algerian crisis. Moreover, the Arabs' terrorism created another problem. Just as repression had sparked the rebellion, terrorism ran the risk of becoming "racist." Terrorism was not exposed to political control and was susceptible to becoming a "crazy weapon of elementary hate."

Terrorism had other serious consequences in France and Algeria. It silenced liberal French intellectuals and played to the advantage of "the party of reaction and repression." Liberals, Camus argued, were finding it increasingly difficult to argue on behalf of Algerians, knowing that FLN members slit French and Algerian peasants' throats and set schools (which housed French soldiers) on fire. Furthermore, liberals realized that in Algeria the FLN's isolated acts of violence caused collective repression against the whole population.

To escape the infernal cycle of terrorism and blind repression, Camus called for a conference, a Round Table, for the leaders of the various Algerian political movements and the French government. Since Camus, like many other French intellectuals, refused to grant the FLN unique authority to represent Algeria's Arabs, he argued that all Algerian factions—the Union Démocratique du Manifeste Algérien (UDMA), 'Ulamas, the FLN, and the MNA—would have to be brought together. [26] This union, Camus claimed, would chart the possible reforms and work for a peaceful solution to the Algerian drama. Only through acts like this could the Arabs and the French be allowed to choose something other than "solitude and resignation."

Camus's Vision of Cultural Fusion in Algeria

As Camus continued to militate for peaceful coexistence in Algeria, he became preoccupied with the relationship between West and Orient. His statements on Algeria during the war acknowledged the differences between the Arabs and the French but celebrated a special type of cultural fusion there. On July 23, 1955, he followed his essay on terrorism with an essay on Algeria's future. Algeria's Arabs, he wrote, had been put in an extremely difficult position by extremists because they had been forced to choose between "silence and violence." [27] Here he is not far from Algerian writers such as Feraoun; however, Camus insisted that colonialism could be viewed positively only if it "favors the personality of the colonized people." Reminiscent of the Comité d'Action themes during the Salle Wagram meeting, Camus suggested that the Algerian drama needed to be seen as one "particular case of a historical drama." This drama was ultimately "a great movement" that forced the "oriental masses" to conquer "their personality." [28]

The awakening of the "oriental masses" meant that France could no longer casually neglect Arab needs. Camus advocated political federation between France and Algeria. "The future of our world," he claimed, rested on a solution to this new challenge. Federalism was the only real solution because it would incorporate aspects of both civilizations. In fact, the power and strength of North Africa resided in the mélange of civilizations:

> In this common country, of which the Mediterranean is always the living heart, the fusion of the Orient and the West is realized several times as the occasion for a creative synthesis. As there was once an Arab vocation [for France], there is now a French vocation, which is both historic and cultural; it draws out the resemblance between the Orient and the West, and, therefore, federates the overseas territories with metropolitan France.

While Camus reflected on the synthesis of the Orient and the West in Algeria, the facts of the war did little to encourage others to believe in Camus's imagined Algerian federation. Moreover, the Philippeville massacre of August 20, 1955, destroyed possibilities for Franco-Arab elections and reforms. The violence continued to separate the two communities, and Camus admitted that after Philippeville the *colons* knew Soustelle's programs were doomed. Association was outdated because it had never truly been attempted, and "the Arab people had kept its personality which cannot be reduced to ours." [29] The choice, as Philippeville had shown, was between "association" and mutual "destruction." According to Camus, "the choice in Algeria was not between resignation or reconquest, but between a marriage of convenience and a marriage of death for two xenophobias" (977).

In order to reach the Algerian audience, in October Camus published his "Letter to an Algerian Militant" in the first issue of the Algerian journal *Communauté algérienne*. [30] In his letter to Aziz Kessous, the "militant" director of *Communauté*, Camus again addressed the problem of Philippeville. Now that the French and Arabs were "pitted against each other," it was impossible, he wrote, to forget the tragic effects of this division. Deeply angered by the massacre, he continued, the "French fact" could not

> be eliminated in Algeria, and the dream of a sudden disappearance of France is childish. But there is no reason either why nine million Arabs should live on their land like forgotten men; the dream that the Arab masses can be canceled out, silenced and subjugated, is just as mad. The French are attached to the soil of Algeria by roots that are too old and too vigorous for us to think of tearing them up. But this gives the French no right, in my opinion, to destroy the roots of Arab culture and life. Throughout my life I have fought for sweeping and profound reforms—and you know that I have paid for this with exile from my country. But people refused to believe because they cherished the dream of power that is supposedly eternal and forget that history constantly progresses; and now those

reforms are needed more than ever. Those which you point out represent an initial effort, and an indispensable one, to be made quickly, before its chance of success is drowned in French blood and Arab blood.

For French and Arabs to avoid drowning in a suicidal bloodbath, both sides would have to transcend the divisions caused by violence. This, he argued, meant saving innocent civilians: "You Arabs must spare no effort to show your people that when they [members of the FLN] kill civilians, terrorism not only raises justifiable doubts as to the political maturity of men capable of such acts, but also strengthens the anti-Arab elements" (129). If Algerians did not cease terrorism, he warned, French liberals could no longer support them.

Camus either was not fully conscious or cared little that by publicly blaming Arabs for terrorism in Algeria, he was losing the respect of Algerian intellectuals and leaders. But he did not give up the hope of influencing Algerian leaders, and on October 28, 1955, he again tried to reestablish dialogue with the rebels. In "The Reasons of the Adversary," which appeared in L'Express, Camus offered an imaginary deal to Algerians: French liberals would condemn repression if the militant nationalists would condemn violence against civilians. This condemnation of political violence meant that even for victims of oppression (as the Arabs clearly were) there were "certain limits" to justice. [31] At the heart of his efforts to restrain violence was his belief that the Algerian Arabs were being misled by fallacious Egyptian pan-Arabism. It would be a monumental mistake to move in the direction of Nasserist, ideological rejections of the West because Algeria's future, according to Camus, was tied to the technological advancement of France. The nefarious "dream" of pan-Arabism would only serve to isolate the already underdeveloped population from the necessary reforms. "It is not," Camus stated, "by the Orient that the Orient will physically save itself, but by the West, which, in the end, will find nourishment in the civilization of the Orient" (979). Hence, like Soustelle, Camus argued that the impact of the "retrograde" doctrine of the "Arab movement" on Algeria would further separate the Arabs and the French and, therefore, fatefully tear the Orient from its sole means of economic and social progress: the West.

Truce for the Civilians, or Liberalism's Eleventh Hour
During January 1956, Camus claimed that not a day had gone by when he had not heard of Algeria's pain in the letters addressed to him, in the press,

or by phone.[32] As a result, he broadened his campaign against violence in Algeria by joining other liberals in forming the Comité pour une Trêve Civile en Algérie. This committee was composed of both prominent Muslims and French Algerians.[33] Because the extremism of the war continued to destroy hopes for a reconciliation, Camus argued that a high-profile, liberal group was needed to bring the cause to the public's attention. He also asked Algerian nationalists to take the higher moral ground and condemn the killing of innocent civilians. With the aid of the committee, Camus reiterated his pleas to Arab militants and Algeria's colons to stop the killing. In short, Camus and other liberals invested in the idea of a "civilian truce." "Because every death separates the two populations a little more, we have to create, for good, a truce for the massacres of civilians. . . . There is no other solution. . . . Aside from that, there is nothing left but death and destruction."[34]

Above all, finding a civilian truce meant being willing to condemn the violence of the French and Algerians. In a letter to Prime Minister Guy Mollet, the Comité pour une Trêve Civile en Algérie applauded his denunciation of the Algerian terrorists' killing of French women and children, but urged him to be equally vigorous in denouncing French abuses. Mollet had to clarify his intentions to negotiate with the rebels if he desired peace in Algeria. Only through such negotiations, held equally with Muslims and French of Algeria, could the "absurd dream of a total rupture with France" and the "establishment of a fanaticism" be avoided.[35]

On January 22, at great personal risk, Camus delivered a speech in the Cercle du Progrés building located in the grounds of the Place du Gouvernement in Algiers. The audience was composed of equal numbers of Muslims and French. Ferhat Abbas even attended, and, after the audience applauded his entrance, Camus embraced him. Throughout Camus's speech, however, the angry ultra crowd could be heard yelling "Camus to the wall."[36]

During his speech, Camus repeated many of the same arguments he had made in L'Express and elsewhere and said that his identity as a writer and an "Algerian" called him to the podium that day. His appeal, he claimed, was not linked to any political party but resulted from a true concern for Algeria's innocents. "Whatever the ancient and deep origins of the Algerian tragedy, one fact remains: no cause justifies the death of the innocents."[37] The task was now to keep those who did not want to resort to violence from being forced to choose between suffering from or practicing terror (142).

According to Camus biographer Herbert Lottman, Camus did not know that Muslims on the committee were FLN members until he was actually in Algiers for the meeting. When he found out, he wanted to cancel but was advised not to do so. Emmanuel Roblès, in his *Albert Camus et la trêve civile*, published in 1988, also notes that Camus quickly understood that the Muslims participating with the committee were all in the FLN and that their participation extended only as far as the FLN allowed. [38] By March 1956, according to Roblès, the "illusion of civil truce" was dead. Just as the French politicians had claimed that the Muslims would never comply with a civilian truce, the Algerians claimed that the French would refuse to give up their attacks on innocent Algerians.

The project of the civil truce was doubtless anachronistic to Algerians and French alike. On February 3, 1956, Mouloud Feraoun, who was no advocate of violence, noted in his journal his distaste for speeches from Camus and from members of the Comité pour une Trêve Civile en Algérie. After confessing that he had "a lot of admiration" for Camus and "brotherly affection" for Roblès, Feraoun wrote that the French liberals' moment for setting right France's past colonial lies had already passed. According to Feraoun,

> they are wrong to talk to us when we are waiting for generous hearts if there are any; they are wrong to talk to us when they cannot express their thoughts completely. It is a hundred times better that they remain quiet. Because, in the end, this country is indeed called Algeria and its inhabitants are called Algerians. Why sidestep this evidence? Are you Algerians, my friends? You must stand up with those who fight. Tell the French that this country does not belong to them, that they took it over by force, and that they intend to remain here by force. Anything else is a lie and in bad faith. Any other language is criminal because, for several months now, crimes have been committed in the name of the same lies; for several months innocents who have accepted these lies and asked for nothing more than to live within these lies have died. . . . And these innocents are primarily indigenous people. The people who do nothing to escape their condition and who get shot so that others will remain silent. [39]

Since Camus and Roblès were not Algerians, in other words, they had no right to speak for Algerians about decolonization.

Algerian Muslims were not the only ones criticizing Camus's position. In a January 10, 1956, letter addressed to Camus at *L'Express*, a man of French and Italian origin living in Algeria and who identified himself as Monsieur Bret wrote to Camus that, despite his European heritage, he (Bret) was Algerian. Bret wrote that he now chose to be Algerian and had even converted to Islam, not by "religious vocation" but by "reflection." [40] His choice of Islam, Bret continued, allowed him to integrate into the new world, the next Algeria. "I know," he told Camus, "that tomorrow there will be France and Algeria."

Bret suggested that only those who fought for the new Algeria could maintain the title of Algerian. Like Feraoun, he suggested that citizenship in the new Algeria required, above all, a willingness to combat France and the West. "I am ready to fight against France—because I have deliberately broken with my own genealogy, my cultural and above all racial links. And now I am Algerian and I will remain so." Bret concluded that France would not solve the Algerian drama, but that each Algerian, each citizen of the new Algerian nation, would do so together.

The day after the Algiers speech Camus replied to Bret. There could be no doubt, Camus acknowledged, that "the racial and religious gulf is what most profoundly separates French and Arabs in North Africa."[41] Yet, despite these differences, Camus cautioned, it was necessary to seek a "plan for moral rapprochement."

Camus's dream of a civilian truce remained unachievable and hopelessly idealistic because it lacked structural support and because Camus had fundamentally misread the degree to which violence against civilians had become part of French and Algerians' armory. The war's unfortunate logic of violence had rendered the truce utopian even before it began. Even more ironically, although Camus did not understand it at first, many Algerians who participated in the committee did so with the hope of showing that the liberal solutions to the war were no longer acceptable. Algerians thought that the public failure of the committee would force moderate Algerians to fight for independence because it would be clear that there was no longer a viable liberal alternative.

Budapest and Soviet Imperialism

Although Camus was unwilling and unable to see justice in Algerians' desire to be rid of French aggressors, he was more than willing to speak out against the Soviet oppression of Hungary. [42] Not accidentally, Camus had been among the first French intellectuals telegraphed by Hungarian insurgents. [43] On October 31, 1956, he sent a letter to François Fejtö expressing his support for the Hungarian intellectuals. He pledged that he and others "will never leave the October insurgents as long as liberty is not given back to the Hungarian people. It is this sermon of fidelity that should unite us tonight."[44]

Camus blamed the West for sacrificing Hungarians to Moscow.[45] On November 10 he wrote that it was a disgrace to forsake the Hungarian intellectuals who were dying for justice. In order for their sacrifice not to be in vain, intellectuals the world over had to do what they could to protest against the "butchery" and demonstrate that justice still existed in Europe.[46]

Reactions to Camus's statements varied. On the same day that his article protesting Hungary appeared in print, Roger Martin du Gard wrote Camus that he agreed with his statements in *Franc-Tireur*. Regardless of his distrust for the "efficacy of these manifests," Martin du Gard averred that it was necessary to show the West's resolve to stand against the Soviets.[47] Another Frenchman wrote to Camus, expressing his "distrust for intellectualism." Instead, the man wrote, it would better to respond to "those Russian bastards" with violence.[48] In his reply, Camus thanked the man but also warned against provoking more bloodshed.[49]

Camus continued his crusade for Hungary. At a public gathering of French students on November 23, 1956, he delivered a speech titled "Message in Favor of Hungary." The only thing the past twenty years had taught him, Camus said, was the value of liberty. Now that the truth of Stalinism was open for public inspection, and after Hitler's tyranny, freedom had to be preserved. On March 15, 1957, Camus delivered a speech in the Salle Wagram, citing the West's failure to stand up to the Soviets in Hungary as a sign of moral weakness.[50] Yet despite its incontestable weaknesses the West's strength rested on freedom. The fate of Hungarian intellectuals and workers would be a reminder that freedom required the greatest courage to protect.

The Guillotine and Silence

Camus did not seem to notice that his stance against the Soviet occupation of Hungary seemed to contradict his support for a continued French presence in Algeria. The 1957 events forced him to confront this contradiction. In many ways, 1957 was the decisive year in Albert Camus's career: he received the Nobel Prize for Literature and was most severely pummeled with criticism of his position on Algeria. In April Guy Mollet gave Camus the chance to take part in a newly formed Commission de Sauvegarde, designed to investigate the crimes of the French and Algerians in Algeria. Camus refused, saying that the commission was ill-defined and that it lacked the necessary freedom from the French government to be effective. It was also in 1957 that Camus began the campaign against the death penalty.

In an essay "Reflections on the Guillotine" in the June-July 1957 edition of *Nouvelle revue française*, Camus voiced his concern for growing powers of the French state vis-à-vis the individual.[51] This essay was especially important because by 1957 the decision of the French state to use the death penalty during decolonization had become extremely controversial. The subject was so explosive that even the French government had a difficult time defining its position. And whereas Camus doubted the morality of capital punishment, the French government in Paris began to rethink its use of the guillotine because of a profound misunderstanding of the religious beliefs of Algerian Muslims. Under the terms of the Special Powers Act, the French government had been granted the right to use capital punishment in Algeria against convicted rebels. After the first uses of the guillotine on Muslim FLN members, the French government realized that the executions had caused Muslims to turn against France. Incredibly, the government assumed that Algerians' unanimous reaction was a reaction against the guillotine as a mode of execution and not against executions in general. The guillotine insulted Islamic beliefs, the government thought, because under Qur'anic law no one could be executed by decapitation. So the government interpreted the Algerian Muslims' frustration as being based in Islam rather than as a rejection of the French judicial system.

A report to the president of the Criminal Affairs and Pardons Office of the Ministry of Justice (under François Mitterrand) wrote of the problems of capital punishment in Algeria. Under Article 12 of the Penal Code, those sentenced to death were to die by beheading under the guillotine.[52] "Now," the report continued, "this mode of execution can shock the beliefs of Muslims. This is why it appears necessary, from this time on in Algeria, that those sentenced to death should be executed by rifle. This measure is not susceptible to aggravate the condition of the condemned."

Despite this ill-conceived discussion of how best to execute Algerian nationalists so as not to offend Islam, French officials did not want to make unnecessary concessions to the Muslims. On June 13, 1956, the assistant director of the Criminal Affairs and Pardons Office wrote an urgent note concerning the report: the rifle "as a mode of execution for common law is a difficult task."[53] Considering the Muslim response to the guillotine, the note claimed, suspension of the guillotine should be recommended, but might be difficult to make "obligatory." Regardless of Muslim religious practices, the French government did not want to prevent use of guillotines by publicizing concern for the Muslims who protested against it. "On other issues, in underlining in the exposé [on the reforms] the motive that decapitation shocks the beliefs of Muslims, we risk provoking further protest if, in the future, we attempt to return to the mode of execution [the guillotine] provided for by the Penal Code."

Camus's "Reflections on the Guillotine" parted company with the French government and criticized not only the guillotine, which he detested, but capital punishment in general. Capital punishment was an insult to humanity that disgraced France and was part of "its arsenal of repression" (177). It did nothing, as its advocates claimed, to prevent future criminals from killing. If this were truly the intent, Camus argued, then executions should be held in public and the entire population invited to attend. Instead, the executions were held behind the prison walls, and reporters camouflaged them with flowery phrases such as "justice has been done." Regarding Algeria and the potential political misuses of capital punishment, Camus cited the recent execution by guillotine of a French Communist worker for a failed attempt to plant a bomb at an oil refinery. Because of the current climate in Algeria, the French government wanted to "prove to Arab opinion that the guillotine was designed for Frenchmen too and to satisfy the French opinion wrought up by the crimes of terrorism" (215).

Connecting capital punishment with the state's growing power, Camus argued that to defend modern European society it was above all necessary to show civilian resistance to the state. Individuals had to demonstrate their resolve to stand up against the state's oppression, especially this most nefarious type. Civilian opposition to capital punishment would prove that the state could not be considered an absolute value. "Hence we must call a spectacular halt and proclaim, in our principles and institutions, that the individual is above the state" (229).

As sensible as this seemed, in 1957 many of Camus's opponents were happy to seize on his latest writings, even ones related to the death penalty, as long as they could publicly rebuff Camus on the Algerian question. For instance, in his *Bloc-notes* François Mauriac, Camus's longtime antagonist, used the publication of Camus's "Reflections" as an opportunity to ridicule the contradictions of Camus's position on Algeria. Mauriac began by admitting that he shared many of Camus's reservations about the guillotine, yet asked himself, "But why do I feel sick when I read the book?"[54] An intense critic of police brutality against Algerians, Mauriac noted that capital punishment might be a useful weapon against the abusive and corrupt colonial state. In fact, he claimed that, in police-sponsored murders, capital punishment would bring back "dignity and honor." "Abolish the death penalty," Mauriac concluded, "when one reestablishes torture? Let us see a little logic, Camus!" (479).

Not all intellectuals took Mauriac's uncompromising position. Some applauded Camus's piece on the death penalty but saw in it an opportunity to win him to the Algerians' side. Gisèle Halimi, Pierre Stibbe, and Yves Dechezelles—lawyers defending Algerians who faced the death penalty for acts of terrorism—asked Camus for his assistance. On July 26, 1957, Dechezelles wrote that the scheduled execution of three prisoners he had defended were "murders commanded only by political opportunity. They [did] not reveal any conception of justice. Anger, hate, thirst for vengeance, which aroused blind or racists attacks explain[ed] them."[55] Dechezelles continued his plea to Camus, asking him to do anything, to intervene publicly or write personal letters to political leaders to aid his clients. "But, good God, you must cry," he wrote Camus. Two days later Gisèle Halimi followed with her own plea for Camus's assistance. Halimi indicated that she had one current client, Badèche Ben Hamdi, who after interviews in Arabic she was convinced was innocent.[56] In concluding her letter, she urged Camus not to pay attention to Mauriac's criticisms because the book about the death penalty was already a positive choice. Two months later Dechezelles wrote again to Camus, indicating that Badèche had been executed. According to Dechezelles, many of his defendants were certainly "militant revolutionaries" but "animated by a noble idea and not fanatics."[57]

On September 26, 1957, Camus, obviously disheartened with the continued use of capital punishment against Algerians, decided to help the lawyers whose clients faced the death penalty in Algeria by writing directly to Guy Mollet. He had chosen to write on behalf of the accused, he told Mollet, after reviewing the individual cases of those awaiting execution. Camus disapprovingly pointed out that the majority of those who faced execution were not convicted of murder.[58] He explained that his decision to write stemmed from the fact that the crimes were not a matter of "blind attacks nor of repugnant terrorism that strikes *en masse* the civilian population, whether French or Muslim." Camus pleaded with Mollet to intervene to stop the scandalous miscarriage of justice in Algeria:

As a French-Algerian with my entire family in Algiers—conscious of all the dangers that terrorism courts for my family as well as for all the inhabitants of Algeria—the present drama affects me every day so strongly that, as a writer and a journalist, I have renounced all public acts, which, despite the best intentions in the world, on the contrary, risk aggravating the situation. This reserve authorizes me, perhaps, Mr. President, to ask you to use your right to pardon as many as possible of the condemned whose youth and numerous families deserve your pity. I am convinced, moreover, after long reflection, that your indulgence will, in the end, help preserve the future we all want for Algeria.

A month later, on October 28, Camus once again pleaded with the French president to put an end to the executions in Algeria. To prevent the rising incidence of terrorism against French civilians in Algeria, France had to relinquish its heavy-handed approach and cease the execution of Arabs. "Measures of grace," Camus wrote, "of very visible generosity, on the contrary, would aid, I am certain, with the pacification of hearts, and with that, authorize more and more hope."[59] Mollet responded to Camus in November, saying that he was concerned with the problem and that in Algeria it was a matter of being able to distinguish between criminal and adversary.[60] It is clear from his personal correspondence that Camus correctly saw a direct correlation between the escalation of terrorism against European civilians and the uncompromising use of the death penalty—the ultimate abuse of state power—against Algerian nationalists. And he was well aware that he was in a position to use his considerable public reputation (in private) to help the French government see its faults.

Camus's personal campaign against capital punishment was finally interrupted by the trial of Mohamed Ben Sadok. Ben Sadok, a former vice president of the Algerian Assembly and a member of the FLN, had been arrested on charges of killing an important Muslim who apparently was not supporting the rebellion. Camus had initially hesitated to come to Ben Sadok's defense. In late November, Pierre Stibbe wrote Camus, expressing his incomprehension at Camus's unwillingness to help his client.[61] "As much as I am a citizen, I belong to the new left like others of the Mouvement Républicain Populaire (MRP), or the Section Française de l'Internationale Ouvrière (SFIO), or the PCF. But, when I am at the bar, I only belong to the person I am supposed to defend, and if my activity as a citizen should compromise my client, there is no alternative for me but to leave the bar and my place among lawyers." Stibbe explained to Camus that he solicited his help primarily because of Camus's recent writings on the guillotine. He also informed Camus that he did not care about Camus's criticisms of the FLN and wanted Camus's help because he was trying to prevent an execution. Stibbe ended his plea for Camus's help by arguing "that when it comes to punishment of a common law criminal, it is absolutely unjustifiable because it is a matter of sanctioning a political crime, which is always dictated by more elevated ideas."

A few days later, Camus decided to aid in Ben Sadok's defense, but not in the way Stibbe foresaw. Instead of making a public appearance, Camus wrote directly and privately to the judge. Camus made it clear that he did not want his participation in Ben Sadok's case to be made public. The letter distilled most of Camus's previous reflections on the death penalty; more important, it did so without sanctioning the crimes of those fighting for independence in Algeria. "By reasoned conviction," he wrote,

> I am in general opposed to the death penalty, and I have already given, in the form of a book, the justification of this letter. But, under the present circumstances, I am following more my feelings in Ben Sadok's case. As much as I entirely disapprove of his action, it would be both inhuman and unrealistic for him to be executed. As human and as stupidly unreasonable as his act is, it cannot be compared to the terrorist's, which indiscriminately kills the woman and her child in an innocent crowd. Even if one does not approve of or even if one condemns his motives, they are of a different order. I am an adversary of the position and the actions of the FLN. But it seems to me, in the Algerian that I am, that at the moment when France can hope to reinstate a dignified peace in the land where misfortune has turned to sadness, an execution would only serve to compromise the future we all hope for. . . .
>
> For all of these reasons, I have decided to come to you, after painful debates with myself, to confide in you my opinion in the hopes that you would make it known, without publicity, to your jury.[62]

On the same day Camus also wrote Pierre Stibbe, affirming that he had acted on Ben Sadok's behalf. Camus restated to the lawyer his fears that a public pronouncement of his involvement would provoke more crimes in Algeria. Moreover, he confided that he did not want, "under any circumstances, to give a good conscience, by declarations without personal risk, to the stupid fanatic who shoots in Algiers at crowds where my mother and all of my family and friends [les miens] are found. . . . Be that as it may, I confide all this to your loyalty." [63] Camus also contributed, behind the scenes, to the defense of others awaiting the death penalty. Actions of this type were, according to Camus, the only way for an intellectual to avoid provoking more violence. In this respect, Camus's conception of the nonpublic or nonpolitical intellectual overlapped with that of the members of the Centres Sociaux. [64]

At about the same time, Camus gave an important interview to *Demain* that contextualized his idea of himself as a European intellectual and discussed his enigmatic French-Algerian identity. In many ways, his depiction of his hybridity closely resembled that of Algerians such as Jean Amrouche and Mouloud Feraoun, but with a twist. For example, when asked whether his writings as an intellectual belonged to "Europe," Camus stated that he was part of the European tradition but his connections to Algeria rendered him more than merely European. [65] "The more French I feel, the more I believe this. No one is more closely attached to this Algerian province than I, and yet I have no trouble feeling part of French tradition. Consequently, I learned, as naturally as we learn to breathe, that love of one's native land can broaden without dying. And, finally, it is because I love my country that I feel European." [66]

But Camus seemed deeply out of touch with the historical reality of decolonization in Algeria. Algeria, for him, was an ideal that represented the intersection of several diverse cultures and therefore could serve as an ideal model of tolerance in Europe. Algeria was really a secret to celebrate: "Unity and diversity . . . isn't this the very secret of Europe?" (243). But diversity, for Camus, did not mean division. As an intellectual, he wanted to unify the two communities. "My role in Algeria never has been and never will be to divide, but rather to use whatever means I have to unite. I feel a solidarity with everyone, French or Arab, who is suffering today in the misfortune of my country" (244–45).

At the same time, Camus also admitted that he resented the pressure on artists and intellectuals to conform to the masses and that he had grown weary of today's "criticism," its "disparagement," "spitefulness," and "nihilism." The threat, according to Camus, did not come from the common man, but from those who claimed to understand the future and did not respect the individual's right to resist collective passions. In reference to the hostility he felt was generated by his stance on Algeria, he deferred to the human condition:

Doubtless, because I am aware of my human weakness and of my injustices, because I instinctively knew and still know that honor (like pity) is an unreasonable virtue that takes the place of justice and reason, which have become powerless. The man whose blood, and extravagances, and frail heart lead him to the commonest weaknesses must rely on something in order to get to the point of respecting himself and hence others. (240)

Silence, a Nobel Prize, and Camus's Mother

When it was announced in October 1957 that Camus had won the Nobel Prize for Literature, he experienced a brief reprieve. Jean Daniel celebrated the nomination with an article titled "Camus, 'the Algerian.' "[67] Outlining Camus's commitment to resolving the Algerian problem, Daniel acknowledged that after the fall of Guy Mollet's government Camus had lost hope in reconciliation and had resigned himself to silence to avoid inflaming the extremes of violence. Daniel defended his friend by stating that one would have to have "a dose of blind pretension . . . to reproach Camus." "For my part," Daniel continued, "I profoundly and completely respect the position of Albert Camus, but as a position that only he could hold. I respect his almost physical solidarity with the community of which he is a member, and, by that, one understands contact with the Arabs." Nevertheless, Daniel conceded that Camus had not understood the full extent of the Algerian conflict: "sooner or later, [the revolution] would have to rejoin the values of which Camus makes himself the guardian."

Mouloud Feraoun also celebrated Camus's achievement and hailed him as the best of moral guides.[68] He advised his "friend" Camus not to take any apparent Muslim silence concerning the Nobel Prize to heart. After the announcement of the Nobel Prize, Feraoun believed that Camus's inspiration would be one of the sole means of escaping the violence that had become part of Algerians' banal routine of "accepting all the deaths which are not their own." However, in celebrating, Feraoun confessed his hope that Camus could bring peace: "despite the great prize and maybe because of it, the men from our country [les hommes de chez nous] are beginning to construct that fraternal world that you always believed possible. I have a profound conviction in it. In a world that will be ours and yours, you will be the best of guides" (207).

On December 10, 1957, when Camus delivered his Nobel address to the Academy in Stockholm, his glory appeared complete. In recent months Camus had lived in comparative isolation because Algeria had made him doubt his place in French society and his reputation as an international writer. Stockholm turned this isolation into an achievement and allowed him to transcend his solitary position. Hence he was able to claim in his address that art "obliged" the writer not to isolate himself and brought out the most "humble" and "universal" truths.[69] Being the bearer of universals, however, required that art not submit to those who make history. The "nobility" of writing, Camus affirmed, was expressed in two difficult manners: "refusal to lie about what one knows and resistance to oppression." But even after the horrors of World War II it was necessary to exit the void of hatred and pain and reject a philosophy of violence and hatred (1073). Art, if it had a function at all, was to unite humankind and protect the liberties found only in a free society.

Four days after his Nobel address and while still in Sweden, Camus delivered a speech to students at the University of Uppsala that would forever change his life and, for critics, the question of Camus. At the university Camus retraced the theme of societal pressures on the writer. No doubt with his own case in mind, he lamented that silence had become politicized. Even "silence has dangerous implications."[70] And today's artist had been stripped of all refuge. In "history's amphitheater," today's artist had to be aware of his own presence. The artist could no longer remain outside history.

The haunting truth of Camus's own words soon echoed down the walls of the lecture hall into the arena of world opinion. It began with a journalist from Le Monde who questioned Camus about recent comments regarding government leniency toward anticolonialist intellectuals. "There is no governmental pressure in France, but influence groups, conformists of the right and the left," Camus responded.[71] Then he was reported to have said that the French government had committed only minor errors in its Algerian policy and that the liberty of the press in metropolitan France was not in danger.

While Camus responded to a reporter's question about the French-Algerian War, an Algerian student in the audience who was studying in Sweden heckled and criticized Camus. Camus responded: "I have never spoken to an Arab or one of your militants like you have just spoken to me publicly. . . . You are for democracy in Algeria, then be democratic and let me finish my sentences." Camus's statements did little to calm his critic. Camus lost his temper. Forced to clarify why he had been silent for months about Algeria, Camus stated rashly:

> I said and I repeat that it is necessary to do justice to Algerians and to give them a fully democratic regime, until one or another type of hate has become such that it no longer prevents an intellectual from intervening, his declaration no longer aggravating terror. It seems better to wait until the proper moment in order to unite in place of dividing. I can assure you, nevertheless, that you have comrades who live today because of actions that you know nothing about. It is not without a certain repugnance that I give my reasons like this in public. I have always condemned terror. I must also condemn a terrorism which is exercised blindly, in the streets of Algiers, for example, and which one day could strike my mother or my daughter. I believe in justice, but I would defend my mother before justice.
> (1881)

Shaken and unamused, the recent Nobel Laureate returned to Paris not yet realizing how far his voice had carried in history's amphitheater that day. Once in Paris, Camus quickly understood. In a letter to the director of *Le Monde* on December 17, 1957, he offered a corrective to the paper's coverage of the Stockholm incident.[72] He had never, he wrote, claimed that the French government had committed minor errors toward Algeria. As far as liberty of the press was concerned, an issue to which Camus had long since been sensitive, he argued that he did approve of limited restrictions on the press because of the nature of the Algerian drama.

Camus's remarks were followed three months later with government censorship of the press. I agree with David Schalk that Camus's willingness to condone censorship in Algeria is troubling. But I am not in complete agreement that Camus should be given the benefit of the doubt regarding his reply to the Algerian student in Stockholm.[73] This is because Camus never acknowledged that the Algeria he claimed was a French Algeria, whereas the Algeria most Algerians wanted was free from France. In the same letter to *Le Monde*, Camus explained his confrontation with the Algerian student, writing that he felt closer to the student than to the French who spoke of Algeria without really knowing the country. The Algerian knew "what he was talking about and his face was not that of hate, but of despair and unhappiness. I share this unhappiness, his face is that of my country. That is why I wanted to publicly give to this young Algerian, and to him alone, the personal explanations that I had silenced until that time and which your correspondent has reported with accuracy."

Ironically, while Camus claimed that the Algerian critic reflected the face of Camus's country, Algeria, not all Algerians agreed with Camus or even among themselves on the Camus question. On the same day that Camus wrote to *Le Monde*, the Association for Algerian Students in Sweden wrote Camus, distancing itself from the outspoken Algerian and apologizing to him for the Stockholm incident.[74] The association was "disturbed," it wrote, to learn that an Algerian was the cause of the affair, and it affirmed that the critic had acted as an individual, belonging neither to the association nor to a nationalist organization. Because of this, the association claimed, he was not "representative" of Algerians.

Regardless of Camus's corrective to *Le Monde* and the Association of Algerian Students' apology, Camus's reputation was irreparably stained. On December 18, the French-Spanish-Algerian poet Jean Sénac fired off a letter to Camus and enclosed a copy of an article intended for publication in *France observateur*.[75] Sénac told Camus that out of personal respect he had hitherto abstained from public criticism of him and that he had written Camus many unsent letters concerning his silence. "All of this is so unhelpful," Sénac wrote:

> That is why I have decided to speak in a public place. Above all our little ambitious persons, there are others. We speak for them. If I am not in the [Algerian] resistance in the mountains, it is because after three tries, they won't take me. But I serve my people in my own way (this people of nine million Arab-Berbers and a million Europeans and Jews). I try to serve love and not hate, at heart, even with violence. I know that I am true to both the oppressed Arabs and the blind Europeans. Our face is not of despair. That of unhappiness, maybe, but also that of an undamaged hope. And already a great many young Europeans are preparing to share the city with our fighting brothers, each in his own way. *My mother also joins me in this hope.* This is one of the greatest joys of my life. The word becomes flesh, it lives among us. . . . We will conquer with confidence, with love, and despite the appearances. . . . I am not "of the FLN."
>
> Tomorrow in Algiers, it's Jean Daniel who will receive great pomp from the independent republic, and you, Albert Camus. Not me. Even if I have the joy to see my people finally liberated. I chose poetry, frankness with all, love, and not their masks.

BIEN SÛR !.. LA PRESSE EST LIBRE !

Figure 2. "No question! There is freedom of the press." One of eight cartoon post-cards created between 1958 and 1961 by Siné (Maurice Sinet), published by François Maspéro in Paris. Courtesy of Maurice Sinet.

But already the young surround me and like me. Others will be born who will know me. My victory is not of this world. My world is combat and fraternity. I will try to defend my mother and justice together.[76]

The manuscript—"Camus to Lacoste's Rescue?"—that Sénac sent with this letter was equally devastating. Sénac confessed that he had long respected Camus's silence. Yet it was necessary to talk about his silence. For those (Europeans and Arabs) engaged in the liberation of Algeria, every day of Camus's silence was painful, but they tried to understand it. It was now time to drop sympathy for that silence and admit that it was undignified. "To protest against the Nazi camps, Soviet's and Franco's too, but to be silent about the colonial camps, to raise your voice against the Russian tanks in Berlin and Budapest, and to be quiet about the massacres . . . [in Algeria], to consecrate a work about the admirable scruples of Kaliayev [Les Justes] but to refuse to testify for Ben Sadok . . . there is the person who holds to the dignity of his work or silence."[77]

According to Sénac, Camus's claim that Algeria was part of France was "gigantic cultural imperialism" (4). The issue for Sénac was not to show that everything belongs to Europe; Algeria certainly knew what it owed Europe. The problem was that Camus continued to ignore Arab culture and civilization altogether. For Camus, Sénac wrote, "Arab civilization and culture is not important. . . . For him, what is important is that Dib, Mammeri, Kateb are 'Europeans.' It makes you believe he has never read them!"

Camus, Sénac criticized, was a perfect example of Eurocentric paternalism, and his solidarity with the European minority in Algeria only helped "maintain Europe in its illusory intellectual supremacy." Camus symbolized the ignorance of Europeans about the Algerian people and represented one of the worst aspects of Western thought. "Misunderstanding the Arab-Berber universe in North Africa, distrustful of its profound values, and thinking that Europe alone has a mission to protect the world because it alone possesses the truth, it is normal that Camus can see the issue of Algeria, thanks to the French presence, only in light of the triumph of Europe. Camus is not very far from the crusade of Soustelle against the obscurant Orient and its cloudy following" (4).

As for Camus's mother, Sénac said that apparently her enemies were "terrorists" and her protectors were the politico-military and police apparatus that sought to pacify the Algerian people. Unfortunately, Camus had joined company with the "pacifiers" who played into Lacoste's politics. Could Camus not see that his mother and justice should be simultaneously defended?

> This is the result of the serious confusion of the spiritual values of a civilization and a government's political use of these values. Nevertheless, for Camus, it seems to be the case that the admirable message of the West is tied to a certain French domination. We finally understand that [according to Camus] to raise a voice against the concentration camps, torture and repression, is to give power to the Revolution's engine, to betray the European community, and to aid in avenging the Barbarians. In fact, it's all there, and Camus, in the name of a humanism that he believes is in peril and with the help of the nihilists, is joining the side of the "pacifiers" and the politics of the lesser of the two evils of Lacoste. Like them [the pacifiers], he cannot trust "the Arabs." He thinks that he must take action against the nefarious Revolution. In order to do this, in order not to hinder the actions of the Crusades, he talks about the injustices. A noble end justifies the dubious means. That is what I call the silence of Civilization's Reason. And that is where Camus finds himself very simply opposed to his own morality. (6)

As a result, Sénac said in conclusion, Camus and the French like him refused negotiations for peace. In order to move to peace, Sénac insisted, fundamental confidence in the West and the Orient, inspired by love, would have to be at the center of Algeria's future.

Camus shot back a letter on December 19. Charging that Sénac had used the Stockholm incident to cripple him publicly, Camus attacked Sénac for not allowing him to work to rectify his name before the damages were beyond his correction. Because of his article in *France observateur*, Camus wrote, he would not be able to keep his better memories of Sénac. Their friendship had been destroyed. "Too bad," Camus commented, and continued, "accept at least this last counsel from your old friend: if you want to continue to speak of love and fraternity, don't write any more poems to the glory of the bomb which indiscriminately kills the child and the frightened, 'blind' adult."[78] Camus ended his letter and his friendship with a simple "bonne chance!"

Sénac, however, was not the only displeased writer in North Africa to correspond with Camus after the Stockholm address. The Algerian writer Kateb Yacine wrote a compassionate letter to his "dear compatriot," asking

Camus: "Are we going to appease the specter of discord together, or is it just too late?"[79] Kateb confessed that he was not expecting a response. Unlike Sénac, Kateb did not want to bring the problems with their "hypothetical coexistence" to the daily presses, but he did offer a similar warning: "If one day a Family Council is called, it will certainly be done without us. But it is (perhaps) urgent to reestablish the waves of communication, with the air of never having disturbed anything before the mother is completely dead."

For the French journalist Gilles Martinet, the Stockholm incident provided the perfect occasion to discuss Camus's shortcomings. In his article "Let Albert Camus Finally Take a Position," Martinet suggested that many in France now found Camus to be a "hypocrite" who was no longer in a position to be "considered a just man."[80] This, Martinet claimed, was not merely his own opinion. "Your silence," Martinet wrote, "is not only disconcerting for those who combat colonialism." Too many people had confidence in Camus and too many were baffled by his hesitation and silence. Martinet also noted that Camus's refusal to defend Ben Sadok openly out of fear that his testimony would provoke more violence in Algeria was unreasonable since a man's life was at stake.

With regard to Camus's mother, Martinet stated that he understood what Camus had intended to say. Having had his own mother arrested by the Vichy police, Martinet agreed that no one wanted to see his family in peril. But it was no longer a tenable position for an intellectual, especially of Camus's stature, to condemn with equal force the violence of throat-slitting and torture without offering a real chance for peace. Getting to this stage required the erasure of silence because the great phrase " 'fraternity of the two communities' " now rang hollow. What France observateur—one of the most important left-wing papers in France—now asked was that Camus take a clear and unambiguous position. Camus never granted this request.

As if these attacks were not already enough to drive Camus into further isolation, he fell immediately into another polemic with Pierre Stibbe. Camus had made it clear that he would intervene in Ben Sadok's case, but only if his involvement was not publicized; Martinet's recent article had revealed that Stibbe had indeed told others (Martinet specifically) of their private conversations. Infuriated, Camus realized that Stibbe had been underhanded, further damaging Camus's public standing. As a result, Camus broke all contact with Stibbe and felt he had no alternative other than to return to his former silence and reject future pleas to intervene in the Algerian crisis.

Now almost completely isolated, Camus felt betrayed, persecuted, and misunderstood. Completely disheartened by the recent attacks against him, but especially by the tactics of Stibbe and the so- called new left, Camus described the contemporary "frightening intellectual society" in a speech written by him and presented by someone else in his absence. [81] This society, according to Camus, was a place where "reflex had replaced reason" and where "entire sects make disloyalty a point of honor." The left accused Camus of being too "aristocratic"; the right accused him of being too "humanitarian." "Remain an artist or have shame of being one, speak or shut up, no matter what, you're condemned." Rather than resign from this disenchanting society, he confessed that he would never willingly separate himself from it. Instead, he would hold fast to his ideals and refuse to condemn "many generations" to a greater injustice in the name of justice. "Without true liberty," he wrote, "and without a sense of honor," Camus would be unable to live (3).

Despite his recent bitterness, Camus did not regress to complete silence, but his vision of Algeria did become more chauvinistic. For example, in his brief essay entitled "Algeria 1958," he admitted that the Arabs were correct to denounce colonialism's abuses, the "trumped-up elections," the injustices of agrarian allocation, and the "psychological sufferings" resulting from the "complex of humiliation." [82] He disagreed with Algerian nationalists' claims that Algeria constituted a nation. The Arabs were wrong, he claimed, to think of national independence as romantics. Algerian nationalism sprang "wholly from emotion. There has never yet been an Algerian nation" (145). Arabs, according to him, had the right to "claim kinship" with Algeria, not in the form of a nation but in relation to the Muslim empire. Algeria in this sense comprised several cultural elements, and each (including the French) deserved to have a voice in Algerian society. The fiction of the Arab empire, which Camus claimed was Abdel Nasser's dream, could only be realized through a "Third World War" (146). Hence the claims of Algerian nationalists were the illegitimate offspring of Arab imperialism inspired by Nasser and backed by the Russians. In spite of this, Camus did not prognosticate a grim future for Algeria. The Algerian-French federalist future could be maintained if proper economic structures and investments infused Algerian society. This new federalism, Camus argued, was the only way to keep Algerians and French alike from suffering the consequences of the loss of Algeria to Egyptian and Soviet imperialism.

May 13, 1958, to January 4, 1960

De Gaulle's questionable return to power in May 1958 brought new hope and new cause for concern for Camus. Not long after the coup d'état, Camus returned to Algiers. While there, he wrote to his friend Jeanne Sicard, the director of foreign affairs, confessing that for a year he had thought that only de Gaulle had enough prestige and authority to settle the Algerian affair. [83] Yet, consistent with his earlier thoughts, Camus revealed his disdain for the ultras and the military who helped de Gaulle return. He warned that the French and Algerians were sitting on a volcano in which the defense of the French Republic was inextricably entangled with the Algerian crisis. Unfortunately, there were now three powers in Algeria: "De Gaulle, the Government, and Algiers' authorities. They are on the same ship and we must seal off the watery leaks." Camus confessed his skepticism in the government's ability to keep the ship afloat but admitted that France could be on the path of integration, provided that the French government protect its democratic heritage from de Gaulle.

On the eve of de Gaulle's 1958 coup d'état, Camus's *Actuelles* series (the re-publication of his writings on Algeria) was already in press. In March and April Camus worked on the introduction, in which he articulated his response to critics, especially "those who . . . continue to think historically and think that it is better to have a brother perish than principles." [84] Obviously still smarting from the Stockholm incident, Camus returned to the problem of supporting terror as a revolutionary agent of change. Terror changed everything, according to him, by reversing the "order of terms" and by deifying violence (893). Innocents were slaughtered because all other principles, such as honor, had been abandoned.

Camus drew from this that, since the FLN was the greatest instigator of violence, it needed to be repressed by the French state. Hence, showing his dislike for blaming the Algerian conflict on the French settlers in Algeria, he claimed that it was unjustifiable for the FLN to decry the use of torture at the same time that it mutilated European children. In his words, it was ridiculous to think that Europeans would pay for their standing "on the stomach of the Other" through violence against the French.

Then, turning his attention to his French peers, he argued that intellectuals shared partial responsibility for the violence. And here Camus touches the heart of the question of intellectual legitimacy: "Part of our opinion thinks obscurely that the Arabs have acquired the right to . . . slit throats and to mutilate" without limits. Rather than taking part in excusing excess of one or the other, or taking part in the violence itself, intellectuals should remain the voice of reason and attempt to assure that reason's voice be heard in the din of knives. Unfortunately the intellectual nihilism of contemporary France justified this intoxicating violence. And, finally, Camus admitted that colonialism's time had justifiably passed, but that being the case, it was likewise time for reconciliation.

After the re-publication of his writings on Algeria in *Actuelles III*, Camus again disappeared from the public's political eye. As it became clearer that de Gaulle was following the road to negotiation with the FLN and as the French community became more and more violent in its opposition to the French government and Algerian nationalism, Camus retreated more than ever. He continued to work on his plays and devoted a great deal of attention to his work in progress, *Le Premier homme*, which was not published until 1994.

However, as Camus's silence from 1958 on became noticeable, so did reactions against him. After the publication of *Actuelles III*, Mouloud Feraoun sent him a blistering open letter titled "The Source of Our Common Misfortunes." Although Feraoun clearly approved of Camus's decision finally to address the Algerian drama again, he called into question Camus's annoying and imprecise use of "Arab" to describe Algerian nationalists, and he criticized Camus's overburdensome concern for the French in Algeria. "Know that I am an 'Arab' teacher," Feraoun wrote, "that I have always lived in the heart of the country and for four years in the center of the drama." However, Camus's (mis)use of the word "Arab," Feraoun argued, displayed a profound ignorance of indigenous Algerians and was "nonetheless not very exact."[85]

In 1958, Feraoun argued, everyone was suddenly interested in Algeria and in Algerians ("Arabs" and "Kabyles") only "in order to kill them, to put them in prison, to pacify them or, recently, to integrate their souls." Camus had once been important, despite his youthful and feeble voice, he wrote, because he had been the first willing to take Algerians' situation seriously. Yet this did not mean that one could now place undue faith in Camus because neither Camus, nor Feraoun himself, nor anyone else could protect the Algerians from the "evil that could come" to them "from others."

Perhaps the most powerful criticisms of Camus came from Ahmed Taleb Ibrahimi, an imprisoned Algerian nationalist who later became the first minister of education in independent Algeria. Testifying to the Algerians' loss of patience for Camus, Taleb wrote an open letter from prison to Camus in August 1959. Where was Camus, he asked, when Roger Martin du Gard, André Malraux, and Jean-Paul Sartre brought their international voices out in protest against the use of torture against the European Jew Henri Alleg, whose family had been in Algeria since the end of World War II?[86] One voice was missing: "yours, Albert Camus!" (68). "Your silence," Taleb deplored, appeared "surprising to those who love you and who admire you. Why Camus, the 'Algerian,' why does he not take a position against torture in Algeria? . . . But we, Algerians, will not lose ourselves in conjectures because we have known, for a long time already, that one more time you will be silent" (69).

Taleb's letter is painful because it marks the fall of a hero. Only ten years before, Taleb remarked, he had read Camus in school. For "the first time, we said to ourselves, a non-Muslim Algerian writer has become aware that there was more to his country than bright sun, magic of colors, mirages in the desert, the mystery of the Casbah, enchantment of the souks, in short, all that has given birth to that exotic literature that we generate—but that Algeria was also, above all else, a community of men, capable of feeling, thinking, and acting" (69).

Taleb confessed to Camus that after reading his writings concerning the French Resistance, the Algerian people expected Camus to understand the exigencies of their war. Algerians had hoped that Camus would not only work for a rapprochement between "Europeans and Muslims but also to create a vast movement in France for the settlement of the whole colonial problem." Unfortunately, after ten years, it had become clear that Camus would never become the eloquent spokesman for the Algerian resistance that he had once been for the French during the German occupation. However, Taleb wrote, the Algerians had the same justifications to resist oppression and that, as with all nationalist revolutions, "arms were not taken merely for pleasure" (73). Indeed, Taleb wrote that it was only now that he had understood that Camus never wanted to see that Algeria was in the midst of a nationalist revolution:

> In reality, what you never wanted to admit was the existence of the Algerian nation fighting to freely build its destiny. Loyal to an anachronistic opinion, you continue to distinguish between "Arabs" and "French," to speak of the *Arab revolt*, even when the facts reply that it is a matter of an Algerian revolution in which Christians and Jews fight along side their Muslim brothers in the

resistance groups and in the camps, in the prisons, and in the cities. Everyone is working for the independence of their country with the consciousness that independence will be nothing other than a step towards the edification of a happy and democratic Algeria. (74)

It was morally disgusting to Taleb that Camus wanted to halt the rightful independence of Algeria with vague talk about ensuring Europeans' rights in the future Algeria. This talk, Taleb claimed, reminded him too much of "Soustellian jargon," which brought out the fallacious issue of pan-Arabism in order to make sure that the "profound aspirations" of the revolution remained unheard. The move to this language was especially curious for Camus since he was one of the few intellectuals who claimed to express an extreme attachment for his " 'Arab' brothers" while, at the same time, he absolutely distrusted "all that is Arab, Muslim, and Oriental." All this so-called brotherhood and Camus's claims that Algeria was his country was nothing more than a "superficial knowledge" of Algerian history.

Moreover, Camus's talk about terrorism, Taleb wrote, was an expression of bad faith. In denouncing so-called Arab terrorism and leaving aside the effects of the French pacification on Algeria, especially since the outbreak of the war, Camus played directly into the euphemistic politics of extermination. To talk about the limits of justice when one's mother was at risk was to use the politics of innocence to deny the original oppression and violence done to the non-European Algerians by the Europeans. Taleb attacked: "You, the man who condemns terrorism for fear that your own [family] will be victims of it, you who speak often in moving terms about your mother, do you know that some of ours have lost their entire families because of the searching [ratissages] of the French army, that others have seen their mother (yes, Camus, their mother!) humiliated by French soldiers, and in the most ignoble fashion?" (79). The greatest irony, Taleb continued, was that the man who received the Nobel Prize had become the "support" and a theoretician for the ultras.

In closing, Taleb agreed that Camus had once been able to influence Algerian Muslims, but his actions, his silence, his intellectual and moral sterility had since rendered him impotent. Today's Algerians, Taleb concluded, were not so easily duped by the man who had once written that Algerians have "more heart than brains." The children who had once been impressed that Camus had been the first to recognize their existence as humans could no longer be placated by jargon and prudent silences; rather, only because of those revolting today, "thanks to their resistance fighters, would Algeria in the near future be free" (83).

While Algerian intellectuals such as Feraoun and Taleb lamented Camus's shortcomings, some liberal French intellectuals praised him. In an article in *Preuves*, Germaine Tillion paid little attention to the comments that had provoked Feraoun's and Taleb's outrage. Tillion applauded Camus for his undying commitment to Algeria, especially his writings from the 1930s and 1940s. Yet she did also acknowledge that the war in Algeria called for a novel assessment. Realistically, Tillion wrote, the problem was no longer confined to imagining agreements between the two peoples; it was to "make" peace between two armies and the political parties behind them.[87] In this respect, Camus's analysis had erred only because he tenaciously denied the existence of the FLN. For the moment, whether he acknowledged the FLN's legitimacy or not, it was the only real political power in Algeria capable of representing Algerians and advancing peace. Having recognized the reality of the FLN, Tillion, like Camus, criticized it for running Algerians into a disastrous economic cul-de-sac from which they would be unable to escape. What was needed now, she insisted, was an honest humanistic effort to think through the crisis and a deeper understanding of the people fighting against France (72).

Camus's Death and the Posthumous Life of an Intellectual

Camus would never have the chance to see how history would judge the French-Algerian War and his place in it. When he died at forty-six in Michael Gallimard's Fecel Vega sports car in southern France on January 4, 1960, there was a universal but contradictory sense of loss among intellectuals. Despite the manifest ambivalence concerning his silence, Camus's reputation as a calm, humanistic liberal brought a great deal of praise during the many eulogies. Not surprisingly, Sartre paid his last respects to his old friend on January 7, 1960, in *France observateur*. Sartre wrote that just six months earlier he had said to someone that it was necessary to respect Camus's silence because "One day, he will talk."[88] "[It was] his silence," Sartre continued, "according to the events and my disposition [humeur], that I often judged too prudent and sad; it [the silence] was an everyday quality, like warmth or light, but human." However, there was more at stake than silence because, Sartre wrote, Camus was this century's inheritor of "the long line of moralists"; and as a "headstrong" moralist, Camus affirmed in the "heart of our epoch," the "existence of the moral fact."

Camus's silence also "had its positive side: this Cartesian of the absurd refused to leave the fields of morality in order to take the untested paths of practice [pratique]." In this respect Camus reflected perhaps better than anyone else the history of France and the present century. What made Camus's death so tragic was precisely its impact on France and on his time. It was imperative that Camus live, Sartre argued, because "for us, for him," and for many others it was "important that he abandon his silence, that he decide, that he conclude." "Rarely," Sartre affirmed, have "the characters of a work and the historical conditions of the moment demanded so clearly that a writer live." Hence, if there was an absurdity to Camus's death, it was that no one would ever be able to ask about "that silence, which is not even silence any more."

Even his fierce opponents at France observateur publicly expressed their regret at losing Camus in this critical moment of decolonization. In an article titled "Camus or Clean Hands," Claude Bourdet admitted that he and others like him were in part to blame for Camus's reclusion during the last years of his life. Ironically, the left's criticism prevented Camus from seeing the weaknesses of his own position:

> What a loss of human capital, in an epoch where there are not enough men who refuse to participate in the symmetric crimes of one and the other! It seems to me that it is our fault: if some of us who criticized him and suffered from his attacks, had known how to convince him, maybe he would have understood, himself, that it is necessary to keep a clean heart, but it is not so preciously necessary to keep our hands virgin pure, away from all tainted contact, if one wants to change something in the world.[89]

In an entirely different vein, his longtime friend and close companion Jean Daniel wrote a moving testimony of the tremendous loss Camus represented for France. "His disappearance is the bitter chill of our generation."[90] When asking himself how he would think of Camus in the future and what lessons would be Camus's legacy, Daniel claimed that Camus would be remembered as the voice of reason.

As for Camus's position on Algeria, Daniel admitted that he had over the past eighteen months diverged from Camus, but that he and Camus addressed the issue from the same perspective: as a "non-Muslim Algerian." Daniel defended Camus by insisting that he was the first French journalist to write about Algerians' oppression and suffering; with Camus many anticolonialist intellectuals (including Daniel) began to speak out against French policies in Algeria.

After the failure of the civil peace and Camus's eventual public disengagement from the Algerian drama, Daniel acknowledged, he continued to respect Camus's desire to stop the violence. Camus's work had proved that if peace were to be realized, it would be essential to maintain friendship between the Muslim and European communities and to reflect on the morality of action. This, according to Daniel, was Camus's legacy, and the youth would always be able to turn to his works, in this respect, for guidance.

Mouloud Feraoun also paid his intellectual and public respects to Camus in Preuves. Like the French commentators, Feraoun stated that Camus's untimely death was a loss for all Algerians. Feraoun recounted that in the last letter Camus sent him he had tried to maintain his strained friendship with Feraoun by writing that someday they would be "separated neither by injustice nor by justice."[91] Having heavily criticized Camus's silence, Feraoun in 1960 admitted that "stupidity [was] tearing up" Algeria. This murderous stupidity was nothing other than a "catastrophe."

But Feraoun, who would shortly become a victim of this catastrophic violence, had other motives for his "melancholic" reflection on Camus's death. The night before he wrote his comments on Camus, Feraoun recounted how he had heard an ultra Algerian deputy on the radio describe the choice Algerians faced between "integration and massacre" (46). The same right-wing deputy cited Camus and Saint Augustine in order to show how Algerians were "passionate, and ferocious, difficult to reason with." What disgusted Feraoun was that Camus could be read in this way to justify the ultras' extremist politics: "They are afraid of Arabs and [afraid] that France, due to its irresolution . . . appears to be emancipating them. They [the ultras] do not want France to emancipate the Arabs" (47).

In order to understand the ultras, Feraoun wrote, he would have to put himself in their place. "Them, yes, I can interrogate them and even imagine their own responses because, since they are accustomed to putting themselves in our place, to speak like us and for us, they have many times had the courage to say very loudly what the most clairvoyant of this country have thought" (47). It was time, Feraoun argued, to upset this paternalistic and racist habit of speech. Interestingly, for this reason, Feraoun returned to Camus.

It was no longer possible, Feraoun wrote, to think that by ending the war the revolt could be suppressed. Writing about Camus during the colons' barricade revolt, Feraoun commented that the *ultras* behind the barricades were attempting to demonstrate that "Algeria was theirs." Was it now necessary for France to speak reason to those behind the barricades who "dreamed of exterminating" Algeria's Muslims? Camus, perhaps alone, Feraoun suggested, may have been able to speak this language.

If Camus could no longer speak for himself, could others speak for him? One of Camus's close friends and a fellow French-Algerian, Jules Roy, believed he could. A novelist, playwright, and former officer in the French army, Roy returned to Algeria four months after Camus's death. Feeling obliged to continue Camus's dialogue on the Algerian question, in October 1960 Roy published *La Guerre d'Algérie*.

Until Camus's death, Roy expressed his unflinching confidence in his judgment, but Camus's passing had forced him to break his own self-imposed silence on Algeria. In *La Guerre d'Algérie* Roy recounted that he was horrified by the tremendous excesses of the French army and ashamed of the extent of its abuses of the Algerian people. Roy also admitted that he was ashamed of the *colons'* desire to "close their eyes" to all the abuses in Algeria.[92] Since France and public opinion had also been "chloroformed," was it possible to revive reconciliation?

Reconciliation, Roy replied, would be possible only if arranged immediately, but, unlike Camus, Roy did not rule out the FLN's importance in arriving at a negotiated peace. In order to arrive at peace, however, France would have to make the first concessions. To begin, it was wrong to look at the FLN as a group of assassins: "All French treat the men of the FLN as assassins, and to a certain extent, they are right, but they do not want to understand why the men of the FLN became assassins. No one wants to understand that the assassin, that abominable thing, is the only means for the Muslims to express their revolt because, on the military level, they are defeated."[93] To have acted as if all the Algerians were "assassins, throat slitters, or fanatics, as if we did not have, we too, our own" is purely "ignoble."[94]

But what bothered Roy even more was the way Camus's last words had characterized the French-Algerian War as a conflict between the West and the Orient. Roy claimed that if Camus were still alive in 1960 he would have realized how different the situation was from the time of his last words on Algeria in the spring of 1958. It was possible to recognize that no one wanted his or her family threatened in Algeria and everyone would protect family members from acts of violence. Without openly criticizing him, Roy implied that Camus had been wrong to make the division between immediate family and others living in Algeria because "our brothers are not only our brothers, but all those who suffer from inequality" (219). Invoking the West in order to protect one's family was, according to Roy, a facile and naive way of excusing abuses and excesses. "Among us, in Algeria, no one receives another in the name of human liberties. . . . And we do not fight in the name of the West." The real issue was not a matter or family versus principles, as Camus had led people to believe, and it was here that Roy found it necessary to part company with Camus in order to seek peace in Algeria. Speaking directly to Camus's memory, Roy writes: "For me, I ignore Camus, if I am like you capable of placing my mother above justice. How can I dare speak of this? Your mother lives still while mine. . . . It's not a matter of preferring his mother to justice. It's a matter of loving his justice as much as his own mother" (226).

Camus's position on Algeria clearly remained a stumbling block for his closest friends, including Jules Roy, and yet Camus's reputation was pivotal to many intellectuals.[95] In Roy's and others' writings, very few French and even fewer Algerian intellectuals were satisfied with the positions Camus had left behind. In many senses, he had let them down, let France down with his comments in Stockholm, his misplaced idealism, his out-of-date paternalism.

Camus's stance placed liberals engaged in a war against colonial occupation under an unflattering spotlight. Camus's death released those respectful of his friendship and mindful of his opposition to the FLN from his shadow. Yet his shadow never left their pronouncements or actions. For example, the publication of Roy's La Guerre d'Algérie received generally positive reactions. Alain Jacob's review of the book in Le Monde claimed that it was an "overwhelming" description of the war's reality: "torture and repression."[96] Patrick Kassel's review in France observateur picked up on Roy's decision to write the book as a means of escape from Camus's shadow and indicted Roy's gesture as a treason against their friendship.[97] However, Kassel admired Roy for offering an alternative to Camus's image of the French-Algerians, especially since Roy had gone beyond Camus's nearsightedness and had demystified the notion of pacification. But, as Kassel pointed out, Roy had offered readers a balanced opinion because he had denounced with equal force the violence of the FLN nationalists and the French government.

Claude Roy in his review for Libération also wrote a great deal about Camus's silence and Jules Roy's desire to escape from Camus's shadow.[98] Sadly, only Camus's death had liberated Roy from Camus's rhetorical prison of "justice" and his "mother" and allowed him to return to Algeria unbridled. It was thus a personal and national triumph that Jules Roy had returned to confront Algeria and his friend's ghost.

Even Charles de Gaulle congratulated Jules Roy for his book on November 13, 1960, telling him that they shared the same hopes for a resolution of the Algerian drama. The drama had to be resolved, de Gaulle wrote, because it was, "in effect," a choice between "reconciliation or a common evil [malheur commun]," the price of which would be "a universal cataclysm." [99] De Gaulle added that he understood why Roy had chosen to focus on certain "facts," which showed even more clearly that "writings [les lettres] were not impartial."

Roy's appropriation of Camus's unfinished business had received mostly applause from France; other attempts to write for Camus quickly provoked polemics. In 1961 Jean Daniel published an article in L'Express in which he suggested that Camus would have approved of the peace talks between the French government and the FLN. In response, a mutual friend of Camus and Daniel, professor of philosophy André Benichou, wrote to the director of L'Express to criticize the recent statement that Camus would have endorsed talks with the FLN's Ahmad Boumendjel. As a friend, Benichou argued that Camus was above all a French-Algerian. Therefore it was natural for Camus to hope for a new and peaceful Algeria. Benichou also noted that it was perhaps up to France alone to correct its many mistakes in Algeria and forge a renewed fraternal relationship. [100]

Benichou went on to explain how Camus disliked L'Express's equation of French Algerians with fascists and colonialists. Moreover, according to Benichou, Camus believed that attempts to rectify an injustice by giving power to the victims was the worst possible medicine. Violence, Camus would argue, could never remedy injustice.

For these reasons, Benichou claimed, in addition to Camus's dislike for the totalitarian character of the FLN, Camus would never have supported negotiations between the FLN and the French. For Camus, the FLN was simply too violent and its violence was no more just than the French injustices. One would have had to neglect Camus's writings, Benichou stated, in order not to be certain about this. Consequently, Benichou asked the director to rectify Camus's name in order to clear his name from the abuse that betrayed his prestigious memory.

On August 8, 1960, Daniel responded privately to Benichou, arguing that the letter's importance went beyond both Daniel and Benichou. From an "amicable" point of view, Daniel did not want to engage in an open polemic with Benichou because it would carry with it the price of prejudicing "the memory of the person that we intend—both of us—to defend."[101] A month later the French-Algerian poet and mutual friend of Camus and Daniel, René Char, wrote to Daniel, stating that he did not agree with Daniel's reply to Benichou.[102]

In many ways, Camus represented one of the central paradoxes of French liberal intellectuals during the war. As spokesmen for the oppressed, the liberals as a whole felt it their obligation to speak out against the injustices of the French government in Algeria. Camus did not hesitate to accompany other liberals along this path, but he stopped where others continued. As a French-Algerian, Camus never allowed his attachment to Algeria to be separated from his attachment to France. For him such a separation would only provoke the destruction of both communities.

It is impossible to guess what Camus's actions might have been if he had lived to see the conclusion of the war. Many speculated and felt that to preserve an untarnished memory of Camus it was necessary to reinvent his position. Given Camus's firm refusal to negotiate with terrorists and his complete attachment to his family in Algeria and to French Algeria itself, it is doubtful that he would have endorsed the results of the war.

It is telling that thirty-four years after Camus's death the question of Camus reemerged. When, in 1994, his daughter Catherine finally published the unfinished novel at his side during his accident, Le Premier homme (First Man), it sold more than one hundred thousand copies during the first week in Paris.[103] Most of the major French newspapers carried reviews, and his old and faithful friend Jean Daniel, now director of Le Nouvel observateur, expressed his praise, stating that Camus had, in opposition to Sartre's fading shadow, maintained his importance as a voice of reason in an unreasonable era.[104]

With Algeria confronting civil war and daily assassinations by Islamic fundamentalists, Camus's assessment of the result of violence and the possibility that antidemocratic tendencies of the FLN would make stability unlikely seems all too prophetic to today's audience. Faced with the new challenges of Islamic fundamentalism, both French and Algerian intellectuals have revived Camus's reputation. Algeria's governmental debacles, in part due to its totalitarian nature, are seen by many modern observers as the root of the corresponding rise of Islamic fundamentalism. Intellectuals' attempts to recover Camus, then, should hardly appear surprising. Camus had condemned the FLN because it used violence even against its own people to achieve its power and because it refused to share power after independence. Even if he had questionable motives for rejecting Algerian nationalism, the fact remains that his predictions about Algeria came true: the Algerian government would never be able to free itself from the violence and its totalitarian foundation.

Just after the publication of *Le Premier homme*, Mustapha Chelfi, an exiled Algerian journalist, wrote that because of the Islamic fundamentalists' terrorism, he and other Algerians fleeing to France for refuge had become the "new *pieds noirs*."[105] Chelfi admitted that, after the self-destruction of post-independence Algeria, he understood Camus's famous statement about placing his mother above justice. In citing a conversation between an Algerian poet and Jules Roy, Chelfi confessed that the Stockholm incident was the only time Camus had shown himself not to be absurd because "the mother is above all else."

Camus's specter even resurfaced elsewhere, including Bosnia. A Polish-Lithuanian *pied noir*, Czeslaw Milosz—who had been on the same side as Camus regarding Communism—responded to the publication of Camus's posthumous novel, stating that he had always "admired Camus's courage. I understand very well his attitude about Algeria. It was that of a man torn apart."[106] Even the Bosnian ambassador to Paris, Nikola Kovac, argued that Camus, were he alive, would have denounced the Serbian massacres. The "just man that he was," Kovac insisted, Camus "obviously would have demanded the end of military aggression against the [Bosnian] population."[107]

No doubt Camus's legacy will live in the future. Regardless of the unpopularity of Camus's political stance concerning Algeria and its apparent neocolonialism in the 1950s and 1960s, as Rachid Mimouni has argued, a certain retrospective honesty is now required.[108] Mimouni points out that, just as Sartre tried to atone for his political miscalculations with his famous phrase that he was wrong, but he was right to be wrong, one has to ask a similar question of Camus. Was he right and was he wrong to be right? These are questions that, no doubt, will be the focus of Camus's revival as liberals, the right wing, and the left wing alike return to the question of Camus as we move from the century that shattered the dreams of revolutionary mythology into a new and uncertain millennium.

PART TWO

Representing Rupture

5. SHIFTING VIEWS OF RECONCILIATION
A Liberal Retreat from Empire?

Whether liberal, socialist, conservative or Marxist, our ideologies are the legacy of a century in which Europe was aware of the plurality of civilizations but did not doubt the universality of its message. Today, factories, parliaments, and schools are springing up in every latitude, the masses are in ferment, the intellectuals are taking power. Europe, which has finished conquering and is already succumbing to its victory and the revolt of its slaves, hesitates to admit that its ideas have conquered the universe but have not kept the form they used to have in our own debates and controversies.

RAYMOND ARON, 1955

It is now necessary to ask how intellectual legitimacy and identity merged with the debates over reconciliation and the issue of violence for French intellectuals. As will become apparent, there were significant shifts in the representations of Algeria and a growing skepticism among moderate French intellectuals concerning the possibility of reconciliation. These shifts were triggered by a fundamental concern for France and its political, economic, and moral status in the world. In contrast with Camus, the intellectuals discussed in this chapter (except Jacques Soustelle) came forth on the Algerian question because they could no longer remain silent about French colonial policy or the unquestionable and immoral abuses of the French army in Algeria. Yet, as with Camus, their decision to break the silence in 1957—which made that year perhaps the most critical for the reconciliation debate during the war—ultimately related to intellectuals' views of the integrity of France, French national identity, the role of violence, and the issue of intellectual legitimacy.

As we have seen in part I, most anticolonialist intellectuals maintained ambivalent attitudes toward the complete separation of France and Algeria throughout the initial stages of the war. However, in the middle and final years many intellectuals realized that the chances of achieving peace were remote and that an alternative to Franco-Muslim reconciliation would have to be found.[1] Important voices addressed the issue of reconciliation, entirely aware of the importance of intellectual legitimacy and of the problem of violence. However, as will be shown below, it was not only the violence of the Algerian nationalists but also the violence done with impunity by the French military that fostered a reconsideration of reconciliation.

Raymond Aron and the Ambivalence of the Third World

Perhaps no voice better captured the shifts within modern France than that of Raymond Aron. In many ways Aron represents the antithesis of Camus, for while Camus refused to bend with the winds of change, Aron experienced a monumental change of heart regarding Algerian independence. Aron's sudden decision in 1957 to favor independence had a decisive impact on the French intellectual community.

Aron's staunch resistance to leftist ideology and his constant, informed criticism of the Soviet regime during the postwar years had made him an intellectual emblem of sorts for French conservatives and liberals. He maintained that he was a liberal, but many conservatives felt comfortable enough with his criticism of Marxism and Communism to claim him as their own. Furthermore, because many nationalist movements had come to rely on Marxist rhetoric to legitimate their own claims for independence, Aron's anti-Marxist position was easily interpreted as profoundly antinationalistic.

It is easy to understand why many of his critics believed that Aron was against Third World nationalism. For instance, when he published L'Opium des intellectuels (The Opium of the Intellectuals) in 1955 he argued that the French left and Third World nationalists were being led astray by Marxist revolutionary mythology. Attacking the French left in the mid-1950s had its price, however, especially before Aron was elected to the Sorbonne's chair of sociology in 1955. [2] As with Camus, Aron faced great challenges from his intellectual peers because he did not fit easily into the mainstream of French thought. Admittedly, Aron faced additional obstacles because, unlike Camus, he was both an academic and a journalist. In an era when the vast majority of leading academic intellectuals adhered to the left, being perceived as a right-wing intellectual posed undeniable complications. What made Aron particularly irritating for many French leftists was his biting challenge to their intellectual legitimacy. In Opium Aron claimed that intellectuals had become especially important. The twentieth-century revolutions, he wrote, "have not been proletarian revolutions; they have been thought up and carried out by intellectuals." [3] The paradox, Aron argued (and Paul Ricoeur later echoed), was that as intellectuals became more important in directing revolutions, they lost universality. Because French intellectuals since the Enlightenment had made special claims to be the bearers of universalism,

Aron's criticism stung. Unfortunately, according to him, intellectuals tried to compensate by relying on ideology: "This is where ideology comes in—the longing for a purpose, for communion with the people, for something controlled by an idea and a will" (323).

The ideological Marxism that had overtaken the French intelligentsia, Aron wrote, was based more on historical "optimism" than on historical materialism (xv). Like Camus, he criticized the French left (to which he claimed to belong) for its idolization of a Marxist-Hegelian notion of history that "teaches violence and fanaticism" (xv–xvi). Insofar as this optimism and violence affected decolonization,

> African and Asian graduates [of universities] and intellectuals have borrowed our mistakes and our illusions together with our values and our ideas. The sanction given to Stalinism by a fraction of the French intelligentsia is not without influence on the destiny of the colored peoples. The European intelligentsia's final emergence from its ideological captivity would certainly not be sufficient to liberate its pupils in other continents from it as well. (xix)

In 1955 there was little doubt that Aron supported continuation of Franco-Algerian relations. Instead of leaning on the crutch of ideology, Aron argued, French intellectuals should work for concrete unity, not abstract divisions. In speaking of how this applied to North Africa, he wrote:

> Many of the tasks which should compel the attention and the energies of France in the middle of the twentieth century would have a significance far transcending our frontiers. To organize a genuine community between Frenchmen and Moslems in North Africa, to unite nations of Western Europe so they are less dependent on American power, to cure the technological backwardness of our economy—such tasks as these might well arouse a clear-sighted and practical enthusiasm. None would revolutionize the condition of men on this earth, none would make France the soldier of the ideal, none would rescue us from the tiny foreland of Asia with which our fate is indissolubly linked; none would have the glamour of metaphysical ideas, none the apparent universality of socialist or nationalist ideologies. By placing our country in its exact position in the planetary system, by acting in accordance with the teaching of social science, our intellectuals could achieve the only political universality which is accessible in our time. . . .

[handwritten marginalia: "Wow, this guy knows his shit.... FR bein that shit"]

To these immediate and attainable prospects, the French intellectuals seem indifferent. One has the feeling that they aspire to
recapture, in a philosophy of immanence, the equivalent of the lost
eternity, and that they murmur to one another: "What's the point of
it all, it isn't universal?" (318)

If this was Aron's criticism of French intellectuals, he was equally critical of Third World nationalism. Aron wrote a poignant *Le Figaro* article
on the Bandung Conference, published a few months before his election
to the Sorbonne. What troubled him was not the coming together of nations under colonialist oppression or nations recently liberated from it, but
rather their inability as a bloc to denounce all forms of colonial oppression. Hence, echoing the issue of "impartiality" that eventually paralyzed
the Comité d'Action des Intellectuels, he noted that the countries gathered
had no difficulty condemning French imperialism but were reluctant to denounce Soviet-style aggression. For instance, leaders such as India's Prime
Minister Jawaharlal Nehru played a double game against colonialism, condemning it when it suited ideology (as in the case of French and British
colonialism) and falling into silence when it did not. At the "risk of shocking
our friends," Aron wrote:

> The Bandung Conference, despite its being Afro-Asiatic, strongly
> resembles a Western conference of intellectuals or diplomats: the
> same disproportion between the importance of the gathering and
> the weight of the conclusions, between men's pretensions and the
> insignificance of unanimous motions, the same repetition of
> clichés, the same invoking of principles (fundamental human
> rights) by the same people who distrust these [principles] or violate
> them.[4]

Aron addressed the North African problem more specifically in his October 1955 *Figaro* articles. By late 1955 he had already noted the abundance
of missed chances for Franco–North African reconciliation. Exhibiting a
curious combination of French chauvinism and self-criticism, he lamented
the lost opportunities. For example, having first taught the North African
elite the spirit of liberty, France could have formed powerful allies by assimilating them fully into French society if it had not been for "racist ideologies,"
which had kept the two communities in Algeria in an "infernal circle of
hate."[5] The contradiction was obvious for Aron: France inspired a desire
of liberty among the elite educated in France, but it denied liberty abroad.

If France wanted to escape the violence resulting from this contradiction, Aron argued, changes had to be made, but these changes did not require unqualified abandonment of North Africa. But Aron maintained no illusions about France's ability to deal with the changes in contemporary Algeria. Huge social forces were at work and things were already very different. Although Algerians had hoped for assimilation some fifty years ago, they were now too affected by poverty, demographic conditions, religion, and nationalism to continue waiting for a better life from France, and moderate Algerians who had supported the idea of federalism had lost credibility.

Aron and the Liberal Turn

By 1957 it had become apparent to Aron that all hopes for a Franco-Algerian solution were gone. In effect, his important work *La Tragédie algérienne* (published in mid-1957) was the culmination of his growing pessimism and his shocking frankness with respect to the Algerian question. It was above all its shock value that made it fall like a bomb on the French intellectual and political community. This explosion and the reactions to it tell a great deal about the constitution of the intellectual milieu in France and the visions of rupture and politics to which this vision gave rise.

Because of Aron's unique stature in the French intellectual community, his basic argument that France could and perhaps ought to abandon Algeria provoked acrimonious debates. This was due in part to the way he presented the book. It was composed of two long essays, the first written in April 1956 for a group of friends (later he admitted that it was given to Prime Minister Guy Mollet), the second in May 1957 (and immediately placed in a drawer). According to Aron, he did not want to publish either essay at the time of writing because he felt it was already too late for them to affect French policy. When he did publish the two essays under the same cover—with criticism, not policy, in mind—they provoked a whirlwind of contradictory reactions, from glowing praise to caustic disapproval. Aron even claimed in the preface that he would never have published the book had it not been for the negative reactions to an essay he published in another 1957 book, *Espoir et peur du siècle*. Furthermore, Aron contended that after three years of hesitant and undirected warfare in North Africa it was his turn to tell the truth. He was, he wrote, a citizen of a country that did not "oblige" anyone to "lie for it" and he lived in a country "where the search for truth, as difficult as it is, could do nothing but add to the common good."[6]

Hearkened by the sirens of truth, Aron thus believed that his work explicitly and successfully navigated through the shoals of partisan analysis. A sociologist, he claimed to present an argument based not on morality but on seemingly straightforward, positivistic "facts." And the first fact the French had to understand was that the revolt against the "Westerners" by Asians and Africans was the symbolic rejection of all foreign domination (7).[7] The revolt was as inevitable as it was justified because the West had long since proved itself indifferent to its humiliation of colonized peoples.

Liberalism was especially in peril because French liberals could not work out the contradiction between their endorsement of the right to self-deter-mination and their support for the state's suppression of Algerian national-ism. Liberalism was floundering theoretically and morally, and this contra-diction within liberal ideology gave birth to a crippling bad conscience. A bad conscience, in turn, affected French liberals differently than it did Mus-lims in Algeria because the Muslims had never been fully assimilated into liberal society. Hampered by their bad conscience, French liberals needed a heavy dose of introspection. Aron intended La Tragédie algérienne to induce this introspection.

However, Aron warned that liberals should not become the straw men of the Algerian revolution. Left and right in France shared the blame because both had been responsible for the loss of North Africa.[8] But now that ter-rorism had become a fundamental aspect of the war, Aron insisted, French sovereignty should be abandoned for economic reasons (20). In fact, the argument that Algeria was vital to French economic interests was meant to camouflage the Europeans' "acquired interests." The war simply cost too much and diverted otherwise productive money from France. Hence, Aron insisted, less out of a concern for liberalism than for economic rationale, that even if France could win the war it would be difficult to maintain strong relations between France and Algeria.

Furthermore, because Algerians had become politically self-conscious, Aron argued, French leadership was no longer suited to their needs. Guy Mollet and Robert Lacoste needed to accept that "integration" was "no longer practicable," and that the "constitution of an Algerian political unity was inevitable" (25). In view of the irreversibility of Algerian nationalism, what was to be done about the French population in Algeria? However guilty they were for creating an irreparable situation for themselves, the pieds noirs could not be abandoned without dishonoring France. For that matter, could France honorably sacrifice the "Muslims who were our friends" to a "violent minority" (the FLN)? (27). The only thing France could do to avoid total humiliation and chaos was ensure the gradual and peaceful independence of Algeria. Naturally, Aron acknowledged, this position was sure to provoke furious reaction from Algeria's French population, and they would never consent to the abandonment of Algeria by France.

Neither would the French left, and Aron made it clear that the left, although it pretended to advocate anticolonialism in the interest of the oppressed, was also responsible for creating impediments to the resolution of the Algerian "tragedy." For example, it continued to disguise its real political motives for pandering to an ideology of internationalism by denouncing colonialism and repression. It did this by insisting that "the [Algerian] interlocutors" were "peaceful Muslims," friends of the West, and "impregnated with French culture." But it was necessary to admit the facts:

> The ties with Algeria are not indissoluble. In recognizing the Algerian personality, one ceased to exclude an Algerian State. In recognizing the Algerian State, one can no longer exclude the independence of Algeria. The "loss" of Algeria is not the end of France. Economically, Algeria is a drain. The sole aim of war, after the independence of Tunisia and Morocco, is to find in Algeria the "interlocutors" (yes, I employ the word), for which nationalism will not be xenophobia. It is possible that one only has the choice between pure and simple abandonment and indefinite war. If this is the alternative, one day or another, it is necessary to have the courage for a radical solution: to offer the evacuation of Algeria in voting for the millions necessary for the repatriation of the French or to maintain a French enclave on the coasts that the insurgents will not be able to take. Will we leave chaos in Algeria? It is possible, even probable. But there are limits to the responsibilities that the community can assume for a fraction of itself. Would the evacuated Algeria be invaluable for France, economically if not politically? Once again, it is probable. But France, disowned by half the French and by its allies, can no longer continue to fight without a tangible objective, even if the adversaries are acting against their own interests without knowledge. (32–33)

After the atrocities of World War II, Aron's suggestion that reservations (enclaves) for Europeans be created along the lines of apartheid in South Africa seems rather curious, if not naive and dangerous. He could have meant the statement as a means to stress the very impossibility of resolving the present dilemma, to shock the pieds noirs into realizing that the reservation/apartheid system was the only real alternative to their repatriation to metropolitan France. Using terminology similar to Camus's, Aron argued that it had become impossible to deny the existence of the "Algerian personality," but the recognition of this personality implied the recognition of an "Algerian state." Unable to stop the Algerian state, France ought to escape from the financial costs of the war as soon as possible. Prolonging inevitable independence, Aron predicted, would destroy French society and discredit France in the eyes of world opinion. Clearly, he acknowledged, France without Algeria would be different, but the only chance to restore national unity and dignity was to repatriate the pieds noirs. To a large degree, Aron was correct in arguing that French politicians were responsible for the unnecessary continuation of this undeclared war, but some of Aron's conclusions had a troubling if not openly xenophobic quality.

Aron's apparent cautious and apprehensive feelings toward Algerian Muslims were, ironically, borne out in his criticisms of the French resident minister in Algeria. In fact, Aron was so disturbed by Lacoste's actions that he devoted the second part of La Tragédie algérienne to the failures of his administration. In mid-1957, it was no longer efficacious to talk about what was possible; instead, it was necessary for the French to talk about what was to be hoped for (40). More than ever before, Aron wrote, the idea of "peaceful coexistence" of the French and Muslims in Algeria constructed around the program of "pacification" was a dangerous deception (39). The French had to take an objective view of the facts, and the facts contradicted—on every level—the idea of integrating Muslims into French society. Demographically, economically, and socially the Muslim community could not be brought into a parallel existence with the French. In other words, the blind violence from both communities had ensured that peaceful coexistence would never be achieved. Moreover, and despite efforts to ameliorate the Muslim population, Islamic social practices like polygamy ensured that its birth rate exceeded chances for corresponding economic growth.[9] Hence, without "Malthusian measures," Algeria's French and Muslim populations could never be brought to the same level (43).

In addition, as long as French capitalists refused to invest in Algerian factories, the political and social reforms envisaged by Lacoste and Mollet would remain illusory. Although Aron did not mention it by name, he condemned programs such as the Centres Sociaux because Algeria's prospects for rapid, large-scale industrialization were unrealistic. Since such reforms were doomed, it was necessary—for France and Algeria's sake—to abandon reformist projects currently in place. Instead of imposing the French educational system (scolarisation) on Algeria, it would have been better to ask Algerian students to learn to read Arabic over French. Pretending that Algerian and French youth would be rendered equal by placing them in the same school system was a "true injustice" (45). Evincing skepticism about progress in Algeria, Aron argued that Algeria needed a school system that corresponded more to its real needs rather than attempting to elevate Algerians to the standards of the French: "Algeria should be led by a regime different from France" (46).

Liberalism was not workable in Algeria because seeking egalitarian reform there was a sure way of leading both countries to complete ruin. In Aron's words: "All politics inspired by egalitarian justice will be catastrophic: it will ruin France without saving Algeria. Algeria is not a part of France; it should not be; it cannot be: the large size of the population, the poverty makes it an underdeveloped country, and it should be treated as such" (43–44). Aware of liberalism's contradictions and sure that Algeria could never be brought out of its Third World status, Aron argued that France had but one option: to grant Algeria autonomy. Recognition of Algerian nationality provided France and Algeria alike the only means of moving beyond the present impasse. The combined effect of war in Indochina and Algeria had led France into an unavoidable economic and social collapse. Its capital resources had been depleted and valuable economic projects had been diverted from production; a military force of four hundred thousand men (mostly draftees) would also be better off in France than in Algeria.

Yet, Aron claimed, France, as a Western nation, had a moral obligation to come to the aid of Algeria. Relying on the age-old notion of mission civilisatrice, he admitted that "personally" he believed in France's mission in Africa, in its "African vocation" (50).[10] But this so-called African vocation did not oblige France to reject the more fundamental right of Africans to govern themselves. France should not be seen as solely responsible for helping the Algerians escape poverty.

If the Algerians governed themselves in more than just "home rule," where did this leave the French population? According to Aron, the rights of the French depended on social function. Since Algeria's French constituted only a small part of the population and were concentrated in the urban sectors, Aron proposed that those in the Algerian administration should be encouraged to repatriate because their services were not essential to the functioning of a new order. The French who provided technical support should be encouraged to stay because their services and knowledge were essential to the country's progress.

With these criticisms in mind, Aron wrote that Lacoste's pacification program had fully discredited France's moral and social mission. With no hope in honest negotiations, he cited actions such as the forced landing and arrest of five Algerian leaders, including Ben Bella, by French authorities as an example of the politics of "gangsters" (59). Moreover, regardless of its numbers and its immoral methods of attaining hegemony in Algeria, the FLN was an undeniable impediment for French governance. It was no longer possible, Aron insisted, for the French to "touch" this revolutionary minority who had "become conscious of itself *against* the French" without addressing the question of "independence" (63–64).[11] The idea of independence had become part of Algerian national identity. No one could stop the Algerians' turn inward. As a result, with the French population unwilling to relinquish its unjustifiable privileges and the Algerian population set on independence, true reconciliation was *dépassé*, unachievable, and even perilous.

Aron's conclusions appeared perhaps coldhearted but pragmatic. Put simply, for Aron the Algerian crisis was "a matter of choosing between two evils" (69). Cohabitation meant pacification, which would morally, politically, and financially bankrupt France. Unfortunately, the facts had shown that the "less it is possible to have peaceful cohabitation between the two communities, the more we are tempted to prefer war to total abandonment." Aron admitted that he could say this because he was not in Algeria and therefore not conditioned by the political hysteria there. Acquiescing to Algerian independence would, at the very least, bring an end to the bloodshed, whereas refusing independence would eliminate the possibility of a federal system. Finally, he returned to his theme of distancing France from Algeria: one would have to "ignore the universe of the twentieth century in order to imagine that the elevation of the quality of life for Algeria's Muslims is indispensable to the prosperity of our country" (71).

In his conclusion to La Tragédie algérienne, Aron admitted that the rapid changes of the war diminished the prospects for peace (73). The FLN attack on fellow Algerians in the village of Mélouza (see chapter 6) had demonstrated to the world, he argued, the terrorist methods the FLN would employ to crush all internal resistance from the MNA. These horrendous events also demonstrated that Lacoste's repression led nowhere. If Algerians were willing to cut a fellow Algerian's throat, Aron clarified, they would stop at nothing short of independence.

Such strident "anticolonialism" coming from an intellectual such as Aron—who the French left believed was its nemesis—had a bewildering effect on his contemporaries. La Tragédie algérienne's call for rupture contradicted arguments by Camus and Soustelle, which insisted that there was no Algerian nation, and it enraged people from all political spectra. It also reopened questions about intellectual responsibility that Julien Benda's infamous La Trahison des clercs (The Treason of the Intellectuals) had provoked in 1928: Were intellectuals duty-bound to the state and were they not increasing violence, nationalism, and racism by their pronouncements?[12] In this light, Aron's criticisms of Franco-Muslim reconciliation signaled a portentous turning point in the French-Algerian War. By lending the anticolonialist movement his logic but not his heart, Aron's depiction of the Algerian situation and his cynical representation of the Algerian nationalists furthered debates within the intellectual community over the possibility and even desirability of a Franco-Muslim identity.

Reactions to Aron's "Intellectual Treason"

In 1957 those in favor of a French Algeria did not share Aron's detachment. Critics quickly labeled his call for Algerian independence reckless intellectual treason. Furthermore, they claimed that it was shameful to pronounce, in the manner of the Parisian bourgeoisie, judgments on a country that he had never so much as visited.

Some of the best examples of criticism came in the form of private correspondence Aron received after the publication of La Tragédie algérienne.[13] In a letter dated June 20, 1957, to Aron at Le Figaro, Roger Duchet, the secretary general of the Centre National des Indépendants et des Paysans, an editor for the right-wing, pro-French Algeria paper France indépendante and a pivotal intellectual in the May 1958 coup, charged that Aron had defamed France by asking for a policy of abandonment.[14] This position could only lead to massacre, poverty, and dishonor. The French had no choice other than to see Aron's publication as political "defection." In response to this defection, Duchet warned Aron that the French in metropolitan France would more than ever defend Frenchmen and French interests in Algeria.

Aron quickly countered Duchet's accusations in a private letter. What most incensed him was Duchet's self-righteous defense of France. "Nothing," Aron wrote in reply, "gives you the political or moral right to pronounce judgments on the acts and writings of your compatriots, to call into question their intentions, to decide between good and evil."[15] Aron also acknowledged his disdain for Duchet's mode of expression: "What is more, if I thought it useful to enter into a discussion with you concerning the bottom of the problem, it would be easy to show you that invectives do not take the place of ideas and that blindness is more the expression of cowardice than of courage." Duchet acknowledged receipt of Aron's letter, replying that such correspondence was unworthy of a man of quality such as himself; all that Aron's riposte proved, according to Duchet, was that Aron was pretentious and insolent.[16]

Duchet was not the only person who criticized Aron for his "defection." One reader of *Le Figaro* wrote that Aron's book was a "nightmare" and that as "true moral cowardice," it represented a "general treason of the intellectual [*clercs*]."[17] Another correspondent, referring to himself as "a little (Oh! very little) *français d'Algérie*," wrote that "decadent intellectuals, political types, and corrupt journalists" such as Aron were leading to "defeatism."[18] What was worse, the man wrote, was that Aron had "pity" only for the *fellaghas*. Regarding veterans and *pieds noirs*, he continued, "We always maintained, despite the Raymond Arons of the world, a confidence in our country, which we hope will not abandon us because we too have the right to dispose of ourselves, while you would like to dispose of us like livestock with 500 billion francs."

Other critics resorted to blatant anti-Semitism, painting Aron as a nefarious Jew whose actions were part of a larger Jewish conspiracy against France. Robert Brassy wrote that Aron's work on Algeria had given him an uncontrollable nausea; he grouped Aron with other prominent Jews in France: the so-called tribe of Mendèsists, Servan-Schreibers, and other such specimens.[19] According to him, this tribe willing to force an amputated and humiliated France to its knees was undeniably Jewish. Brassy stated simply that he rejected the right of these so-called foreign Jews to speak to France of patriotism. He concluded with a warning that Aron and his abandonment look-alikes would be largely responsible for the rebirth of anti-Semitism in France.

In a less hysterical but no less critical tone, Robert Lacoste wrote to Aron from Algiers that he often sought out opinions contrary to his own in his efforts to reach a critical understanding. However, he confessed that he could not "tolerate" the "injustice" of Aron's work.[20] With regard to the "policy of pacification," Lacoste retorted:

You know very well that my responsibility here is to prepare the best possible conditions necessary for a political solution to the Algerian problem. You know very well that the force of terror is part of the political system of the rebellion and those who support it throughout the world. It is not possible for me to recognize that no one can abstract themselves from the realities, let alone think of shameful negotiations which would place our country in a derisory situation of a bed trampled by the feet of our adversaries. . . .

As for your saying that you have never met anyone who has shared my confidence, that's a lie that I would have thought impossible of you.

From this moment, you are no longer a man of science or an intellectual of good faith. You are close to too many blind and superficial politicians who do a lot of damage to France by speaking wrongly about what they do not know and by acting as if false hopes were reality.

Not all the letters Aron received after the publication of La Tragédie algérienne shared Lacoste's sense of reality. On June 19, Jean Fabiani, the director of Combat, praised Aron and insisted that it was "impossible to demonstrate with more clarity, intelligence, and above all courage . . . the realities of the Algerian Tragedy." [21] Another admirer wrote that Aron's writing was "perfect" and that it captured "the thoughts of most of the French people."[22]

What did Algerians think of Aron's sudden turn? Jean Amrouche, while confessing how the war was destroying him, wrote to Aron of his growing dissatisfaction with the way French intellectuals discussed Algeria. [23] What disturbed Amrouche the most—as an intellectual and as an Algerian nationalist—was the paternalistic tendency of French intellectuals who wanted to speak for Algerians. Even Aron, Amrouche noted—but more specifically intellectuals such as Maurice Schumann and Jacques Soustelle—had to be reproached for talking of Algerians in the third person. According to Amrouche,

It is a question of them [Algerians] being referred to in the third person or even less; it is not [a question of] who one speaks of, but that one speaks of [them] as if it were a matter of things and not human beings.

The great patriots like Schumann and Soustelle still do not understand:

1st that the soldiers of the ALN are Algerian patriots.

2nd that terrorism is a response and the only possible one to 127 years of repression.[24]

Jacques Soustelle Attacks Aron

It was no accident that Amrouche also mentioned Jacques Soustelle in his letter to Raymond Aron. In fact, the most public and polemical reaction to Aron's La Tragédie algérienne came from the ex–governor general, Jacques Soustelle, who had since returned to his teaching position at the École Pratique des Hautes Études and to his seat in the National Assembly as a representative from Lyon. Soustelle's vitriolic attack, under the title of Le Drame algérien et la décadence française: Réponse à Raymond Aron, returned to many of the themes that had obsessed Soustelle during his tenure as governor general. In particular, he contested Aron's intellectual authority, questioned his patriotism, and publicly rebuffed his former friend and Resistance colleague, arguing that Aron's thought was a symptom of the declining intelligence of the West. In Soustelle's words, "certain intellectuals, proud of their skull," testified, like Spengler, to the "true 'decline of the West.' "[25]

Soustelle was particularly concerned with Aron's change of heart because he understood that Aron was a major intellectual whose defection from the so-called French cause reflected a serious setback for French Algeria. According to Soustelle, if intellectuals such as Aron entered the conflict on the side of the Algerians, the war would be lost because the "Algerian conflict" was an "80 percent psychological war where the adversary finds his arsenal among us" (2). In condescending to the Algerian nationalists, Soustelle claimed, it was France's own daily press and its "intelligentsia" who offered the revolution its "arguments, slogans, and propaganda themes." Aron was guilty of aiding the enemy by joining the "phalanx" that sought to destroy the "mooring ropes" connecting Algeria to France. Even worse, according to Soustelle, Aron was far too intelligent to be unaware of the consequences of his writing, and he had dishonored France immensely by advocating the abandonment of the ideal of a Franco-Muslim community. Aron's decision represented the ultimate intellectual and social treason because he consciously pursued this course knowing in advance what effect it would have on the Algerian debate.

If Aron was conscious of his own actions, that did not mean, according to Soustelle, that he understood the "truth." In fact, Soustelle claimed that Aron had besmirched his intellectual status by preaching the same decadent defeatism as the French left: "A professor at the Sorbonne, a great opponent of communism, an admired oracle of the stock market and industry, a regular collaborator of a well-respected daily. In sum, a paragon of bourgeois virtues, [Aron] has just given his benediction to the thesis of abandonment and has dressed it in the measurable prestige of his speech" (4).

Hence, dressing his words in professorial prestige and so-called patriotic duty not to lie for his country, Soustelle announced that Aron's mistake was sobering for all intellectuals because Aron did not understand that the truth should not be wielded against France. Soustelle went further in attempting to discredit Aron's reputation as an objective intellectual: "Behind his willfully measured style is hidden an uncontrollable passion, but the passion of a non-being (*passion du non-être*), a belief in the degradation of France, and the revelation of decadence" (12). For Soustelle, then, it was clear that the truth could only be useful if it worked to the advantage of the French of Algeria. And if Aron truly wanted to help France out of its present impasse, he should have grasped that "no one [was] obliged to write, and [one] could be quiet for the country" (7). [26] Even worse, as an intellectual and a social scientist, Aron had shown that he possessed only a "superficial" knowledge of Algeria founded on the "most conventional view." The result, Soustelle scoffed, was that Aron had not produced a book on Algeria, but a "book on himself":

> In the mirror, which he holds up to us, we see neither the earth nor the men on the other side of the Mediterranean. Only Raymond Aron. And as others believe in paradise or hell, he believes that the truth condemns us, that the order of the world is against us, that the historical *factum* should run France over like the chariot of the Juggernaut.
>
> It is a type of metaphysical revelation, a Pascalian "wager" not on God but on a nothingness, which fascinates, terrifies, and attracts at the same time. (7)

Aside from proving that patriotism was "incongruous" with abandonment, Soustelle used Aron's writings in order to argue that, once again, the true victims of the prophets of abandonment were the Algerians. For example, in his chapter titled "Algerians, Our Brothers . . . ," Soustelle insisted that Aron did not "understand the Algerian people" or comprehend the specificity of the Algerian crisis (21). "Friendship," Soustelle argued, "is a good thing, but here [in Algeria] it is a matter of family. I feel myself closer to an Arab or Berber Algerian than I do to certain people in mainland

France" (22). In short, the crux of Soustelle's argument was that Aron was profoundly ignorant of Algeria and Algerians. This bottomless ignorance, Soustelle claimed, led Aron to believe that the FLN was the true representative of the Muslim masses.

The present confusion was explicable because Aron's ignorance and misunderstanding hinged on the issue of identity. Since Algeria was inhabited by both Europeans and Muslims, they shared a common heritage, which, according to Soustelle, was French. Put simply, holding dear to his belief in the universalism of French culture, Soustelle claimed with all the paternalism he could muster that for these "French Algerians" and "Algerian French," France was "their nation [patrie]," and Algeria was "their country [pays]" (22–23). French and Algerian identities were bound together. Allowing Aron's "Olympian indifference" to subject the "French Algerians" to repatriation and condemning the Muslims to the "discretion of the FLN, of those killers, of those throat slitters!" would be an utterly inhuman act (45).

Ironically, as paternalistic as Soustelle was, he widened his attack on Aron by pointing out, as others had, the troubling xenophobic tone of Aron's book. Even worse, Soustelle stated, only racism could prevent Aron from believing in Franco-Muslim reconciliation. According to Soustelle, as policy, Aron's writings proved that he liked neither Europeans nor Muslims; furthermore, Aron's abandonment of Algeria to the FLN illustrated that he had "succumbed" to the belief that Christians and Jews could not live in an Arab state. The future Arab state Aron supported (in Algeria) would condemn all non-Arab peoples to exile because only a regime on the scale of Stalin's could effectively carry out the transfer of all the politically and religiously unwanted (45). The end result was so clear that Aron could not see it: with the help of men like Abdel Nasser, "evacuated Algeria would be pan-Arab, communist, or American, or perhaps the three simultaneously" (55).

In Soustelle's opinion France could not abandon the French and Algerians to a void of hatred and division. Unwilling to relinquish the idea of the Franco-Muslim community, Soustelle insisted that France would continue to support all Algerians—whether named "Pierre," "José," or "Belkacem"—because the "French of Algeria" deserved France's "affection" (61–62). As difficult and as dangerous as it was, he continued, the French must transcend the defeatism of the "new left" (Bourdet) and the "new right" (Aron) to fulfill their national calling. The struggle to maintain the Franco-

Muslim community would continue "until, inch'Allah," France and Algeria found "together the peace and happiness they [would] never find again if they [were] separated" (63).

Soustelle's book triggered its own responses. One of the most telling is a letter he received from de Gaulle, who wrote to his friend Soustelle that his response to Aron was eloquent and moving.[27] De Gaulle expressed his appreciation of Soustelle's courage to resist Aron's claims and his fear that Algeria would be lost if the current tide of French opinion could not be altered. Soustelle's book was a positive and a necessary step. For this reason, de Gaulle noted, it would be useful in the future. Rather ominously, de Gaulle concluded his letter by suggesting that no solution could be found without completely changing the current political and moral regime.[28]

De Gaulle was not the only one who thought that a "complete" political change was needed if a solution to the Algerian crisis were to be found. In his response to Aron's La Tragédie algérienne, Jean Daniel argued that Aron's pessimism was warranted if the present leaders—Bourgès-Maunoury, Lacoste, and Mollet—maintained this "diabolic perseverance in error."[29] Daniel argued that a change of "French opinion" could modify the future such that a confederation could be built. But Daniel's objectives differed from de Gaulle's: "It is simply necessary for France to find again the same force and the imagination to decolonize that it once had when it colonized."

Germaine Tillion's Changing Views on Reconciliation

Although Aron's turn did represent a significant event for French intellectuals, there was still one other major intellectual (besides Camus) not yet willing to endorse the Franco-Muslim community's divorce. In continuing the themes of her earlier public works for Franco-Muslim reconciliation, Germaine Tillion offered her Algérie en 1957 (Algeria: The Realities) as an alternative to Aron's program of separation. Like Aron's La Tragédie algérienne, Tillion's book was originally intended for a private audience of close friends and politicians. According to Tillion, her friends considered it so important that they set about getting it published almost without asking permission.[30] Her manuscript was an attempt to work through the unhealthy combination of conflicting representations of Algeria. As it stood in 1957, the information concerning Algeria was "a fantastic farrago, rather as if a careless publisher had got hold of the proofs of three or four paper-back thrillers and got them mixed up before sending them to be bound."[31]

The method of Tillion's book resembled Aron's because it was not intended to provoke polemics; rather, as director of studies at the École Pratique des Hautes Études and as a Maghrib ethnologist, she intended to present an objective analysis of the crisis in Algeria. For Tillion—contrary to the recent right-wing and left-wing hysteria—there had been many "victims but few criminals" in the Algerian crisis (viii).

As a liberal intellectual, Tillion believed that to elucidate the path toward reconciliation it was first necessary to present an accurate representation of Algerians. And, if reconciliation was still possible, it was necessary to address the issue of racial categories. But how could one better represent Algerians when there were already many distortions? The answer was simple: one should stress similarities, not differences, between French and Algerian identities. For example, it was analytically and morally inappropriate to identify an inhabitant of a country as a "native." Researchers did not refer to the French in France as "natives," nor, for that matter, did the term "settlers" adequately represent the fewer than two thousand original settlers whose numbers had grown to over 1.2 million (4). Tillion was, however, willing to use both terms to identify the two communities, which she argued "might almost be twins" because of the characteristics they shared: "a sense of honor, physical courage, faithfulness to their word and their friends . . . violent dispositions, unbridled love of competition, vanity, suspiciousness, jealousy" (5). Not surprisingly, Tillion's efforts to define her subject put her in conflict with other intellectuals such as Soustelle and Aron.[32]

Besides the divisions between "settlers" and "natives," another critical obstacle to understanding Algeria was the use of the term "Muslim." According to Tillion, efforts to classify Algerians as Muslims and non-Muslims had led to a confusion of religion with race. To overcome the tendency to represent Muslims as radically different from, if not incompatible with, European civilization, she overstressed commonality and criticized the argument (seen in Aron, Camus, and Soustelle) that the nationalist Muslims were controlled by religious fanaticism. And, although she was correct to take issue with this "racist" argument, her vision of Algeria in 1957 was somewhat close to Camus's and Soustelle's. Like them she insisted on traditional ties between the Muslim and French communities and emphasized the closeness of the Muslim elite to France: "I can assure you that a Moslem intellectual, and a practicing Moslem at that, whether he be professor, doctor, lawyer, or teacher, has a religious attitude far closer to that of a Christian intellectual than to that of his illiterate fellow countrymen" (7–8).[33] And, although it was true that most of the Muslim populations inhabited areas that were not technologically advanced, the racist-like efforts to connect Islam with fanaticism was, she wrote, nothing more than the "nonsense that is talked about Islam" (9).

Tillion located the principal source of conflict in *pauperization*, a term she coined to explain the decline in the standard of living for Algerians. Many of the areas that had suffered from pauperization during the postwar epoch had very little contact with French civilization in Algeria. As a result, one could not cite colonialism's abuses as the principal cause of pauperization, nor of the war. This did not excuse colonialism because, as she wrote, "the slave trade" was the "greatest crime of the eighteenth century," just as colonialism was the "corresponding crime of the nineteenth century" (29). But the real crime would be the "pauperization of three quarters of the human race," which would be ensured by the French withdrawal from Algeria. She argued that historically, just as colonialism arose from the antislavery campaigns of the eighteenth century, an incurable pauperism was going to be born from the anticolonialism campaigns of the twentieth century.

Tillion was genuinely convinced (in perhaps an overly optimistic way) that this closeness between the Algerian Muslim "elite" and Europeans could still foster an opportunity for Franco-Muslim reconciliation. In fairness to her, she wrote this in an effort to combat the charges by French politicians and some intellectuals that Algerian Muslims were engaged in a jihad against the French state. As commendable and correct as she was about the lack of a real jihad in the FLN ideology, she did not realize just how far the revolution had moved out of the control of the so-called Muslim elite to become a genuine twentieth-century mass movement.

In many ways, therefore, Tillion's work represented a blend of sociological analysis and French humanism. Sociologically, out of a profound desire to escape from the xenophobia implied by current religious and ethnic categories, she separated Algeria's populations into different social groups based on economic status, then made a further distinction between "archaic" and "industrial" civilizations. Nevertheless, she insisted that all civilizations, though divisible, shared a culture in contemporary Algeria. Indeed, they were so symbiotic that any fracture would lead to their complete destruction. Yet, as a firm believer in Western progress, Tillion did not think that codependency equalized the archaic and the modern. Thus, to displace the devastating efforts of the anticolonialism movement, which posed rupture as the solution to the Algerian crisis, it was necessary to recognize that archaic Algerian society (the Muslim majority) could not survive unless it could be swiftly integrated into industrial society (the French minority and metropolitan France).

Tillion's writings demonstrate that even within the French liberal community there was no single interpretation of the Algerian "tragedy." For example, whereas Aron had concentrated on the effects of the war on France to justify disengagement, Tillion focused on the effects on Algerians to justify cooperation and Western-oriented modernization. In doing so, she offered two principal reasons why France and Algeria should not be separated. First, France was part of a globalized technical civilization. This civilization was an overwhelming force, which could not be resisted by archaic societies. Second and equally important, more than four hundred thousand Algerian workers in France depended on the privileges of the French identity card, which would be revoked if Algerians gained independent status. The immediate and long-term outcome of this loss of employment in France, according to Tillion, would be disastrous because the incomes of the four hundred thousand Algerian factory workers in France supported more than two million Algerians in Algeria (72). The end would be catastrophic. [34]

For practical and economic reasons, Tillion argued, both French and Algerians had to accept that their ties should not be broken. Moreover, despite the harm the pieds noirs in Algeria inflicted on its archaic society, their survival there was crucial to its fragile infrastructure and the transition from archaic to modern society. Without the French there would be little if any capital investment and no means to realize this transition. Placing the French on "reservations," as Aron had suggested, by granting the Algerians independence but keeping the French minority secluded from the majority of Muslims, was an absurd and inhuman idea. This "Palestinian solution" was inhuman because it would be impossible to guarantee their safety and ridiculous because it would prevent the necessary interaction between so-called archaic and modern societies (74).

Finally, Tillion attempted to discuss how the clash of civilizations became the mechanism of violence. Through their extensive exposure to French society (one of every two Algerian men had worked in France), frustrated Algerians had seen the advantages of technical civilization without ever benefiting from it. Furthermore, technical civilization had introduced a biological revolution (a decrease in mortality and an increase in fertility) and worsened the Algerian situation because, according to Tillion, Algeria was socially and economically only halfway evolved, and the consciousness of this partial evolution ultimately resulted in violence and hatred (75). Put simply, the Algerians were forced into the resignation of revolt that resulted from exposure to (but few benefits from) technical civilization; closed off from a sense of progress, Algerians would naturally hate the French (94).

However, even Tillion could not escape the familiar penchant of French intellectuals to view Algerians through the lens of French, progressive paternalism. Refusing to acknowledge that Algeria and France should be separated, she argued that Algeria's sickness could be treated only by becoming more Western, thus requiring a "great mutation." Although two of three Algerians had never benefited directly from the fruits of French democracy and society, they had at least tasted them and appreciated their value.

Ironically, according to Tillion, the very deprivation that was in part responsible for their resignation had sensitized them enough to prepare Algerians better than the Asians or other people of Africa to use these democratic and economic fruits to their fullest advantage. If the Algerians were prepared and willing, she argued, they could catch up sociologically as long as France took its responsibilities seriously. Rather than using colonialism as a "scapegoat," she agreed that colonialism's legitimacy had long ago perished and that it was imperative to move beyond the colonial paradigm. However, simply acknowledging the death of colonialism did not relinquish France of its responsibilities toward Algeria.[35] Since traditional Algerian society had been destroyed by the French, France was obliged to increase its efforts to prepare Algerians for the competitive needs of the future. The choice was simple: prepare for "immediate conversion" (to Western modernity) or "swift decline" (104).

The conversion required the French to relinquish their old privileges and assume new burdens. Likewise, Tillion argued that Algerian nationalists would be equally to blame for the impending catastrophe if the two communities were irreparably severed. In particular, nationalists had to face the fact that they had wrongly interpreted public opposition in France to the war as a sign of moral and political support for Algerians; rather, the truth was closer to Aron's position, that the French were tired of the fiscal drain Algeria represented and were no longer willing to offer economic aid to Algeria (106). If the Algerian people opted for the illusory dreams of the Algerian nationalists who preached the separation of the Franco-Muslim communities, Tillion warned, the results would be disastrous for Algerians: they would lose their incomes from French employment and Algeria would face starvation.

In many ways, Tillion's vision of Algerian progress was simply a revisiting of the familiar French notion of *mise en valeur*—written about eloquently by Alice Conklin—which became the bedrock for the French *mission civilisatrice*.[36] For example, Tillion's mandatory three-point reform called for Algeria to make good on its potential. Its focus was on increased spending on educational and technical training (the Centres Sociaux); agrarian reform (including legal division of land), necessary since farming had become impractical due to uncertainty over ownership; and creation of an additional three hundred thousand industrial jobs in Algeria. Tillion estimated that this plan, which was essential to the survival of the Franco-Muslim community, would require "over 2,000 billion francs' worth of capital investment in Algeria within the next five years" (111–12). In addition, Tillion insisted that two years of "compulsory service" for some high school graduates and the guarantee of the Algerians' rights to work in French factories—"nothing less"—was necessary to "reverse the current" (112). If both communities were willing to work together to ensure a common future, it was possible, Tillion claimed, to move Algeria into the future.

Tillion also noted that successful mutation from archaic to modern society required special effort from Algeria's intelligentsia. If intellectuals refused to continue their alliance with France, France would have no alternative other than to prepare for the exodus from Algeria and "make room in France for whomever we want to save in Algeria, whatever their race or their religion may be" (115). There was no choice, Tillion argued, because the "Algerian boat," as it now existed, "has ceased to be seaworthy, and there [was] no time to lose before the final wreck. But the disaster could have been avoided, and perhaps it still [could]."

Honor and the Army: Shame, Silence, or Speech?

While Germaine Tillion, Raymond Aron, and Jacques Soustelle each weighed in on the Algerian crisis in 1957, important challenges to the notion of Franco-Muslim reconciliation emerged from other well-known French intellectuals. And despite the efforts of key intellectual figures such as Tillion to keep the bridge between the two communities open, horrors of warfare could not be kept away from the floodgates of public opinion. Indeed, while Tillion insisted on pursuing reconciliation, revelations of the French army's despicable tactics of pacification galvanized public outcries. While Camus retreated into silence and Soustelle attacked Aron for not being silent enough, other intellectuals suddenly broke ranks and insisted that revelations of torture now compelled them to speak out. Although they

... QU'UN SANG IMPUR ABREUVE NOS SILLONS!

Figure 3. "May an impure blood flood our furrows!" One of eight cartoon postcards created between 1958 and 1961 by Siné (Maurice Sinet), published by François
Maspéro in Paris. Courtesy of Maurice Sinet.

admitted their discomfort about speaking badly of their nation, they found the French state's use of violence to be so revolting that they believed that silence disgraced France.

Like many, Jean-Jacques Servan-Schreiber, editor of L'Express, was initially hesitant to criticize the policies of the French state. [37] After serving in the French army for six months, Servan-Schreiber found himself bound by his conscience to act, which he did on March 8, 1957, when he published the first section of his autobiographical novel about his experiences in Algeria, Lieutenant en Algérie (Lieutenant in Algeria), in L'Express. Appearing in France simultaneously with several other works about the French military involvement in Algeria, Servan-Schreiber's depiction of his military tour (which began on July 16, 1956) provoked enormous debate in France. Above all, his high profile as editor of L'Express and frank style of writing lent his work unusual importance.

Servan-Schreiber admitted that, as a recalled soldier, it was difficult to speak ill of his country. So why did he decide to write? According to him, he did so in "the name of his quiet comrades," the men who wanted to but who dared not. [38] He claimed that he would recount what he had seen, but confessed that he had not seen everything. For example, he had not seen torture applied to Algerians, although he knew many incontestable witnesses of it. His real intent was to represent everyday military life in Algeria, an everydayness situated symbolically somewhere between the two extreme artifacts of French society now extant in Algeria: torture and the miracle of the modern skyscraper.

Servan-Schreiber's commentary is important here because it directly addressed the eclipse of reconciliation. According to him, reconciliation was endangered in Algeria not by violence per se but by its lack of justification. The French army's sloppy and careless aggression against innocent Algerian civilians gradually chipped away at reconciliation's foundation. Servan-Schreiber argued that this same aggression also destroyed army morale and prevented its soldiers from acting in reconciliation's interests. Even superpatriotic military men no longer wanted to stay in Algeria because they knew that the army was randomly destroying the country. With a few important exceptions, he continued, the French high command was irresponsibly plunging the French army deeper into an unpopular war. Real reconciliation was unmistakably jeopardized because the military's pacification campaign generated twenty fellagha for every one killed. [39]

Besides the everyday harshness, his novel revealed more threatening problems by highlighting the divisions between military and civilian authority in Algeria. The military was so embarrassed by its failures and so suspicious of civil authority that even the highest French civilian authorities knew nothing of the military realities in Algeria. As Servan-Schreiber wrote, "Even the Minister didn't know the facts: they didn't dare tell him" (52).

Servan-Schreiber's representation of Algerians and Franco-Muslim reconciliation was not all that different from Camus's or Tillion's. In fact, he suggested that, if it were not for the abuses of the French army and the French colons, Algerians might be willing to work with France. In other words, it was due to the army's deliberate misinformation and its abuse of power that the Algerian "Arabs" were being lost to the Algerian nationalists. "What the Arabs hated was the colonial setup"—the powerful colons, "rottenness of the administration, the corrupted police, the dishonest mayors." Perhaps reconciliation could have been possible because the Arabs "didn't really hate France" (54). What they hated was the colonists; and they had a right to, because the local French population in Algeria also corrupted the purity of the French army.

Reconciliation was ever difficult to pursue for several reasons. According to Servan-Schreiber, although the Algerian masses did not hate France, most French soldiers saw the Algerian as a bicot (87).[40] This point underscored why the army pacification plan and the politico-liberal notion of reconciliation were incongruous. Yet the problem was not entirely one-sided. The French army militated against reconciliation, but Algerian rebels did their part to make reconciliation impossible. According to Servan-Schreiber, the Algerian nationalists relentlessly persecuted Algerians who remained amenable to a Franco-Algerian community. As a result, the rebels targeted moderate Algerians because they wanted "to do the most possible harm, to destroy any attempt at reconciliation or compromise" (70). This was in part a result of what Servan-Schreiber aptly called the influence of "totalitarianism" and the Stalinists in Algeria (72).[41]

Servan-Schreiber portrayed the difficulties of a military presence in Algeria. Settlers and Algerians distrusted the army if it showed preferential treatment toward the other group. "This soldier should therefore be an umpire—not exclusively the defender of one side against the other" (132). This was easier said than done, given that it required soldiers to reflect on the origins of the revolt. This reflection necessitated another equally perplexing choice. The soldier had two choices. He could believe that the current revolt was led by groups of isolated gangs and was an "Islamic plot," "armed and financed . . . by foreign interests" such as Abdel Nasser, "the Russians, the Tunisians, the Moroccans, even the British and the Americans through their cartels or oil kings." Or he could believe that the revolt originated in "popular resentment, and that the only way of ending it [was] by treating the people as human beings" (133). Either way, the soldier would be demoralized by his choices.

The image of the soldier Servan-Schreiber presented was thus a man who confronted a Janus-faced Algerian; depending on the soldier's view, the Algerian could either have a legitimate right to revolt or be manipulated by exterior Communist or religious forces. The dilemma was simple: since there was no real policy in Algeria except the settlers' insistence on pacification, the army was a prisoner of settler politics and therefore had to ignore the Algerians' humanity. Lacoste's authority rested on the support of the hysterical settlers, and because he remained in power only at the mercy of the army in Algeria, there could be little doubt of his position or of the future of reconciliation.

Servan-Schreiber, in offering his fictionalized but historically accurate account, insisted that he had simply done his moral duty to his comrades: to tell their story after he resumed his position as a prominent Parisian journalist. Aware that he would report his experiences in the military after he returned to L'Express, the army and Lacoste had tried to blackmail him. According to Servan-Schreiber, he received a threat from the resident minister's office issued by a messenger, who stated that if he attempted to criticize the French pacification policy, the army would bring out a dossier of supposed "treasonous" connections between him and the FLN. After a meeting at the French government headquarters in Algiers with a man he identified only as "Major B.," Servan-Schreiber was also told that the military's plan was to claim he had run a brothel for the military men. Major B. warned him how the public would react to his immoral act: "They'll say that you used your time in uniform to go in for the white-slave trade and that you haven't wasted your time here in view of the commission you drew from this racket" (195). In response, Servan-Schreiber claimed, "I looked at the man opposite me in fascination. . . . I was concerned with the way in which a man, and a French officer at that, could suggest over a table a connection between what he had just said and my silence after I go back to France."

Rather than discouraging Servan-Schreiber, the "degree of vileness" of the encounter encouraged him to tell his story. He wrote of the French high officials:

If they had become blind, it was by dint of despising people. In theory, of course, they despised only the Arab. But the Arab, however much a gook he may be, is still a man—an unalterable fact. And what you think of the gook, in the final analysis, affects the way you look at the whole world. You start by kicking an animal that looks like a man but is really of another species, and, unconscious of the transition, you end up by treating a French officer as if he were a Place Pigalle pimp and asking people at the point of a Tommy gun whether they are Catholic. The truth is that contempt for human beings cannot be rationed or controlled—because eventually it corrupts. . . .

It made me realize how, without any Franco-style landing from overseas or any spectacular coup d'état, a subtle, progressive poisoning of the Frenchman's way of thinking could lead from the degradation of this war to the degradation of France itself. (197)

Servan-Schreiber was not the only French intellectual to speak out against the army in 1957. In March, Jacques Peyrega, dean of the Faculty of Law at the University of Algiers, resigned from his post after he witnessed a French soldier beat and murder an unarmed Algerian suspect. Like Servan-Schreiber, Peyrega claimed it was his duty to bring abuse to the public's attention because it harmed not only innocent Algerians but also the French nation. To ensure the public's awareness, he sent a copy of his letter of resignation to Serge Hurtig, a maître de conférences at the Institut d'Études Politiques de Paris. Hurtig forwarded it to Pierre Mendès France, indicating that the letter was not originally intended to be made public, but that Peyrega had consented to let Mendès France publish it if he thought it would be useful. [42] In response, Mendès France wrote: "I hope with all my heart that testimonies of this kind will contribute to alert the so very misinformed public opinion of our country." [43]

Two days later, Peyrega's open letter to the minister of national defense appeared in France observateur under the heading, "The Dean of the Faculty of Law of Algiers writes to Mr. Bourgès-Maunoury." [44] Peyrega relates that as he entered a boutique in Algiers he heard someone yell, "Arrest him." Within seconds the police had trapped a Muslim suspect. After hearing a few shots, Peyrega left the boutique and approached the man as he stood with his hands against the wall yelling, "No, don't shoot." Minutes later, the Muslim was surrounded by parachutists and began to walk away with them. Suddenly, a parachutist smashed the man in the kidneys with his rifle butt, and the man fell to the ground just in front of Peyrega. The parachutist, still in a rage, walked over to him, pointed his machine gun at his kidneys, and fired.

Shocked, Peyrega advanced and asked why the parachutist had shot the man. The parachutist simply turned and ran away. Peyrega was even more appalled when he read the next day in the newspapers that after two "terrorists" attempted to throw a grenade in a store, one of them, Ahmed Ben Ali, twenty-two, was killed. As a professor of law, Peyrega could not countenance such willful disrespect of the French judicial system and flagrant and criminal abuse of power. It was therefore necessary to expose the injustice of these events, Peyrega wrote, because France's methods were now approaching those of National Socialism, and it was important to have the courage to be among the "first to recognize them [the methods] and to disavow them":

> A former member of the Resistance, a reserve officer, a professor of the Faculty, a University representative, ought not to be content in a country like France to deplore such facts in thought or in private conversations, nor even in order to underline his conscience by a confidential confession to a higher authority. He should, in his attitude, his thoughts, and his writings contribute to the spiritual and mental maintenance of the moral values and juristic principles, which are the strength of France and of the superiority of our civilization. . . .
>
> Now how do you respond, Mr. Minister, when a Muslim, after seeing what the soldiers are doing, says to you that he is ashamed to be French? When a father of a family tells you that he is afraid for his sons? When a Kabyle declares that it is better to take a gun and shoot in order to die as a man: what do you say? . . . When we are here, when we hear the rumors and have some examples to prove their probable veracity, we are seized by fright. We say to ourselves that even the Nazis did not know or did not want to know that they were accused of horrors, and that they thought, even they thought, that it was only a matter of a few abuses.

The timing of the letter could not have been worse for the image of the French army. Only a week earlier General Jacques de Bollardière had published a letter supporting Servan-Schreiber's courage to depict the realities of the French military operations in Algeria. Criticisms of the French operations coming first from a distinguished military figure, then from a distinguished academic and former officer, served as important measuring sticks of public opinion. But the army's moral case also worsened as a result of its actions. It responded to de Bollardière's request for a transfer back to France just before he wrote his open letter to *L'Express* by sentencing him to sixty days of house arrest, severe punishment handed to a senior officer during the war.[45]

These criticisms of the French army, along with the writings of Tillion, Aron, and Soustelle, form part of a larger ensemble of visions on the possibility and conditions of reconciliation. Critics of the army were beginning to come from a more moderate spectrum of the French intelligentsia. For example, the same month that Peyrega resigned, the Comité Résistance Spirituelle published a devastating document, *Des Rappelés témoignent*, written by officers and soldiers who had served in Algeria.[46] The testimonies in the pamphlet were assembled by intellectuals of unquestionable moral and public stature such as Henri Marrou (professor at the Sorbonne), Jean-Marie Domenach (editor of *Esprit*), Paul Ricoeur (philosopher), and some former members of the Comité d'Action des Intellectuals. According to the Comité Résistance Spirituelle, it assembled letters from former military men in order to show the degree to which the war in Algeria represented the collective crimes of all French people. The goal was to help arrive at Franco-Muslim reconciliation. It was possible that the "recognition of our errors may be . . . the key that will permit the opening of hearts to pardon and reconciliation" (5).

How could *Des Rappelés témoignent* ameliorate the Franco-Algerian relations? To begin, it was necessary to show that the military's central problem related to lack of comprehension of Algerians as a people—a concern Servan-Schreiber also evidenced. As proof, it cited an excerpt of a soldier's journal entitled "The Two Worlds Which Do Not Come Together":

> I am still incapable of a personal judgment about North Africa; it is frighteningly cruel to find yourself bewildered [*désemparé*] in front of the native [*l'indigène*] because we know neither his language nor his morals nor if he is Chaouia, Kabyle, Berber, or Arab. For the army [*l'armée d'opération*], there are only *bicots, bougnouls,* and *krouyas*; will we kill them, "make them pay," one or two, because there are so many of them or because we have arrested one, a suspect? and we don't know what else to do. . . . One of my platoons has killed their first Arab . . . but who was that man? Suspect? Fugitive? Without a doubt, an innocent like another man we have wounded. (11–12)

Story after story in Des Rappelés témoignent described the army's cruel and inhuman violence against Algerians. Ironically, without the Comité's awareness and contrary to its intention, each story also bore witness to the fading hopes for Franco-Muslim reconciliation. One soldier put it this way: "The situation is irredeemably screwed up. We have not known how to save one single Muslim friendship, nationalist or not. What a waste! Poor France! We have strangled all the voices of wisdom and honor, and have baptized them 'Progressivists,' 'Communists,' and what do I know? What a waste!"[47] Another described a systematic search (ratissage) on a village in the Aurès as a "pigeon shoot of civilians."[48] "One day," the same soldier wrote, "we burned a nomad's camp in the desert, shot all the men, and left the women and kids with nothing in the desert." With more than twenty-four such entries, Des Rappelés témoignent was a devastating condemnation of the French army. It was the first such disclosure of military abuses as a collection of former soldiers' writings, and therefore added momentum to the argument that reconciliation was dépassé.

Throughout 1957 the French state was helpless to curb growing dissatisfaction with its policies in Algeria. This became even clearer when René Capitant, a former minister in de Gaulle's government and professor of law at the University of Paris, suspended his course on hearing the news that a former student of his, the popular Algerian lawyer Ali Boumendjel, had suspiciously committed "suicide" in Algiers. However, as much as Capitant disliked the clear abuses of the French army and France's postwar "political incoherence," he refused to despair over France's future and hoped that his actions would contribute to a clarification of purpose for the French.[49] It was true, he wrote, "that the nation [had] never been as passive as today." But this passivity could be overcome because it was part of France's "destiny" to "open its doors to a new prosperity and a new influence and to destroy the mask that hides it from the face of History." Arriving at this point, at history itself, required the French to revolt "against the injustices that have been committed in its name." Returning to the theme of reconciliation and the reestablishment of French grandeur, Capitant wrote, "The mission was not to restore the domination of the Whites with the aid of Europe, but to unify Whites, Blacks, and Yellows in a new community reciprocally and equally desired. The French miracle is that, despite colonial domination, despite the atrocious wars, which have marked [colonialism's] end, the profound desire for fraternity exists in the populations that have lived under our flag."

As if Peyrega, Servan-Schreiber, de Bollardière, Des Rappelés témoignent, and Capitant's suspension of courses were not already enough to question the integrity of the French military in Algeria, another publication further challenged the army's moral wisdom. Just after Capitant suspended his course, a brochure called *Le Dossier Jean Muller: De la pacification à la repression* made public the letters of a Christian soldier killed during service in Algeria.[50] In explaining their decision to "intervene" in the Algerian tragedy by publishing *Le Dossier*, the editors of *Témoignage chrétien* claimed that the letters of Jean Muller had stripped away their right to silence. Furthermore, and perhaps scandalously, while the editors acknowledged the necessity of publishing Muller's dossier, they also made a remarkable confession. They were aware that the many stories concerning the army's abuses "confirmed the extreme violence of what we call the Algerian war. Out of respect for the honor of our country," *Témoignage chrétien* wrote, "we remained silent, accepting for ourselves the responsibility of our own silence." But now *Témoignage chrétien* took a firm position on the war: "There is a type of moral imperative to speak; some will accuse us one more time of bringing instability to the national drama; the accusation has no more validity than it did yesterday. Before such aggressions, to speak the truth is to remain true to the honor of the country. If we had refused to publish the testimony of our friend, we would have simply reneged on our national responsibility" (3).

Le Dossier is a self-reflective look of a Christian soldier, and, as with *Des Rappelés témoignent*, it presented a firsthand account of the Algerian tragedy from within the military. Muller wrote: "Summary executions happen very often, that is to say that the military commanders have given us orders not to bring the men out, but to bring them to justice. This war is a dirty thing; when will we be able to stop it? We, here, are in a corner, obligated to follow the movement, we only have the recourse to refuse immoral orders" (10).

What, exactly, made the war so dirty for Muller? Lacoste's "pacification" program, which Aron had also criticized, was making the French army into a fascistic machine. Besides the orders to kill Arabs on the spot, Muller witnessed the use of torture. One suspect, Muller wrote, had been tied to a tree all night by his feet with his back against barbed wire. He was given only dirty laundry water to drink (17). Other forms of torture Muller reported witnessing included pushing a knife slowly into the flesh of a man, suspending a man from a very high helicopter, administering electric shock, leaving a man in the hot sun in a metal cage, and severe beating. Often, torture did not stop the atrocities, and after being tortured, suspects were given back to the "paras" and liquidated (18). The consequences were obvious: "We

Types of torture

are far from the pacification for which we were recalled to duty [rappelés]," and, Muller continued, "we are in despair when we see just at what point the French employ the processes, which calls to mind the Nazi's barbarity."

Trapped, Muller could not reconcile his military responsibilities with his Christian beliefs in justice, truth, and charity. He confessed that his beliefs frequently put him at odds with the French military and that the army tried to "break" him three times. Yet he also admitted that his commander had not openly attacked him in front of the men; when the army tolerated Muller's abstention from these acts of "barbarity," it did so because Muller's actions were interpreted as "Christian" and not as "political" (19).

Whether Christian or political, Muller's letters in Le Dossier and the testimonies of the soldiers in Des Rappelés témoignent resonated loudly in the world of French intellectuals. It was no longer possible for French public opinion to ignore the ignoble deeds of the French army. In April 1957, François Mauriac directed his Bloc-notes article at the French government: "We too will not accept that in covering the crimes of a few, you dishonor the army, and through it, France."[51] Sartre added his comments in an essay titled "You're Wonderful" in the May 1957 issue of Les Temps modernes. Written mostly about Des Rappelés témoignent, he applauded the soldiers' courage to write about the collective crimes and the "cynical and systematic exercise of the absolute violence" of the French army.[52] Because the brochure denounced crimes witnessed directly by the soldiers, and because it demonstrated the extent of the moral plague that had overcome France, Sartre recommended that all French read the brochure to overcome this great moral sickness: "It is because we are sick, very sick; burning and prostrated, obsessed by the old dreams of glory and by the foreboding of its shame; France is fighting herself in the middle of a confused nightmare that she cannot escape or decipher" (58).

Because the French army was fighting in the name of France, Sartre argued, each French person was personally responsible for the collective crimes against the Algerians. Importantly, he added, cynicism and hate were not responsible for the demoralization of France; rather, "false ignorance" demoralized and kept the French both unaware and in line with the French government's policy of cruelty (59). Who was to blame for this false ignorance? The French press was largely responsible because it had done a very good job portraying the massacres of the Europeans by the fellagha, but when, for example, an Algerian lawyer suspiciously committed suicide, the French public believed what it was told. Something, Sartre argued, had clearly gone awry. Moreover, he continued, an even more poignant example of how the public responded to unflattering news was Peyrega's testimony. When he told about the summary executions, the French public believed him only because he was French. What this had proven, therefore, was that for French policy in Algeria, as shown definitively in the soldiers' writings, there were no holidays for executioners.

The French people, according to Sartre, were confused and twice guilty as a result of the misinformation concerning the government's policies and the desire to believe in the justness of their own government. They refused to give the government their complete confidence and, at the same time, "counted on it to dissipate" their "distrust" (64).[53] Besides being guilty, the French people were condemned by the use of torture in Algeria. "But the torture? Can someone retain a friendship with someone who approves it?" Sartre asked. Since everyone remained silent and looked at neighbors with suspicion, a generalized distrust had overcome the French. "Distrust has taught us a new solitude: we are separated from our compatriots from the fear of distrusting them or of being distrusted by them."

Perhaps worse than the distrust, a collective guilt hung over France. The testimonies had been spoken, Sartre claimed, and had removed all the protection pure innocence could secure. Not only was the military guilty, but so were the French people. "It is we," Sartre wrote, "who are in question today" (65). Drawing an analogy from European denial of reports about Dachau and Buchenwald, he argued that current French experiences were the same as during the Nazi era because "the information was uncertain" (66). Yet with documentation now coming from Algeria attesting to torture in the name of France, it was impossible and inhuman to remain silent. "That is why I believed it necessary to call the public's attention to the soldiers' brochure. Here is the evidence; here is our horror: we cannot see it without tearing it from us and destroying it" (67).

There is no question that Sartre was angry and that he and others like him felt compelled to write with vigor against the injustices being committed in Algeria under the French flag. It was this turn against silence in 1957 that made Camus's case for silence even more objectionable. The moral current within French intellectual circles was clearly moving against silence. Pierre-Henri Simon's Contre la torture in April 1957 echoed Sartre's concerns. But Simon's voice registered on a different moral key in France. Distinct from the other pamphlets on torture and Sartre's writing, Simon offered a mixture of personal testimony and intellectual reflection on the problem that loomed over the French horizon.

As a graduate of the École Normale Supérieure, a former Resistance hero, a prisoner of war, and an officer in the French Legion of Honor, Simon confessed that he wrote Contre la torture with no "gaiety of heart" because he was "never one of those intellectuals who have complained about the French army."[54] Torn by both his obligations as a citizen and a former officer, Simon admitted that like so many other intellectuals, he had decided to make public his recent experiences in Algeria because the practice of torture by the French army was "intolerable" and disgraced the uniform that inspired "love and respect" in him (16).

Since the army's practices questioned the integrity of the French nation, and those who opposed the army risked being called traitors, it was certainly no accident that Simon made an analogy between the intellectual activity during the French-Algerian War and the Dreyfus affair. Simon claimed that, just as in the Dreyfus case, the real defenders of the army in Algeria were not the jingoistic ultras but the "rigorous moralists" like himself (16). Furthermore, since the army's real mission was to ensure the safety of the inhabitants of Algeria and deplore the "spirit of cruelty and vengeance" that prevented "reconciliation," the army had to play a pivotal role in mending the divisions between the French and Algerian populations.

Simon also urged Algerians not to follow the nationalists who ignorantly demanded the irreparable separation of the two peoples. Having said this, Simon was careful not to argue that unification should come at the cost of torture and disgrace. For society's benefit, Simon insisted, the police and the army could not be allowed to "reverse the fundamental rules, which give the social pact its value" (48–49). If society were to allow for this harmful reversal, it would certainly be put more at risk by its own action than it would by its "external enemies" (49). Intellectuals and individuals had a special role to play in bringing this internal threat to the public's attention. In fact, the individuals harbored in them a fundamental liberty; the individual had to be allowed freedom of dissension because if the "solitary conscience" were unequivocally replaced by the collective conscience, society risked becoming totalitarian.

Simon most feared that the army's unlimited violence in Algeria would create "myopic fascism." If the public lapsed into a "general silence," nothing could be more damaging for French honor (108). Each French person, Simon argued in the same tone as Sartre, would first have to admit to a collective guilt in order then to fight successfully against the impending danger to French democracy. Accordingly, and in response to the Dreyfusard charges, the actions resulting from individuals' opposition to policies of the French army in Algeria could not be interpreted as acts of treason (115).

Conversely, Simon argued, noble actions such as those of the Centres Sociaux ensured the survival of the friendship because their goals were antithetical to the effects of the French army. Unfortunately, as the social assistants worked for a "peaceful coexistence and pacification," the police conspired to destroy this work (117). The government idea (inaugurated by Soustelle after the Philippeville massacre in 1955) that the Muslim community would have to "pay" collectively for the crimes of their compatriots who fought against the French was absurd and pushed Muslims into the enemy camp. Exhibiting perhaps more concern for the effect of torture on the French nation and French youth than for the Algerians being tortured, Simon continued:

> Even if the torture of an Arab did pay, I would still say that it was criminal, that it was intolerable and a mortal stain on honor in the sense that one says that sin is mortal. Something more essential than force will have been achieved and destroyed; a defeat more intimate and more irreparable than the destruction of the army [would be] sustained. . . . I think, in effect, that a certain ethic of total war, a certain rallying to Machiavellian methods without conscience and without pity are the only possible outcome of the criminal forgetting, in the treason of the soul, of France's vocation. What can we fear from the boys who have fought in this war in this spirit? (122–23)

In later editions of his book, Simon was pressed to defend himself. For example, in the fourth edition's epilogue, written on April 22, 1957, he responded to both French and Algerian misuses of his work. This edition also included two Le Monde pieces in which he defended his book against both the French ultras and the FLN militants. In the first article, "The Plot," published on April 17, he defended himself (just as Raymond Aron was forced to do) against French superpatriots who had labeled him a defeatist and denounced his writing as a "defamation of the army."[55] If he were considered a traitor by his detractors, so be it, but then so would thousands of other men, women, and young people who had the courage to speak the truth. And, he asked, if he was really a traitor, why was he not imprisoned? Ironically, he wrote, he might have the opportunity to see Guy Mollet in the same cell, since it had been Mollet who had said he "wanted to know the whole truth" about Algeria (136). This desire for truth, he claimed, if it militated against the army's actions, was the real origin for a treasonous plot. The truth and those who spoke it could not be guilty of treason.

In his second article, "Where the FLN Is Wrong," published on April 19, 1957, Simon showed equal disdain for the FLN's use of his work and claimed that the "Algerian national movement [was] trying to exploit the vague opinion against France."[56] Since it was clear that Simon never rejected the French goal of building friendships with North Africans, it should not be surprising that he attacked the FLN for trying to use the scandal over torture to back its claims of political legitimacy and destroy reconciliation. The conscience that motivated him and others to speak out against torture for the honor of the country also exercised the right to "protest if foreign propaganda" attempted to "deform the sense of their position" (138). The FLN could not assassinate and bomb innocents in cafés and then expect these terrorists to be martyred as Algerian heroes: "If on the contrary, the leaders of the Algerian revolt persist in ignoring the question posed by the choice of their means . . . to prefer the language of a virulent nationalism to that of a realistic politics, one will never exit this impasse" (139). As a result, the FLN would have to allow for the possibility of continued French-Algerian relations and to understand that protests against "cruelty and injustice" did not "imply any adhesion to the Arab racism or barbarity which would only displace and accentuate them [cruelty and injustice]" (140).

The Military Responds to French Intellectuals

In April the armed forces issued a message intended for internal use titled, "The Moral of the War and the Morale of the Army." According to the army, the problem of the war arose from a fratricidal struggle in Algeria, and it was clear that both "national interests" and "even the cause of civilization" depended on the army's efforts there.[57] As the protector of "civilization," the army's mission was clear: to win the war so that French interests and democracy could be preserved. The army in Algeria was not driven by the "colonialism complex" but was inspired by its "honor" not to let the French and the Muslims in Algeria be victimized by "fanatics." In its opinion, to protect those threatened by fanatics it was above all important to recognize one significant change in wartime tactics. Ominously, the author of the note explained that the real problem for the army was the absence of a responsible civil authority. It was due to the "guilty silence of the authorities" that "the French army was forced to take initiatives. . . . This explains, if not justifies, any of the excesses that may have been committed" (2).

According to this report—which foreshadowed the army/settler-sponsored coup in 1958—the military sensed that civil authorities in France had distanced themselves from their professional obligation to the French army. In response, the military distanced itself from the actions of the feeble and unprepared Parisian metropolitan government. Since the void created by the absence of strong civil authorities strengthened "rebel" forces, the army thought itself obliged to fight against terrorism and protect the lives and property of both French and Muslims in Algeria.

The recent "campaign against torture," the army claimed, was orchestrated by the press to obscure the reality of the Algerian rebellion and disgrace the army by marring it with the psychological stain of "collective responsibility." From the army's point of view, this effort to link individual problems arising from isolated cases to a program of "collective responsibility helped the rebels" and smelled of "political exploitation" (3). The majority of the writers involved in the campaign to disgrace the army were trying to avoid their "elementary responsibilities to their country." It was a particularly dishonest intellectual effort because, given the degree to which "violence had become systematized" by the rebels, this new type of "subversive warfare" (terrorism) demanded the suspension of the normal legal protocol. Hence, the author concluded, it was now again up to Parliament to decide how it was going to combat the Algerian rebels and to redefine the legal structures with which it was willing to bring an end to the rebellion. The question was whether Parliament would do what was necessary to win the war.

As we have seen, by 1957 French intellectuals of all stripes were beginning to reconsider the possibility of reconciliation. Moreover, revelations of torture acted as a primary force for many moderate French intellectuals to rethink reconciliation. Torture certainly broke the barriers between anticolonialist intellectuals and the intellectuals who had tried to maintain political neutrality, but it rendered French intellectuals more cognizant of the difficulty of sustaining reconciliation. And, while the army continued to defend itself with the argument that it was protecting French and Algerian lives and property in Algeria, it was clearly also beginning to acknowledge that pacification had hardened the rebels' hatred of France and weakened the chance for reconciliation. The emergence of the antitorture campaign fused with debates over the future of French Algeria sparked by intellectuals such as Aron, Soustelle, Simon, and Tillion. This fusion of ideas and concerns forced many to ask whether the current government was fundamentally incompetent. Could it also protect the future of democracy in metropolitan France? Any reply to this question indicated that the future of France hung in the balance with the Algerian question. As the number of intellectuals willing to engage in an open polemic against the French state grew, it was clear that the French government was uncomfortable with the sudden turn in public opinion away from the horrors of Algerian nationalists and toward the revolting tactics of the French military. With this in mind, we turn to a discussion of how the French intellectuals responded to the escalation of violence and how their responses triggered a further demise of reconciliation.

6. VISIONS OF RECONCILIATION, VISIONS OF RUPTURE
Violence, Propaganda, and Representations of Difference

It must be pointed out that not a single attempt at an explanation is undertaken on the level of the population of the colonialist country. Because it has no hold on the people, the democratic Left, shut in upon itself, convinces itself in endless articles and studies that Bandung has sounded the death-knell of colonialism. But it is the real people, the peasants and the workers, who must be informed. Incapable of reaching the millions of workers and peasants of the colonist people and of explaining and commenting on the realities of the drama that is beginning, the Left finds itself reduced to the role of a Cassandra. It announces cataclysms, but because public opinion has not been adequately prepared, these prophesies, inexplicable in the pre-insurrectional period, will, at the time of the explosion, be regarded as proof of complicity.

In France, among the Left, the Algerian war is tending to become a disease of the French system, like ministerial instability, and colonial wars a nervous tic with which France is afflicted, a part of the national panorama, a familiar detail.

FRANTZ FANON, 1961

When the war's violence increased drastically in 1957, the French project of reconciliation encountered an even greater deterrent. After having taken firm positions against the torture of Algerians by the French military, French intellectuals were forced to take issue with the Algerian nationalists' use of terrorism against other Algerians and against the French. Not surprisingly, as criticism of Algerian nationalist violence increased, Algerians offered ripostes—all of which led to the eventual collapse of the idea of Franco-Algerian reconciliation within French and Algerian intellectual communities. For this reason, we now investigate how the representations of violence ultimately devastated liberal hopes for reconciliation and led to the radicalization of identity politics during the French-Algerian War.

Massacre at Mélouza: The "Whodunit" of the French-Algerian War?
Just before the publication of Tillion's and Aron's books, which underscored the shifting attitudes concerning the possibility of reconciliation, a

massacre of more than three hundred Muslims took place in and around an Algerian village called Mélouza at the end of May 1957.[1] Mélouza was a very remote area of five small villages in a mountainous region of the southern part of Kabylia on the border of the Sétif and Médéa departments. Approximately 700 people lived in the center, known as the "mechta Kasba"; the estimated population of the total area was 3,395. According to most reports, the massacre started on the afternoon of May 28, 1957, when a group of armed men entered from the eastern part of the area and began moving through the smaller villages, killing some men, taking others, and pillaging along the way. At the end of the day, the victims (all men) were assembled in the central village. At this point, the systematic execution of all the captured men over fifteen years old began with guns, knives, and axes. The incident became known in the press as the Mélouza massacre. The French military were in the immediate vicinity but did not investigate the site until some forty hours later, giving some reason to suspect French involvement. The French government immediately blamed the FLN for this most frightful massacre in the history of the war.

Two days later, in an area known as Wagram and d'Aïn-Manaa, about twenty kilometers from the city of Saïda, in the west of the department of Tiaret, another massacre took place, also attributed to the FLN. A group of men seized approximately eighty Muslim workers on a local farm and began killing them in the same way as at Mélouza. A total of thirty-five men were killed and twenty-four wounded. About thirty managed to escape.

After the May 30 massacres President René Coty asked in a radio broadcast that the French and the international community join in denouncing these "abominations." Addressing himself "to civilized people," Coty pleaded to the world to reject all negotiations with the agents of this "hideous terrorism."[2] But Coty also used the opportunity to assure listeners that France would continue to protect all the "Muslim compatriots" in Algeria and would send even more military personnel there to ensure everyone's safety.

According to most historians, the Mélouza massacre, which was in fact perpetrated by the FLN, arose from the FLN's fear that the revolution was beginning to falter. The French SAS troops—designed to strengthen reconciliation by helping Algerian peasants with agricultural, educational, and social concerns—had begun to build confidence among the Algerian population. Meanwhile, in the region where the massacres took place, the rival MNA had developed a significant following called the Armée Nationale du Peuple Algérien, led by an Algerian named Si Mohammed Bellounis.[3] Hence the FLN ordered the assassination of all Bellounis's men at Mélouza to demonstrate its control over the revolution.

At the time of the massacre, responsibility was difficult to attribute, especially given the series of disclosures concerning the French military's penchant for unwarranted brutality against Algerians. The French government had much to gain politically from orchestrating such an event. Moreover, in 1957 there was an equally good chance, as far as French intellectuals could know, that the French military or the FLN could have carried it out. The FLN propaganda machine did, after all, attribute the massacre to the French authorities. Given the lack of irrefutable evidence, then, it is interesting that French intellectuals so quickly accepted the French version, which happens to be true but at the time could not have been known to be so. In 1991, on Benjamin Stora's television program *Années algériennes*, Mohamed Saïd, one of the leaders of the FLN in 1957, did finally admit that the FLN was responsible.[4] But in 1957, in the absence of this (and other confessions), the eager acceptance of the French government's version is illustrative of many issues relating to the representation of identity. The massacre also represented a unique moment during the war for all concerned.

Soon after the Mélouza massacre, in a secret police report dated June 24, 1957, French officials even understood that Mélouza could lead to a possible cease-fire between the Algerian MNA and the FLN. Both nationalist groups, following the public outrage over the massacre, had agreed not to engage in conflict with each other because in the upcoming United Nations session on Algeria they wanted to give the world the impression of a unified nationalist movement.[5] In effect, the police report claimed that, if their cease-fire were successful, "the two rival groups think that France would not be able to stop the UN from intervening in Algeria." In other words, from the point of view of the French intelligence officers, a temporary truce between the FLN and the MNA could hurt the French efforts to block intervention by the UN and the international community in the conflict. The report concluded: "Another failure of extremist nationalism at the UN would cause the leaders of the FLN to modify their intransigence and to seek an accord with France." The implications are clear: French officials in Algeria were fearful that the cease-fire would affect UN discussions and turn world opinion even more against France. The report also noted that the proper authorities had been notified, and the "opinion of the Service" was: "It is not necessary to insist on the importance of this information, which can, in a large measure, influence the position that France can take before or during the UN session." The note was transmitted to the Sûreté Nationale in Algeria on June 28, 1957.

Curiously, and despite the importance of the Mélouza massacre for French authorities, French intellectuals, and Algerian nationalists, historians have not devoted much attention to its impact on the French intellectual community and public opinion.[6] Without question, representations of the Mélouza massacre and reactions to it rendered it one of the most crucial events of the war.[7] The massacre caused an important and noticeable shift in the representations of Algerian nationalists and Algerian identity, depicting Algerians as more Oriental and therefore more "barbaric." Mélouza was also quickly and effectively used by the French propaganda machine as the textbook example of Muslim extremism. In fact, as we shall see, intellectuals' changing views on Algerian nationalists and the French government's propaganda campaigns were closely linked. For example, Lacoste's administration in Algeria tried to capitalize on the violence as a means of representing Algerians as "savages" who would stop at nothing to bring about their "Islamic" and "Arab" revolution. The French propaganda associated with the massacre became a key factor behind the shifting representations of Algerians; it solidified the intellectuals' positions toward the conflict and served as a means for the French state (and indirectly French intellectuals) to recover from the moral losses resulting from the highly damaging antitorture campaign. Moreover, because the massacre was such a charged political event, it became an equally important source of conflict between French intellectuals and Algerian nationalists and helped both groups (as well as important Algerian intellectuals) move swiftly against reconciliation.

In looking at the effects of the massacre on the changing representations of Algerian nationalists and on the idea of Franco-Algerian reconciliation, it is important to point out that the FLN vehemently rejected French criticisms. Meanwhile, the French military maintained that those massacred were from the MNA. The major French dailies quickly fell in line and blamed the FLN. The FLN denied responsibility. World opinion moved against the FLN. Most French intellectuals did not believe the Algerian denials and were moved by world opinion and Lacoste's propaganda. In fact, intellectuals' negative reactions toward Algerians regarding Mélouza can be attributed to Lacoste's tactics, because in a morbid bid to ensure international condemnation of the massacre he granted French and foreign journalists, and especially photographers, immediate access to the bloody site.

At the same time, leading spokesmen for Algerian nationalists, such as

Frantz Fanon (the former chief of psychiatry at Blida's hospital then writing for the FLN newspaper El Moudjahid) went on the defensive and rejected the French accusations.[8] In his own propaganda move, Fanon argued that France realized that its so-called good works projects (efforts to destroy the rebellion by providing economic support) had failed to regain the allegiance of the Algerian masses. This meant that the French administration would resort to drastic means to bring about the "counterrevolutionary" currents in Algerian society. "Mélouza and Wagram developed, to an ultimate point of cruelty, methods in which rapes and massacres ostensibly perpetrated by the FLN, clean-ups of entire douars [villages] were aimed at provoking the outrage of the entire population and the condemnation of the revolutionary movement."[9]

In other words, according to Fanon, the French government choreographed violence on the Algerian stage in order to turn world opinion against the revolution. It was therefore ridiculous to blame Mélouza on the FLN because Mélouza was controlled by FLN forces. Therefore the French authorities had made a significant error in trying to convince people that the MNA, not the FLN, was attacked because the "husbands of the women who had been raped were in the local FLN group" (59). Since the French did not understand FLN operations, they thought they could say that anything could happen in the mountains. As part of his proof that the FLN was not responsible, Fanon claimed that wartime logistics could not have allowed for a random FLN massacre at Mélouza. "Because they had no knowledge of" FLN logistics, "the French authorities let loose their soldiers and their harkis on the Algerian civilian populations" (60).[10]

According to Fanon, blaming the FLN for Mélouza was just another indication that France was unable to take the realities of the war seriously. Mélouza was a construction that lapsed into prophecy and political illusions; it denied the importance of Algerian nationalism. Depicted as a factional conflict, it represented an effort by French authorities to dispute the broad-based support for the revolution. Mélouza, for Fanon, represented a French ploy to convince the world that there was no monolithic nationalism in Algeria. And Fanon predicted that French efforts to stop the FLN would fail. Just as the FLN could not be swayed by the economic arguments, neither could it be stopped by French propaganda. Fanon concluded: "Without any grasp of reality, unable or unwilling to recognize the Algerian national will and to draw the inescapable logical conclusions, the French authorities today live under the domination of desires and prophecies" (63).

Other Algerian nationalists supported Fanon's argument that Mélouza had been orchestrated by the French-backed *harkis*. For example, on June 3 *L'Humanité* published a declaration of the FLN representative in New York, Mohamed Yazid, which claimed that "[t]he French authorities have launched a campaign on the so-called massacre [*prétendu massacre*] of Mélouza."[11] Yazid asked for an international investigation of the massacre to be led by the United Nations (which he knew France would reject) and pledged the FLN's full cooperation in the investigations: "We are certain that all impartial inquests will demonstrate the false character [*caractère mensonger*] of the French accusations" (3).

On the same day, a French journalist, Yves Moreau, was one of the few French intellectuals to impute responsibility for the massacre to the French military. In *L'Humanité* he supported FLN demands for an international commission to investigate the massacre and claimed that the "wisely orchestrated campaign" was devised by the French government to divert attention from a ministerial crisis.[12] "The only solution that conforms with national opinion," Moreau wrote, was "to end the killing and engage in immediate Franco-Algerian negotiations." On June 4, *L'Humanité* published a second article that reinforced the claims that Mélouza had been the dirty work of the French army.[13]

Algerian nationalists certainly understood that Mélouza could damage their cause. On June 17, a lieutenant colonel of the French army's Fifth Bureau of Psychological Action reported the interception of a document entitled "Letter to our French Friends."[14] The "Letter," written on June 9 by Bachir Hadj Ali, secretary of the PCA, urged his French "friends" not to be persuaded by the government's propaganda concerning Mélouza.[15] According to Hadj Ali, the accusations were a political smoke screen with which the *ultras* attempted to silence critics of torture by using "terrorism" to counterbalance the horrors of the French military. Few French people, Hadj Ali admitted, were able to see through the propaganda. He commended *L'Humanité* for being one of few French newspapers to refute the French government's claims. Appealing to Marxist sympathies, he advised the French left to show more solidarity for the Algerians because the "community of interests" of those exploited by the "bourgeoisie" demanded a sense of unity among the oppressed.

As for clarifying the "facts of Mélouza," Hadj Ali argued that the area had been too heavily patrolled by the French military for the FLN to have carried out the massacre in broad daylight without being caught. Hence Mélouza had very likely been the work of the French troops, the *goumiers* (Algerians serving in the French army), or the *harkis*. But, as he suggested, motives were perhaps the greatest proof of the FLN's innocence. After all, he asked, was it not the colonialists and the *ultras* who profited most from the massacre? The colonialists had successfully diverted attention away from recent scandals. Algerians lost the most from the public's perception of violence. World opinion, which was sympathetic to Algerians, now doubted the FLN's judgment and condemned its violence. Furthermore, new controversies were likely to emerge among Algerian patriots, questioning the leadership of the FLN; French liberals and leftists were confused about how to proceed with anticolonialism, given the recent atrocities. Any way one looked at it, the FLN was discredited by the violence and hence could not have been behind the killing.

In a propagandistic maneuver, Hadj Ali continued, the FLN would not have massacred its own Algerian people because its cause was just and did not need these methods to triumph over the French. Having made these arguments, he acknowledged that he did not expect all French democrats to be convinced of the FLN's innocence, but he did encourage the French to "reflect" on the issue. "The blood of our own people is too precious," he claimed, for Algerians to kill themselves so brutally. Then he issued a call to arms: "The Algerian will no longer accept to live as a foreigner on his own soil. I prefer to die standing up than to live on my knees." In an effort to internationalize the conflict, Hadj Ali also demanded that an international commission be created to investigate the massacre. Presumably, if the French government did not accede to this demand, it would be proof enough "that they are afraid of the truth and that their version is built on lies."

On June 13, *France observateur* published the findings of a group of independent reporters not officially commissioned by the United Nations or recognized by France. The report, written by Mohamed Ben Smaïl, editor and director of the Tunisian newspaper *L'Action*, was based on a number of interviews with military personnel and a few survivors. Ben Smaïl determined that probably neither the FLN nor the French military actually carried out the massacre; rather, it most likely had been a band of *harkis*, supported by the French army, who had disguised themselves as FLN *fellagha*. One witness reported that the leader of the band had said repeatedly that his name was "Abdelkader Sahouni, the leader of the FLN" and that he was going to "kill the sons of bitches who had sold out to France"; the report concluded that these actions were obviously an attempt to frame the FLN. [16] The claim made sense because the FLN had long since regarded anonymity as essential. Moreover, Ben Smaïl continued, since it was widely known that the psychological warfare division of the French military had already been active in recruiting "contre-fellaghisme," it was more likely that the troops that had carried out the massacre were trained by the French.

Furthermore, there were simply too many problems with the French military's recollection of the events. The army had waited nearly forty hours after detecting that the village was under siege before it sent in troops to investigate. Consequently, not one suspect was captured. This was unusual because the French army usually responded immediately. And since the MNA-FLN rivalry was well known in the area surrounding the massacre, this provided opponents of the FLN with "an ideal alibi," thus making it easy to blame the Algerians.

Most important, as Hadj Ali had, the article speculated about motives. Mélouza had undeniably hurt the Algerian cause on both national and international levels. Taking into account problems with the French military's records, the political damage that imputing the Mélouza massacre to the FLN would do to the Algerian cause, and the known psychological warfare of the French army, it was reasonable to deduce that a group of French-backed harkis had orchestrated the killing. In the interests of certainty and to test the sincerity of both French authorities and Algerian nationalists, the journalists called for the creation of an international commission to investigate the massacre. This commission never materialized.

French Intellectuals Criticize the FLN

Despite the claims that the FLN was not responsible for Mélouza, the massacre was a turning point for French intellectuals. To understand just how Mélouza affected the tenor of the debates during the war, it is helpful to consider first its impact on Jean Daniel. From the beginning of the war, Daniel had been active in the anticolonialist movement, but he had never endorsed the FLN. Following Mélouza, his lukewarm position became hostile as he deplored the FLN's "terrorist" tactics. After Mélouza, he wrote in L'Express, Algeria had become a land of "savage assassination" and everyday violence. [17] What distinguished Mélouza from the everyday terror and horror of the war was the sheer number of victims and the fact that "the attitude of the FLN . . . did not hesitate to impute responsibility for the crime on the French units." Blaming the French was, he claimed, even more disgraceful than the murders themselves. As for the killing, Daniel was unequivocal: the FLN could not justify its own crimes by using means more reprehensible than colonialism. As he put it, "it is not sufficient to kill a certain number to rally the others to their cause" (4). The FLN murdering other Muslims merely gave Lacoste and the *ultras* more justification to use excessive force; this in turn increased extremism among the Muslim population and delivered "Algerian nationalism more and more to the rebellion's fanatics."

Daniel was not alone in criticizing the FLN. On June 7 Joseph Folliet asked in *Témoignage chrétien* how one could face the "nausea of rage and disgust" when "thinking about Mélouza?"[18] According to Folliet, the FLN was clearly responsible, and the massacre showed the degree to which the FLN had become a totalitarian movement bent on destroying reconciliation and its own people:

> There are no excuses for this killing. It reveals neither racial passions because Algerians have sacrificed other Algerians nor religious fanaticism because Muslims have butchered other Muslims. It is only the frightening episode of a sordid political quarrel and a terrorist progression toward domination. It comes down to a question for the FLN of "reabsorbing" a pocket of the MNA in its zone of influence. A great means of defining the rivalries! And a great preface to future domination!
>
> We are the few Christians and Muslims who have never wanted to despair for peace in Algeria, a peace of justice, of the equality of all the populations, and a fraternal collaboration in a common future. . . . The butchery of Mélouza is the worst defeat that we have sustained since the beginning of the revolt. If certain "hardliners" of the FLN want to burn the last bridges, render all reconciliation not only impossible but inconceivable, they can rejoice: they have just marked a decisive point with blood.

Without question, Mélouza forced many French intellectuals to rethink the possibility and especially the desirability of reconciliation. The French left, despite the uncertainty of the villains' identities, refused to listen to the Algerian denials. But just how much had Mélouza cost Algerian nationalists in the eyes of their supporters? In a communiqué issued in the June 6, 1957, *France observateur*, the so-called new left claimed to support ending the war in Algeria through recognition of Algerian rights, but it distanced itself from the "atrocious" means of solidifying Algerian nationalism.[19] And like other groups, the new left called for an international commission to investigate the massacre.

Claude Bourdet, one of the principal leaders of the new left, acknowledged that Mélouza had placed intellectuals sympathetic to Algerians in a rather uncomfortable position. According to him, the dilemma was simple: how was it possible to provide intellectual and political support to the Algerian rebels who disgraced their own cause and the reputation of their supporters by massacring innocents? In the interest of intellectual legitimacy would it not be important for French intellectuals to condemn the FLN's violence? The answer was certainly yes, but it was qualified. Before condemning Mélouza, he argued, it was most essential to recall that French repression and collective reprisals were really the original sources of nationalist violence. [20]

Algerians were in a desperate situation, Bourdet insisted, and violence could be justified as long as it came in the form of individual acts of resistance to French domination. In other words, there were "qualitative" differences between individual acts of violence and collective acts of violence (massacres). Mélouza was "different" because it was a massacre of innocents, not an isolated attack carried out on an individual target.

Bourdet's distinction between legitimate and illegitimate violence was meant to keep moral pressure on the French government as well. The French army's use of torture, systematic destruction of villages, and large-scale killing were different from individual and isolated assaults on Algerian nationalists and immoral on the same grounds. For most French intellectuals, it was never a question that the army's use of torture was immoral, but now Mélouza placed the same cloud of suspicion over the Algerians. Just as torture had done to the reputation of the French high command, Mélouza's violence suggested the moral depravity of the FLN leaders. Rather than giving credence to the FLN's denials, Bourdet noted that Mélouza had pointlessly provided conservative French forces with just the right excuse to "fix the problem" with even more force.

If Algerian leaders were truly interested in leading a just revolution, Bourdet implied, they would have to understand an elementary political rule: know one's allies' (in this case French intellectuals and the international community's) moral limits. He made another realistic but patronizing observation: since the nationalists were not a political force with a long-standing nation-state to support them, they would have to show even more discretion than France because France could rely on its "status quo" authority in the international community and Algeria could not. He acknowledged that "theoretically" it did not make sense for the Algerians to have committed the massacre since it only "blackened" their name. But "history," he conceded, was comprised of "facts and errors" that ultimately made little sense.

If the new left was horrified by the lack of political discretion the massacre had shown, more conservative liberals such as Jean-Marie Domenach, editor of the influential monthly, Esprit, upped the ante. Just as Bourdet had argued, Domenach suggested that Mélouza was morally "different" because it represented a collective, not an individual crime. [21] Admitting that responsibility for the massacre remained uncertain, he did think that, since the FLN-MNA conflict was well known, it appeared likely the FLN had organized the massacre. He conceded that it could have been the harkis, but this would be somewhat ironic since until then, the FLN had repeatedly denied their existence out of desire to show the unity of the Algerian people against colonialism (105).

Despite the overall negative reactions Mélouza sparked in France, it would be tremendously misleading to argue that only French intellectuals condemned Mélouza. Mouloud Feraoun, for one, disapproved but was shocked to see how quickly the massacre had turned international opinion against the Algerians. On May 30, 1957, he noted that when the radio first announced the massacre in Mélouza it was given only a "small space" in the dailies "among all the other communiqués." [22] By June 3 he described how world opinion had been awakened: "Alas! All the newspapers are talking about the Mélouza massacres. Horrible photos are splashed across front pages, and world opinion, now vigilant, is beginning to express anger and disapproval. A disgrace! A disgrace, a stupid act whereby an entire nation is condemned, and its people shamelessly reveal their inhumanity." Despite the possible "psychological" or "political explanations," he noted that the human costs were too great: "In any case, the victim's blood needs no explanation. There is no justification that will dry the children's tears or blot out the unspeakable horror that hellish night fixes forever in the haggard eyes of those women" (212).

A week later, on June 10, Feraoun wrote in disgust how both French and Algerians were denying responsibility and attempting to use the massacre for propaganda. There was something tragically farcical about this propaganda war. On one hand, President Coty represented the Algerians to world opinion as "barbarians." On the other, the FLN appealed to the pope (of all people) to stop the "genocide" in Algeria, and cited the Mélouza massacre as the most recent event in the long list of French collective crimes against the Algerian people. Added to this feast of immorality, Feraoun found the position of the French intellectuals particularly vexing. He noted with sarcasm the French pleas for Algerians to denounce the massacre. Those who refused to consent to French requests were deemed "bastards" by the French, but if by bastards the French meant that Algerians were determined to keep Algeria Algerian, then the Algerians certainly welcomed the epithet (212). He admonished the French:

> —Gentlemen, for us, it matters very little whether you are this or that. And while we are at it, let us say that we are bastards, just like you. This is not the point. What matters is knowing whether or not we are at home, whether or not you are in our home, and if you want to leave us the fuck alone. . . .
> Everything else is nothing but casuistry, tragic hypocrisy. (213)

More than two months later, on August 30, Feraoun commented that he had seen a propaganda brochure compiled by Lacoste on the Mélouza massacre and noted how even then the French and the FLN shrank from responsibility: "[N]obody has the courage to admit to this crime" (222). Given the circumstances, he challenged the authority of the French government's propaganda because all the journalists' accounts recorded in the publication were based on official French sources (223). All this, he commented sadly, demonstrated that real chances of reconciliation had been wasted and there was nothing but the wolf left in man, since both sides were doing everything possible to destroy a common future. Regardless whether it was the "Gentlemen of the FLN or the Gentlemen of the Fourth Republic," Feraoun asked both sides tough questions: "[D]o you think that a drop of your blood is really worth anything more than a drop of anyone else's blood—blood that, because of you, is being shed on the scorched soil of Algeria? Do you truly believe that, with your dirty hands, you are going to build the better future that you are promising us in your hysterical speeches? You, who have manufactured our misfortune, do you think that you will not also share in it?" (223).

Demonizing the Enemy

Rather than commission an international investigation of Mélouza, as everyone had called for, Resident Minister Robert Lacoste saw an opportunity to exploit the tragic deaths at Mélouza. He wanted to discredit the FLN and turn French intellectuals, the French public, and world opinion against its leaders. Photographs and provocative text were his choice weapons of propaganda.

According to Alistair Horne, Jacques Soustelle may have had something to do with the use of photographs in the press. When he had been sent by Guy Mollet to New York as part of the UN delegation to defend French colonialism in Algeria, Soustelle supposedly "complained" to Mollet that he had found in the delegation's offices a "cupboard stuffed with unused material and photographs on the FLN atrocities, in Algeria." Soustelle is quoted as saying: "But these were never used by us, for fear of offending the niceties of diplomacy. So could you win the diplomatic war when you were fighting with your hands tied like this?"[23]

Aware of the political windfall his administration could gain from swift propaganda, Lacoste followed Soustelle's lead and immediately allowed reporters and photographers to cover the site of the massacre. Soon thereafter, horrible photographs surfaced in the French and Algerian press. Algerian corpses with crushed skulls, brains splattered onto the dirt, bodies tossed on top of each other like cattle, and body parts next to rotting corpses were omnipresent. The appearance of these shocking images was sanctioned by Lacoste's government. But then Lacoste's administration in Algeria decided to take the ghastly display of violence to another level when he had other more explicit photographs printed and sent to high government officials and influential persons.[24]

Trying to get political mileage out of the dead, in August 1957 Lacoste's propaganda machine published a small brochure titled L'Opinion mondiale juge les sanglants "libérateurs" de Mélouza et de Wagram (World Opinion Judges the Savage "Liberators" of Mélouza and Wagram). This publication shows that the French colonial government was beginning to understand how it could exploit violence in order to redirect public attention away from the crimes of the French army and police. "On 30 May 1957, the civilized world heard the name Mélouza spoken for the first time," the pamphlet noted; "this village was destined to be ignored by men if it had not been the theater of one of the most atrocious crimes in history: the Front de Libération Nationale has just deliberately exterminated every man over the age of fifteen."[25] It threatened that the FLN would seek power with a logic similar to Nazism and with "the most inhuman means" of "terror." What could be done to stop this terror? It was important for world opinion to be alerted to the myth that the FLN represented liberation and democracy for Algerians. Next to a gruesome photograph showing the mutilation of the corpses at Mélouza, the editors concluded: "The words 'democracy,' 'national liberation movement,' behind which the rebels try to hide their criminal actions, sound cruel to the ears of those who have heard only once the names of Mélouza and Wagram."

The pamphlet also contained articles from the world press condemning Mélouza. One such article was signed just after the massacre by a group of some of the most vocal anticolonialist intellectuals responding to the FLN's denial of responsibility.[26] It declared that the FLN had not shown sufficient proof that the French army was responsible for the atrocities. "Without calling into question" their earlier positions against the war, they wrote, the group asked the FLN and the ALN to "publicly disavow similar means of combat" (12).

By autumn 1957 Lacoste and his administration in Algiers had put together an even more revealing piece of propaganda, Aspects véritables de la rébellion algérienne (The True Aspects of the Algerian Rebellion).[27] Dubbed the "Green Book" (livre vert) because of its green cover, the booklet was the most explicit propaganda effort launched during the war. Its goal was to turn readers against the rebellion, and its authors tried to achieve this through a shocking combination of gruesome photographs of massacred victims (from Mélouza and elsewhere) and textual descriptions of the Algerian "rebels" as brutal and irresponsible monsters. But according to the resident minister's office, its goal was "to show in concrete and conclusive fashion, by irrefutable documents which can easily be verified, the methods employed by the rebels."[28] Assisted by Michel Gorlin, the technical consul to Lacoste's cabinet, the resident minister's office distributed the brochure to influential intellectuals and individuals across France and even abroad.

Introducing the Green Book, the government announced that it intended to destroy the "mask" of Algerian propaganda (5). On the second page the brutal truth behind the mask was reflected in a photograph of a corpse in full rigor mortis, its hands in the air around its neck, its arms covered in its own blood in a hopeless attempt to stop the flow of blood from its slit throat to the parched earth. On the chest of the corpse was pinned a simple note, stained by the victim's blood, which read in both Arabic and French:

> YOU HAVE BETRAYED THE NATIONAL CAUSE. THE TRIBUNE OF
> THE PEOPLE CONDEMNS YOU TO DEATH. THE BLACK SWORD
> IS SUSPENDED FROM YOUR HEAD. COMING FROM OUR ARMY.
> IT WILL PURSUE YOU AND STRIKE YOU TO DEATH WHERE YOU
> ARE. THE HOUR OF JUSTICE HAS ARRIVED. (7)

According to the government, this note was found on a victim named Hadj Brahim Larbi, the mayor of the village of Bouchagoune, "whose throat was cut by the rebels on the 12th of April 1957 because he refused to resign."

In order to illustrate that for the French and Algerian populations alike, Algerian nationalism translated into Islamic fanaticism and pan-Arabism, the government divided the booklet into five principal sections: (1) "The Struggle for Arabism," (2) "The Struggle for Islam," (3) "Servitude in the Name of Liberty," (4) "The Struggle against Humanity," (5) "The Struggle against Colonialism." Each section combined brutal photographs with descriptions of how the Algerian Muslims posed a danger to France, other Algerians, and humanity.

The booklet outlined the "Definition and Characters of Arab Nationalism" with quotes out of context from sources such as one that defined Arabism in the following manner: "I, Arabism, I am a terrible force, a revolt, which cannot be extinguished, a volcano always rumbling" (13). Along with a poetic commentary on Arab unity by Ahmed Saïd taken from the Cairo-based radio program, The Voice of the Arabs, the minister's propaganda showed a charred and mutilated Algerian corpse (15). In a subsection devoted to "Racial Hatred and Xenophobia," Lacoste's team mixed excerpts from other broadcasts ("The heart of every Algerian is filled with hatred for the French." "Oh colonialists and imperialists! Leave the country, leave Arab Algeria before you are chased out, before you are thrown out like ferocious and harmful beasts") with photographs of European men, women, and children murdered in their homes, in their beds, with their throats gashed open (21). Images in "The Struggle for Islam," recorded the same attempt to make the conscious link between Islam and brutality by mixing quotes from radio transmissions and the like, connecting "Arab" words of violence to images of corpses. For example, the corpse of René Falourd, a French soldier, was shown with his entire right arm's muscles shaved off to the bone. "The muscles of the right arm and forearm had been torn out, laying bare the bones," the caption read (31). As far as the French government's propaganda machine was concerned, the corpse's mutilated arm was the direct result of the supposedly Islamic dimension of the struggle.

Another part of the Green Book was devoted to showing the effects of the FLN's interdiction to work for the French administration, to smoke or drink, or to go to movies. It was a well-known FLN practice to punish those who broke such FLN prohibitions by assassination or cutting off noses or lips. To demonstrate this, Lacoste's men printed horrifying photographs of lipless and noseless Algerians, all "victims" of "fanaticism." One photograph profiled an Algerian whose nose had recently been chopped off; the same victim, still alive, was also missing his ears (52).

By far the most terrifying of the photographs (if it is possible to make such a distinction) were in the chapter "The Struggle against Humanity" in the subsection "Assassinations (Mutilations and Tortures)." Filled with gruesome images, this section was meant to revolt onlookers and convince readers that reports of the French military torture paled in comparison to what Algerians were capable of. For example, the book displayed a photograph of two decapitated Muslims' heads on the ground, each mouth stuffed with a penis. The caption read: "On the 27th of May 1956, in the douar [village] of Zenata (Remchi) two Moslems, Bouhassoun Benmrah and Mohamed Beneli, were tortured by the rebels. They were decapitated with a hoe after having their penes cut off and thrust into their mouths" (112).

Algerians, according to the minister-endorsed text, would attempt to win their liberty through the most grotesque means possible. The authors pretended to present the facts of the rebellion objectively: "We have seen in what terms the rebels interpret the struggle for liberty; let us examine the way in which they seek to impose their conceptions of liberty by a terror which we leave to our readers to judge for themselves" (76). To set the mood, this chapter opened with a picture of the face of a murdered Muslim—a burned face without lips and exposed teeth, a face without a nose—with a quote from Radio de l'Algérie Libre et Combattante (Free and Combatant Algeria), the Voice of the FLN and the ALN: "We are fighting for a just cause, a humanitarian cause" (75). The chapter then began with other FLN directives taken from Radio de l'Algérie Libre et Combattante dated March 13, 1957, stating that women, children, the old, religious figures, and doctors were to be assassinated (77). The photographs in this section showed dead children with vocal cords hanging out, murdered women, mutilated old men, murdered doctors and military men, other random victims, and finally victims of various massacre sites throughout Algeria.

The government's attempts to demonize the Algerian nationalists seemed to climax with the massacres of Wagram and Mélouza in the Green Book. Making no mention of the FLN's request for an international investigation of the massacre or the French government's newly created Muslim concentration camps (euphemistically called "relocation camps") in Algeria, it cited Mélouza as the worst evidence of the FLN's monstrous behavior. According to the Green Book, the FLN simply arrived, descended on Mélouza, and murdered more than three hundred victims in an effort to stamp out the rival MNA. The administration wrote that it was clear what the FLN meant when it claimed that the masses were "solidly behind" it— only "in subjugation by terror," the fire of a "machine gun, the hatchet or the knife" would Algerians remain loyal to the FLN (118). The Green Book concluded with further descriptions and images of urban terrorism and mass destruction and a brief comment by Lacoste's administration restating the intent of the book: "The facts which we have presented should enable the fair-minded reader to be a better judge of the fantastic tales spread by the propagandists of the rebellion. Our aim will have been achieved if each one, after closing these pages, can discern the true face of the Algerian rebellion behind the mask of its principles and pretensions" (157).

Intellectuals Respond to Lacostian Demonizing
Most of the letters Michel Gorlin received following the mass mailing of the Green Book testified to the effectiveness of French propaganda and to the perceived need (among some intellectuals) for Lacoste's administration to rein in the terrorists. In a letter dated November 15, 1957, Louis Marin, president of the Académie des Sciences Morales et Politiques, thanked Gorlin for the "beautiful work" that showed "what the Algerian rebels really are."[29] Louis Papy, a professor of geography, responded that the document used to "make the rebel methods" known was "sadly evocative," and that it "had to be made known."[30] The general director of secondary education for the Ministry of National Education, Charles Brunold, applauded Lacoste's administration for his careful "objectivity" in writing about the "atrocities committed by the rebels."[31] A member of the cabinet of the dean of the Faculty of Sciences in Lille claimed that after he and his colleagues had read the book they were "better informed on what Algeria is and they could better understand the reasons that we have in not abandoning it, and it was even in the interest of the North Africans" for the French to stay.[32]

Realizing that the American and British audience was especially susceptible to the Algerian demands for international recognition but that neither would endorse terrorism, Lacoste's administration (not surprisingly) saw the Green Book as a means to disengage American and other international support from Algerians. Even F. Charles-Roux, the French ambassador to the United States and a member of the Institut de France, suggested to Gorlin on November 27 that the book was perfect for turning foreign opinion against the Algerians. "My opinion is that these booklets are very useful because of the horrors and atrocities they represent, and that it will be of great interest to diffuse them abroad, especially in America and in Great Britain."[33]

Despite the euphoric optimism of government officials for their new propaganda weapon, some French disagreed with the use of the Green Book. Paul Vienney, an attorney in the Court of Appeals, wrote to Lacoste on November 16, 1957, expressing his distaste.[34] Vienney admitted that he was more "sensitive" to the book than most because he had lived in Algeria for sixteen years and that he was disturbed to see the evidence of the "most atrocious aspects" of the revolution. But, he wrote, it was not in these atrocities that one would find the "bankruptcy" of the moral world because the "bankruptcy is precisely that of colonialism." The book should have contained the "counterpart, the photographs of the ravages in villages and communities caused by the blind repression about which much was spoken—before his investiture—by President [of the council] Guy Mollet." Vienney went further, suggesting that without much effort the government could most certainly find in the "army archives photographs of infant cadavers, old people, and native women brutally mutilated by French bullets and bombs." These were the "truths," Vienney concluded, that could have convinced the French people to finally end a war that had already been declared "unjust and unnecessary" by the president.

Perhaps even more despicable than the massacres themselves, Jean-Marie Domenach added, was the nauseating degree to which both the French and Algerians had used them in their propaganda efforts. "This propaganda war," Domenach wrote, "was ignoble." Ultimately, it discredited both sides and showed how victims could be exploited for the sake of politics. As Domenach stated, "In this day, there is no horror that cannot be used."[35]

After publishing his criticism of the propaganda campaign in Esprit, Domenach must have found it ironic to receive Gorlin's letter asking him to accept the same pamphlet designed to "make the methods of inspiration used by the rebels better known."[36] Gorlin's letter continued:

> Only misunderstandings, confusions, and errors determined by ignorance of these horrible realities which we have placed aside for a long time out of a concern for humanity, can now incite us to deliver these atrocious images to [public] opinion. We know though,

moreover, that it is our responsibility to inform the enlightened opinion.

I think that, with your intellectual network and with your moral authority, you can, better than anyone, spread these truths which surge with brutality in these few pages out around you. Because this work is only meant for limited distribution, I am ready, if you think it useful, to make it known to people of your choice by sending you a few extra copies.

Domenach did not respond directly to Gorlin's letter, but he did publish a letter written by Casamayor addressed to "an ultra." Casamayor attacked Lacoste and Gorlin for distributing propaganda aimed at inciting hatred between the European and Muslim populations. "Mr. Gorlin," Casamayor wrote, "hopes that we will become like him by showing us cadavers torn to bits [and that] he will arouse in us a spirit of revenge."[37] Simply by "singing the *Marseillaise*" and showing devastating photographs, Gorlin was hoping to turn the French against the Algerian people (276).

For Casamayor, the Green Book was simply another sign of the government's stupidity because it continued to think of the Algerian crisis in purely militaristic terms. In "traffic[ing] the mutilated corpses," the government was once again denying the social and political aspects and hoping to provoke enough animosity to unleash an avalanche of hatred. In short, it was clear for Gorlin and his type that, "It was not a matter of respecting the dead [*des cadavres*] but of mobilizing them" (277).

Casamayor's criticisms of French propaganda did not mean that he endorsed the FLN's political violence. His comments echoed Feraoun's, and he argued that the French and Algerian people were wedged between two extreme enemies and were being forced to choose between two equally nefarious regimes. Moreover and equally crucial, Casamayor suggested that the war was becoming increasingly abstract because the enemy was being dehumanized. At the same time that the extremists on both sides were trying to demonize the "enemy," Gorlin was also trying to consolidate French power by pushing the moderate French in Algeria into the *ultras'* camp. In fact, Casamayor claimed, Gorlin was attempting to "*fabricate the ultras*" (279). The result was despicable: Algeria had become a "land of violence" where a "brutal contrast" between "the Europeans" and the "natives [*autochtones*]" had been ushered in by the "total incomprehension" of one group by the other. Hatred had therefore become the mediator of relations between Europeans and Algerians. With the Europeans being traumatized into "ultra robots" by propaganda campaigns, the exterior reality of the "Algeria-Object" had crumbled into irreconcilable differences (280).

After living in Algeria for twenty years, Casamayor concluded, it had become difficult, if not impossible, to address himself to a Muslim because the Muslim had ceased to exist. What was now left was a "billboard covered with slogans. . . . The real Muslim [l'homme musulman véritable], I do not know him. I fear that the war, if I can judge it by its effect on us, will not permit him to know himself" (287). As proof of this, Casamayor cited the rise in group and collective consciousness that had overridden the individual who carried the sacred words of "liberty and the fatherland [patrie]." Finally, because he did not know the Muslim who had become the adversary of the French, Casamayor said, he had addressed himself to the adversary he did know, Gorlin, in the hopes that by criticizing one the other would also be properly illuminated.

Mélouza and Lacoste/Gorlin's propaganda had a tremendous impact on the French intellectual community. Although there were obvious differences among intellectuals, violence obliged anticolonialist intellectuals to reevaluate and clarify their sympathies for Algerian nationalists. Since nearly all, if not all, French intellectuals believed that the FLN was responsible for the massacre, they were forced to choose between accepting the FLN's revolutionary methods and salvaging the idea of Franco-Algerian reconciliation. In many ways, their anger after seeing the FLN atrocities was a form of displaced anger on both sides of the colonial divide. Both the pro-Algérie française and the anticolonialist intellectuals seemed to rely too much on good faith—either in the French government or in the direction of the FLN. Certainly both attempted to make sense of and use the violence. However, although the anticolonialists did not seem to glorify FLN violence, their reactions did suggest a weakening of moral standards when confronted with direct evidence. Perhaps an uneasy awareness of their discomfort with violence was responsible for French intellectuals' reassessment of their political alliance with Algerian nationalists. This ambivalence is probably also to blame for nationalist intellectuals' desire to distance themselves from their French counterparts. What Lacoste and Gorlin did not realize was that in turning the French against Algerians, they would also turn them, indirectly, against the idea of French Algeria.

Frantz Fanon, *El Moudjahid*, and the Bad Faith of French Intellectuals

In the politicization of violence, Frantz Fanon emerged as perhaps the single most important critic of the French anticolonialist movement.[38] Born in Martinique but educated as a psychiatrist in France at the University of Lyon, Fanon took a post at the Blida-Joinville Psychiatric Hospital in November 1953. A year before he assumed his new post, Fanon's first important work, *Peau noire, masques blancs* (*Black Skin, White Masks*), was published in Paris.[39] Its highly autobiographical tone captured Fanon's personal experiences with European racism against blacks. In order to depict the impact of this racism, Fanon employed a cultural dialectic of the Self-Other. In the section titled "The Negro and Hegel," Fanon described the principal agent of the dialectic: "reciprocity." "In its immediacy, consciousness of the Self is simple being-for-itself. In order to win the certainty of oneself, the incorporation of the concept of recognition is essential. Similarly, the Other is waiting for recognition by us, in order to burgeon into the universal consciousness of Self" (217).

After siding with Algerian nationalists during the war, Fanon soon realized that a universal consciousness of Self would never develop under the colonial structure of oppression. More specifically, he had become aware of a shortcoming in his own theoretical work. Whereas he had previously believed that recognition was an essential element in the dialectic, the problem he encountered in Algeria was that the *Homo occidentalis* was not concerned with recognizing the Other. Unfortunately, the war and colonialism had demonstrated that the French were lost in Eurocentric rhetoric and concerned only with the war's effect on the French conceptions of selfhood. Fanon phrased this in the following manner in a letter to a French friend who was leaving Algeria because of the war:

> Concerned about Man but strangely not about the Arab . . .
> For there is not a European who is not revolted, indignant, alarmed at everything, except the fate to which the Arab is subjected.
> Unperceived Arabs.
> Ignored Arabs.
> Arabs spirited away, dissimulated.
> Arabs daily denied, transformed into the Saharan stage set.[40]

What Fanon had not counted on in his earlier theoretical work on racism and began to work into his new theory was the denial of the reciprocal exchange of consciousness (intersubjectivity) between the oppressed and the oppressor.

With the revolution swirling around him, Fanon worked for three years to humanize health care for Algeria's mentally ill. By 1956 he could no longer endure working in an administration he considered racist and expressed his frustration in a letter of resignation to Lacoste. It was no longer possible, Fanon wrote, to perform his duties as a psychiatrist in Algeria. He would no longer take part in efforts to reintegrate the mentally ill, since the principal source of their illnesses was colonialism itself:

> Madness is one of the means man has of losing his freedom. And I can say, on the basis of what I have been able to observe from this vantage point, that the degree of alienation of the inhabitants of this country appears to me frightening.
>
> If psychiatry is the medical technique that aims to enable man no longer to be a stranger to his environment, I owe it to myself to affirm that the Arab, permanently an alien in his own country, lives in a state of absolute depersonalization.
>
> What is the status of Algeria? A systematized dehumanization.[41]

When Fanon was expelled from Algeria in 1957, he joined the FLN's political and intellectual elite in Tunis, becoming an important contributor to the newly formed Algerian nationalist newspaper El Moudjahid. By 1957, as demonstrated in his writings on Mélouza, he was one of the most vocal critics of the French left. According to him, the French commitment to decolonizing Algeria was based on bad faith. In September, after Mélouza, he began to publish anonymous articles in El Moudjahid. One such article, "Algeria Face to Face with French Torturers," charged that French intellectuals had to give up their double game of condemning torture in Algeria and refusing the FLN's legitimate demands for independence. [42] Torture went hand in hand with today's colonialism and was simply a principal means of maintaining France's continued domination of Algeria; it was "an expression of the occupant-occupied relationship" (65). Since torture was an "expression," not an "accident, or a fault, or an error," French intellectuals' first duty was to admit that the claim that torture was "exceptional" was a lie (66). Only after intellectuals saw why the colonial system had to be completely overthrown could they understand that the objective of the Algerians' struggle was "from the outset total and absolute" (72).

By December Fanon had become even more disillusioned with the French because they maintained the illusion of reconciliation. Because they believed in reconciliation, they would always interpret the revolution negatively. He unleashed an unprecedented polemic in a three-part series published in El Moudjahid. In the first of these articles he caustically reassessed the shortcomings of French intellectuals.[43] Since it was clear that they were driven by democratic paternalism and would try to influence revolutionaries by criticizing the nationalists' methods, Fanon insisted that "[o]ne of the first duties of intellectuals and democratic elements in colonialist countries is unreservedly to support the national aspirations of colonized peoples."

Thematically, Fanon broke the French participation in the rebellion into two phases. In the first phase (which immediately preceded the rebellion), the French left enjoyed "the status of a prophet." With Cassandra-like instincts, they sat back and predicted the impending explosion. In this stage there was a "partial communication between the people in revolt and the democratic elements" (77). The left also felt close to those revolting because in many cases they had known each other personally.[44]

The second phase shows evidence of a shift in the relationship between the democratic left in France and Algerian revolutionaries attributable to violence. As violence intensified, repression increased and the people in revolt had no choice but to react to the "genocide campaign" waged against them. According to Fanon, this presented a paradox for the French left when "ultrachauvinistic, nationalistic, patriotic propaganda" created an artificial opposition between the colonized and the French nation (77). To neutralize French intellectuals' sympathies for Algerians, conservative forces used the charge of treason (see Chapter 5).

French government propaganda was able to offset intellectuals' participation in the anticolonialist movement, but intellectuals' arguments increasingly weakened and lost vitality. The idea of terrorism as presented in propaganda militated against the Algerian nationalists' cause: "The propaganda [concerning terrorism] became orchestrated, wormed its way into people's minds and dismantled convictions that were already crumbling. The concept of barbarism appeared, and it was decided that France in Algeria was fighting barbarism" (79).

The second article was more forceful in attacking French intellectuals for meddling in the affairs of the colonized. Fanon reduced French intellectuals' behavior to the Eurocentric desire to dominate every aspect of the colonized lives. This desire ran so deep, he argued, that it was essential not to mistake French intellectuals' apparent devotion to anticolonialism as an indicator of solidarity. This so-called solidarity, he continued, was merely the culmination of the French intellectuals' inability to affect politics in their own country; this, in combination with their "ill-repressed desire to guide, to direct the very liberation movement of the oppressed," led them to blackmail Algerian nationalists with ersatz humanism (80).

From this perspective, he argued, the injustices of colonialism could not be redressed by Algerian nationalists through liberal philosophies of the Self. In other words, ending colonialism could not be achieved through liberal reforms; it required independence. However, Fanon called for a re-thinking of the human relations forged under colonial rule; it was neces-sary to reject the liberal view that colonialism was ultimately about an in-dividual's relation with other individuals. Since colonialism was an act of collective, not individual, oppression, he insisted that collective violence against all Frenchmen in Algeria could be justified: "Colonialism is not a type of individual relations but the conquest of a national territory and the oppression of a people; that is all. It is not a certain type of human behavior or a pattern of relations between individuals. Every Frenchman in Algeria is at the present time an enemy soldier" (81).

For France, moreover, colonialism constituted an integral dimension of French history. Since all colonial relations between the French and Algeri-ans were predicated on the basis of force, France was de facto implicated in colonialism's violence. Yet, for the democrat faithful to France's historic (and imaginary) past, a past impregnated with mythic grandeur and false ideas of equality, it was difficult to understand that the very same colonial-ism he or she condemned as "dying" and "inhuman" had been an integral part of France's development (83). Consequently, the French had to realize that in condemning Algerian independence and French colonialism, they were simultaneously implicating themselves in the collective guilt of polit-ical oppression, a guilt that further implied the decaying nature of French society itself.

In the third article, published on December 30, Fanon widened his crit-icism of French intellectuals and focused on the problem of identity. He argued that, while France's intercourse with the continent of "Africa" had largely been a function of "property" relations, Algeria was different be-cause the French conquest and continued domination of Algeria was deter-mined by "the relations of identity" (84). This could be clearly demonstrated by the fact that Franco-Algerian relations had been contaminated by the ubiquitous idea that "Algeria is France," and as a result the Algerians were "up against instinctive, passionate, anti-historic reactions" (85). These re-actions conditioned the debates and weakened the French people's resolve to act in their best interests and release Algeria from the burden of military occupation.

The problem of identity had now become critical, Fanon insisted, for both the Communist and non-Communist left confronting the problem of decolonization. For non-Communist intellectuals it was important that Algeria be kept within the Western orbit and not be allowed to fall under the control of Abdel Nasser or the Eastern bloc. But these intellectuals did not understand that Algerians were determined to liberate themselves from the "French colonialist yoke" with the aid of sympathetic nations (86). Not comprehending the urgency, non-Communist French intellectuals "implore us to combine the two efforts: rejection of French colonialism and of Soviet-neutralist Communism."[45] Paradoxically, the French Communist left made antithetical demands on Algerian nationalists, issuing an ultimatum that it would help in the Algerian liberation only if they could be guaranteed that the Algerians would remain faithful to Communist ideology and goals.

As these conflicting demands illustrated, extraneous motives for the French to engage in the anticolonialist campaign had been tainted by considerations and politics internal to French traditions. Algeria, Fanon claimed, had become a "bone of contention" between two jealous supporters. It was therefore with sarcastic irony that he asked, "For whom, indeed, is Algeria going to be liberated?" (86). The answer was just as simple: "For three years the Algerian people have not ceased repeating that it proposes to liberate itself for its own sake."

What Algerian nationalists resented most, Fanon claimed, was the conditional nature of French intellectuals' support. Rather than pledging to help the Algerians on principle, French intellectuals held Algerians hostage to the "restrictions" that they, not Algerians, placed on the nationalists' objectives. The crux of the matter could be traced to the inability of the entire French left to recognize the legitimacy of the Algerians' demand for independence. In effect, the French left wanted to ensure that the intellectual and political links between France and Algeria would remain intact. Unable to relinquish political or cultural control of Algeria, the French had devised the insidious argument that without French technology and industry Algeria would regress. This, Fanon claimed, was disguised "technocratic paternalism" (88).[46] Wrapped in a contorted identity that had been falsified by the hidden desire to dominate Algeria, the French were bewildered by the nationalists' demands for freedom. In Fanon's words:

The colonialists tell the French people in their propaganda: France cannot live without Algeria.

The French anti-colonialists say to the Algerians: Algeria cannot live without France.

The French democrats do not always perceive the colonialists, or—to use a new concept—the neo-colonialist character of their attitude.

The demand for special links with France is a response to the desire to maintain colonial structures intact. What is involved here is a kind of terrorism of necessity on the basis of which it is decided that nothing valid can be conceived or achieved in Algeria independently of France. In fact, the demand for special links with France comes down to a determination to maintain Algeria eternally in a stage of a minor and protected State. But also to a determination to guarantee certain forms of exploitation of the Algerian people. It is unquestionably proof of a grave failure to understand the revolutionary implications of the national struggle. (88)

While their support had been admirable in many cases, French intellectuals had to bring it to the final crescendo of commitment by helping Algerians attain independence. This required them to struggle against their own state, but did not necessitate national betrayal. Only by completing the circle of belief in their own revolutionary past by joining rhetoric with action could French intellectuals truly help Algerian nationalists.

Philosophizing the French Way: Intellectuals Respond to Fanon

Few French intellectuals on the left appreciated Fanon's criticisms, and, as he came to learn, criticizing these intellectuals meant opening himself (and the FLN) to a whole set of equally powerful accusations. Nevertheless, by fashioning a precise attack on the left, Fanon brought the latent tensions between the FLN and French intellectuals into the open.

François Mauriac, never shy from polemics, was one of the first French intellectuals to attack Fanon's anonymous articles in El Moudjahid. He began by agreeing that the Algerian revolution was taking a toll on the French Fourth Republic. Fearful that France was sitting on a political volcano, he admitted that the "Algerian sickness" weakened French institutions, dishonored the French left, and fostered a fascist atmosphere in both France and Algeria. Mauriac also admitted that after a plane carrying Ben Bella and other Algerian politicians was skyjacked by the French military while traveling from Morocco to Tunisia in October 1956, the real possibilities for a cease-fire had greatly diminished.[47] Ironically, Mauriac correctly noted that, by attacking the French left as El Moudjahid had done, the Algerians had created a worse situation for themselves: French right and fascist elements would make gains that would damage the possibility for peace talks. "But what do you gain?" Mauriac asked. "You deliver us, you deliver French politics to your worst enemies, the least capable of listening to reason—so obstinate that even the loi-cadre revised by Soustelle renders them furious."[48]

To avoid an all-out catastrophe, Mauriac urged the FLN to come to a compromise with the French. This, however, did not mean that he fully endorsed Algerian independence. Unwilling to accept independence, he simply argued that if the FLN would relinquish this idea, the French would be willing to make a concession on the "myth of French-Algeria." These concessions from both France and the nationalists, he concluded, were mandated by the situation because "The health of the two peoples existed somewhere between them."

Gilles Martinet and the France observateur also did not take El Moudjahid's criticisms lightly. On January 2, 1958, Martinet published "Response to the FLN" along with the third El Moudjahid article. According to him, the nameless author was obviously a "recent intellectual convert" [un intellectuel "rallié" de plus ou moins fraiche date] to the FLN who had a "taste for verbal outrages and psychological striptease."[49] Thinking that the articles could not possibly have been written by the same person, Martinet argued that the author of the final article appeared to be a "political man who had a sense of responsibility."

Besides lack of continuity between the different "personalities" expressed in the articles, Martinet argued that they exhibited a poverty of argumentative sophistication. The first article had been overly polemic and naive; the last article suffered from undisciplined arguments. The portrayal of the FLN in the most recent article, he wrote, exhibited the same deprived logic as the French government. Instead of being willing to make the concessions necessary for peace, the FLN refused all compromise. This intransigence represented an important shift in FLN politics. In the past the FLN had been willing to recognize the individual rights of the colons living in Algeria, but now (with Fanon speaking for the FLN) all the French people living there were to be considered enemies of Algeria. Martinet did acknowledge the left's weaknesses with regard to formulating a unified political stance on Algeria. However, he also commented that France observateur had already written extensively about these faults and that, although the left's weaknesses did certainly justify some of the FLN's new criticisms, these weaknesses did not give credence to the FLN claim that all French inhabitants of Algeria were enemies.

Investigating this critical shift away from reconciliation, Martinet asked what the chances of victory were for the opposing forces and what future Franco-Algerian relations would consist of. He argued that, although the FLN army (the ALN) was capable of sustaining the conflict, it lacked the military prowess to defeat the French army. Without giving the FLN "advice," he maintained his previous position that a compromise would have to be arranged since no direct military solution was available:

> For our part, we are in favor of approaching a compromise not because we desire to save the position of French colonialism in North Africa but because, on the one hand, we believe that from the moment when negotiations are opened, the reality of the Algerian nation cannot be questioned and because, on the other hand, we think that the pursuit of the war heavily menaces French democracy and also—we will say very frankly—the future Algerian democracy.

Martinet's question about the future Algerian democracy pressed the FLN to face the reality of reconciliation. It was common knowledge, he suggested, that the Europeans in Algeria would try to maintain their place on the basis of economic and technological functions. However, did the fact that the French right wing used this reasoning to maintain their economic and social status invalidate the argument? "Was it true or false that independent Algeria would find itself facing economic problems very difficult to resolve, and that it would benefit from the aid of other nations?" These questions could not be "evad[ed] by the FLN." Consequently, Martinet continued, the best way to avoid what the FLN called "neocolonialism" was to confront the reality of Algeria's problems and arrange for a possible association of the different peoples on the standards of equality. This was an extremely important point, he argued, because "total rupture" had not yet occurred between the Algerians and France, and therefore it was still possible to hope for some kind of reconciliation or relationship.

In concluding his argument, Martinet distanced himself (as a member of the so-called new left) from the traditional left, which he acknowledged was influenced by neocolonialism. In doing so, he stated that the FLN had its own idiosyncrasies to reconcile. The ultimate goal was to provide an arena in which ideas could be discussed "openly and frankly. Not as French 'friends' of Algerian nationalism or as Algerian 'enemies' of the French left, but as French and Algerians concerned with finding an acceptable path leading to true friendship between the two peoples."

Jean-Marie Domenach's response to Fanon's criticism of the French left was equally bellicose.[50] Fanon, identified patronizingly by Domenach as the "FLN's philosopher" (Domenach did not know that Fanon had authored the criticisms), had committed a serious blunder and had misread the nature of the Algerian conflict. "Did it make any sense," Domenach asked, "to open a calm dialogue between French intellectuals who have no military or civil responsibilities and the Algerian nationalists?" Since the French intellectuals were critics and not policy makers for the French government, he chastised the "FLN's philosopher" for overstating the culpability of the French intellectuals in the Algerian drama. More to the point, he emphasized that the "FLN's philosopher" was naive about French toleration for violence.

The El Moudjahid articles made it more difficult, Domenach claimed, for French intellectuals to help Algerians in their struggle because the FLN had given up the goals of peace by embracing violence. Violence, as celebrated by the FLN, was nothing but a "caricature of power: it testifies only to the absence of authority that sacrificed the final goal for instantaneous shock" (248). By arguing that Algerian nationalists ought to resort to "blind terrorism" against all Europeans, the FLN alienated its supporters in France. The "FLN's philosopher" was destroying the FLN's support, and so demonstrating a philosophically untrained mind.

Domenach insisted that the articles demonstrated faulty logical reasoning because the "FLN's philosopher" fabricated an unbalanced and incomplete dialectic. The "philosopher" had made two central claims in his criticism of the French left: (1) "the colonizing people are universally colonists," and (2) in Algeria all French were to be treated as "enemies." The result was the creation of a "totalizing dialectic" in which everything was mediated through violence. This being the case, there was no possibility for being "innocently French" in Algeria, and therefore even the "children merit the grenades that gut them on the street corner." In effect, Domenach refused to reduce guilt to ontology.

Another of Fanon's philosophical shortcomings, according to Domenach, had been that in condemning the French intellectual left he had condemned only a part of the French population in France. Since supposedly all French people were inherently bad in France, and since all French in

Algeria merited "grenades," the FLN was wrong to focus exclusively on French democrats, the left, and the intellectuals in France. This unbalanced condemnation, Domenach argued, represented the "degeneration of the dialectic."

Whereas the FLN was claiming that it was necessary to expel the Europeans in Algeria on the basis of the preexisting "Algerian nation," the FLN's philosopher argued that the Algerian nation was "ahistorical." The problem, Domenach wrote, was that there were undeniable "historical" facts about French colonialism. In denying the factuality of colonialism, the FLN denied the social transformations Algeria had gone through over the 125-year "invasion." In positing this ahistorical temporality of the Algerian nation, the FLN attempted to deny Europeans' right to live in Algeria. Ironically, Domenach continued, if it were possible to deny the historical developments of Algeria for more than a century, then it would also be philosophically necessary to deny the existence of the very conditions and foundations of modern Algerian nationalism. Hence, in response to the charge that French intellectuals undermined Algerian nationalism by constantly emphasizing the historical connections between France and Algeria, Domenach countered that undeniable historical characteristics had to be accounted for if a solution to the Algerian drama were to be found. The FLN's mistake, therefore, was to justify violence on the grounds of absurd and illogical arguments:

> We must make liberty from what exists and not from historical impossibilities. In its second article, El Moudjahid reproaches the French left for mortgaging the liberation of Algeria in the name of necessary connections with France. It is true that we have been a little too self-indulgent in this respect. The necessities do not exist less because of this, and it is with liberty and not before, that they will be recognized. Nevertheless, it is important to say this clearly: the liberty of the Algerian nation can exist only if those who fight for it do not start by submitting it [liberty] to the exclusive determinations taken from eternal definitions. Worse than the terrorism of the necessary, there is a terrorism of essences. It is not a revolution but a parody. It prepares generic murders, total war. It is a bad philosophy, indignant of a people struggling for liberation.

Turning Fanon's argument about abstractions against him, Domenach pointed out that the El Moudjahid writer had outdone the French in reifying the conflict. As a result, terrorism was being justified with abstractions, and while the FLN was condemning the French for their failure to see the Algerians as individuals and as humans, the flawed dialectic of Fanon's thinking replicated the very fascist-like logic in Algeria that the FLN attacked. To avoid violence, Domenach concluded, greater clarity and political realism would have to replace dehumanizing abstractions.

Whither Franco-Algerian Identity?

Perhaps what made Fanon's attacks so insufferable for anticolonial French intellectuals such as Mauriac was that they were not isolated incidents. For example, Mauriac in March 1957 had already rebuffed an Algerian he called the "Grand Inquisitor of French Writers," Jean Amrouche, when he insisted that the FLN was the true representative of the Algerian people and that the Algerians needed to construct their own national identity.[51] Mauriac condescendingly dismissed Amrouche's comments and argued that Amrouche's dual Algerian-French identity—"French himself and baptized"—betrayed his right to speak for the Algerian people. Mauriac wrote: "This is what a man of high culture thinks who carries in his mind and in his body the double, Kabyle and French filtration."[52]

What Mauriac contested most with regard to Amrouche's hybridized identity and his analysis of the conflict was the potential for breaking ties. Mauriac challenged Amrouche's belief that Algerians wanted to rediscover their "historical personalities" and that this rediscovery necessitated the rupture of French-Algerian connections. The contradiction in the formula, Mauriac wrote, was that the national fact of Algeria (le fait national algérien) was imposed in tandem with the "fact of the Franco-Algerian community [le fait de la communauté franco-algérienne]." A resolution could not be achieved without the recognition of both "facts," and this resolution could not be found in the violent conquest of one community by the other. "It is forbidden to us Christians to give our consent to these two confronted despairs—because that which is childish is squalid" (32). Algeria must have free elections in all areas already or about to be "pacified," Mauriac concluded, to avoid future massacres and unnecessary violence. In order for that to happen, the FLN would have to renounce its claim to be the sole interlocutor in Algeria.

Having previously attacked French intellectuals for their paternalism and been rebuffed for it, Jean Amrouche not surprisingly emerged to defend El Moudjahid's position. He offered one of the most lucid analyses of the relationship between the FLN and the French anticolonialist left, decried the demise of efforts to work for Franco-Algerian reconciliation, and framed his analysis around the question of identity. He began by indicating that the debate between the French left and El Moudjahid was "irritating" because instead of allowing for a fruitful dialogue, it had degenerated into serious "misunderstandings," which would only harm the "Franco-Algerian future."[53] The most immediate point to understand, he suggested, was the truth behind the FLN's claim that the French had "a long tradition" of excluding Algerians from their own conversation—as if the Algerians were "deaf."

According to Amrouche, given this tradition of exclusion, the French left's indignation at being criticized for their paternalism vis-à-vis the Algerians' revolution was all for the better: "Rudeness is salutary, and a little violent writing is liberating." It was salutary and liberating, he wrote, because "before every effort of rapprochement and reconciliation, it is good for the interlocutors to take a little distance and define their positions in plain language." Once the appropriate distance had been made between the French and the Algerian nationalists, they would quickly understand that they were not at the same level. Moreover, the French language, which parodied revolutionary action, masked "innumerable traps" of comprehension. In other words, "an Algerian patriot" was not "an anticolonialist in the same manner as a man of the French left." The difference, Amrouche wrote, could be reduced to the difference between the lived experience of suffering colonial oppression and having "sympathy" for the oppressed. No one could deny that for the French left the Algerian tragedy was a pressing concern, but it was important only as a collection of "political, social, and economic problems." In other words, the French anticolonial left had approached the French-Algerian War as a theoretical problem, not as a lived one. The difference lay in the separation between authentic and synthetic commitment:

> The French left participates in the Algerian tragedy as a doctor who helps the sick. It does not live it. For the Algerian, the Algerian war is not an armed conflict the same as any other. It is a sacred war that puts into question his entire being, his very existence, and the foundation of that existence and not only certain modalities of that existence.
>
> This translates into a human attitude and into language. Their consciousness [conscience aiguë] of their situation adds to the ex-

treme susceptibility of Algerians, to their excessively proud character [leur caractère ombrageux], something tight and strained.

In this debate, France does not run the risks of disappearing.
For Algeria, on the contrary, which has already sacrificed hundreds
of thousands of its own, it is really a matter of being or not being. This
alone is enough to create a distance that is difficult to do away with
between the French and Algerians.

To suggest, as Martinet had, that FLN criticisms of the French left were
equivalent to a "psychological striptease," Amrouche argued, grossly un-
derestimated the ontological dimensions of the conflict for the Algerians.
The ontological claims continually repeated themselves during the war because Algerian identity had become part and parcel of the autonomy of the
Algerian nation. For this reason, the left had to understand that all paternalistic comments would be rejected by Algerians engaged in a struggle for
their own country and therefore for their own existence. Rather than engaging in "paternalism" and "fraternalism" by trying to give " 'disinterested' "
advice to the FLN, the left should have moved French public opinion against
its own leaders who were fighting an "unjust and stupid war" (14).

In reply, Martinet acknowledged Amrouche's dual French-Algerian identity, but insisted that the French could not be indifferent to the necessity of
peace.[54] Yes, there was the unquestionable racism of Europeans in Algeria,
the fact that the left did not authentically "live" the conflict as the Algerians
did, the irrefutable paternalism of the left, and the chauvinism of French
workers. However, as a militant anticolonialist, what had "struck" him the
most in the El Moudjahid articles was the predominately "negative" presen-
tation of the French efforts by the FLN. To believe that the FLN could erase
French interests from Algeria's future was to live absurd political naiveté.
Martinet admitted that some French were prone to give the FLN advice "as
if they were Algerians." But he rejected the FLN's dismissal of French anticolonialists because these French "patriots" had worked hard to stop the
war and to "profoundly transform the structure and the face of their government" (13). Furthermore, the French had other, transcending interests
in the Algerian crisis:

> But here precisely is the important point: our patriotism ties the
> future of France to the saturation of socialism, that is to say, to the
> victory of a cause, which is international. This is the deeper reason
> for our interest in the evolution of Algerian nationalism, nation-

alism with its origin in the proletariat and which is developing in a country where the national bourgeois is extremely weak. Different issues are possible: independent Algeria could know a system similar to Bourguiba's, a military regime of the Nasser type, or a socialist republic. It is not a matter of indifference—to the ensemble of the French left—to know which is the solution which has the most possibility of being realized and which are the factors that are susceptible to play in favor of one or the other. (13)

In the debates between French intellectuals and Algerian nationalists, one other important French voice was unwilling to allow for the sudden erasure of France by the FLN. For the Muslims, Jean Daniel wrote in September 1957, terrorism was "profoundly unpopular," and despite all "myths of the holy war," Algeria's Muslims were not ready to accept "indiscriminate and blind terrorism."[55] The reason Muslims hesitated to support revolutionary efforts (including terrorism) was their lack of conviction that the blind terrorist violence that threatened innocent Muslims was truly revolutionary violence. For the French left, the problem of terrorism was to deal with what it considered the regressive nationalist aspects of the Algerian revolution. In addition, the French were even more baffled by the claims of "authenticity" made by the revolutionaries. Hence according to Daniel, the French had difficulty accepting the "colonized telling them [the French] that they wanted the right to be 'themselves': but what could that mean for a member of the French left: 'to be yourself?' " (29).

Resurgent Divisions among French Anticolonialists
In one of the most important interviews with Sartre during the war, Daniel continued this line of questioning just after the publication of the El Moudjahid criticisms.[56] When asked whether he agreed with the FLN's articles, Sartre confessed an uneasiness with the question, but admitted that French intellectuals had made some significant mistakes in dealing with the FLN. For example, Sartre argued that the intellectuals had been wrong to condemn the FLN after Mélouza because the French had not understood, at the time, that it was "necessary to hide things when one plays politics. We must accept that politics implies a constraint not to say certain things. Otherwise one is a 'good Samaritan' [belle âme] and then one does not engage in politics" (251).

In this extraordinary statement, Sartre explained why it was necessary, if one wanted to win political games, to overlook massacres. French intellectuals mistakenly first "denounced the tortures among us" and then "denounced the atrocities among them." Without knowing it, these intellectuals had played directly into the hands of the real enemies in Algeria, the French *ultras*. In the interest of anticolonial politics, French intellectuals ought to have looked the other way regarding Mélouza.

Daniel retorted that if these crimes "appeared unacceptable to the French intellectuals, partisans of an independent Algeria, it was not because they [the intellectuals] had suddenly become 'good Samaritans' but because, for the first time, they were forced to question the choice that they had made. [These were the] first doubts about the FLN" (252–53).

This exchange between Sartre and Daniel helps point out growing strains between the different factions of the French anticolonialist left. Since for Daniel the FLN's moral authority was put in question by acts of "blind terrorism" (252), it was important that French intellectuals rethink their own motives for supporting the FLN. On the contrary, Sartre insisted that it was not an issue of supporting or not supporting the FLN: "Listen, whatever the FLN is, it is there, the Algerian Revolution is it. We have to take it how it is." Despite his willingness to accept the FLN as the embodiment of the Algerian revolution, however, Sartre did admit his frustration with the recent FLN criticisms of French intellectuals and told Daniel that he had even gone so far as to ask the FLN not to circulate widely the issues of El Moudjahid that had attacked the French left in France. Ironically, and as an example of FLN unwillingness to listen to French intellectuals, Sartre said that the FLN responded to his request by sending him "two copies!"

This interview also demonstrates how little French intellectuals such as Sartre understood the FLN's present and future goals. From Sartre's comments we are able to see the degree to which some French intellectuals were willing to follow the FLN merely because it fulfilled the requirements of revolutionary action. "You know," Sartre confessed, "we do not know what the FLN wants. The relationship with them is similar to the one we had with the communists. One day they come to see you, shake your hand, propose you some articles, and then you never see them again. Two months ago I waited for an article on the future institutions of independent Algeria. They never wrote them. Or perhaps the one who wrote them was afraid of being disavowed."

According to Daniel, the Algerians were denying their past by pretending that the French in Algeria occupied the country as enemies: "They want to do this because they want to reconstruct their past" (253). Moreover the

Algerians were fictionalizing their status as a nation by arguing that France had "denationalized" them. Because Algeria constituted a "state" but not a "nation," Daniel rejected the FLN's right to refuse rights to the French because they represented "the occupant" (254).

Disagreements over the Algerians' identity also surfaced in the published conversation between Sartre and Daniel. Whereas Daniel did not want to reduce the Algerians' revolt to psychoanalysis as Amrouche had done, Sartre argued that this dimension was important. The "Algerians' situation is tragic. They do not know who they are. They are making themselves with the help of the past. The psychological facts [données psychologiques] are more important here than elsewhere." Consequently, Sartre continued, their "revolutionary future" depended on France, but the question was, "which France?" Since it was obviously the "French revolutionary forces" that would help the Algerian nationalists, it was essential to ask what the French could do to advance Algerian nationalism. But the French first had to admit that their influence on Algerian nationalists had reached its limits. In other words, Sartre agreed with Fanon's articles, and explained it to Daniel thus: "No, we are only powerless intellectuals asking them to pay attention to moral values, and they no longer have any confidence in us; they distrust us, they have treated me like a 'worn-out intellectual' [intellectuel fatigué]. They want a rupture. And that is because of our impotence" (254).

It was certainly not a coincidence that Sartre then cited Fanon as an example of the changing relationship between FLN revolutionaries and French intellectuals. As someone who used to visit him, Sartre lamented that Fanon no longer corresponded or visited. Fanon and others like him were "in the machine" and no longer had time for the French. But did the fact that French intellectuals had very little influence on FLN revolutionaries mean that the French should abandon the Algerians altogether? No, Sartre argued, adding that if French intellectuals were going to fight effectively against colonialism they would have to do it on their own terms and not in an attempt to control or appease Algerian nationalists.[57]

How did this play out in concrete terms for French intellectuals? For some, it meant that representations would become Orientalistic. The same month Daniel interviewed Sartre, Daniel also recognized the improbability of reconciliation and began to deplore the effects of the war. Because Algerian nationalism was a "contingent" and not a "necessary" fact, he argued, France once had a chance to combat the impending rupture between the "Orient" and the "West," but the "bet was lost" because France had not integrated the Algerians into the West. As a result, Algerian nationalism now appeared to be a "necessary" phenomenon. [58] Furthermore, he explained that because the nationalists could give Algerians "a destiny" and France could not, the Algerian revolution had become increasingly "anti-Western." The end result, he argued, was that, although they had initially taken arms against France in the name of the values France inspired, the revolution's leaders were now in a powerful enough position to reject those same values. Thus the last occasion to "help build a Western Algeria" was lost (30).

Violence and French Self-Criticism

As French intellectuals gradually realized that they could do little to influence Algerian nationalists, they focused on what they could sway: French public opinion. As they confronted the rebellious and anonymous critic at El Moudjahid, two incidents—the Maurice Audin affair and the publication of Henri Alleg's La Question (The Question)—quickly redirected attention back onto France's internal problems. [59] Both cases undermined the French government's moral and political authority and provided intellectuals another venue with which to demand an end to the conflict.

Despite the French government's rather vulgar propaganda efforts against the Algerian "rebels," most French intellectuals did not take their eyes off of the growing abuses of the French army. The Question and the Audin affair did little to ease the pressure. Maurice Audin, a Communist and a mathematics professor at the University of Algiers, had been arrested the day before Henri Alleg. Alleg was imprisoned and tortured, while Audin— after being incarcerated by the French paratroopers—disappeared. The army denied the use of torture against Alleg, and after torturing and killing Audin, claimed he had escaped and was in hiding.

François Mauriac was one of the first to link Audin's and Alleg's cases to what he called the "new Dreyfus affair" in his Bloc-notes for L'Express. [60] The efforts to embed both cases in Dreyfusard symbolism were deliberate. The historian Pierre Vidal-Naquet, who immediately published a booklet about the Audin case entitled L'Affaire Audin, later stated that the symbolism of the Dreyfus affair "was well and badly chosen" as an analogy for Audin. [61] As a European intellectual, Audin and his case could mobilize French public opinion in a way that torture of an Algerian could not. [62] Furthermore, Audin's youth (he was twenty-five), the fact that he was a promising young scholar, and his affiliation with the PCF all increased the likelihood that a large portion of the French population would be shocked by his treat-

Figure 4. "Justice." One of eight cartoon postcards created between 1958 and 1961 by Siné (Maurice Sinet), published by François Maspéro in Paris. Courtesy of Maurice Sinet.

ment. However, the Dreyfus symbolism was not entirely analogous to Audin's case, Vidal-Naquet noted, because Audin was not truly a representative "victim of oppression in Algeria" (31). But the claims of similarities between the Dreyfus affair and the crimes committed in Algeria were powerful motivators for public opinion.

The two cases were also important for contemporary French politics because both men were Communists. The PCF attempted to appropriate the cases as evidence of the persecution of Communists. On December 12, 1957, Josette Audin and Gilberte Alleg, the men's wives, were received by the PCF. Jacques Duclos greeted them with a speech in which he told Josette Audin she should be proud of her husband's efforts to fight "for the cause of the independence of Algeria" and to fulfill his "communist and patriotic responsibilities."[63] According to Duclos, the actions of men such as Audin worked to "unite all Algerians without distinction to origin." "We, French communists, we are on the side of our brothers, the Algerian communists. Our actions have contributed to bring out the truth and to organize the masses of French men and women against the tortures and the violence which have become generalized in Algeria."

In order to clarify the circumstances and the events of Audin's arrest, the Comité Maurice Audin was formed in November by Vidal-Naquet and the French mathematician Laurent Schwartz.[64] In an article written for the January 16, 1958 edition of L'Express and used also as the preface to Vidal-Naquet's L'Affaire Audin, Schwartz also compared the Dreyfus case to Audin's.[65] The principal difference, Schwartz argued, was that Dreyfus's case was isolated whereas Audin's was not. In this sense, Audin's case was even more damaging to the French nation than the Dreyfus affair had been. Schwartz praised Vidal-Naquet's L'Affaire Audin for its impartial analysis of Audin's disappearance, saying that the book represented nothing less than "public opinion's coming to consciousness of the danger of democracy disappearing in France" (56).[66]

Others lamented the loss of French status as reflected in these two cases. Writing in L'Humanité about a gathering of academics at the Sorbonne in honor of Maurice Audin, Georges Bouvard noted that it was a shame France was motivating intellectuals to speak out against the state's abuses of power.[67] Yet he claimed that those gathered for Maurice Audin illustrated a great level of cultivation in keeping with the Sorbonne's highest traditions of liberty. In addition to the Sorbonne elites, French democratic opinion would continue to honor Audin's memory and show solidarity for the young man who was sacrificed "to the worst of wars."

Audin's story was powerfully described by Vidal-Naquet. In contrast, what made Henri Alleg's story so compelling was that he described his torture at the hands of the French military on pieces of paper that were smuggled out of prison. The notes, immediately published as The Question, received the dubious honor of being the first work banned by the French government since the eighteenth century. [68] Alleg, besides being a member of the PCF, had been the editor of the Algerian Communist daily Alger républicain until he was forced into hiding by French authorities in 1956. He was arrested by General Massu's men in the Tenth Paratrooper Division on the charge that by going underground he had evaded prosecution as the editor of a banned publication. The title chosen to describe his ordeal was especially significant because it invoked the outdated practice of torture known as "la question" during the ancien régime.

Alleg began with a confession that "[i]n this enormous overcrowded prison, where each cell houses a quantity of human suffering," he considered it almost "indecent" to talk about himself. [69] However, in making the horrors known, Alleg believed that his story might "serve a purpose," which was to help bring about "a cease-fire and peace" (41). At the first torture session, the paratroopers ("paras") ridiculed him as a Frenchman who had sold out to the "rats." This exacted a heavy penalty, which he described thus:

> J-, smiling all the time, dangled the clasps at the end of the electrodes before my eyes. He attached one of them to the lobe of my right ear and the other to a finger on the same side.
>
> Suddenly, I leapt in my bonds and shouted with all my might. C- had just sent the first electric charge through my body. A flash of lightning exploded next to my ear and I felt my heart racing. I struggled, screaming, and stiffened myself until the straps cut into my flesh. All the while the shocks controlled by C-, magneto in hand, followed each other without interruption. . . . Between two spasms, I turned my head towards him and said, "You are wrong to do this. You will regret it!"
>
> Furious, C- turned the knob on the magneto to its fullest extent. . . . And as I continued to shout, he said to J-: "My God, he's noisy! Stuff his mouth with something!" >
>
> J- rolled my shirt into a ball and forced it into my mouth, after

which the torture continued. I bit the material between my teeth with all my might and found it almost a relief.

Suddenly, I felt as if a savage beast had torn the flesh from my body. Still smiling above me, J- had attached the pincer to my penis. The shocks going through me were so strong that the straps holding me to the board came loose. They stopped to tie them again and we continued. (54–55)

The Question became even more important when Sartre took up his pen and introduced it to the French public. His scathing commentary, "Une Victoire" ("A Victory") was also immediately seized by the French government. [70] As he noted, The Question was the first document during the war written by a Frenchman that described being tortured by the French military. Until the publication of The Question, men returning from military service and priests were the only people capable of revealing the horrible truths about the French army. Alleg's case was extremely important because, Sartre claimed, it demonstrated that not even French citizens were safe from torture. The lessons were obvious: that "fifteen years were enough to turn the victims into executioners" and that "anybody, at any time, may equally find himself victim or executioner." [71] This did not mean that the French were *necessarily* doomed. Ironically, Sartre argued that, although it was true that the Algerian revolution had focused the French people's attention on the "whirlpool of inhumanity," a careful look at Alleg's book could help the French save themselves from the "vertigo" leading them to ruin.

Torture, Sartre continued, was by far the worst aspect of this vertigo, and it gave even the most dispassionate young French soldiers a fascist's "taste for violence" (24). Torture, which he blamed on Robert Lacoste, had the capacity to destroy the fabric of society by locking both victim and executioner in the "grip of a violent and anonymous hatred" and by making the youth susceptible to becoming fascists. To protect their nation from fascism the French had to understand that they were not exempt from the same forces that plagued "totalitarian" nations. Specifically, he claimed, since torture had Lacoste's blessing, the French nation was no better or worse than the Soviet Union under Stalin or Egypt under Abdel Nasser. In other words, "Hitler was only a forerunner" (26), and the French had to be willing to fight against their own state to keep the gangrene of torture from spreading.

Demonstrating how seriously he took his own warning about becoming a "good Samaritan," Sartre insisted that it was necessary to clarify what was meant by torture and to distinguish it from revolutionary violence. "Torture is senseless violence, born in fear. The purpose of torture is to force from a tongue, amid screams and the vomiting of blood, the secret of *everything*" (29). The French had created a situation in which the only choice left to the Algerians was to affirm their identity as humans ("manhood") by violently rejecting "French values" and "French nationality." The Algerian nationalists' new claims to "manhood" threatened, diminished, and cheapened the French claims to superiority by "divine right." By claiming that there were "two kinds of human beings" (the French and the Arabs), the French could justify torture; torture in Algeria was thus an expression of French "racial hatred" for the Arabs (32). As such, it was at the "essence of the conflict" (36). This meant that the conflict could not be resolved through dialogue or reconciliation efforts. In other words, in returning to the themes of *autocritique*, Sartre intended to show that the payoff for France came in seeing how racial and national boundaries of institutionalized racial violence were beginning to blur and migrate. Only declaring Algeria independent would resolve the conflict and free the French from spreading fascism. As Sartre wrote, "Our victims know us by their scars and by their chains. . . . It is enough for us that they show us what we have made of them for us to realize what we have made of ourselves" (13).

On February 23, 1958, Mauriac used *The Question* to attack Camus's silence: "Camus prefers his mother to justice. I would too, I am afraid, if I were confronted with the choice. That is not the case: every injustice with respect to men, committed in the name of France, overwhelms our mother, France. But is it really a matter of our mother in the flesh, as with Camus?"[72] On March 28, after another governmental confiscation of *The Question*, Mauriac again asked in frustration what was happening to France. This time, he focused his anger on Lacoste, who, according to him, dishonored France by repeatedly denying Alleg's torture. By letting this disgraceful abuse continue, Mauriac stated, Lacoste and the entire French nation were to be held responsible. Although Alleg was a French Jew and not an Arab, Mauriac, like Sartre, argued that the application of torture in Algeria was carried out by Frenchmen who "hate men of other races" (53).

Unlike Sartre, however, Mauriac did not make a moral distinction between "torture" and "revolutionary action" as a means to "find solidarity with Algerians."[73] In fact, Mauriac wrote to Denise Barrat on August 24, 1957, that he wanted to end the war in Algeria and stop the abuses of the French government, but that he was equally opposed to the Algerians' use of "terrorism": "I am not for the murders of one side [and] against the murders of the other" (339).[74] The Algerians who murdered their own, he continued, could not be defended under any circumstance. Moreover, he wrote, France could not be expected to renounce its "right in Algeria," which was secured for it by more than a hundred years of contact. Refusing to give up the idea of reconciliation, he wrote to Barrat that he "loved" the Algerians "as people," and he asked God for the chance to see peace delivered between the French and the Algerians before his death.

A month later, Jean-Marie Domenach described a recent confiscation of The Question as being the "last and the most flagrant testimony of the imbecility of power."[75] It had been easy to make Audin disappear, Domenach claimed, but Lacoste could not erase Alleg's writing without seeking out every existing copy and "washing out the brain of everyone who has read it." As impossible as it was to erase The Question from everyone who had read it, it was equally necessary for everyone to read it because it concerned all citizens. Alleg's book, he wrote, placed everything in perspective and showed why the French could no longer tolerate the army's abuses "without renouncing" their "dignity."

In the army's internal informational note, written by a lieutenant colonel in the Fifth Bureau, Alleg's book was nothing other than leftist propaganda "orchestrated by those who fight for the systematic destruction of the established order of the Western world."[76] According to the French military, The Question was merely intended to divide France from the rest of the Western world. Even worse, the army claimed, as a Communist Alleg was allowing his work to be exploited by non-Communists in France so that it would be seen as "irrefutable testimony" to the abuses of the French army. The army concluded: "This simplification is a diabolical trap, this division of the French, this attempt to divorce France from the Western world is the work of the civil war and the tearing apart of the Christian world for the profit of the revolutionary war" (3).

The effects of the Audin and Alleg scandals on the French Fourth Republic were dramatic. One of the most telling signs was the "petition" sent to the president signed by André Malraux, Roger Martin du Gard, François Mauriac, and Jean-Paul Sartre. These four celebrated writers protested the government's confiscation of The Question and asked for a complete investigation of Alleg's case.[77] It was Alleg, after all, who had written that he wanted the French to read him so that they would understand that the Algerians were indeed being tortured but that the Algerians were not confusing "their tortures with the great people of France" (122). The French had to know, quite simply, Alleg claimed, so that they would "know what is done In Their Name."

While Alleg and the Audin affair no doubt helped contribute to the fall of the republic and, indirectly, to de Gaulle's coming to power in May 1958, de Gaulle's rise again fractured the French intellectual community. Jean-Jacques Servan-Schreiber and Claude Bourdet violently attacked his seizing the government, whereas Mauriac supported him. Sartre and members of the new left detested de Gaulle's rise through "fascist" forces originating from the extreme right wing and the army. As Sartre stated: "The Algerian colons want to colonize France"; they were holding de Gaulle as their "hostage." [78] In order to fight against this crime, France had to be "demystified." To demystify, intellectuals had to show that the French-Algerian War had destroyed the French Republic and that the colons together with the army were conspiring against the republic. Specifically, intellectuals had to inform public opinion against the travesty of justice. [79] Demystification of the war by committed intellectuals would show, for example, that torture was not only criminal, it was also not useful. Since torture "destroys what is human in the Other," and since "it will necessarily destroy it [what is human] in the Self," torture itself had to be eradicated. All journalists and writers were obligated, Sartre concluded, to speak out in favor of the true France, the France of "the Rights of Man and Citizen" and the right of every man "to be a human and a free citizen in his own country." [80]

Besides L'Affaire Audin and The Question, several other important works also pushed French intellectuals to confront the realities of torture in Algeria. Pour Djamila Bouhired, written by Jacques Vergès and Georges Arnaud, two French lawyers working at the Algerian bar, appeared in October 1957. Bouhired had been tortured extensively in April 1957 during "interrogations" by French paratroopers. An active member of the FLN, Bouhired had been caught carrying the correspondence of Yacef Saadi and Ali La Pointe—two known FLN leaders during the infamous Battle of Algiers. Her torture involved having electrodes attached to her breasts, vagina, and elsewhere. And during her interrogation Bouhired was reported to have signed a confession, which she later denied. In taking up her case Arnaud and Vergès described her treatment in detail. Bouhired was accused, along with Djamila Bouazza, of planting a bomb at the Coq Hardi in Algiers. She was eventually condemned to death; Arnaud and Vergès explained that they had written

Pour Djamila Bouhired in order to provoke an outcry against her treatment and keep her from being executed.[81]

In June 1959 Minuit took a huge risk and published another scathing critique of French torture in Algeria entitled *La Gangrène (The Gangrene)*. The *Gangrene* documented the cases of five Algerian men, most of them students, who had been arrested and tortured in Paris by the Direction de Surveillance Territoire (DST), the French secret police under Roger Wybot. That these men had been tortured in Paris, in metropolitan France, was a tremendous shock to French public opinion. The French government immediately banned the book and the French press was forbidden to mention it, which it did in great detail anyway, and criminal charges were brought against Minuit's director, Jérôme Lindon. The book reviews by most of the French dailies and several newspapers suggested that there were disturbing parallels between the Nazi occupation of France and the DST's use of torture in metropolitan France during the French-Algerian War. Without question, this migration of torture to metropolitan France via the DST and the de Gaulle government's desire to suppress all such reports at any cost gave most French intellectuals reason to pause and fundamentally reevaluate the effects of the war on French society and French law. As a writer for *Le Monde* put it, "These students seem to have been tortured with special mercilessness, precisely because they were intellectuals. Nothing was done to prevent these acts of torture—everything on the contrary was done to facilitate them—the indifference of public opinion, and French law itself."[82]

At about the time that the French government tried to counteract the damage caused by *The Gangrene*, Gisèle Halimi—another lawyer defending Algerians accused of revolutionary activities—received a letter from Djamila Boupacha. Boupacha (a young Muslim woman) was under arrest and being held at Camp Bousset, outside Oran. Boupacha, like Algerians in *The Gangrene* and like Alleg and Audin, had been tortured, but with one difference. A virgin before being arrested, she was raped by a French soldier with a bottle, after being tortured in other unimaginable ways. Boupacha's trial and *Djamila Boupacha (Djamila Boupacha: The Story of the Torture of a Young Algerian Girl Which Shocked Liberal French Opinion)*, a book eventually published in French and English in 1962, by Simone de Beauvoir and Gisèle Halimi, also sparked intense national and international controversy. This controversy was largely anticipated by de Beauvoir's June 3, 1960, letter to *Le Monde* about the case; it amounted to a battery of attacks on the French judicial system in Algeria. Other French intellectuals came to her defense, includ-

ing Germaine Tillion, and twelve important figures provided testimonies—
including Henri Alleg, Josette Audin, General Jacques Paris de Bollardière,
Daniel Meyer, Jean François Revel, Jules Roy, and Françoise Sagan—that
were reproduced in Djamila Boupacha.[83]

The Jeanson Network, the Manifesto of the 121, and Treason of the French Self

Given the increasingly radicalized frustrations with the French state, it is
not entirely surprising that a few French intellectuals decided to join the
Algerian nationalists fully in their struggle. Nor is it very surprising that
Francis Jeanson led the French intellectuals in the underground activity.
Collette and Jeanson's L'Algérie hors la loi was undoubtedly on the forefront of
support for the Algerian revolution already in 1955. Jeanson continued his
avant-garde support for the Algerian nationalists' cause, eventually providing financial, intellectual, and moral support to the FLN and to deserters
of the French army. He was driven underground in 1957.[84] Having lived
in Algeria for several years, Jeanson had also been one of the first French
intellectuals to write about the impending revolution. In his articles in Esprit
in 1950, Jeanson attempted to bring the French out of their "sleepwalking"
with respect to the reality Algeria posed.[85] As an editor at Éditions du Seuil,
Jeanson had written the introduction to Frantz Fanon's first work, Peau noire,
masques blancs (Black Skin, White Masks) in 1952.[86] As discussed in chapter 2,
Jeanson's involvement in the Comité d'Action had been important, especially his polemic with Jean Daniel.

While in hiding, Jeanson began to assemble a vast network capable of
aiding Algerian nationalists.[87] The "Jeanson network" (always referred to
in the press as "réseau Jeanson") was discovered about a month after the
barricades scandal at the beginning of 1960. In total, twenty-three members
of the network, seventeen French and six Muslims, were arrested, while
five—including Jeanson—managed to avoid the police. Their trial, which
began on September 5, 1960, provoked an unprecedented national debate
on the limits of intellectual engagement and on the question of treason. For
the first time since their split after Budapest, Jeanson and Sartre were joined
in a common cause: motivating French public opinion and using the threat
of a civil war in France to rejuvenate the French left.[88]

Jeanson's decision to enter into an alliance with the FLN was therefore
taken with two primary objectives in mind: ending the war in Algeria by
supporting the only effective Algerian revolutionary movement, and unify-

... JE DIS INTELLECTUEL, PARCE QUE JE
SUIS INTELLECTUEL ! JE SUIS FIER D'ÊTRE
INTELLECTUEL, D'UNE VIEILLE FAMILLE
D'INTELLECTUELS : TROIS GÉNÉRATIONS
D'INTELLECTUELS ! TOUS MORTS POUR
LA FRANCE !..

Figure 5. "I say intellectual because I am an intellectual! I am proud to be an intellectual, from an old family of intellectuals: three generations of intellectuals! All dead for France!" One of eight cartoon postcards created between 1958 and 1961 by Siné (Maurice Sinet), published by François Maspéro in Paris. Courtesy of Maurice Sinet.

ing the French left in order to save French democracy. The problem Jeanson faced as a clandestine intellectual trying to achieve these two aims was simple. Since his alliance with the Algerian revolutionaries was forged underground, public opinion was not aware of his network. In his words, "our technique of clandestineness, evidently indispensable, risked keeping us in political clandestineness." [89] For that reason Jeanson created his journal, Vérités pour . . . , at the beginning of 1958. It was to be the vehicle for bringing the clandestine activities to the surface of French political life and showing the political unity of the French left and the Algerian resistance. This unity was particularly important because the issue for the French left was no longer merely one of cultural and political reconciliation with the Algerians; rather, unity was to be found in political and universal revolutionary activity.

The obvious risks of printing Vérités pour . . . , according to Jeanson, were part of its intrinsic merit. Being chased by the police only added to the validity of the publication's claims. The French public had to have access to writings "condemned by official justice" to show that there was indeed an alternative to official justice and that this alternative was supported by solidarity between Algerians and the French (1541). To bring about this cooperation between the revolutionary French and Algerian public, Jeanson advocated political engagement not just based on "theoretical" concerns but also "inscribed within an everyday context." It was possible to bridge the gap between "action" and "practical reflection" by illustrating to the French public that there really was "something to do" for the Algerians.

Because most French leftist intellectuals were unwilling to make the first moves toward a solution, it was now up to what Jeanson called "avant-garde" intellectuals to take the first step (1542). Since the war was France's primary concern, the French left had to maintain "solidarity with a people fighting for its liberation" (1543). This solidarity, this "Franco-Algerian friendship," had hitherto remained unattainable, he claimed, only because the French left defined political engagement as a "choice between clients." The left could no longer stall by insisting that the Algerians had to present an alternative to the FLN.

Aware that taking the FLN's side would lead to the charge of treason, Jeanson claimed that the charge was false because, according to France's official rhetoric, the rebellion was merely a civil war in which the Algerians were considered "French citizens" (1544). The "crime" of collaborating with the Algerians was worth the penalty, he claimed, if the alternative was to admit that he belonged to the same "community" as men such as General Massu and Prime Minister Debré. Moreover, since it was indisputable in 1960 that the Algerians would achieve political independence and that France was heading toward fascism, he argued that it was in France's political interest to guarantee future relations with the Algerian government by "sav[ing] France at the side of Algerians." Saving France and ensuring that the French would not be condemned *en bloc* by the Algerians after independence would forge a new Franco-Algerian solidarity (1546–47).

In February–March 1960 *Les Temps modernes* published a provocative editorial titled "The French Left and the FLN," which continued the themes of intellectual commitment espoused by Jeanson.[90] Specifically, it attacked de Gaulle's policy in Algeria and depicted him as a fascist threat to French democracy. The French left, specifically intellectuals such as Jean Daniel and Maurice Duverger (a professor of law in Paris who had criticized the French left), were intentionally misrepresenting the Algerian situation by arguing that peace should be the sole objective of French policy. According to *Les Temps modernes*, this was illusory because de Gaulle's peace would destroy the French left and be unsatisfactory to the Algerians. Thus, to save France from de Gaulle's fascism and from the "incompetent" left it was necessary for the revolutionary left to proclaim "the political solidarity of the French left with the FLN" (1172–73).

In the May issue of *Esprit*, Jean Daniel fired back at his attackers. Defending his position as a respectable journalist, Daniel claimed that it was in the public's interest for him to describe and to analyze the possibilities of peace under de Gaulle.[91] Unlike Jeanson and Sartre, Daniel cited the FLN's political recalcitrance as one of the most important reasons for the stalled peace process. Moreover, he disagreed with the avant-garde's position on violence. "Violence," he declared, "had posed the problem; it did not suffice to solve it" (810). As far as the *ultras* and the FLN were concerned, violence could achieve nothing because the two sides were balanced against each other in a hideous fight to the death.

Contrary to what Sartre and the radicals believed, Daniel wrote, the left had always been on the side of imperialism and therefore "integration." Hence Soustelle was not altogether wrong when he once claimed that "integration was a 'thesis of the left' " (811). The fact, Daniel charged, was that the French left wanted to profit from the revolutionary spirit of Algerian nationalism and this "intellectual slippage was very perceivable" (811).

As for unwillingness to accept the FLN as the interlocutor of the Algerian people, Daniel again expressed his fear of the FLN's "Arab-Islamic" orientation (812). While the avant-garde of the French left was willing to overlook this pernicious element, it had aligned the FLN with the Arab league, which "hoped for the disappearance of Israel."

The FLN orientation especially threatened the non-Muslim community in Algeria. As a result, Daniel continued, the French avant-garde left had overlooked fundamental and disturbing facts about Algerian nationalists in order to blindly "sacralize" the FLN as a revolutionary movement. This activity was no better than "Stalinist intellectuals [who] sacralized the Parti Communiste" (813–14).

This was simply not the case, Les Temps modernes replied in its next issue.[92] Admitting to desiring the unification of the left with the FLN, Sartre's journal stated that it was important not to accept de Gaulle's peace because "if de Gaulle makes peace, it will be good for the Algerians, but bad for the left." Les Temps modernes did not deny that it and the avant-garde left wanted to make use of the Algerian situation; however, since "pacification" was de Gaulle's goal, the left and the Algerians remained united in their opposition to the government's policies. Moreover, in response to Daniel's claim that the FLN was anti-Semitic, Les Temps modernes wrote that, although the left had fought for the Jews during World War II, it was now necessary to show the same enthusiasm to fight for people facing a similar threat of torture and execution. The real problem was simple: "Peace . . . did not justify the Gaullist order" (1534).

The rift between the avant-garde French intellectuals and moderate left was finally brought to full public attention on September 4, 1960, when Le Monde announced that 121 intellectuals (writers and artists) had signed a manifesto for the "right of insubordination" and draft resistance.[93] It was doubly important because it was made public on the day before the Jeanson network trial began in Paris. The manifesto was intended to derail or at least disrupt the trial, and the two events had an enormous effect on France. In the words of Sartre's biographer, Annie Cohen-Solal: "The trial of the Jeanson network was a masquerade, a farce, a circus, a political happening, a series of challenges of an insolence and a violence rarely seen in a courtroom, a vaudeville revue, and on the part of the lawyers [Jacques Vergès and Roland Dumas], a provocation of justice, the army, and the Gaullist government—in short, a platform for the partisans of the Algerian independence to voice the implacable urgency of their appeal."[94]

Although circuslike in atmosphere, the trial illustrated the importance of intellectual unity. The Manifesto of the 121 had mobilized a significant group of France's most prominent leftist intellectuals, including Robert Barrat, Simone de Beauvoir, André Breton, Marguerite Duras, Michel Leiris, Jérôme Lindon, Dionys Mascolo, Jean-Jacques Mayoux, Jean-Paul Sartre, Pierre Vidal-Naquet, and many others. For these intellectuals, intellectual legitimacy mandated that they stand together with Jeanson.

But not all prominent French intellectuals who were asked to sign the manifesto could do so, for fear that they would tarnish the movement. The highly controversial novelist Jean Genet had been involved in 1955 (along with others such as Marguerite Duras, Edgar Morin, and Jean-Paul Sartre) in creating an anticolonialist petition against the war in North Africa that was eventually signed by the likes of Mauriac, Sartre, and Françoise Sagan. Genet was "bitterly attacked in the press as a 'professional pederast, habitual offender and thief,' and as a 'police informer' whose name brought disgrace to the 'gentle-men-ladies' who had signed the petition." [95] Genet explained how he feared his affiliation with this 1960 manifesto supporting the soldiers' right to desert could compromise the manifesto's ability to mold public opinion: "I deserted twenty years ago after stealing the bonus money from joining up, then I had eight or ten sentences for theft. Therefore I don't think that I can give moral guarantee for the men who are struggling for idealism and who could moreover take exception to my statement. In fact their morality is that of those who condemn them. Except that they—the first ones I've named—put this morality into practice. What could a thief, pornographer, etc., do in their midst?" [96]

Jean Genet regretted his inability to join his comrades on the left in support of desertion; another group, led by Merleau-Ponty, quickly countered the Manifesto of the 121 with a more moderate manifesto. This group signed a less provocative manifesto that underscored the moral choices the government was forcing on the youth, but did not advocate the right of desertion. The signatures totaled more than a thousand French intellectuals and educators, among them Raymond Aron, Roland Barthes, Georges Canguilhem, Jean Cassou, Jean-Marie Domenach, Jean Dresch, Claude Lefort, Jacques Le Goff, Maurice Merleau-Ponty, Edgar Morin, Daniel Meyer, and Paul Ricoeur. This split in the French intellectual community showed how important debates over the military had become.

Writing about the trial and the Manifesto of the 121, sociologist Edgar Morin, one of the founders of the Comité d'Action, claimed that a hidden duality in the French left's identity had been revealed. This duality created tension between the left who wanted "peace" and the left who wanted to "adhere to the Algerians." [97] The division demonstrated the "ideological dynamism" that "adhesion to the Algerian revolution" provided. As a result, the Algerian revolution was interpreted by the French revolutionary left as the "decisive moment of socialist progress in the world," which required immediate participation. This was why the Jeanson network and especially the youths in the university who supported the FLN had opted for this so-called committed position.

The essential problem facing intellectuals now, according to Morin, was lack of perspective. Put simply, intellectuals were making the Algerian revolution stand for something other than the mere struggle for Algerian emancipation: "[T]he Algerian war was not only the resistance of a colonizing nation to the emancipation of an oppressed nationality; it had become part of the global game" (6). Unfortunately, the Algerian people would be the ones to suffer for this "theoretical" argument, because the "radicalization of the process would not bring a 'permanent revolution,' but, on the contrary, would accentuate the preponderance of the system and methods of the military in the political system." To avoid this political disaster, it was important that the "party of peace" (de Gaulle) come to its senses; likewise, avant-garde intellectuals had to come to their senses to find a solution that would avoid the dictatorship of the "party of the revolt."

The following week, on October 13, 1960, Dionys Mascolo (a Comité cofounder) responded to Morin in a letter published in *France observateur*. [98] In attempting to clarify the role of the manifesto, Mascolo admitted that the closeness of the dates might have led readers to believe that the manifesto was intended to support the Jeanson network. But it was intended to uniquely support those drafted into the military if they wanted to refuse compulsory service. One did not lead to the other, he claimed. It was important to understand that the right of youth to refuse military service was an "essential" step in ending the war and ensuring that the youth not be judged by the international community as the Nazis were judged at Nuremberg.

There were tremendous changes in the relationship between Algerian nationalists and French intellectuals. The first French reactions against torture in 1957, the Mélouza massacre, the Audin, Alleg, *Gangrene*, *Pour Djamila Bouhired*, and *Djamila Boupacha* scandals, as well as the Jeanson trial and subsequent Manifesto of the 121 all helped define the new relations and positions within the French left. Violence and the perceptions of those who employed violence were the key factors in altering alliances between the French left and the Algerian nationalists. But, as we have seen, the threat of fascist violence in Algeria and France along with the desire to use the Algerian revolution for their own ends motivated the avant-garde of the French left to reclaim this important alliance. These constantly shifting alliances deepened the divisions within the French intellectual community.

The French left began to rethink its relationship to the Algerian nationalists especially after de Gaulle came to power. By 1960, as the extreme right was beginning to demonstrate its impatience for de Gaulle's politics of self-determination, the French avant-garde left had found in the Algerian revolution a means to rejuvenate itself. It was clear that the FLN would continue to reject the paternalism of the French left as it continued to meddle in FLN affairs and make moral pronouncements on the FLN's nationalism—especially after Mélouza.

Out of this changing relationship in the French left and between the French and the Algerians, a central question emerged: Whose war was the French-Algerian War? Whether it could be truly the Algerians' or the French left's was a matter of great dispute. Jeanson tried to answer this question with his book published at the end of 1960, *Notre guerre*. Jeanson's position, so similar to that of others like Sartre and Mascolo, was that the Algerian war had put French identity into question. It was in order "to really be French" that intellectuals like him were "now working to reconstitute a national community" by fighting alongside Algerians. [99]

Hence, for Jeanson, the issue was not whether the war was a French or an Algerian war, but rather how the French could engage in the war on the Algerian side in order to reconstruct their own national community without becoming less French. He did not deny the risk involved—losing one's French identity during the struggle. In Jeanson's words, those working with the Algerians "faced two inverse risks: that of being so accepted that we become submerged, absorbed, lost, Algerianized; and that of being rejected for having kept our distance" (14–15). The network members tried to account for this, he said, by attempting "to be totally *with*, and in consequence, totally *ourselves*. . . . For three years, we have worked *for* the FLN . . . *without being 'under its orders,' or without being 'for sale'* " (48). Thus the problem was reduced to showing solidarity with the Algerians while maintaining autonomy from the Algerians.

Jeanson argued that the French who refused to participate in the war because the FLN was not "socialist," because of the supposed Islamic threat, or because of FLN-MNA rivalries were only using alibis (30). It was essential to demonstrate that the French people were willing to negotiate with the FLN in order to ensure any future for France in independent Algeria.

As for the charge that the French people involved in the Jeanson network were betraying their national community, Jeanson claimed that "*the real Treason* was the renunciation—active or passive—of the profound resources of the country, the only chance to realize an effective community, of everything that can, in the end, constitute a real showing of France at work" (117). Only working for a warranted peace, a real peace, could assure continued cooperation and friendship between the French and Algerians and dispel the "Gaullist magic." That was the true meaning of the war for France. It was, in fact, according to Jeanson, the only way to restore France's real significance in the world.

For Jeanson and the French left, the realities were clear. The left had been ambushed and trapped by de Gaulle's illegitimate rise to power in 1958. French intellectuals were trapped by the illegalities of the French army, the unstoppable use of torture and mass killing, and by a desire to take an active role in a revolution that was not their own. The paradox could be reduced to this simple question: How could the French avant-garde left not be, as Jeanson said, "Algerianized" through its involvement in the Algerian revolution?

7. THE POLITICS OF OTHERING

It is difficult to distinguish clearly between what is affected and what is neglected by colonial history. One paradoxical result is that in their respective situations, each of the two opposing groups may refuse to admit the other's place in history. By his actions as well as through his knowledge, the European disputes the native's share in the evolution which is now taking place under his eyes and which he has to a large extent provoked. He reacts with authoritarian conservatism to archaic, traditionalist Muslim attitudes; he explains them by an ethnology that is obsessed with the primitive, or by a pluralistic psychology. On the other hand, the European often appears to the native merely as a deus ex machina, a god or rather a devil brought forth by the machine, a tempter and a destroyer, incapable of human adaptability. Utilitarian requirements on the one side, metaphysical prescriptions on the other thus prevented the two opponents from understanding the history confronting them. It is true by then the depth of men's feelings, the violence of their acts was to confer on history an anthropological dimension. When that time came, generosity and cruelty, sexual ardor and revolutionary faith, critical awareness and tumultuous passion would be fused in the same violence.

JACQUES BERQUE, 1962

With a few notable exceptions, the French were never fully Algerianized by their involvement with Algerian revolutionaries. In fact the reverse could be said to be true. Algerian were in many ways profoundly influenced—despite repeated warnings by many intellectuals—by the theories of non-Algerian writers such as Jean-Paul Sartre and Frantz Fanon, who focused on negative dialectics, violence, and radical Otherness as a means of reconstituting Algerian postcolonial identity. Ultimately, and without being reductionist, this proved disastrous for the emerging Algerian nation after independence, especially as Algerian leaders such as Houari Boumediene (who spent most of the war with the FLN in Tunis) eagerly grafted Sartrian and Fanonian theories of identity and belief in the revolutionary potential of the Algerian peasantry onto Algeria's political programs.

This is not to imply, of course, that there were not other factors (such as the economy, industrialization, agricultural problems, the OPEC oil crisis, failure to allow for a multiparty political system, and demographic changes) that led Algeria into its present postcolonial condition. But we cannot neglect the effect of theories of identity formulated during the war on Algeria following decolonization. The single most important theoretical concern of decolonization, alterity or the issue of Otherness, has also continued to resonate clearly in nearly all Algerian debates since independence in July 1962. For this reason, I believe it is instructive here to underscore how the political, cultural, and intellectual uses of the concept of the Other and the notion of Otherness fit into the history of the French-Algerian War.

In many cases political Othering rose from the ashes of the idea of Franco-Algerian reconciliation. [1] Said differently, the use of Otherness by intellectuals generally came to the fore after reconciliation efforts had been sufficiently exhausted. Nevertheless, there were also intellectuals (both Algerian and French) who used the concept of the Other and the notion of Otherness (alterity) without implying that tolerance was a thing of the past and, in fact, argued that the proper understanding of Other or Otherness could keep nonviolent reconciliation alive even after independence. And although the concept certainly antedates the French-Algerian War (some of the intellectuals discussed had already used it in formal, phenomenological discussions of identity), Othering takes on specific meanings in the identity politics that emerged during the decolonization of Algeria. [2] In fact, there were generally two camps of Otherers—those who used the concept to foster tolerance and those who used the concept to destroy tolerance. There were also those who used "Other" in specific, or Otherness in general, to highlight the relationship of decolonization to identity during the war.

To facilitate this discussion, this chapter is divided loosely into two sections. The first treats the use of Other as a formal concept in philosophy and the social sciences. The second focuses on popularized discussions of Otherness, which relates most directly to the issue of anticolonial violence. The two uses were of course connected. However, the rise in popularity of discussions of Otherness during the French-Algerian War—especially when the Other was used as both an analytical tool and a political ploy—related directly to political events in Algeria and to ideological issues that intellectuals confronted in metropolitan France and elsewhere.

Representations of the Other's identity in most cases went in tandem with representations and the projection of the Self. In fact, as will become clear, when intellectuals began to Other Algerians (or vice versa), both conceptually and politically, disagreement among intellectuals over questions of intellectual legitimacy reemerged and were entangled in endeavors to represent French and Algerian identity. There is in this sense something postmodern in these debates, and, without question, the emergence of postmodern theories relates to the questions raised below.[3] In other words, an explicit relationship existed between Otherness and the problem of intellectual legitimacy or power, and this relationship polarized the debates in extreme ways. Moreover, because debates relating to use of Other, identity, and violence antedate today's discussions of Orientalism and Otherness, they should alert readers to issues implicit in present-day identity politics. This chapter is therefore intended to encourage today's researchers to pause before using the concept "Other" and think through its political, social, and epistemological repercussions.

Using the "Other" Word

Just after the Mélouza massacre in May 1957, Maurice Maschino—an early draft resister living in exile in Tunisia—used the concept "Other" to locate nationalist violence within the dehumanizing problem of colonization.[4] According to him, violence had to be explained through a phenomenological analysis of the worldview of Algerian identity. This required a detailed explanation of the significance of the lived experience of the Algerian nationalists, which in turn had to be understood by the French as an ontological problem.

Ontology, or the problem of Being, Maschino argued, was especially important for Algerians. He explained that violence was an artifact of this problem because it was merely an expression of the Algerians' effort to "recuperate their lost being."[5] French colonialism was to blame for the violence because Algeria's French had enjoyed extraordinary privileges challenging the core of Algerians' sense of being. "What are the Algerians revolting against?" he asked. "Against being treated by the Europeans as second-rate beings [d'être-au-rabais], which has been an important factor correlatively and until now in ensuring [the Europeans'] an excessive and hypertrophic form of being. For the Algerian, it [the revolt] is a matter of being; for the European, it is a matter of being superior." In short, the revolt was an attempt to equalize *difference* between the hypertrophy of the colonial European's ontological Self and the atrophy of the Algerian's ontological Otherness.

Colonization, according to Maschino, had robbed Algerians of their most basic material properties. Colonialism, by this definition, was "the pure instrumentalization of men and the physical riches of Algeria; the Algerians had become just another material source to be exploited along with the minerals and the cows." But colonization had done much more than that; it had also robbed them of their souls, their Being. Hence the fight against the colonial system was really a struggle to regain true selfhood:

> The being that they [the Algerians] are reconquering with weapons is not mythical; it is not a philosophical abstraction; it is the era of man, his humanity, the sense of his existence and his substance. The acquisition of rights is secondary, the fundamental [right] is not the right to live, but the right to be a man. To treat a man as a man, to take charge of his own human existence, is to cease to be an instrument of the Other. The Algerian Revolution is first a demand for humanity.

In Maschino's analysis, the Other was the Frenchman, the outsider, the pernicious colonialist, and the thief of Algerian Being. The Algerians' struggle had become an ontological problem because denying Algerian nationalism meant rejecting the Algerians' Being or identity. For this reason, the French-Algerian War was not merely a question of rights in the French republican sense; rather, revolution represented first and foremost an effort to reclaim "humanity" (read Being) for Algerians.

Within this logic, independence, not reconciliation, was the first step toward Algerian selfhood. And if any people should be familiar with this ontological mandate, Maschino insisted, it would be the French. In fact, Maschino took French rights-of-man theorists at their word and suggested that the freedom found during the French Revolution had produced the modern French soul. Since revolutionary freedom was part of the French national psyche, the French could not legitimately continue to deny independence to Algerians without doing tragic damage to the so-called universalism of the French soul. In short, Maschino brilliantly used the specific claims of French universalism both to subvert the age-old mission civilisatrice ideology and to protect the universalistic message of freedom found within the French Enlightenment.

It is fair to say that efforts to understand identity, decolonization, and the Other through serious abstract analysis such as Maschino's eventually became one of most important intellectual developments during the French-Algerian War. It is also reasonable to say that such efforts would leave enduring paradigms for understanding human identity, paradigms that continue to inform discussions of identity today.

Jacques Berque: The Other, the Orient, and the Collège de France

Many readers familiar with Edward Said's monumental work *Orientalism* might think that Said was the first writer to call European Orientalism into question. Although *Orientalism* is arguably the single most important book published on the subjects of power, knowledge, and identity vis-à-vis imperialism, Said was not the first to doubt Orientalism's future. One of the most influential writers to announce the deconstruction of Orientalism was Jacques Berque. Not surprisingly, Berque's questioning of Orientalism was tied directly to the decolonization of North Africa. The son of the well-known French North African administrator and writer Augustine Berque, Jacques Berque testified, as did so many others (Camus, Daniel, Feraoun, Amrouche, Memmi) to a dual identity. Born French but raised in Algeria, he had firsthand experience with the problems of identity and assimilation well before the outbreak of the war. In a study written for the French government on March 1, 1947, "A Study for a New Political Method for France in Morocco," Berque suggested that the French attempt to gain administrative acceptance among North Africans (Moroccans) did not place sufficient weight on the "soul" of the people. Because of the present-day "psychologism," the project of assimilation was at an "impasse": "In our system, in effect, there is no freedom for the Muslim to identify with us."[6] In order to compensate for the inability of Muslims to identify with the French, Berque suggested a systematic reform based on respect for the Muslim community. Unfortunately, liberalism as practiced in North Africa was analogous to a "political Esperanto which [was] impossible to undress." Moreover, he added, "We have not affected anything in North Africa with our garden-variety humanism [*notre humanisme de jardiniers*]" (9). Frankly, as he assessed the situation in 1947, the continuation of this brand of liberalism would lead directly to "our immediate eviction."

Nearly ten years later, on December 1, 1956, as Berque addressed the crowd assembled to hear his inaugural address at the Collège de France, the truth of his early predictions had prevailed. Not only was the "political Esperanto" he had once claimed liberalism to be undergoing hostile attacks, but France had since lost both Tunisia and Morocco, entered into war in Algeria, and just faced the Suez crisis.[7] Berque admitted in a later interview the awkwardness of delivering his inaugural address on assuming his chair in social history of contemporary Islam during the immediate aftermath of the Suez invasion. Talking about the "survival of a Franco-Arab future" in a room that was "black" and "charged with resentment" because of the recent debacle of the Anglo-French expedition and Gamal Abdel Nasser's oratorical excesses presented a very arduous task.[8]

In the tense atmosphere imperiling the future of French-Arab relations, Berque tried to speak of reconciliation by offering a theoretical analysis of Arab identity and by arguing that reconciliation required true understanding of the Arab world. This understanding, he argued, needed to be founded on a better comprehension of the world in general. "Our world is no longer cantonal. It does not reward the virtues of the gardener. We have believed this too late! But the Maghreb is devouring ideas and men." Hence Berque suggested to his audience that the task of addressing Islam today required caution and respect for historical demands. The present conditions required a special ability to live "in contact with these men [the Arabs]." Because Berque was a scholar, his contact with the Arabs obliged a twofold action on his part: long prodigious study and a "pact of sympathy and engagement" (7).

As a former "citizen of the Maghreb" and representative of the government in the Orient, Berque told the audience that his essential task of understanding and imparting knowledge about the Orient had not changed on entering the Collège. His coming to the Collège did signify a change in the way this knowledge would be acquired. Orientalism as it was traditionally practiced could no longer be justified because it was impossible to study "Arab civilizations without the support [concours] of the Arabs" (9). In short, the study of the Arabs and the Orient would have to be revamped because conventional Orientalism was methodologically outdated.

Since Berque was speaking of a new and more acute means of investigating sociological questions and since this new methodology was affected by current political conflicts, Orientalist methodology, or the "optic between the Orient and the West," had to be reconsidered. To begin, scholars had to understand that the Arabs marked the beginning of their modern history with the end of World War I. Above all it was imperative to see that the West had played a negative role in the origins of the modern Arab world because Arabs now defined themselves against the West and in favor of the Orient. Cautioning his listeners not to fall into the trap of defining the Arabs through "gross definitions" such as "nationalism, pan-Islamism, fanaticism, xenophobia, or other comfortable labels," he continued, "we must see that among them [chez lui] the reformism of some, the conservatism of others, the very progression of thinkers are very often only the effects of positions taken with regard to the West. Alterity, as our philosophers would say" (13).

Since alterity (Otherness) was a crucial aspect of the scholar's study,

Berque focused on his concerns for the representation of the Orient. The Orient was marked by its language (Arabic) and the influence of the "techniques of the industrial age" (14). In its attempt to maintain its identity, the Orient was able to use Western inventions such as the printing press and the radio against the inventors.[9] In fact, he continued, the words that expressed the power, magic, and feelings of the Orient were transmitted with the help of these Western mechanical inventions, but these inventions had also since become characteristics of the Orient's "personality." Importantly, the Orient did not entirely abhor the appropriation and objectification of its personality by the West: "The Orient resents less than us this bite of the object, this bite of the Other, the creator among us of attention, objectivity and many other working dispositions."

Nevertheless, this objectification by the researcher required a certain degree of intellectual honesty and epistemological clarity. For example, Berque argued, it was necessary to account for the observer's social and investigative limitations. "The researcher is a man, [a man] from a certain place" (30) The social embeddedness and historicism of the observer, "I" in other words, could not be "neglected" without "hiding a lie." As Berque said, "The I reappears here, or more to the point the *we*, so difficult to strip." This raised a particularly important question for today's researchers because there had been an "awakening" of the Oriental peoples, but they had not completely rejected Western civilization. Western researchers could still work toward reconciliation between the West and the Orient in North Africa if they could look dispassionately at the particularisms of culture in the Maghreb.

Unlike Sartre and others, Berque was not advocating universalism. For this reason, accounting for the particular context of analyses of the Oriental world, whether North Africa or Iraq, was all the more important because it was the first step in determining the "responsibilities" of the researcher toward his "country," "science," and himself. As a caveat to his listeners at the Collège, Berque argued that scholars had to distinguish between a citizen's and a scientist's responsibilities. This meant that researchers had to objectify their political positions with regard to their objects of study. This would not be easy because politics is omnipresent: "If the citizen's initiative extends beyond all the parts of his methodological reserve, it is his business. . . . But in his research it is both fatal and vital for France, Arab countries, and civilization—everywhere he encounters politics in studying subjects equal to him [qui *affrontent de pareils sujets*]. He should neither hope for nor run from these encounters. He should distinguish between his personal opinion and his scientific opinion."

Closing his inaugural address, Berque reaffirmed his belief that the "alliance" between the world of the Arabs and France was likely to endure through today's turbulent conditions. The long history of friendship between the two civilizations and the successful penetration of French culture and language had, for better or worse, made this alliance possible. Most important, he showed his optimism that the Arab and European common "Hellenistic" heritage would be sufficient to mitigate existing hostilities. If it appeared paradoxical to reaffirm his belief in a Franco-Arab future given the current crises with Egypt and Algeria, this paradox legitimated the special task entrusted to him by the honor of his position at the Collège.

Two years later, in an article titled, "Arab Anxiety in Modern Times," Berque continued his efforts to describe the relationship between the Orient and the West. [10] By 1958, however, it was clear that his essential methodological and social questions had shifted as a result of the war. For example, instead of demonstrating how a common heritage could join the Orient and the West, Berque concentrated on how this common heritage, expressed often by the West's domination of the Orient, forced people in the Orient to struggle with their notion of selfhood. So deeply had the West entrenched itself in the psyche of the Oriental person that "In liberating itself from the West, the Orient conquers only its own demons. It passes from there to the positive critique of itself. Here we are in the current period. A new cycle is starting."

With the commencement of the "new cycle," a fundamental reevaluation and remaking of Arab identity was set in motion. Berque focused on the issue of time to demonstrate how the new cycle translated into Arab reevaluation of history in both traditional and temporal terms. The questioning of their tradition with respect to their newly projected future shattered the Arabs' "authenticity" because it had been so closely allied with traditionalism. The traditionalism of their parents was now interpreted as a product of the West's political usury. Hence politics—as history—was a product of Others and, as Maschino had also argued, the Others were the Europeans. Berque wrote:

> Politics [was] plotted by Others. That is the horizon on which the Arabs' eyes open. For him nature is Others. . . . European history launched the ideas of liberty, equality, and revolution, in a profitable

coincidence with valorization [*mise en valeur*] of the world. It only had to stomp its feet, according to the ancient image, for the legions of workers, consumers, retailers to crawl out of the earth to answer its call. Exactly in the inverse, the history of the Arab does not start until its first strike against the world is already inventoried, appropriated, tied up: hence, the Suez affair. The West's denomination had even drawn a type of authenticity, and definitely its efficacy, from the scientific hold on the "fields of action" [*champs d'action*]. (100)

Since the Arabs, according to Berque, were to reappropriate history and the world, they would inevitably face an internal contestation of their own identity. Having long identified themselves with a world and a tradition appropriated by the West, the Arabs had had to battle against the external and psychological worlds that the West had penetrated equally. Hence, according to Berque, being curious about himself and about the Other (*autrui*) (101), the Arab found himself in a predicament that posed not only "sociological" questions but also "psychoanalytic" ones (102).

The Arab revolt, Berque concluded, was not merely a revolt against the individual who oppressed but also against the "destiny" that had created oppression. The Algerian revolution provided Arabs with a means to reconstruct an image of man that had been mutilated by oppression. The issue in Islamic societies such as Algeria, Berque noted, was that the Arab had been so deeply penetrated by the West that the present revolution had become "ontological" (106). Confronted with an ontological revolution, the Arabs' search for authenticity forced a difficult choice between "idealizing" and "exorcizing" their "great past" (107), In other words, this ontological search for selfhood forced the Arab into a constant "interrogation of his essence" during which a defiance of Others represented his source of strength. As Berque stated it, "His force is his cry," However, one question remained: "Would the Others [the Europeans] hear this cry of ardor and exile?" (107).

If Berque presented the problem of Algerian identity as a conflict between the Arab Self and Western Other, how did he explain violence? From this phenomenological standpoint, violence stemmed from the Algerians' attempt to work through the internalized contradictions of identity, historical oppression by the Western Other, and internalized absence of historical time. The violence Algerians employed thus originated from an ontological rejection of the West's external and internalized domination. The repudiation of the West was not without paradox because the Arab-Algerian struggle against the Otherness of the West was also a conflict with the very part of the West that had been internalized in Arab identity and had therefore become part of the Arabs' fundamental ontology.

Understanding how to overcome the paradox required objective scientific precision with which the problem of difference and the cultural bifurcation of the Arabs' ontology could be examined. In analyzing the revolution, violence, and identity in this way, Berque claimed, a methodological transition from ethnology to sociology had to be made. He acknowledged the social scientist's indebtedness to Sartre's phenomenological formulation of the concept of the Other, which had transformed modern social science. For example, the concept of the Other was a much needed tool for research on " 'Jews,' 'the proletariat,' 'Negroes,' or 'colonial peoples.' " [11] Yet Berque hinted that Sartre's formulation lacked methodological precision because modern social scientists still needed to distance themselves from the process of decolonization. The researcher's inability to place an objective distance between him or her and his or her subject rendered the study of racism and difference extraordinarily onerous (24). Most important, Berque warned that the social scientists should not overlook the "lesson" to be learned from the current conflict: "It has already substantially altered the background to the study by substituting, in some measure, for the dialectic of origin and religion, a dialectic of nationality, which is not based on the ethnic factor but is already differentiated by class and party" (25).

Not all Islamic and Arab scholars agreed with Berque's view that the problem of identity had to be understood in dialectical terms. For example, speaking about the position of the social scientist at a university colloquium held the week after the Mélouza massacre, Berque's colleague at the Collège de France and a proponent of Gandhi's philosophy of nonviolence, Louis Massignon, argued that the object of scientific inquiry should be the uncovering of "truth" and should prevent the "unleashing of blind violence that creates 'its own truth' through the refusal to understand 'the Other.' " [12] Indeed, according to Massignon, achieving peace would come through the "comprehension of the Other" as a "Stranger," and only with a nondialectical concept of the Other could productive understanding of the Orient be achieved. In other words, reconciliation was still necessary and possible because by recognizing the "hospitality of the Other"—a recognition that came through working and living together—one could understand the truth of the social unity. Ultimately, this suggested that the problem of Algerian identity could not be represented as a violent, dialectical confrontation of the Algerian with the world and with history. On the contrary, the goal was not to understand violence, since violence was the obstacle to a peaceful agreement between the Arabs and the non-Arabs in Algeria.

To arrive at mutual comprehension of Otherness, according to Massignon, Arabs had to seek out common or communal ties through a relationship with "Strangers" or "Foreigners" based on "hospitality" and comprehension. In phenomenological terminology, Massignon's representation of the Arabs as Other strove to minimize the possibility of conflict by putting the question of Algerian identity in the framework of the problem of "existing-for-Others." For Berque, the problem of Arab identity could not be explained in terms of "hospitality" (existing-for-Others); it had to be seen primarily as a question of "existing-for-oneself."

These differences between Massignon and Berque illustrate how central the issue of reconciliation remained for intellectuals concerned with the representation of Algerian identity; they show how intellectuals who believed in reconciliation suggested that difference was a positive, nonviolent artifact of identity. The opposition between Berque's and Massignon's conceptions of Otherness and interpretations of the Arab-European, West-Orient conflict is best shown in a direct debate between Massignon and Berque published by Jean-Marie Domenach in Esprit in October 1960. [13] In this "dialogue," moderated by Domenach, Berque extended his definition of the Arab in order to explain the growing distance between the Arabs (the Orient) and the European technological civilizations (the West). Berque again argued that, despite the Arabs' desire to distinguish themselves from the Western world, they could not completely reject industrial civilization without remaining "eternally opposed to the Other." And, since the Other's (the European's) civilization had so deeply entered the Arab world, this technological civilization could not be rejected because "in refusing the Other, they [were] refusing themselves" (1506).

Where did this leave Franco-Algerian reconciliation? To address this question both Berque and Massignon turned to genealogy, and, interestingly, both relied on the notion of monotheism to substantiate their claims. Berque argued that Arabs were bound to European civilization through a common Greco-Oriental heritage or culture; Massignon insisted that Europeans and Arabs were linked by a common Semitic and religious heritage. Hence, according to Massignon, respect for this common religious past mandated that a nonviolent, nonconfrontational understanding save the two peoples from rupture. Moreover, since the Arabs held three principles to be fundamental to their culture—the Abrahamic tradition, the spoken word, and the right of exile—it could not be true that the Algerians were incapable of showing "hospitality to the French *colons*," nor could it be claimed that the Arabs had lost their respect for the spoken word (1519). These traits, Berque answered, had already been long lost and it was up to "us" (Westerners) to restore this "plentitude." In other words, Massignon's notion of a common Franco-Algerian culture based on religious mono-genesis would restore reconciliation, while for Berque reconciliation was a remnant of the past and a disguise for the Western status quo.

Refining and Defining Otherness

Orientalists and Islamic scholars were not alone in assessing the impact of the French-Algerian War on Algerian society and identity. In fact, the French anthropologist (and later a sociologist) Pierre Bourdieu—who returned to Algeria to teach at the University of Algiers after fulfilling his military service there—offered an important contribution to the identity debates. The young *agrégé* in philosophy from the École Normale Supérieure and student of Raymond Aron surged into these debates over Algerian culture and identity in 1958 with the publication of his highly praised *Sociologie de l'Algérie* (*The Algerians*).[14]

In his structural attempt to depict Algerian society, Bourdieu could not have agreed more with Berque's call for scientific precision. To make his analysis more precise, Bourdieu diagnosed Algerian identity by introducing the terms "acculturation" and "deculturation."[15] Taking the debate over identity still further, he also divided Algerian society anthropologically into four main peoples—the Kabyles, the Schwia, the Mozabites, and the Arabic-speaking—to show how a "kaleidoscopic mechanism" had both united and separated Algerians. According to him, the diversification of ethnic groups within Algeria created separate Algerian cultures with "intense cul-tural interpenetration" (93). The war had bonded the three groups behind the common front of nationalism, which had objectively transformed Alge-rian society. Put simply, the war had irrefutably affected the kaleidoscopic mechanism because the different ethnic groups—which had historically attempted to differentiate themselves from one another—were now moti-vated by a desire to dissimilate themselves from the Europeans. In other words, the war and the colonial situation had "aided in breaking down the particularisms and fostered the development of national consciousness" (94n2).

Bourdieu's concern for Algerian identity and nationalism, however, linked him in important ways to Massignon and Berque. The Algerians, Bourdieu wrote, exhibited a "stage personage" (96). Similar to Massignon's argument, Bourdieu suggested that this stage personage required that Algerians "reveal to others not one's inmost being but a semblance of oneself." As a result, Bourdieu wrote, the Algerian was primarily understood as a "being who exists for others [être pour autrui]." This formula was exemplified by the notion of honor because it symbolized constant scrutiny or the act of being constantly subjected to the gaze of others. As an individual, the Algerian was "also 'a being who exists through others' [être par autrui], who is, as it were, the point of intersection of many relationships, and who has much difficulty in thinking of himself as an autonomous personality" (96).

Because Algerians were inspired by a profound sense of communalism and were capable of existing for and through others, Bourdieu insisted that pinpointing the source of the current conflict required grasping how individuals acted as social conduits. The social conflict in Algeria—the rebellion—was not merely the culmination of the kaleidoscopic forces uniting against European domination, nor was it a unique outgrowth of individual passions. Then, if the conflict could not be explained uniquely in terms of a change in the kaleidoscopic forces or as a reaction against colonialism, could Islam—as many intellectuals believed—be held responsible? According to Bourdieu, despite the fact that the Islamic "imprint" was clearly legible within Algerian society, it was wrong to see Islam as the "determining or predominate *cause* of all cultural phenomena," just as it would be wrong "to consider contemporary Western religion as being merely a *reflection* of the economic and social structures" (108). Thus, although several factors linked the irruption of the war to individual concerns, he located the real source in the totality of Algeria's objective social structures.

About the same time that Bourdieu published The Algerians, Germaine Tillion made one final effort, in Les Ennemis complémentaires (France and Algeria: Complementary Enemies), published in 1960, to ensure peace by trying to clarify the meaning of Algerian identity. Without a doubt, according to her, the revolution had created "cruel evils," which had only "one cure: it [was] called reconciliation." [16] One of the problems her work underscored was growing division among intellectuals. [17] Moreover, Tillion believed that to end the war and work toward reconciliation required reexamining the most fundamental distinction of human identity: division between "*We* and *the Others*" (60). Tillion stated that Otherness was a universal phenomenon and therefore just as applicable from village to village within France as between nations, cultures, religions, and races. Nevertheless, she also acknowledged that time was running out. She began by distinguishing herself from the phenomenological method and, without attacking it directly, left little room to doubt that she questioned the division between Algerians and the French based on the "Self-Other" dialectic. In attacking this dialectical distinction, she revisited the idea of universal humanism:

> Each human being's conception of the relations—both real and ideal—that unite or oppose him to the rest of humanity is the profound basis of his personality.
>
> Once—and that situation still survives, here and there—humanity was divided into two coherent and stable groups: *We* and *the Other*.
>
> *We*: an entity not to be judged, or seen, and in which each individual melts like a piece of sugar in hot coffee; *the Others*: unknown monsters who don't talk "like everyone else," who eat disgusting food, who pray the wrong way, who dress absurdly, do unexpected things. . . .
>
> In 1960, what is *We*? We French? We workers? We intellectuals? We owners of fifty acres? We officials of such and such a grade? We African Negroes, or Senegalese, or citizens of Mali? We champions of the West against other cardinal points of the compass? We Marxists? We pacifists? We career soldiers? We Mormons? (60–61)

What had happened historically, according to Tillion, was that the growth of the "We's" had fractured and disconnected universal society. However, because today's world required more than ever the global coming together of individual societies and nations, it was nearly impossible to avert the impending "shipwreck" of humanity. She warned that for democracy to survive, the "rights of the human being" had to be protected (68). France's problem as it faced the Algerian question, she continued, was that it was not ready for "Volume Two of human history" (69).

Volume Two of human history challenged universal humanism because individuals at this stage lost their prior importance. Overshadowed by the uncontrollable crowds, which were led by a smaller number of leaders, individuals could not protect themselves from the vicissitudes of war. Moreover, this new historical stage also presented problems for France, Tillion acknowledged, because it had been outflanked by "the stupendousness of giant nations" (the United States, the Soviet Union, and China) (82). Nevertheless, even with France's declining status in the world, Tillion's vision of "human history" was unquestionably Francocentric. "France," she wrote, was "tired of playing the boogeyman, and I believe she possesses all that the peoples of Africa are seeking: the rich language, well established in every latitude, a civilization open to the future, the vitality necessary for the creative ferment to continue" (84).

Hence, despite her pessimistic appraisal of France's position relative to the "giant nations," she still believed (in a maternalistic or paternalistic sense, but many Algerian intellectuals agreed with her) that "Africans" and the citizens of the Third World looked to France for cultural, linguistic, and political inspiration. And, as if her Francocentrism were not already enough to make African and Algerian nationalists uneasy, she claimed that Paris was the "master trump" of French civilization: "Whereas France finds herself outdistanced by giants unknown to the foregoing centuries, Paris remains the capital of the world" (84).

Tillion acknowledged that Algerians, victimized by oppression from nearly every angle, had clearly distanced themselves from France."[18] Algerians desired revenge. The problem was that reconciliation and friendship were no longer the primary issues. The most important matter was peace, and for peace to be achieved it was necessary to negotiate with the enemy (the FLN). In other words, although Tillion insisted that the French ought to maintain an open dialogue with Algerians because France was the bearer of universal human rights, she had finally realized that reconciliation could not be achieved without peace and that, to arrive at peace, France had to compromise and acknowledge a separate and different Algerian identity. This did not mean that there could be no true friendships between Algerians and French, but the friendships that did exist were marked by a distant "theoretical character" between the French left in Paris and the Algerian nationalists in Algeria (177).

The theoretical character the friendship between the Algerians and French had acquired (and which Tillion clearly regretted) was perhaps best exemplified by Sartre's representation of the Algerians as Other. Even before Tillion's comments, Sartre's former colleague at Les Temps modernes, philosopher Maurice Merleau-Ponty, had already warned in 1955 of Sartre's dangerous and politicized use of the concept of Otherness as a means to unveil the dynamic of history. As he wrote about Sartre and the Other in Les Aventures de la dialectique (Adventures of the Dialectic):

In going from personal history or literature to history, Sartre does not for the time being believe that he is meeting a new phenomenon which demands new categories. Undoubtedly he thinks that history, like language in his view, does not pose metaphysical questions which are not already present in the problem of the other. The class "other" is so established a phenomenon that the individual other is always in competition with it. . . . Is not action made up of relations, supported by categories, and carried on through a relationship with the world that the philosophy of the I and the Other does not express?[19]

Hence, in Wittgensteinian fashion, Merleau-Ponty called into question the ability of the concept of the Other to envelop the reality of the phenomenological worldview of the individual.

Merleau-Ponty suggested that Sartre's specific use of the concept as a means to explain reason in history was racked with ulterior motives. Sartre's newfound concern for history explained his use of the Other, and the philosophy of commitment, in this sense, merged and determined Sartre's interpretation of history. Alterity, in other words, was a means for Sartre to steer a clear course through an otherwise unclear historical process. Sartre

decides to look to history only for the illumination of a drama whose characters—the I and the Other—are defined *a priori* by means of reflection. By taking as his own the gaze that the least-favored casts on our society, by his willingness to see himself through these eyes, by extending an open credit of principle to the party and the regime that claim kinship with the least-favored, Sartre seems to have the greatest concern for the Other. But Sartre hides his reasons from the Other. (195)

Sartre used the Other conceptually, according to Merleau-Ponty, in order to invent independence of consciousness, which "justifies," "limits," and "terminates" the Other's intervention in the life of the I.

By July 1958, Merleau-Ponty went so far as to claim that both Sartrian and right-wing radicalism, if unchecked, would produce fascism in France as they had in Algeria. If we are to take Merleau-Ponty's warning seriously, it is essential to look at Sartre's most important theoretical work written during the war, volume 1 of the *Critique de la raison dialectique* (*Critique of Dialectical Reason*).[20]

Critique tells us a great deal about why Sartre appropriated the Algerians as Other to prove that a negation of a negation (the destruction of colonialism's destruction) was an affirmation. It also reveals how Sartre combined several problems (ontology, violence, and class) in an effort to have Algerian nationalism *stand for* the Marxian view of history: "There is in fact a deep relation of ontological identity, of practical ubiquity and of contradiction in movement; and, as a developing process, this is what, in Marxism, is called proletarian self-emancipation" (692).

In order to lay the foundations for the proletariat's self-emancipation, Sartre distinguished between analytical (scientific) and dialectical reason. He claimed: "Scientific research can in fact be unaware of its own principal features. Dialectical knowledge, in contrast, is knowledge of the dialectic" (20).[21] This meant that dialectical reason alone could penetrate the contours of history. This assertion was epistemologically critical for Sartre because, in order to properly understand man's relationship with history and with the world, it was essential to understand that true knowledge came through dialectical, not analytical, reason. Placing dialectical reason over analytical reason thus had tremendous implications for "man." Specifically, the dialectic overpowered man at the same time that man empowered it. Going yet further, Sartre argued that there was "no such thing as man; there [were] people, wholly defined by their society and by the historical moment" (36). In short, Sartre combined historicism and particularism with historical universalism by arguing that while there were "*several collectivities, several societies*," there was only "*one history*," which was "woven out of millions of individual actions."

Sartre explained how historicism and universalism had produced the French-Algerian War, but the war was only one aspect of the totalizing essence of history. The Algerian, as a colonized Other, participated in a particular revolution that belonged to *one* history. Sartre used "Other" to explain the colonists' capitalistic exploitation of Algerian "natives," and that this exploitation permanently suspended the colonial situation in a dialectic of violence. However, in Hegelian fashion, Sartre concluded that the dialectic of logic created a situation in which the colonialist and the Algerians were Other:

> The only possible way out was to confront total negation with total negation, violence with equal violence; to negate dispersal and atomization by an initially negative unity whose content would be defined in struggle: the Algerian nation. Thus the Algerian revolution,

through being desperate violence, was simply an adoption of the despair in which the colonists maintained the natives; its violence was simply a negation of the impossible, and the impossibility of life was the immediate result of oppression. Algerians had to live, because colonialists needed a sub-proletariat, but they had to live at the frontier of the impossibility of life because wages had to be as close as possible to zero. The violence of the rebel *was* the violence of the colonist; there was never any other. The struggle between the oppressed and the oppressors ultimately became the reciprocal interiorization of a single oppression: the prime object of oppression, interiorizing it and finding it to be the negative source of its unity, appalled the oppressor, who recognized, in *violent rebellion*, his own oppressive violence as a hostile force taking him in turn as its object. And against his own violence *as Other*, he created a counter-violence which was simply *his* own oppression become *repressive*, that is to say reactualized and trying to transcend the violence of the Other, in other words, his own violence in the Other. (733)

As Sartre argues in this complicated passage, the violence of the Algerian revolution originated in the original sin of colonialism (read capitalism). The only possible escape from colonial oppression for the Algerians as Other was to battle against the colonial Other's praxis of violence, which was part and parcel of the "process of exploitation" (733). Under these conditions where the dynamic of the dialectic required the violent psychological and physical confrontation between the colonial Other and the Algerian as Other, reconciliation would be impossible because radical difference was an essential characteristic of history. Hence, in Hegelian fashion, the dialectic of violence and counterviolence doomed the colonial situation to self-destruction because the oppressed would undoubtedly consume the oppressor. In this case, the concept of the Other abstracted the Algerians from their particular revolutionary setting and contextualized their historical struggle against colonialism as one step in the culmination of history and reason. Since all violence with regard to colonialists was self-referential, pointing back to the original violence of capitalist oppression and colonial domination, the violence of the "native" (Sartre's term) was automatically qualified and venerated through dialectics and through history.

In response to Sartre's celebration of dialectical reason and violence, anthropologist Claude Lévi-Strauss devoted the final chapter, "History and the Dialectic," of *La Pensée sauvage* (*The Savage Mind*) to refuting Sartre's theory. Lévi-Strauss's bout with Sartre was in many ways his only significant contribution to the debates over the decolonization of Algeria."[22] According to Lévi-Strauss, Sartre's *Critique* mostly demonstrated that Sartre employed sloppy logic and that he had misunderstood the distinction between analytical and dialectical reason. What angered Lévi-Strauss the most was Sartre's claim that the scientists utilized only analytical reason. In reply, Lévi-Strauss insisted that the "savage mind" could only be understood by anthropologists via dialectical reason because "it is in this intransigent refusal on the part of the savage mind to allow anything human (or even living) to remain alien to it that the real principle of dialectical reason is to be found."[23]

Equally important, Lévi-Strauss attacked Sartre's separation of dialectical and analytical reason. According to Lévi-Strauss, dialectal reason accompanied analytical reason and could not be understood as existing independently. This distinction was especially important because it pointed to a disciplinary polemic between Lévi-Strauss as an anthropologist and Sartre as a philosopher over the constitution of "man." Sartre claimed that his dialectical method showed how humans were constituted, whereas Lévi-Strauss argued that the human sciences were supposed not to "constitute, but dissolve man." Hence Sartre aimed to refashion human identity while Lévi-Strauss only wanted to examine it. "The preeminent value of anthropology," according to Lévi-Strauss, was "that it represents the first step in a procedure which involves others" (247). The problem with Sartre's dialectics, then, was that in constituting man Sartre had given a nonterrestrial quality to history. According to Lévi-Strauss, Sartre's vision of history, in this sense, posited history as something that was not of this world and possessed metaphysical qualities:

> Seen in this light, therefore, my self is no more opposed to others than man is opposed to the world: the truths learnt through man are "of the world," and they are important for this reason. This explains why I regard anthropology as the principle of all research, while for Sartre, it raises a problem in the shape of a constraint to overcome or a resistance to reduce. And indeed what can one make of peoples "without history when one has defined man in terms of dialectic and dialectic in terms of history? Sometimes Sartre seems tempted to distinguish two dialectics: the "true" one, which is supposed to be that of historical societies, and a repetitive, short-term dialectic,

which he grants so-called primitive societies while at the same time placing it very near biology.

This imperils his whole system, for the bridge between man and nature which he has taken such pains to destroy would turn out to be surreptitiously reestablished through ethnography, which is indisputably a human science and devotes itself to the study of these societies. (248)

Lévi-Strauss continued, ridiculing Sartre's politically motivated appropriation of the Algerian people:

Alternatively Sartre resigns himself to putting a "stunned and deformed" humanity on man's side . . . but not without implying that its [the Algerian people's] place in humanity does not belong to it in its own right and is a function only of its adoption by historical humanity: either because it has begun to internalize the latter's history in the colonial context, or because, thanks to anthropology itself, historical humanity has given the blessing of meaning to an original humanity which was without it. Either way the prodigious wealth and diversity of habits, beliefs, and customs is allowed to escape. (248–49)

According to Lévi-Strauss, who had argued that anthropology possessed the key to understanding man, Sartre's dishonesty neglected the originality of Algerian culture and beliefs and replaced Algeria's real place in the world within a supposed historic place. History as prophesied by Sartre ignored local Algerian cultures under the pretext that the Algerian revolution was a step in the longer dialectical process. In fact, according to Lévi-Strauss, rather than making the process of history philosophically transparent, Sartre's use of history and Third World cultures demonstrated that he was merely a "prisoner of his own Cogito." More to the point, Lévi-Strauss claimed that Sartre mixed ontological questions with Marxian notions of class struggle and history, and Sartre's use of the French-Algerian War left one conclusion: "To the anthropologist . . . this philosophy (like all the others) affords a first-class ethnographic document, the study of which is essential to an understanding of the mythology of our time" (249n).

Unfortunately this Marxist "mythology" also posed serious epistemological problems, especially relating to the problem of Otherness. As Lévi-Strauss pointed out, it was wrong to conclude that "others are wholly dialectical" simply because "knowledge of others is dialectical" (250). This problem became clearer when one looked at Sartre's confusion over the type of history—history as analysis or history as life. Speaking more directly about the problem of history and addressing the idea of history as present-day "mythology," which made use of Others, Lévi-Strauss showed how dialectical theory as advanced by Sartre ultimately, if not ironically, turned against itself. Since "truth" depended on context, it was impossible to locate and isolate truth historically before it disappeared. This was clearly a problem for today's left, he continued, because "[t]he so-called men of the Left still cling to a period of contemporary history" that bestows "the blessing of a congruence between practical imperative and schemes of interpretation" (254).

In effect, Lévi-Strauss was caricaturing Sartre's notion of intellectual legitimacy because Lévi-Strauss was directly attacking the French left's notion of political commitment, or praxis. For example, rather than clarifying problems with history, the left's praxis rendered it impossible to see necessary distinctions between the past and the present. This was because history had become intertwined (hence confused) with the intellectuals' conceptions of their own identity.

Because historical knowledge had merged with the individual's own "inner sense" of time and continuity, "it appears to reestablish our connection, outside ourselves, with the very essence of change" (256). But this was only an "illusion" based on the "demands of social life." These demands (the idea of political commitment and the desire to make sense out of the world, for instance) meant that history had to be understood as "history-for" (257). This was a critical point because this very conception of history-for explained the penchant of the French left to appropriate local or national histories, to cast them into the global or transcultural Geist of history. In a footnote, Lévi-Strauss summed up the problem of history-for:

> Quite so ["History is therefore never history, but history-for"] will be the comment of the supporters of Sartre. But the latter's whole endeavor shows that, though the subjectivity of history-for-me can make way for the objectivity of history-for-us, the "I" can still only be converted into "we" by condemning this "we" to being no more than an "I" raised to the power of two, itself hermetically sealed off from the other "we's." The price so paid for the illusion of having overcome the insoluble antinomy (in such a system) between myself and others consists of the assignation, by historical con-

sciousness, of the metaphysical function of Other to the Papuans. By reducing the latter to the state of means, barely sufficient for its philosophical appetite, historical reason abandons itself to the sort of intellectual cannibalism much more revolting to the anthropologist than real cannibalism. (257–58n)

The obvious problem for understanding Otherness, according to Lévi-Strauss, was that for dialecticians such as Sartre, whose work attempted to discredit scientific knowledge, history would be appropriated to fulfill the "demands of social life." In appropriating history in this manner, Sartre had rendered understanding between Others impossible and cast the Other as a concept into the mold of a useless metaphysical abstraction that held no claim on historical truth. Asserting his own professional and intellectual legitimacy, Lévi-Strauss argued that it was up to the anthropologists to bring out the historical dimensions and the reasons behind the expansion of this Marxist "mythology" within the modern French left.

Seasoned academic contemporaries such as Raymond Aron understood the importance of Sartre's and Lévi-Strauss's debate about the representation of the Other for French intellectuals. But in his 1973 *Histoire et dialectique de la violence* (*History and the Dialectic of Violence*)—originally given as a series of lectures at the Collège de France in the early 1960s—Aron disagreed with both men because they had oversimplified the issue.[24] He agreed that Sartre's dialectical attempts to understand the Other were probably useful if one wanted to find "meaning and salvation in an existence that to ourselves seemed noise and perdition" (184). Yet, because Sartre's method emphasized an ontology and an epistemology based on praxis or constituting dialectic, which meant the dialectic of individual consciousness, it was theoretically flawed because Sartre had fatally merged the idea of intellectual praxis with Third World violence. Furthermore, it was entirely disingenuous, according to Aron, for a writer or intellectual to attempt, by pen, to create a dialectic of violence without suffering threat of torture or violence to him- or herself. Aron pointed out that of the French intellectuals in Paris it was Francis Jeanson, not Sartre, who through his contacts with the FLN had truly been able to effectuate intellectual praxis. Even worse, Sartre's ontological understanding of the world "would condemn the historian or ethnographer, as Sartre reproaches Lévi-Strauss, to see only himself in the other or to see only the other with respect to himself, and consequently to destroy what constitutes for the historian or the ethnographer their task and reward *par excellence*, which is to succeed in keeping their distance from their own ego or, in other words, to recognize alterity" (197).

As a practicing social scientist, Aron claimed that he could not leave Sartre's contemptuous, praxis-based attack on analytical reason and the positive sciences unanswered. Aron insisted that Sartre, by placing too much emphasis on praxis and dialectal reason, had misunderstood the possible contributions analytical reason could make to debates over identity and consciousness. However, on this issue, he was not aiming his criticisms only at Sartre. Lévi-Strauss, he argued, "dreams of a science of man comparable in its structure to a science of insects or microbiology. At the end of *The Savage Mind* he upholds, at least hypothetically, a materialism that establishes the possibility of a science" (204). Hence Sartre and Lévi-Strauss, Aron pointed out, were unwittingly connected through their emphasis on historical materialism. [25] The difference between them was that for Sartre the "ontological primacy of *praxis* leads to the primacy of understanding or dialectical Reason," whereas for Lévi-Strauss the "epistemological and perhaps the ontological primacy of structures" had skewed the real meaning of lived experience (205).

If Sartre's insistence on praxis, Lévi-Strauss's reliance on structuralism, and Aron's search for an alternative way of knowing and dealing with Otherness left important questions unanswered, was there a better way to explain the relationship between human identity, alterity, and violence? Of the other scholars who addressed the problem of alterity during the war, perhaps no one was more concerned with this question than Emmanuel Levinas. One year after Sartre's publication of *Critique*, Levinas's 1961 *Totalité et infini* (*Totality and Infinity*) conceptualized the Other without the violence implicit in the Hegel-Heidegger-Sartre dialectic. Although he never, so far as I have been able to find, mentioned the Algerians specifically in reference to the Other, Levinas's epistemological and ethical theories point to an alternative to dialectical violence discussed often in reference to colonial warfare. His work, above all, represents the antithesis of Sartre's vision of war as emancipation: "War is not only one of the ordeals—the greatest—of which morality lives; it renders morality derisory." [26]

War, according to Levinas, had particularly serious repercussions for the problem of identity because war "suspended morality" and so threw human identity into chaos:

> The trial by force is the test of the real. But violence does not consist

so much in injuring and annihilating persons as in interrupting their continuity, making them play roles in which they no longer recognize themselves, making them betray not only commitments but their own substance, making them carry out actions that will destroy every possibility for action. Not only modern war but every war employs arms that turn against those who wield them. It establishes an order from which no one can keep his distance; nothing henceforth is exterior. War does not manifest exteriority and the other as other; it destroys the identity of the same. (21)

Consumed by the importance of war in 1961, Levinas shared Lévi-Strauss's concern about a totality in which violence answered to violence. For both Lévi-Strauss and Levinas, Sartre's view of totality and history hermetically sealed off the Other from other Others, thus reducing the individual to stasis. In other words, in a totality where the "ultimate meaning counts," the individual's actions would appear "in the already plastic forms of the epic" (22). This ontological plasticity denied individuals responsibility for their actions, and it proposed that violence would be part of the "epic" of imperial warfare.

This point was critical because the West was experiencing a crisis of morality that directly affected the lives of the colonized. "The peace of empire issued from war rests on war. It does not restore to alienated beings their lost identity." Philosophers confronting empire had to reintroduce the idea of infinity to address the issues of identity and morality. Levinas did this by concentrating on eschatological meaning, which allowed individuals to think of their relations with other individuals as "being beyond the totality or beyond history, and not as being beyond the past and the present." Eschatology was even more important because it alone could extract humans from the "totality of wars and empires" (23). By focusing on the "vision" of eschatology and the Cartesian notion of infinity, Levinas understood subjectivity as being rooted in the very notion of infinity. The goal, Levinas argued, in moving away from the violence of totality was to illustrate how subjectivity allowed for and, in fact, mandated "welcoming the other, as hospitality" (27).[27]

Moreover, directly opposed to Sartre, Levinas argued that the concept of infinity, not totality, allowed for the possibility of "activity and theory" (27). This was a crucial point because Levinas also challenged the idea of praxis. It was also important because Levinas wanted to ensure that consciousness would not be thought of as equating "being with representation." In specific reference to Heidegger, Levinas here was trying to avoid the ontological reduction of the Other to the same. Again, the idea of infinity, which meant acknowledging the Other's radical and insurmountable stance, was, according to him, the only way to arrive at the possibility of ethics.

Levinas also opposed Sartre's fundamental ontology as presented in *Being and Nothingness* because Sartre's ontology deprived "the known being of its alterity" (42). However, there were parallels between Levinas and other thinkers discussed above. For example, Lévi-Strauss believed that Sartre's use of ontology posed a danger because Sartre always placed the Other in a position sealed off from others. Similarly, Levinas argued that ethics required both recognition of and respect for the Other, even at the expense of individual freedom. The idea of freedom *from* Others posed substantial problems for the possibility of ethics, and Levinas demanded that this idea be eradicated prima facie.

Most important, Levinas claimed, the issue of the Other had been wrongly analyzed by Sartre, especially the later Sartre of the *Critique*. Violence was *not* attributable to the Self-Other dialectic. Violence represented the breakdown of the moral code, not the celebration of man's all-or-nothing question for humanity. The reason for this was simple. For Levinas, ethics were derived from the calling into question of "my spontaneity by the presence of the Other" (42). This prohibited the reduction of the Other to the same via the concept of Being and thus opened the possibility of ethics by calling Sartre's very notion of history into question. "When man truly approaches the Other he is uprooted from history" (52). History was therefore not a dialectical source of conflict but something to overcome.

In the same way, Jacques Berque offered his own historical alternative to the radicalism of Sartrian philosophy. He did this by using the concept of the Other; however, unlike Sartre, he realized the danger (if not impossibility) of postulating the idea of a new identity through violence. Rather than neglecting the Arab-Islamic dimensions of decolonization, Berque analyzed them historically. As the French-Algerian War concluded, Berque's *Le Magreb entre deux guerres* (1962) (*French North Africa: The Maghrib Between Two World Wars*) offered the most comprehensive analysis of Algerian and North African history. Distancing himself from intellectuals such as Sartre, Berque claimed that the problem confronting many intellectuals was that they were acting in "bad faith" by trying to shed their "imperialistic egoism" while "identifying themselves with 'the Other,' which implies the failure to recognize this difference." [28] Perhaps this bad faith (Sartre's, for example) could be reduced, he suggested, to epistemological imperialism or to a misunderstanding of history, especially the meaning of modernity. Since modernity was marked by "mutual exchange and conflict," the very division between observer and observed had been altered to the point that it was "no longer valid" (16). Hence the idea of difference had become both stronger and weaker: stronger in that conflicts such as the French-Algerian War highlighted distinctions between the West and North Africa and weaker in that the principle of self-awareness reminded "mankind of its unity."

Even more pressing, Berque wrote, since colonialism and decolonization had become the most important questions of the twentieth century, intellectuals' approaches to these issues would seriously affect their own future. As long as Muslims and Europeans continued to deny each other's place in the history of decolonization, there would be little possibility of resolving some of the fundamental questions now confronting everyone (99). This did not mean that North Africans were not affected, which Sartre tended to argue, by their religious considerations. For example, in writing about Tunis in 1961, Berque noted that "The very appearance of the town thus reminds us immediately of that key which serves to interpret the whole of contemporary Islam: a two-fold questioning of The Other and of oneself" (189). Berque explained this in basic terms such as the very visible effort of changing the names of streets from "Rue de l'Église" to "Rue de la Mosquée" (190).

Berque, who had learned his historical methods from the Annales school, took great pains not to erase or generalize the historical and local dimensions of North African history. This put him in direct opposition to Sartre's ahistorical method, which worked from the general to the specific in an extremely functionalistic manner. Berque was concerned with a history of the relationship between Europe and North Africa, but he did not believe eliminating Europe and European culture from North Africa could create an entirely new North Africa. Yet Berque did think that "European domination merely reflected, and to a certain extent usurped, the expansion of technical culture. Now this expansion brought with it social and mental relations historically in advance of the civilization which it affected. . . . The so-called 'civilizing' character of colonization resulted not only from its direct achievements but still more from the reactions it aroused in the native population" (331). Consequently, nationalism had to be understood as a response to domination linked to technical culture—a view that incidentally directly contradicted Tillion's. In line with Aron's criticism of

Sartre, Berque continued, the problem with the French was that, reared in "the French Jacobin tradition, they were saved from chauvinism only by an internationalism itself in advance of nationalist aspirations." This helped explain the historical move of the French left to internationalist aspirations for the colonies and why many French leftists (and nationalist intellectuals such as Fanon) had misunderstood the real (local) dimensions of the conflict.

Despite the various misunderstandings of the French left and nationalists, it was really the local European settler community, the "administrators, colons in Algeria and petit blancs" who undoubtedly "bore the blame, rather than France itself," for the eventual eruption of the conflict in North Africa (383). By squandering their achievements and hoarding their privileges, the Europeans had been granted "carte blanche to exploit the country" (387). As many intellectuals had done throughout the conflict, Berque argued that two visions of France had grown up side by side in the Maghrib: the ideal of France and French civilization and the reality of the exploiting, abusive colonial France. The result of this contradiction was clear:

> The day would come when the tension between the two would become intolerable; in other words, when the growing influence of French models, among them those of the Revolution and the Resistance, would have lost all plausible connection with the colonial situation. And then, as other hitherto repressed or down-trodden forces emerged, offended Arabism would unite with disappointed pro-French sympathies to produce a terrible explosion. (386)

The contradictions of the colonial situation, according to Berque, hinged on the problem of identity. The colons realized that they would have to adapt their identity to that of the local Algerian population, but they never completed the process. The Algerians were also alienated from the dominant colonial community and were thought of only as objects to be manipulated and whose land should be appropriated. [29] Thus the Algerian was kept at a distance to be excluded as the Other, but that was precisely the problem with the colonial system. "Excluding any future for 'the Other,' it jeopardized its own future" (388).

Berque's most important point was to demonstrate that the origins of the conflict were local concerns about colonialism in Algeria, not external ones such as the Middle East, pan-Arabism, and pan-Islamism. Although he did not deny the influence of the Middle East on the current crisis, he did insist that "the nationalist movement was based to a large extent on what it was fighting" (389). Since the nationalists fought against French colonialism and French repression, nationalism mirrored, in this sense, its French counterpart.

The systemic contradictions of colonialism and its sheer anachronism ultimately forced France to answer unanswerable questions. This did not mean, Berque concluded, that the "Latin" element (his word to describe the power politics of the Roman, and by extension French, empire) of the Maghrib would forever disappear (394). It was clear, Berque claimed, that there would be residues from colonialism that could not be resolved overnight. It was equally clear that, through its own stupidity, France had lost its hand in the region's future. The Maghribi people were now in search of their own authentic identity. Without a doubt, Berque conceded, they would look toward the Middle East. Hence their search for authenticity had arrived at the all-important question of being, of identity. "For this reason, according to one ancient interpretation of the term jihad, holy war, their fight [was] not so much against 'the Other' as against them selves—against a certain aspect of themselves" (394–95).

Decolonization, Otherness, and the Question of Violence: Albert Memmi

In moving from analyses of the Other and alterity to general discussions of identity and violence during decolonization, it is helpful to keep in mind that there was a relationship between writings on the Other and writings on violence. In fact, in some cases, there was significant overlap because many intellectuals wrote on both subjects. The writings that follow concentrate primarily on the relationship of questions of identity and identity politics to anticolonial violence.

One of the most influential theoretical contributions to the question of identity vis-à-vis colonialism and decolonization was Albert Memmi's *Portrait du colonisé précédé du Portrait du colonisateur* (*The Colonizer and the Colonized*), first published as two installments in 1957 in *Les Temps modernes*.[30] Memmi's influence extends well into present-day discussions of identity and, in many ways, subsequently informed the theoretical analysis of internalized and externalized responses to colonial oppression—the colonized's and the colonizer's. Before considering Memmi, however, it is instructive to consider the first appropriation of Memmi's theories by Sartre because Sartre's comments give us, once again, significant insights into a Marxian and militant anticolonialist's uses of identity politics to justify revolutionary action. As will become clear, Sartre's writings on Memmi tell us as much about the former as the latter.

In his introduction to Memmi's book Sartre claimed that Memmi's authority on the question of identity came from a hybrid identity that was "a twofold liability," which meant that Memmi was simultaneously colonizer and colonized.[31] Sartre approached Memmi directly from Memmi's comments about himself. As a Tunisian Jew, Memmi admitted that he had been granted a higher civil status than Muslims in North Africa—yet his status was lower than that of Christian Frenchmen. As a result, he claimed to know the colonizer from the inside almost as well as he knew the colonized. Not surprisingly, this so-called liability, according to Sartre, turned out to be a theoretical blessing because Memmi's hybridized identity could "enlighten others through his self-examination: a 'negligible force in the confrontation,' he represents no one, but since he is everyone at once, he will prove to be the best of witnesses" (xxii).

In bearing witness, Sartre insisted that Memmi exhibited another extraordinary quality: Memmi could use his hybridity to transcend his particular colonizer-colonized identity and move toward the "universal" (xxii).[32] Here Sartre adapted the familiar Hegelian dialectic and the Marxist notion of systems to the age-old Enlightenment claims of universal reason but with a slight twist: Memmi would carry readers toward not universal man but a "rigorous reason enforcing its claims on everyone." Importantly, Sartre acknowledged that Memmi would not agree with his analysis of The Colonizer, and the Colonized because Memmi wrote of the particulars of identity, whereas Sartre aimed to "universalize" identity:

> I have always thought that ideas take form from things and that the ideas are already within man when he awakens them and expresses them to elucidate his situation. The colonizer's "conservatism" and "racism," his ambiguous relations with the mother country—such things are given first, before he revives them into Negro complexes.
>
> Memmi would no doubt reply that he is saying nothing else. I know that. (Does he not say, "The colonial situation manufactures colonizers as it manufactures colonies"? The whole difference between us arises perhaps because he sees a situation where I see a system.) Moreover, perhaps it is Memmi who is right in expressing his ideas in the order of discovery; that is, starting with human intentions and felt relationships, he guarantees the genuineness of his experience. He has suffered first in his relations with others and

in his relations with himself; he encountered the objective structure
in thoroughly studying the contradiction that was rending him, and
he delivers structure and contradiction up to us just as they are, raw
and still permeated with his subjectivity. (xxv)

The genuineness of Memmi's experience—the lived quality of his analysis—lent his writing stinging clarity. Thus, according to Sartre, writing of
his personal suffering at the hands of others, especially the French, rendered Memmi's Self and subjectivity transparent to readers. With this trans-
parency Sartre was able to transform Memmi's definition of the colonizer—
as an illegitimate "usurper" who maintained power by denying the basic
rights of the colonized in Algeria—into a systemic critique of colonialism.[33]
This would mean that the important issue for decolonization, according to
Sartre, was not reconciliation but the necessity for the colonized to reclaim
his identity, dignity, and power in his own country. In short, the first act of
reconstituting colonized identity would be the replacement of reconciliation with rupture.

Indeed, Memmi's analysis of colonial identity points out why rupture is
so important. And at the forefront of this reconstitution of identity are the
issues of time and representation, which made it easier for Sartre to take
Memmi's conception of history and translate it into a Hegelian notion of
history. Being dehumanized by the situation, the colonized had been denied
his place in history; unable to participate in public affairs, the colonized was
outside "the game" (92). However, being forced out of history ultimately
opened up for him the possibility for political subversion because the colonized had not internalized the crucial norms necessary for a functioning
society such as citizenship. Hence, at the most fundamental level, the colonized and the colonizer did not conform to the same ideals of nationality
and citizenship. In the end, according to Memmi, oppression and denial of
basic rights were diseases that could not be remedied and destroyed colonial
society's ability to regenerate itself. And, more important, from within the
dying structures of colonial society, the colonized youth faced the choice
between absolute decay and absolute revolution.

Condemned to the eternal present and excluded from historical processes, the colonized became conscious of their situation through nationalist literature and language, which allowed "the colonized to resume contact with his interrupted flow of time and to find again his lost continuity
and that of his history" (110). In the immediate case, Memmi admitted,

plugging into the "lost continuity" was done with the colonizers' language, French. Nevertheless, nationalist literature pushed the colonized back into time and unmasked the decay of colonial society. Ironically, Memmi wrote (as had Berque), colonialism was responsible for its own death because it had forced the colonized to live outside colonial society and, therefore, kept the colonized from exalting the colony. A foreigner in his own land, the colonized was "dropped off by the side of the road—outside of our time" (112).

For Memmi, placing the colonized back into historical time rendered the outdated politics of integration and pacification (Jacques Soustelle and Robert Lacoste respectively) purely illusory and had tremendous import for the question of identity. Perhaps, he admitted, assimilation might have been possible, but present conditions left the colonized only one option: he will revolt. Abandoning assimilation led to a "recovery of Self and of autonomous dignity" (128). Recovering the Self—as Aron had also once claimed in *Opium of the Intellectuals*—meant that the colonized would use the same techniques, the same demands for justice, that the colonizer used against him. Yet not all aspects of the reconstitution of identity were to be celebrated. For example, when the struggle to recapture the colonized Self turned violent, the colonized's xenophobia and racism surfaced. This, Memmi argued, was not to be credited to the revolt; in fact, this new racism and xenophobia was self-delusory and was used to justify absurd and unnecessary aggression toward others, including those who have been colonized (130). In other words, the colonized had to exercise caution to fight against surges of rage that resulted from the same hatred of others that the colonizer used to justify colonial violence. [34]

The injustice of this excessive aggression toward others had to be understood as an effort to reconstitute the Self. The colonized, having shown repeatedly that he was not capable of assimilating into the dominant society, had come to define himself through the characteristics of difference. As a result, when the colonized asserted himself, he did so on this basis, because "those differences, after all, are within him and correctly constitute his true Self" (132). As the process of self-definition unfolded, the negative aspects of the colonized's culture became positive. Notwithstanding this transformation, recovering fully from the sickness of colonialism required termination of the revolt and colonialism. Only at that point would the postcolonial framework provide the conditions necessary to rethink the relationship between France and its former colonies.

Memmi's closing remarks suggested an alternative to total rupture. Since colonialism was ultimately a European disease, the Europeans could eradicate the sickness. As for the Algerians, overcoming the colonial situation meant that the colonized had to "reconquer himself," to "cease defining himself through the categories of the colonizers" (152). [35] Having achieved this basic freedom by using new categories to define himself, the colonized could achieve freedom from the tyranny of the colonizer's concepts (and of the colonizer directly); the final step was to become a "free man" with all the "ups and downs" of freedom (153).

Memmi's analysis of the colonial situation and the process of decolonization was an important event in the intellectual history of the French-Algerian War. As part of a larger movement by intellectuals to study the war through complex questions of identity, Memmi's work, in many ways, marked an epistemological watershed for popularized discussions of the problem of identity and of analyses of difference.

Frantz Fanon and Jean-Paul Sartre

In his L'An cinq de la révolution algérienne (A Dying Colonialism), published in French in 1959, Frantz Fanon acknowledged, like Memmi, that decolonization had brought unprecedented violence to Algeria and that this violence was a legitimate reaction against the French army and settler intransigence. Yet Fanon argued that regardless of the government's efforts to dominate the Algerian people with "unlimited exploration of new means of terror," the essential task at hand was to determine the degree to which Algerian identity and the Algerian nation had been born during the revolution. [36] At every level, Algerian society was being remade: families, traditions, dissemination and production of information, settler politics, medical practices, and even metropolitan France, he argued, were now being "colonized by Algerian activists"—a claim that evoked Jeanson's comments on the Algerianization of French intellectuals (150). Fanon's Dying Colonialism also described Algerian society as a revolution within a revolution, and Fanon characterized this as being as inevitable as it was positive.

A year later Fanon addressed the problem of violence and identity in a speech delivered at Accra, Ghana. [37] Speaking about both colonized people in general and Algerians in particular, he argued that the colonized's violence could be understood as "three-dimensional" violence, whose components included everyday violence, violence aimed against the past, and violence aimed at the future impregnated with colonial oppression (4). The logic of this three-dimensional violence generated the need of the oppressed to overthrow the colonial regime by any means necessary. In this sense, violence was a manifestation of a basic interior, animalistic rage. The colonized's violence, he said, was becoming, "very simply, a manifestation of his own animal existence. I say animal," he continued, "and I am speaking as a biologist because such reactions are only . . . defens[ive] reactions, translating into the most banal instinct of self-preservation." Since it was clear that the FLN and its principal spokesman, Fanon, were going to use revolutionary violence to achieve liberation, most French intellectuals who listened carefully understood that reconciliation was stillborn.

In 1961 Fanon plunged further into the identity debates with his best-known work, *Les Damnés de la terre* (*The Wretched of the Earth*). Not surprisingly, as with Memmi's *The Colonized and the Colonizer*, Sartre again used a Third World writer to make his case, this time for violence and against reconciliation.[38] In many ways, Sartre's preface to Fanon's *The Wretched of the Earth* finalized the issue of reconciliation during the French-Algerian War. On the surface, Sartre's stated motives for writing about the Algerians' violence differed little from his motives in 1955 and 1956. What had changed was his perception of Algeria's relationship to France. It was clear to Sartre that Algeria would become independent, and he believed (based on his relations with revolutionaries like Fanon) that Algerians wanted nothing to do with France or French culture. In 1961, after the Melun Conference in June 1960 and before the Evian Accords in February–March 1962, it was already evident that the FLN would reject all last-minute reconciliation efforts.[39] However, since the *colons* and the French army refused to admit this and since their violence against the Algerians had gone into a frenzy, it was also evident to Sartre that violence and terrorism were the only means left to Algerians to rid themselves of European colonialism.

Despite his previous pro-reconciliation positions, Sartre no longer advocated protecting the ties between Europe and Algeria. In fact, there is a noticeable distance between French and Algerian culture in his preface. He freely admitted that the ties had to be broken, that the umbilical cord of identity had long since been poisoned by the blood of Western culture. Proof of this necessary break came, according to Sartre, when Algerians realized that they were recreating their identity—their manhood—through violence. This emancipative violence would come at the Europeans' expense. "The child of violence, at every moment he [the 'half-native'] draws from it his humanity. We were men at his expense, he makes himself man at ours: a different man; of higher quality."[40]

Without question, Fanon's work and Sartre's preface to it are two of the most influential writings on violence written during the war. Everywhere in both works, identity surfaces to justify, confirm, and distinguish legitimate *native* violence from illegitimate colonial violence. Situated within the context of an impending independence, Sartre follows violence's "boomerang" effect and offers a radical critique of the French left. In its purest form, the Algerians were using revolutionary violence of the "half-native" in order to "recreate" their identity (21). In recreating their identity, the ex-natives could force the Europeans to reevaluate European identity.

European identity aside, what was really important in Fanon's work according to Sartre was that the Third World found *itself* and spoke "*itself* through his voice" (10). As the mouthpiece for the Third World, Fanon was the first person (except for Sorel) since Engels to delineate the process of history (14). The process of history, in turn, revealed the emergence of the dehumanized half-native as fulfilling a dialectical prophecy of violence that was a response to the original European oppression. Fanon's text, as Sartre pointed out, completely reassessed the problem of Algerian identity. This is in fact what Fanon proposed in *The Wretched of the Earth*.

Fanon went the furthest of the theorists by hypothesizing that it was possible to erase colonial identity through anticolonial violence. In other words, the process of decolonization created a tabula rasa of human identity in Algeria. He said the revolution meant a "veritable creation of new men."[41] Not surprisingly, he also wrote that violence would be a fundamental aspect of the tabula rasa. "At the level of individuals, violence is a cleansing force. It frees the native from his Inferiority complex and from his despair and inaction; it makes him fearless and restores his self-respect" (94). The new men would reject all residues of Western culture. Wanting to destroy the boundary of identity that separated the colonizer from the native, the native would simply bury colonial society. For this reason, the native showed great enmity for "Western culture," so much so that when he heard it mentioned he would pull "out his knife—or at least make, sure that it is within reach" (43).

Returning to his attacks against the French left who clung to Western values, Fanon argued that these leftists refused to admit that reconciliation was not possible. This was based on the simple truth that the liberals did not understand that once colonial exploitation was removed, Europeans would have no reason to remain in Algeria. Moreover, and more important, the liberals did not understand that the guiding ideas of Western liberalism—"the triumph of the human individual, of clarity, and of beauty—had become lifeless, colorless knickknacks" (47). Divorced from the brutal reality of violence that hid behind liberalism's mask, these foundational ideas of liberalism were simply "dead words." Europeans did have a role to play in the creation of the new men. Yet to be beneficial during decolonization "the European peoples must first decide to wake up and shake themselves, use their brains, and stop playing the stupid game of the Sleeping Beauty" (106).

It is unclear what Fanon expected Europeans to do once they awakened. He provided no incentives for them to have further dealings with the liberated "natives," not even on the level of commerce. Perhaps Fanon, despite his hyperbole and revolutionary rhetoric, realized that the Third World was more dependent on the West than he would have wanted. Certainly he feared that the capitalist impulse would surge again in Algeria following the war. What he overlooked was the role violence would continue to play in postcolonial society. Hence, although he clearly feared that the Algerian bourgeoisie would mimic the old colonial regime (171), he showed no concern about the possibility that Algerians would mimic the extreme revolutionary violence of the FLN for years to come.[42]

In essence, Fanon wanted to avoid the possibility of giving birth to a stillborn revolution that would replicate the capitalistic social ills of colonial society, but he remained blind to the long-term effects of the revolutionary violence on Algerian identity. Instead he focused on how the prosperity of the revolution would be ensured by the people who *were* the revolution; with this in mind, the intelligentsia in underdeveloped countries had to educate the masses politically and socially. In opposition to European liberalism and reminiscent of the rhetoric of Robespierre and Saint Juste, Fanon argued that, in this new society, the talented or "exceptional" individual could not be cultivated because the goal was to "uplift the people" (197). Curiously, like the Enlightenment credo that suggested that men became men through rationality, in Fanon's logic Algerians were not fully human until they had been converted to the revolutionary creed: "We must develop their brains, fill them with ideas, change them and make them into human beings."[43] Not surprisingly, this political education required ethnicity, or what Fanon called "tribes," to be checked. The "tribalization of central authority" and an "ethnic dictatorship" could destroy the revolution. Hence the revolutionary intellectuals and politicians would have the difficult task of educating the masses, blocking "tribalization" of authority, and preventing the growth of a national bourgeoisie.

The ultimate product to be achieved in the aftermath of liberation was the construction of a national culture, not adoption of pan-African, pan-Arab, or pan-Islamic culture. As such, Algeria's politicians and intellectuals would have to exhibit care regarding the reappropriation of history, especially if it concerned Islam and African culture. The move back to Islam, Arabism, and Africanism resulted from the past colonial lies about the history of the country before colonial conquests. It was understandable, according to Fanon, that men would be drawn to these movements as unifying forces. But the Algerian nationalist leaders would have to consider extranational histories and movements without losing sight of the nation. If they did prefer African unity over nationalism, they would have been hopelessly led up a "blind alley" (214). Here Fanon's conception of Algerian identity was an artifact of his revolutionary theory. Selfhood was, for him, the expression and the lifeline of the revolution. The nation depended in toto on the Self's identification with it. Self-consciousness and self-awareness were, therefore, essential to national culture: "The consciousness of Self is not the closing of a door to communication. Philosophic thought teaches us, on the contrary, that it is its guarantee. National consciousness, which is not nationalism, is the only thing that will give us an international dimension" (247).

If self-consciousness was the determining factor in nationalism, revolutionary violence was simply part of the natural and emancipative logic of the French-Algerian War. According to Fanon, the revolution had become part of Algerian identity. The ideal of the Algerian nation had been so firmly implanted in the Algerians' minds that Algeria, as an ideal, had become an essential aspect of Algerian identity. Fanon wrote: "The Algerian nation is no longer in a future heaven." Focusing on psychological transformations of the Algerian people by nationalism, he continued, Algeria "is no longer the product of hazy and fantasy-ridden imaginations. It is at the very center of the Algerian man. There is a new kind of Algerian man, a new dimension to his existence" (30).

Fanon argued that revolutionary action created a new man. Fanon did not dwell on the lasting effects of violence on Algeria, nor did he attempt to account for the structural embeddedness (unless dealing with capitalism) of traditional Algerian culture in his new man. For Fanon, the genius of revolutionary action rested on its ability to fundamentally and swiftly erase ingrained psychological dimensions of oppression on Algerian identity, which had suffered generations of colonial usurpation. The revolution's power resided "henceforth in the radical mutation that the Algerian has undergone" (32). In other words, the power of the revolution would rise or fall as transformations in Algerians' identities occurred.

In concluding The Wretched of the Earth, Fanon made it clear that Algeria and other colonized nations did not want reconciliation with Europe. "Come, then, comrades," he wrote, "the European game has finally ended; we must find something different" (312). Since the United States had tried and failed to create something better from European ideas, the new man did not want to create a "third Europe" (313). Turning his back on Europe, Fanon urged his "comrades" to do the same in order to achieve the ideal of humanity, which Europe had prophesied but failed to deliver. Fanon confessed that he would be asking his comrades to invent a new identity and enter unexplored territories of man. This search was itself an act of courage: "For Europe, for ourselves, and for humanity, comrades, we must turn over a new leaf, we must work out new concepts, and try to set afoot a new man" (316).

Since Fanon's Manichaeanism and conceptual rejection of European ideas was such an integral part of his mythical new man, it is important to ask why French intellectuals such as Sartre were so taken with his work. Politically, the French avant-garde left (to which Sartre belonged) had curious reasons for aligning itself with the FLN, and the Fanon-Sartre union symbolizes the ultimate unhealthy marriage, a marriage of convenience as it were, between the French left and the FLN. France could, Sartre claimed in the preface, benefit from reading Fanon's provocative text. But Sartre acknowledged in interviews that the French left could also profit from the French-Algerian War.

As mentioned above, Sartre spelled out in the Critique his belief that there was a universal proletarian revolution afoot and that the Algerian revolution was part of it. Hence any cooperation between the French and Algerians would have to be revolutionary in nature. For example, when Sartre spoke of the French youth in an interview in 1960, he claimed that student movements had been important in maintaining contacts between Muslim and French students. [44] In addition, he pointed out that workers' unions played the most crucial roles in maintaining contact between the two communities. In order for the revolution—in France and Algeria—to advance (during and after the war) "it was necessary to create a liaison and a solidarity between the French workers and Algerians" (2). When asked if this did not have an unpatriotic quality to it, Sartre replied that, after the decline of the notion of internationalism following World War I, it was necessary for the French left to appeal to the "underdeveloped world" to revive internationalism:

> In the face of the awakening of the underdeveloped world, the left should on the contrary restore internationalism. It is a primordial question. The French left should be in solidarity with the FLN. Their types are after all connected. The victory of the FLN would be the victory of the left. I have always been a partisan of the independence of Algeria, and it is, according to me, the only internationalist position possible for the left because it is precisely a matter of relations with a certain nationalism of the colonized countries which is rising. (2)

It is important to understand exactly how Sartre intended to use the Algerian revolution as a life support for the French left and a means for the left to resuscitate its imperiled legitimacy. In an interview given to La Voie communiste in February 1961, he pushed the theme further by asking why so many "petit bourgeois intellectuals" were repelled by "the idea of direct negotiation with the FLN."[45] The answer was simple: because the FLN represented a "real revolution, not only nationalist but also social." The violence implied in this "real revolution" should have been understood as "just violence, an anticolonial violence of a disfavored class that many are afraid to deal with in the revolution. They want Algeria for the Algerians as long as it belongs to the bourgeois Algerians."

As long as it was the so-called Third World proletariat that took power, Sartre was for an Algerian Algeria. This, of course, had special significance for the notion of political reconciliation, especially as it applied to the question of assimilation. No one, he claimed, "except a few Muslims at a time when they were not ready to take a role in the revolution," really believed in assimilation. Since assimilation was as undesirable as it was impossible, it was necessary to encourage solidarity between the French workers and the Algerian super-exploited. This was such a pressing issue, he argued, that there were but two immediate and real objectives to meet today: demystification of de Gaulle's referendum and "the fundamental campaign of solidarity, in actions, between the Algerian Revolution and the French workers." This notion of solidarity, Sartre claimed, had motivated intellectuals to draw up the Manifesto of the 121. As he said, "one of the reasons motivating me to sign [the Manifesto] was precisely that we need today a whole series of radical stands, which, whether they're followed or not, make people express their solidarity."

For intellectuals who opposed Fanon's depiction and Sartre's exaltation of violence, the idea of creating solidarity through violence was a flagrant and scandalous political game. Jean Daniel, as a Jewish pied noir who had taken a moderate position concerning negotiations between the FLN and the French state, disputed Sartre's and Fanon's calls for revolutionary violence. Daniel claimed that this really translated into the idea of revenge, which would not help get to the next crucial step of political negotiations. Daniel noted in L'Express: "The colonized's knowledge of his power to avenge suffices to resuscitate his dignity." [46] If any real progress was to be made, it would have to be at the negotiation tables and not through violence. In addition, Daniel attacked Sartre and the French left for appropriating the Algerian revolution for their own self-rejuvenation. By appropriating Algerians in this dubious manner, he argued, the radical left compromised the more important issue of world peace in order to spin illusory and harmful notions of Third World revolution.

In his journal La Blessure, on December 8, 1961, Daniel went still further and wrote that after hearing of Fanon's death he felt that The Wretched of the Earth was obviously the work of a man "condemned" to death who cared little about the effects of his theories on the living. [47] "So Fanon was able to work sufficiently in order to leave something that is not himself, which was already not he, a useful presence for others which is not his own." This was not to say that Daniel did not respect Fanon; in fact, he admitted that he did. Unfortunately, Daniel lamented, Fanon would become a "saint" in Algeria because Fanon had "bothered everyone, because he [had] upset everyone, myself included as I write these lines" (66).

If Daniel thought Fanon's text was bothersome, he found Sartre's preface even more disturbing. Daniel commented that Sartre's justifications for anticolonial violence—which affirmed Algerian identity by killing Europeans—was the worst form of "verbal masturbation!" (67). Sartre's endorsement of Fanon's call to violence was frivolous because one could not justify one's existence by killing other men: "If I kill, if I could, I would be denied; I would deny all men. This would include the rebel Aimé Césaire who presents himself thus: 'My name: offended; my first name: humiliated; my state: revolted; my age: Stone Age' " (67).

What was for Daniel perhaps most discouraging about the Fanon-Sartre duo was that neither Fanon nor Sartre truly understood what types of fruits their absurd theories would bear. In fact, neither could fathom the damage their writings could have on the Third World. If nationalists tried to implement the ideas sketched in The Wretched of the Earth, it could force the Third World into "convulsions." The result could be uncontrollable murdering because "after having found it necessary to kill the colonist, they will find it indispensable to kill those among them who refused to kill. The redemptive assassin will be worse than the crimes of Stalin." The simple fact, according to Daniel, was that Fanon had penned a "terrible book, terribly revealing, and terribly foretelling of barbaric justice." Both Fanon and Sartre had simply supplied unscrupulous terrorists with an identity politics that allowed a new identity to be forged through the act of killing others.[48]

Sartre could anoint this delusional vision of violence with the benedictory pen of a righteous French intellectual only because he lived in abstractions. "For Sartre," Daniel noted in his journal on January 3, 1962, "the Arab is abstract. He sees in him [the Arab] only the oppressed, the humiliated, the alienated but almost nothing 'positive', like a Jew who has been saved from the look of 'anti-Semitism' " (86).[49] The problem with this, Daniel continued, was that Sartre knew exclusively the men of the FLN, the "revolutionaries" who looked like the "French Marxists." This meant that Sartre was profoundly ignorant of Algeria and the "Arab problem" in general. In part, the reason for this miscomprehension was that Sartre's own view of the Algerians came from Frantz Fanon, who was neither Algerian, nor North African, nor French. Fanon was, in short, equally ignorant of "Arabism, Islam, and even the Mediterranean," and his influence on Sartre had been completely negative. It was truly a case of the blind leading the blind, who—though seeming to follow the blessed path to revolutionary salvation—were, in fact, leading the faithful to a grotesque spectacle of cannibalistic fratricide. Together both Sartre and Fanon had neglected the "Arab-Islamic determinations" of the Algerian conflict out of their "passion" to make Algeria fit their "revolutionary and abstract universal" (86). In other words, while Sartre and Fanon certainly believed that they were correct in diagnosing the ills of colonial identity, not all or even most French and Algerian intellectuals agreed.

Pierre Bourdieu

One of the most important theorists who unequivocally rejected Fanon's and Sartre's analysis of colonial identity and anticolonial violence was Pierre Bourdieu. In 1961 Bourdieu—the young French sociologist then at the University of Algiers—once again entered the conversation among intellectuals regarding the source of the Algerian conflict's violence in an essay entitled "Revolution within the Revolution," published in the January edition of *Esprit*.[50] Along with a preface by Raymond Aron, this essay was added to the English edition of *The Algerians*. Aron noted in the book's preface that objectivity was especially necessary because it was now time to admit that the French-Algerian War had been a major strain on France: "For almost eight years the drama of Algeria weighed on the French like an obsession, a guilt, and also like a duty. It precipitated the fall of a regime, split a nation asunder. It imperiled domestic peace and spread throughout the mother country a climate of passion and crime. It could no longer be considered a simple episode in a historically irresistible movement called 'decolonization.'"[51] Rather, the war had become a "tragic moment in the history of France." It was therefore up to those who cared about the "destiny of France" to look to Bourdieu's work in order to find in it the "data necessary for reflection and judgment." Not surprisingly—after his own turn against reconciliation in 1957—Aron argued that the most critical observation Bourdieu's readers must be prepared to accept was that the differences between the French *colons'* "culture" and the culture of the various groups of Algerians expressed "a radical incompatibility" (vi). Hence, for Aron, Bourdieu's work would show decisively that reconciliation was impossible.

Unquestionably, violence was responsible for forcing the collapse of reconciliation, but this collapse was not due to the violence of Algerian nationalists; rather, violence in Algeria was a "logical" part and "completely integrated within the colonial system."[52] Furthermore, Bourdieu wrote that the Algerian revolution was not a product of a few radical nationalists who tyrannized the Algerian masses with violence, so to suggest that the revolution was a result of a "handful of ringleaders" was gross negligence (145). Sociologically the revolt had broad-based support, responding to systematic colonial violence. According to Bourdieu, this meant that the French-Algerian War could not be read as the "mere explosion of aggressiveness and hatred" (149). More to the point, he insisted that even violence expressed in "individual conflicts" was the product of an "objective situation" sociologically constituted in the colonial structure.

Since even individual violence could be interpreted as originating from the objective situation, where did this leave Franco-Algerian relations? And what did violence mean in the context of the identity question? According to Bourdieu, in contrast to Fanon, the Algerians were able to make distinctions between "the true Frenchman" (the "Frenchmen of France") and "the French of Algeria" (151–52).[53] Initially, Algerians had made ontological distinctions among the different types of Frenchmen on the basis of ideal types—the Frenchmen of France believed in and acted on just principles. However, Algerian terrorism and French repression had destroyed any remaining solidarity between French and Algerians. As a result, the war that had been ushered in by objective structures (colonialism) was being transformed by the products of objective situations (revolution).

Like Fanon, Bourdieu recognized that at the heart of the situational and structural transformations of Algerian society, the war produced psychological transformations, which had a profound impact on the identity question. Now, for the first time, the Algerian people had "a voice, a voice capable of saying 'No!'" to colonial relations (157). This being the case, Bourdieu insisted that it was crucial to elucidate this effect on contemporary Algerian culture. Here his analysis also closely paralleled that of Jacques Berque. Bourdieu claimed that one visible effect of the war was erosion of "traditional traditionalism." Traditional traditionalism had originated as an Algerian response to European hegemony and was part of an Algerian identity that had internally rejected colonialism. Colonialism could not fully dominate Algerian identity, and the voice that said "No!" to it came from social actors who could simultaneously borrow and reject aspects of "Western civilization" without "denying [themselves] in the process." The collective appropriations and rejections of Western culture acted as a catalyst for the Algerians' new self-identification and allowed them to experience the feeling of autonomy (163).

Although Bourdieu's structural model of the war emphasized the psychological dimensions of the conflict, he did not want to overstate the importance of subjective transformations within Algerian society."[54] What was perhaps most essential to realize was the extent to which the underlying traditionalism of Algerian society (based on sacred communal values, respect for elders, and the patrilineal system) had been structurally transformed by the war's own internal negative logic. The negative influence destabilized Algerian society and created a gulf, not only between Algerians and the West but also between older and younger generations: "The revolutionary values are those of the younger generation. Schooled by the war, turned towards the future, and completely ignorant of a past to which their elders cannot help remaining attached, the adolescents are often animated (and the part they played in the revolutionary war bears witness to this) by a spirit of radicalism and negativism which often separates them from their elders" (186).

Sociologically, Bourdieu continued, Algeria's youth culture was now part of the society that was to be transformed by the revolution. For example, the new status of women represented one of the most telling breaks within Algerian traditionalism. Given "greater independence" by her new role as a partner in revolution, the Algerian woman was freer to circulate in the ur-ban areas and, importantly, was entrusted with business and administrative affairs. Yet Bourdieu warned that the changing view of women was part of a larger social upheaval and should not be misunderstood. In reality, the changing status of women, the growing distance between the generations, and the rejection of Western values were all the results of the decolonization process. These changes fundamentally altered the social structures and the minds of the Algerian people but had yet to be worked out fully for Algerian society (187).

Bourdieu predicted that Algerian identity and society would be funda-mentally different after the war. However, very much in opposition to Fanon, he insisted that Algeria's leaders could not be naive about the fact that the "whirlwind of violence" had attacked every "vestige of the past" (188). Postcolonial Algeria would be highly revolutionary "because it [had] been highly revolutionized." Because Algerian society would be completely chaotic and the situation so explosive, Bourdieu concluded that it was likely that the newborn nation would have to choose between "chaos" and "an original form of socialism" capable of responding to the unprecedented needs of a postcolonial situation (192).

Where Bourdieu differed most from Fanon was on the relationship be-tween theory and practice. As a practicing academic sociologist, Bourdieu believed that it was one thing to analyze an objective situation and quite another to engage in revolutionary speculation, masquerading it as a socio-logical analysis as Fanon constantly claimed he was doing. Not surprisingly, Bourdieu (as a social scientist, not as a revolutionary) offered a cautious and objective evaluation of the revolution and, as he would say later, thought Fanon's analysis of Algerian identity and the revolution was dangerous and naive because it remained "speculative" and celebratory in nature."[55] Ac-cording to Fanon, postcolonial Algeria would free Algerians, both men and women, from an oppressive traditionalism, even an Islamic traditionalism.

Fanon (as an atheist) had no place for Islam in his speculative postcolonial society. According to Bourdieu, Fanon's and Sartre's incomprehension of the Algerian revolution went beyond the mere misunderstanding of the Islamic dimensions of Algerian society. In a 1994 interview with me Bourdieu put it this way: Fanon's The Wretched of the Earth and Sartre's preface to it not only were inaccurate about Algeria, they were hazardous because they used "Parisian" ideas to explain Algeria. Sartre's preface, Bourdieu said, is a "completely irresponsible text."[56] "Sartre says no matter what," without any regard for the truth. Likewise, what

> Fanon says corresponds to nothing. It is even dangerous to make the Algerians believe the things he says. This would bring them to a utopia. And I think these men contributed to what Algeria became because they told stories to Algerians who often did not know their own country any more than the French who spoke about it, and, therefore, the Algerians retained a completely unrealistic utopian illusion of Algeria. . . .
>
> [T]he texts of Fanon and Sartre are frightening for their irresponsibility. You would have to be a megalomaniac to think you could say just any such nonsense. It is true, of course, that I do not have a lot of admiration for these two here . . . even when they are right, it is for bad reasons.

In fairness, Bourdieu did admit that it was very good that both Sartre and Fanon were "against the war," and he agreed with them on this issue. He noted that it was also "very good" that Sartre took the position he did with regard to the "121"; in fact, it was "extraordinary." But the text that accompanied Sartre's position "was propaganda. It was the symbol of intellectual irresponsibility. It was a la mode." Furthermore, on the level of analysis, both Fanon and Sartre used Manichaean categories of identity that were fundamentally absurd in Algeria given its Islamic history and the dispersed agrarian character of Algerian society. Bourdieu stated, "Sartre did this with regard to Algeria." Moreover, he continued,

> The problems of racism [against blacks and against Algerian Muslims] do not present themselves in the same terms. There is a specificity to the racism against blacks, which is very particular. There are corporeal properties. . . . This is absolute racism. In the Algerian case . . . the problems of corporeal identity that Fanon articulated with regard to blacks are not manifested at all in the same fashion.

I have never heard an Algerian present his problems in the same terms as blacks. There is certainly the inferior treatment, and so on, but not on the basis of corporeal identity, on the basis that Fanon writes about. I think this is very important. . . . The black's problems are not the same as the Algerian's problems. For the Algerians, there are poverty, humiliation, the Frenchification, and linguistic issues, but they are not concentrated to the degree to which Fanon claims on corporeality. There is a huge difference. . . . The Algerian women have a relationship with their body that is not the same. I think that the logic that Fanon develops does not have the same importance for the North Africans [Maghrébins] as it does for Fanon.

Bourdieu's comments on Fanon and Sartre are more than a mere difference of opinion. According to Bourdieu's later, postindependence interpretation, what made Fanon so important in the formation of an independent Algerian state under Colonel Boumediene was the negative effect Fanon's miscomprehension of the revolution had on postcolonial Algerian society. Because Fanon placed an emphasis on the revolutionary and not the traditional residues of Algerian society, his analysis was anti-Algerian, or nonspecific, meaning that Fanon's writings universalized and depersonalized the Algerian revolution by making it stand for something that it was not. Fanon's imposition of non–North African and corporeal categories of identity on Algerian Muslims only complicated matters. Furthermore, Fanon's suspicion of colonialism translated into a general suspicion (if not contempt) of traditional Algerian society because it had been so deeply contaminated by colonialism. In this context, traditionalism posed a tremendous obstacle to so-called true revolutionary activity.

There was perhaps an even greater danger in Fanon's analysis. Not only had Fanon misunderstood the importance of Islam in Algerian society and undervalued the importance of the nuanced and hybrid notions of colonial identity, he promoted the fatal and critical belief that the Algerian "peasantry" represented a "revolutionary class."[57] It was true, and Bourdieu had written it himself, that the Algerian revolution had broad-based support from the peasants. However, the peasants in Algeria were far from constituting a revolutionary class. Here Bourdieu also conceded that Fanon was not alone in his misunderstanding of peasant society. Most of the "Western scholars," Bourdieu noted, "were pulled" by Mao Tse-tung's ideas about the peasantry in China and were convinced that the Chinese model could be grafted onto other emerging nations. "It was the Chinese myth that was forced on the Algerian reality."

According to Bourdieu, reality in Algeria during the revolution was clearly incompatible with Fanon's writings. Bourdieu realized early on that Algerian leaders were all too eager to try to apply Fanon's notions of the avant-garde revolutionary peasantry. In response to these developments, he immediately published *Travail et travailleurs en Algérie* (1963) and *Le Déracinement: La crise de l'agriculture traditionnelle en Algérie* (1964, with Abdelmalek Sayad), in order to help Algerians make the best choices. In truth, Bourdieu stated, the "Algerian peasantry" was "overwhelmed by the war, by the concentration camps, and by the mass deportations. To claim that it was a revolutionary peasantry was completely idiotic." "Sartre and Fanon never understood this." Even worse, Fanon's and Sartre's theories were "maddening" because they had "consequences." "Unfortunately, very important Algerian leaders . . . lived in this utopian delirium, which claimed that everything would be changed by the revolution." The irony of this utopia, Bourdieu said, is particularly sad for contemporary Algeria. Algerian leaders were so eager to reconstitute Algerian society and Algerian identity that they uncritically accepted this "pretentious foolishness." The end result was that Sartre's and Fanon's visions of revolutionary identity and Algerian society epistemologically recolonized Algeria's political leadership after the war. The lingering results are, according to Bourdieu, transparent in many of Algeria's social and political conflicts today. In effect, these conflicts have been influenced by a political Manichaeism and a failed revolutionary utopian socialism. In other words, authenticity, violence, difference, and a lack of hospitality for the Other suggest that Fanon's myth of the new man was strong enough to persuade leaders to follow but naive enough to lead them into one of the most regrettable political cul-de-sacs of the twentieth century.[58]

In conclusion, the questions of sameness or difference were thus important aspects of the identity debates during the French-Algerian War. As we have seen, many intellectuals found the concept of the Other particularly attractive for describing the complexities of the identity question. However, as has been described throughout this work, intellectuals had a wide variety of motives for choosing words and concepts to explain their own feelings on issues that they believed directly impacted their own national community's future. The concept of the Other was in this sense no exception, for it was deeply implicated in the debates over reconciliation and France's future in Algeria. For each of the various intellectuals who used the concept, it was an epistemological means to address the identity question and express their ideological commitments and values.

Similarly, attempts to condemn or condone political violence in Algeria on the basis of the question of identity were extremely contentious and prone to bring out a whole host of political concerns. For the proponents of nonviolence, the Other could be an effective analytical tool. As such, it could be used to help people understand the depths of torment Algerians suffered as a result of colonialism, not as a means to justify tormenting and killing the French colonists. Yet for those who supported anticolonial violence, identity was already in and of itself deeply impregnated by politics. The primary concern of which was to exorcize—through violence—the colonial system from the psyche of the colonized. The Other was in this sense a different and far more lethal kind of tool.

However, as we have seen, the vast majority of intellectuals were committed to understanding how the issues of Otherness and identity related to the process of decolonization. By and large, although these writers repudiated the colonial system, they did not believe that unmitigated violence was Algeria's key to a better postcolonial world. Unfortunately, in these disputes, Othering was often used as a justification for extreme violence. Some, though not all, intellectuals fell prey to the desire to use the Algerian revolution and difference for their own revolutionary agenda.[59] Lamentably this is also one of the lasting legacies of the French-Algerian War, and it remains in Algeria to this day. Using sophisticated theories of *difference* (ethnic, religious, and linguistic) to justify violence became (and still is today) the hallmark of an ongoing, uncivil war.

8. THE LEGACY OF VIOLENCE

Reflections on the Revolution in Two Nations

The fundamentalists invoke Islam to justify a priority and legitimize all their words and deeds. But I don't think any religious text, whatever it may be, contains within itself any orders about how it should be interpreted. It is what men make of it, depending on their political or social ambitions, and on their psychological makeup.

KHALIDA TOUMI, 1995

How to withstand mourning for our friends, our colleagues, without first having sought to understand the why of yesterday's funerals, those of the Algerian utopia? The white of a sullied dawn.

ASSIA DJEBAR, 1995

Today, the long-term impact of the identity politics that surfaced throughout the French-Algerian War cannot be ignored. This is especially true in the postcolonial and post–September 11 world. When I published the first edition of *Uncivil War* in the summer of 2001, I already believed (and still do) that the war had fundamentally transformed how the French and Algerians would think of national identity, their relationship to a joined colonial past, to Islam, and finally to each other.

As a historian who spent much of his adult life in France, I had, to be sure, the benefit of a historian's sixth sense. During the 1980s and the 1990s, when I continued to live on and off in Paris over the course of several years, I could see firsthand the French struggling to come to terms with the memory of the Algerian conflict. The past several years have shown that France is no nearer to turning the page on the Algerian question than it was in 1962. In fact more controversial information about the use of torture by France has continued to emerge since *Uncivil War* first went to press, and these revelations have prompted me to add this new chapter. I offer this as a set of reflections on recent history in which I attempt to sketch out some ways the war has continued to haunt French considerations of national identity.

The reality of colonial violence has no doubt remained a grave problem in France because it has simply taken the French state far too long to acknowledge its actions during the war. This delay has, as William Cohen demonstrated, allowed for a very striking separation of the French public from the French state vis-à-vis the war, with French intellectuals and the public engaging in wide-ranging debates on the war and the French state remaining obstinately reticent. This separation remains all the more clear because French intellectuals had been vocal in their denunciations of torture since the mid-1950s and continue to press the state today for answers. The state, however, has been at pains to keep the past buried and even irretrievable.

I believe it is equally important in this new edition of *Uncivil War* to outline briefly some of the ways that Algeria attempted to assume a new postcolonial identity. On this question, I have the benefit of a historical record showing how the notion of "authenticity," as announced by anticolonial theorists such as Frantz Fanon during the revolution, could be recast as a major cultural issue by Algerian politicians after independence, including Ahmed Taleb Ibrahimi (the first minister of education and the man who once criticized Albert Camus in an open letter written from prison). This historical record also shows how the question of authenticity would resurface with the Islamist movement in the 1980s and 1990s. This is to say that authenticity has, in debates over language, democracy, Islam, and ethnicity, remained the basis for much of Algeria's postcolonial cultural contests and political strife. Yet it is important to keep in mind, as I argued earlier in this book and elsewhere, that the seeds of Algeria's future internal conflicts were clearly sown in the late 1950s and early 1960s, when it became clear to many observers that Algeria was well on its way to political and social upheaval.[1] Even before the Evian Accords were signed in mid-March 1962 and Algeria's independence from France was formalized on July 3, Algeria had begun to move in the direction of a militaristic, authoritarian, one-party, socialist state that, in the words of Hugh Roberts, acted primarily as a "façade party" until it had finally outlived its usefulness.[2]

That France and Algeria would continue to wrestle with the legacy of the French-Algerian War should hardly come as a surprise. After all, among the many wars of national liberation during the era of decolonization, Algeria's was by far one of the most brutal and celebrated. As in many other colonial conflicts throughout the Third World (to use the term crafted at Bandung in 1955 by the agents of decolonization themselves), the identity politics that came along with decolonization in metropolitan France and Algeria have remained central to postcolonial debates about the nation and nationalist politics in both countries. And these debates have taken on added meaning in recent years.

To understand the importance of the shadow cast by colonial violence, I return first to 1962 and to the French writer Jacques Julliard's discussion of how the torture of Algerians would haunt French society. Indeed it can be said that Julliard's essay "La morale en question"—along with Pierre Vidal-Naquet's *Torture: Cancer of Democracy, France, and Algeria, 1954–1962* (1963)—best anticipated the aftereffect of the war on France. Penned for *Esprit* in October 1962—just months after Algerian independence—Julliard's essay (which bears an uncanny resemblance and some important connections to the recent debates about America's use of torture in Iraq) states that while France had begun to forget the "phantoms" of the Algerian conflict, such phantoms "would never disappear."[3] "Today," he noted, "no one discusses seriously the reality of the facts that were furiously contested just a few months ago. No judge protests, even for show, when an officer affirms that he and his colleagues have received the order to torture. The sound is that of realism: all of that is past—and over with." The problem with this attitude was, as Julliard stated, that between four and five million French soldiers served in this conflict, and therefore the problem of a fundamental lack of moral accountability by the French will haunt the nation.

The past could be buried, but the results could not. The soldier who learned how to fight with any means at his disposal, even means that debase himself and the nation, would be conditioned by a "contagious climate and rendered crazy by violence" (361). In the future, Julliard wondered, how could the French (or the modern military) discriminate between Nazi-like actions and actions in the interest of the state? Where would the lines be drawn? Ultimately this ethical confusion would mean that society as a whole would have "assisted with the bankruptcy of a system of moral education." The Algerian conflict, he continued, was a total moral defeat for the French nation, not because Algeria achieved independence but because France had forfeited its morals in the process of defending French North Africa: "The Algerian war revealed us to ourselves: in place of the traditional (and conventional image) of revolutionary France, the country of the rights of man and universal brotherhood, another image has been substituted: that of a petty France, haunted by the spirit of possession and a little too stingy with its means" (362).

In a much more thorough fashion, Vidal-Naquet asked similar questions about how torture had transformed France. As he stated in the opening sentence of *Torture*: "Can a great nation, liberal by tradition, allow its institutions, its army, and its system of justice to degenerate over the span of a few years as a result of the use of torture, and by its concealment and deception of such a vital issue call the whole Western concept of human dignity and the rights of the individual into question?" [4] The answer was simply yes. France had not only degenerated but had allowed its sacred institutions and political structures to be hijacked by the same political necessity that led nations into totalitarianism. This was because the Algerian revolution was an internal problem, and thus France's "machinery of the State" and the "full forces of the nation" could be mobilized. "The willingness to use any means, even torture, was bound to lead to a totalitarian system" (27). The police and the entire administrative apparatus became enmeshed in the application and hiding of torture. Even worse, knowing full well that amnesty would render self-interrogation impossible, the state used amnesty to render the truth unreachable. Hence, by putting an "end to any possible proceedings against the torturers, 'amnesty' set the seal on the hypocritical attitude which the State had always adopted toward this vital problem. It legitimized, a posteriori, actions that the State had neither been able nor willing to stop. The State has, so to speak, decreed an 'amnesty for itself' " (161–62). This would mean, quite clearly, that the only answer to this deliberately created "legal" problem now was "political." And the only honorable political solution was to brand those who had used torture with "some sort of 'national ignominy' " (164).

In addition to the moral quagmire created for France by torture and the state's decision to cover itself with amnesty, the French military (along with the FLN's brutal methods) shared part of the blame for Algeria's premature unraveling because of the sheer terror that military and paramilitary forces brought to bear on the country. After all, once it became clear that the French state was going to negotiate with the FLN, the OAS—as the most organized and violent of the French paramilitary forces—terrorized the civilian populations in Algeria and France in the final years of the war with great effect. As true believers, OAS thugs and killers pursued a private crusade against an independent Algeria and, after the loss of Algeria, against the "treasonous" Gaullist "dictatorship" that had sold out the French colons there. [5] The OAS's war against the French state was taken to extreme measures, including failed attempts to assassinate President Charles de Gaulle, as well as other notables including André Malraux and Jean-Paul Sartre. Before the OAS's schizophrenic rampage was over, it had murdered countless innocent Algerian civilians and set the stage for a profound threat of right-wing violence that lasted in France until 1968.

As I have written elsewhere, this threat of right-wing, if not neofascist, violence only ended in 1968, when the leadership of the reconstituted Conseil National de la Résistance (CNR)—the political wing of the OAS—along with the other imprisoned or fugitive leaders of the OAS, were granted amnesty by de Gaulle. Suddenly and without warning, the three remaining at-large leaders of the CNR—Jacques Soustelle, George Bidault, and Paul Gardy (only Antoine Argoud had been caught, tried, and imprisoned in France)— returned from exile and were allowed to enter France with impunity.

The French state began to forget about the war in very peculiar ways, but now, despite the state's efforts to suppress the truth about torture and colonial crimes, the reality of what happened in Algeria is gradually seeping into the public historical record with a vengeance. One very powerful illustration of how this historical record continues to elude the French state's control is Death Squadrons: The French School (2003), a French documentary film directed by Marie-Monique Robin. As this documentary shows in great detail, members of the OAS and other members of France's elite torturers (especially General Paul Aussaresses, whom we will turn to shortly) became special consultants in the exportation of systematic torture around the world—including to the military juntas in Argentina, Chile, and Brazil as well as to the American military at Fort Bragg in 1961, which was eager to learn the techniques of "interrogation" from the French as it geared up for the impending war in Vietnam.[6]

Perhaps because of the fact that some French officers were already engaged in the business of franchising international torture before the French-Algerian War was even over, it seems fair to say that forgetting (or writing out of the official memory) the numerous crimes committed in Algeria became easier for the French state than forgetting the French crimes of the Vichy era. However, a greater reason is that de Gaulle had decided to grant amnesty to renegade politicians, to known OAS murderers and to military personnel—including those men who had organized failed putsches. Hence de Gaulle's shocking final amnesty decision in 1968—when he lifted the arrest warrants for his own would-be assassins and mutineers—reveals a disturbing pattern of avoidance within the French state. For example, in the spring of 1962, de Gaulle decreed several amnesties for French soldiers and police involved in the war and for the Algerian combatants. As William Cohen has written, amnesty—decided on by de Gaulle for reasons of political exigency—fostered amnesia (by absolving or negating acts) and did little to bring closure to the war. In fact, it was not until 1999 that the French state began to acknowledge that what had happened in Algeria was indeed a real war.[7] Yet as the exiled Algerian historian Mohammed Harbi has said in a recent interview, from his residence in Paris: "They've admitted it was a war but wait! That was because the veterans of Algeria demanded a statue honoring French combatants! It had nothing to do with Algerians" (309).

The cultural, political, and national anxiety about the war has added greatly to the French postcolonial malaise, especially with regard to its North African immigrants.[8] Furthermore, the brutality of the French methods of suppressing the revolution and the deliberate disregard of those crimes (through amnesty) continue to prompt contemporary public discussion in France and abroad. And since the issue of the French military's use of torture has permeated recent debates in France about the effect of decolonization, it is not surprising that General Jacques Massu (commander of the French Tenth Division of Paratroopers during the Battle of Algiers) has often been at the center of these scandals.

In 1962 the publication of Yacef Saadi's memoirs, Souvenirs de la Bataille d'Alger, ignited more controversy. Saadi, the leader of the FLN in Algiers during the so-called Battle of Algiers in 1957, and the man who would appear as himself in Gillo Pontecorvo's classic and recently rereleased film The Battle of Algiers (1966), accused the military of torture and attacked the French for pursuing a brutal, inhumane war against the nationalists. Not wanting to be outdone by this Algerian account, General Massu eventually published his response, La Vraie Bataille d'Alger (1971). As a defense of the French campaign, Massu's reply to Saadi (and the FLN) came very close to being a public justification for the use of torture by the French military during the war, and General Massu made no effort to disguise the fact that the French used torture during the "interrogation" process to get the job done. The job was simply to prevent the terrorists from killing innocent civilians. Furthermore, as Massu phrased it, the "extreme savagery" of the Algerians far outweighed the violence that the French used to get information out of would-be thugs and killers.[9] Massu's book, although penned as a reply to an Algerian FLN leader, provoked several responses, including one from France written by Jules Roy. In his book, J'Accuse le général Massu (1972), Roy indicted Massu (again invoking the Dreyfusard's battle cry, "J'accuse," that became the anticolonial mantra during the Algerian conflict) of dishonoring the French nation and military by allowing for the systemization of torture within the French military arsenal. As Roy stated:

Do you know why I accuse you?

Because the name of Massu has become synonymous with abomination; because one can now confuse the hatred of Massu with hatred of the [French] military. Because when we now try to encourage our youth to serve in the army, they hesitate to run the risk of obeying; because, due to your actions, the scent of our army in the minds of our youth and our intelligentsia is reduced to execration. (90)

Although Massu periodically reappeared in the national media, by far the biggest public storm he caused occurred near the end of his life. As before, his public pronouncements were tied to an Algerian's statements about the conduct of the French military. The most recent controversy involving Massu started in 2000, when Louisette Ighilahriz, an FLN combatant during the war, gave an interview in Le Monde on June 20 in which she accused Massu and another retired French general, Marcel-Maurice Bigeard, of having presided over her torture sessions (which included rape and beatings and which went on for months). [10] However, she also praised the young medical doctor who helped save her life and asked for help in finding him in order to thank him. In reply to Ighilahriz's accusations, General Massu gave an interview in Le Monde on June 22, 2000, in which he finally complied with Jules Roy's three-decades-old request by expressing his regret for sanctioning the use of torture. As General Massu put it in Le Monde: "No, torture was not indispensable in time of war; we could have done without it. When I think of Algeria, it makes me sad, because that is all part of a certain ambiance. We should have done things differently." Without further hesitation, Le Monde continued, the general expressed his "regrets." At the same time, the debate continued to widen in France when other senior French officers broke their silence to either defend or deny the use of torture. On June 22, 2000, General Bigeard even went so far as to denounce Ighilahriz's accusations in her interview with Florence Beauge as "a stream of lies." [11]

Veteran intellectuals from the era of the French-Algerian War again entered the public debate on October 31, 2000. Sickened by the hypocrisy of the recent pronouncements of the French commanders, Pierre Vidal-Naquet, Henri Alleg, and Germaine Tillion among others, referred to as "the Twelve," organized a petition known as "L'Appel des douze" that was published in L'Humanité. The signatories called on French President Jacques Chirac and Prime Minister Lionel Jospin to denounce retroactively the use of torture during the French-Algerian War. The document, entitled "L'appel à la condamnation de la torture durant la guerre d'Algérie," was signed by Henri Alleg, Josette Audin (the wife of Maurice Audin, who was disappeared by the French in 1957), Simone de Bollardière (the widow of General Jacques Paris de Bollardière, who opposed torture during the war and consequently spent ten months under house arrest for his public opposition to the French military's actions), Nicole Dreyfus (a lawyer), Noël Favrelière, Gisèle Halimi (the lawyer for Djamila Boupacha), Alban Liechti (a draft dodger from the war), Madeleine Rebérioux, Laurent Schwartz, Germaine Tillion, Jean-Pierre Vernant, and Pierre Vidal-Naquet. The petition stated that the two peoples on both sides of the Mediterranean would remain "haunted by the horror that marked the Algerian war as long as the truth has not been said or recognized."[12] The Twelve asked for five things: (1) the urgent condemnation of torture, (2) that the truth about the facts be established, (3) the setting aside of a special day for teaching about colonialism in schools, (4) to seek reconciliation between the French and the Algerians, and (5) that a delegation representing the Twelve be met by the president and prime minister. Their request fell on deaf ears.

Meanwhile, General Bigeard, who had been named by Ighilahriz as an overseer of the torture process in her interview in *Le Monde*, went even further a few months later by penning a longer reply to her in the form of his *J'ai mal à la France* (2001), in which he again categorically denied overseeing her torture. While Ighilahriz hoped for some sort of historical closure to old wounds, General Bigeard's words recalled the anger of the war and the military's sense of betrayal. Written nearly forty years after the war as a defense of his actions, General Bigeard's claims in *J'ai mal à la France* sound stale and unseasoned by time: "From the moment that the FLN started its action in 1954, France only had two choices: to fight to the death, or to leave Algeria."[13] But were these really the only choices that the military had?

For Bigeard there had been no question which path the military should pursue, and thus the military was charged, in the face of heinous acts of violence against European settlers, with the protection of the civilian population (as his fictional manifestation in the film *The Battle of Algiers*, Colonel Mathieu, poignantly described it). Moreover, Bigeard continued, the military was charged with police duties during the Battle of Algiers, and during that time, his men never "harassed or inflicted unnecessary violence" (134). Bigeard did admit, however, that the circumstance of having to stop a potential terrorist immediately forced the military to resort to unpleasant "interrogation techniques," including electric shock (181). But he stopped far short of admitting to torture, noting instead that, "[t]hanks to these methods, we were able to check the FLN, despite the fact that its members called us torturers. That's false! The torturers, those were the ones who massacred unarmed civilians with the blind bombs. We didn't like this 'job' at all" (182).

Not surprisingly, but shocking nonetheless, Bigeard recycled some of the very same photographs that first appeared in the Green Book in 1957 under the direction of Robert Lacoste's government in Algeria (covered in detail in chapter 6). Hence, over three decades later, the controversial images of corpses were used again to justify, without remorse, the brutality of the French military; and, in so doing, the Algerian nationalists' humanity was again demonized for the next generation of Frenchmen by the worn-out labels of Muslim fanatics and FLN terrorists. A defiant Bigeard simultaneously reshuffled the photos of mutilated bodies and decried the loss of French patriotism with the age-old refrain that the glories of the France of his youth were being robbed by treasonous bleeding-heart, nonviolent liberalism.

His reply was countered by Louisette Ighilahriz herself in her own book, L'Algérienne (2001), in which she described her torture as overseen by Bigeard and Massu but carried out by another man named Graziani. However, rather than merely laying blame on the French, Ighilahriz's stated intention was to help both nations, Algeria and France, come to terms with the past. As she phrased it:

> With this book, which follows my testimony [from Le Monde], I hope that the truth will break. I hope that the French know that in Algeria, between 1954 and 1962, it was never a question of an operation to "maintain order," nor was it one of "pacification." I write it to recall that there was an atrocious war in Algeria, and that it was not easy for us to achieve independence. Our liberty was acquired at a price of over a million deaths, unknown sacrifices, and a terrible effort of psychological demolition of a people [entreprise de démolition psychologique de la personne humaine]. I say this without hate.
>
> Because the young generations don't know. The grand majority follow [se fie] the official history, now filtrated and disinfected. Now, one cannot elude these tragic years, continue to lie by omission about the subject. . . . Memory is heavy to carry. Atheists or believ-

ers, it pierces both, I hope that we never again hear of mental and physical torture.[14]

A few months after Ighilahriz's story first broke in the summer of 2000 in *Le Monde*, and certainly fully aware that because of the several amnesty deals struck at the end of the Algerian conflict he would be protected from prosecution for torturing, murdering, and "disappearing" Algerians during the war, General Paul Aussaresses brazenly admitted to sanctioning torture during the war and refused to apologize for it. No doubt angry with Massu for expressing his belated regret for ordering torture and the denials of others, Aussaresses decided to make his own public declarations on November 23, 2000, in *Le Monde*.[15] Expressing no contrition whatsoever, he proudly admitted to overseeing torture sessions as well as summary executions of many Algerians. His confessions unleashed a torrent of public debate. As if spurred on by the public's outcries against him, Aussaresses decided to go into more detail about his military views and misdeeds.

General Aussaresses thus joined in the publishing fray with his sensational, best-selling, tell-all memoir, *The Battle of the Casbah: Terrorism and Counter-Terrorism in Algeria, 1955–1957*. Ausseresses's book finally shattered existing illusions about the war and the role of the French state in torture. But far from apologizing, he stated that torture was nothing to be ashamed of. According to him, torture was necessary, systematic, and condoned by the French metropolitan political authorities all the way to the top. Everyone, or nearly everyone, in the political, judicial, and military establishments knew the facts about the systemization of torture—however much they pretended otherwise throughout the war and afterward.

There are many shocking details about the banalization of torture and cruelty in Aussaresses's account, but a few incidents stand out. For example, Aussaresses described how he arrested and murdered Larbi Ben M'Hidi, the FLN's so-called mastermind of the Battle of Algiers: "We grabbed Ben M'Hidi and hanged him by the neck to make it look like suicide. Once I was sure he was dead, I immediately had him taken down and brought the body to the hospital. I immediately phone Massu. 'General, Ben M'Hidi has just committed suicide. His body is at the hospital. I will bring you my report tomorrow.' Massu grunted and hung up the phone. He knew full well that my report had been ready since early afternoon" (140).

Aussaresses also recounted how he ordered the execution of the Algerian lawyer Ali Boumendjel in 1957, and he recorded all this in his private testimony without remorse. In his own words, Aussaresses declares:

> What I did in Algeria was undertaken for my country in good faith, even through I didn't enjoy it. One must never regret anything accomplished in the line of duty one believes in. Only too often today condemning others means acquiring a certificate of morality for just about anyone. I write only about myself in my memoir. I don't attempt to justify my actions, but only to explain that once a country demands that its army fight an enemy who is using terror to compel an indifferent population to join its ranks and provoke a repression that will in turn outrage international public opinion, it becomes impossible for the army to avoid using extreme measures. (xiii)

Ausseresses's defense of murder and torture in his book, as well as in the media before its publication, crossed an unspoken political line in France. President Jacques Chirac, himself a veteran of the French-Algerian War, was eventually forced—no doubt because of mounting public pressure—to reply to the issue of torture by removing Aussaresses from the French Legion of Honor and by forbidding him the customary privilege of wearing his uniform in public. But neither Chirac nor Jospin, who was an antiwar protester at the time, could bring themselves to deal more forcefully with the legacy of the war. Hence, despite growing public pressure for trying Algerian War criminals, Chirac and Jospin stalled. As Jospin put it, "I'll never do anything to harm the memory or the honor of the men who fought for France. In these sorts of events, the best thing is to stand back and let history do its work." [16] Disingenuously passing the problem on to history and the historians' shoulders was an easy course to take, but it would also require opening up all archives and other state documents for investigation, which France has been unwilling to do.

Protected by French laws and a state unwilling legitimately to open the debate, Aussaresses remained steadfast, and in November 2002, during the trial brought against him by human rights groups as a result of his book, Aussaresses again refused to apologize, restating that his "actions appeared justified," and he added that he "would do the same thing again today against Osama bin Laden." [17] Aussaresses's point, as he repeated it throughout his book and to the media, was that military-backed torture represented the only effective means to combat terrorism and that he had a professional duty to protect innocents from the enemy's bombs by any means at his disposal—be it rope, rape, poison, bullets, knives, water, fire, or any variety of sadistic instruments (many of which he invented).

On January 25, 2002, at the age of eighty-three, retired general Aussaresses was finally convicted in a French court, though absurdly, for "trying to justify war," and fined approximately $6,500. What is most startling about his conviction was not the fact that he was put on trial for the confessed murder of dozens of Algerians during the war but rather that he was convicted by a French court for telling his story. Even his publishers (the president and senior editor of the publishing house that brought out his book) were convicted and fined thirteen thousand dollars for letting the story be told. Aussaresses's lawyer, Gilbert Collard, claimed that the court's decision constituted the first censorship of a personal account in French history.

Perhaps even more ironic and troubling, between Aussaresses's trial and his sentencing by the French courts, the highly celebrated American news magazine *60 Minutes* ran an interview on December 18, 2001, in which Aussaresses was allowed (interviewed by Mike Wallace) to pose as the man from whom the United States could learn much in its own so-called war on terrorism in the wake of the September 11, 2001, terrorist attacks. (Wallace was apparently not aware that Aussaresses had already schooled the Americans—North and South—on "interrogation" techniques during the Cold War.) The same *60 Minutes* segment, appropriately entitled "Torture," also featured an interview with the controversial Harvard Law professor Alan Dershowitz. During that segment, Dershowitz made a stunningly rational plea for the legalization of torture in the United States in the form of "torture warrants."

At the same time, Alan Dershowitz's own best-selling book, *Why Terrorism Works: Understanding the Threat, Responding to the Challenge* (2002)—published on the heels of the September 11 attacks as a clumsy and unabashed effort to put the blame of most modern terrorism on the shoulders of the Palestinians—continued to advance the need for "torture warrants" in the United States. However regretful Dershowitz's misuse of history is, in this case, to justify Israel's position vis-à-vis Palestine, it is interesting to note that Dershowitz seems to understand France's real historical failure to deal with torture as a means to combat terrorism. As Dershowitz put it:

> Perhaps the most extreme example of such a hypocritical approach
> to torture comes—not surprisingly—from the French experience
> in Algeria. The French army used torture extensively in seeking to

prevent terrorism during the brutal colonial war from 1955 to 1957. An officer who supervised this torture, General Paul Aussaresses, wrote a book recounting what he had done and seen, including the torture of dozens of Algerians. "The best way to make a terrorist talk when he refused to say what he knows was to torture him," he boasted. Although the book was published decades after the war was over, the general was prosecuted—but not for what he had done to the Algerians. Instead, he was prosecuted for *revealing* what he had done, and seeking to justify it.

In a democracy governed by the rule of law, we should never want our soldiers or our president to take any action that we deem wrong or illegal. A good test of whether an action should or should not be done is whether we are prepared to have it disclosed—perhaps not immediately, but certainly after some time has passed. No legal system operating under the rule of law should ever tolerate an "off-the-books" approach to necessity. The road to tyranny has always been paved with claims of necessity made by those responsible for the security of the nation. [18]

As Dershowitz's comments on Aussaresses help illustrate, many observers have indicated that there are striking parallels between the French position during the French-Algerian War and the dilemmas facing U.S. foreign policy makers in the twenty-first century. Like the French, Americans today are forced to think about the repercussions of their own self-declared war on terrorism. This is especially true in light of revelations of prisoner abuse and torture in Iraq by American soldiers. However, even before this scandal broke, many argued that the French war in Algeria might be used as a case study of how to win or lose the so-called war on terror. One important example relates to the decision of the Pentagon to screen Gillo Pontecorvo's film The Battle of Algiers for Pentagon officials. In an opinion column for the Washington Post, David Ignatius reported that important officials in the Pentagon viewed the film in order to learn how the French "won" the war yet lost the hearts and minds of Algerians in the process. According to the Pentagon's advertisement: "How to win a battle against terrorism and lose the war of ideas. . . . Children shoot soldiers at point blank range. Women plant bombs in cafés. Soon the entire Arab population builds to a mad furor. Sound familiar? The French have a plan. It succeeds tactically, but fails strategically. To understand why, come to a rare showing of this film" (quoted in the Washington Post, August 26, 2003).

Whether or not the Pentagon learned much from the film is a matter of debate, but the overwhelming interest that came as a result of reports about the Pentagon showing have been wonderful for the film itself, which was enhanced and rereleased and is now out in a three-volume DVD collection that includes interviews about the film with directors such as Spike Lee and with Richard A. Clarke, President George W. Bush's former terrorism advisor. However it is also worth pointing out that comparisons between The Battle of Algiers and other current events are not particularly new. In fact, during the late 1960s and early 1970s, many reviewers of the film argued that it could be used to understand the race riots in Watts and Harlem, as well as black women's empowerment. It was also used by Latin American juntas as a training film in the fight against so-called Communist subversion in the 1970s and 1980s. More creatively, the film was used in Marie-Monique Robin's documentary Death Squadrons: The French School as a backdrop to interviews with the French officers most involved in torture during the historical Battle of Algiers, thus bringing the fictionalized characters to life as they are set against their real-life personas. Robin's documentary is of particular interest here because she interviews Paul Aussaresses and Marcel-Maurice Bigeard, among others, about how the French perfected the "interrogation" techniques during the Battle of Algiers and then began, often as officials representing the French government, to export these to other governments. In referring to his work in the military after Robert Lacoste (the French official who served as resident minister from 1956–59) handed over civilian police powers to the army, General Bigeard states that he simply did the "police work quickly." Robin then later asks Aussaresses if he has seen Pontecorvo's film and what he thought of it, and Aussaresses replied gleefully: "Magnificent! Magnificent!" He added that the colonel in the film who oversaw the entire operation was Bigeard. Going even further, Aussaresses brags that the term "disappearing" was invented in Algeria and used systematically for the first time in order to get rid of suspected revolutionaries without a trace. Commenting on the subject of the "disappeared," Aussaresses says to the camera: "Bigeard's shrimp! That's what we called them."[19]

"Bigeard's shrimp," indeed. "Un 'bon mot' des assassins," as Henri Alleg also attested in a compelling set of interviews with Gilles Martin, published in 2001 under the title of Retour sur "La Question", conducted in response to the recent torture scandals.[20] Coming after the public statements and publications of Massu, Bigeard, and Aussaresses, Henri Alleg's statements, as a victim of French torture during the infamous Battle of Algiers, ring with clarity. In speaking of the so-called Battle of Algiers and of Massu's role, Alleg stated that Massu "always presented himself as the victor in the Battle of Algiers. In reality, there never was a battle; only a gigantic police operation carried out with an exceptional savagery and in violation of all the laws" (21).

In response to Bigeard's June 21, 2000, *Le Monde* declarations, in which the general denounced Louisette Ighilahriz's statements as a "stream of lies," Alleg replied:

> Bigeard is the type of roughneck soldier who neither forgets nor learns anything. Never forgets because today he still uses the same lines as if the Algerian war were still being fought. Back then, torturers and assassins at the highest level, like Massu himself, swore, with their hand on their heart, that the statements by victims of torture were nothing but slander. Bigeard and his men had the assurance that in Algiers, with Governor General Lacoste, just as in Paris, President Guy Mollet and his ministers (including François Mitterrand) would not refute them. But today, despite the countless obstacles put up over the years to prevent it from happening, the truth has finally broken out. Bigeard, it seems, never noticed this, and his pigheaded denials are not just indecent, they are also ridiculous. . . . His name has remained associated with the form of summary execution largely used in Algeria and elsewhere [Latin America] and of which I have already spoken: tossing prisoners with their feet in cement out of high-flying helicopters.
>
> During that time, crimes of war did not hinder the career of the colonel. Quite to the contrary, as he continued to earn his stripes until he became a general, and with the benediction of then-president Valéry Giscard d'Estaing, he was even asked to serve from 1974 to 1975 as secretary of state in charge of defense, a quasi–cabinet minister. Who would dare say that the republic is ungrateful to its loyal servants? (35–36)

As France sustained its uneasy dialogue with the past and while Generals Aussaresses and Bigeard continued to justify torture as a necessary method in the French war on terror, Massu died at the age of ninety-four in October 2002. Jacques Chirac paid his respects to the retired and controversial commander and stated very clearly that despite Massu's December 2000 admission of torture, Massu had always acted in France's best interest. "At the sunset of his life, as France engages in a debate over the sad pages of its recent history, General Massu assumed his responsibilities with dignity, courage, and honor."[21]

Others in France, especially many of those who had been at the forefront of the campaign against torture during the French-Algerian War, did not believe that France had yet done enough. On May 16, 2001, having failed to get an audience with either President Chirac or Prime Minister Lionel Jospin, the Twelve again asked both Chirac and Jospin to acknowledge and condemn the use of torture during the war. On March 18, 2002, during the extremely controversial presidential elections, the group published a communiqué in L'Humanité calling for all candidates to denounce the use of torture during the French-Algerian War (a move that was particularly vexing to Jean-Marie Le Pen, who had long been accused of torturing Algerians during his service in Algeria).

Finally, in another attempt to put Jacques Chirac—who became one of Europe's most outspoken critics of the American invasion of Iraq in 2003— on the spot, the Twelve connected the issue of torture during the French-Algerian War to the American occupation of Iraq. Seizing on the worldwide outrage cause by the revelations of the Abu Ghraib Prison abuse scandal that broke in May 2004, the Twelve published a new Manifesto on May 12, 2004, again in L'Humanité, asking the French president to acknowledge and condemn the use of torture in Algeria once and for all. However, clearly understanding that France's own credibility to denounce the use of torture by the Americans in Iraq was called into question by the French government's historic inability to confront its own historical past, the Twelve also acknowledged that, despite the American actions, the Americans had at least had the courage to made the abuses public and to deal with the scandal in a public manner. France never had this courage, and, as a result, its right to speak about atrocities in Iraq was crippled by its own moral failures. As the Twelve put it:

> This urgency concerns all the citizens for whom over the course of the past forty years the question of intervention has played a major role in the open debates in our country. But if France wants to have its voice heard at the highest levels, it is imperative that it not be content merely to deplore practices "among others," in as much (d'autant) as the Americans and the British who have been shocked by what happened [regarding torture] in Iraq and by the conduct of their governments who knew how to act without waiting. It [France] must firmly condemn the torture for which it was

responsible in Algeria. They [the concerned citizens] demand for this reason that the authorities of our country no longer delay this recognition, thereby setting an example that rejects the use of such practices that stain [entachent] the honor of an entire people. [22]

If the French state's failure to come to terms with its deeds during decolonization has continued to haunt French society with such ferocity, it is also appropriate to ask in concluding this work how Algeria fared after the war. To address important aspects of Algeria's part of this story, it is now necessary to briefly sketch some of Algeria's intellectual and political responses to changes in the postcolonial era.

The Algerian Troubles

By the time Jean-Paul Sartre's lungs collapsed on April 15, 1980, at the age of seventy-five, Algeria had begun its political free fall. In fact, during that fatal spring, the Algerian state was gearing up for an unavoidable duel with the Kabyles, who comprised over 20 percent of Algeria's total population. The troubles began in mid-March, when the FLN forbade the Algerian intellectual Mouloud Mammeri from giving a lecture on ancient Berber poetry in Kabylia's capital city, Tizi-Ouzou. This refusal made sense within the monolingual logic of the Algerian National Charter of 1976 (which ignored the Kabyle population's demands for cultural and linguistic recognition) but incensed Kabyles and set off a wave of protests that culminated in the occupation of the University of Tizi-Ouzou by protesters and a general strike throughout Kabylia. Only five days after Sartre's death, the crisis, later known as the "Berber Spring," erupted in full force. [23] Before this protest against the linguistic policies of the Algerian government was over, more than thirty protesters (mostly Kabyle) had been killed by the state authorities, with over two hundred wounded and many more jailed.

These protests would continue to simmer until 2001, when the Algerian military would again crack down on Kabylia by killing dozens of unarmed protesters there. After years of conflict, the Algerian government finally made the long-awaited concession to the Kabyle by naming Tamazight (the Berber language) an officially sanctioned national language in the summer of 2002.

The language issue had been brewing in Algeria since before the revolution, but it was with the help of Ahmed Taleb Ibrahimi, the man who once wrote to Albert Camus as "Ahmed Taleb" in his letter from prison (and whose request to found an Islamist party was denied by the Algerian government in 2000), that the language issue took center stage immediately after the war. In an article published in December 1962, Ibrahimi cited Aimé Césaire and others in his efforts to demonstrate that Algerians had been "deculturated" by colonialism. It was up to Algerians to discover their true identity. As he put it, "The Algerian should therefore seize the richness of his past and he cannot do this without knowledge of Arabic."[24] Appointed to the post of the first minister of education for the newly independent Algeria, Ibrahimi thereafter pushed hard for a progressive Arabization program that would use bilingualism only as a transitional tool. As Ibrahimi put it: "Only bilingual instruction can assist in the transition from colonial education to authentic national education" (19). Three years later, in a speech to Algerian students, entitled "Rootedness and Authenticity" ("Enracinement et authenticité"), Ibrahimi stressed the need for Algeria's youth, and especially its intellectuals, to reconnect with Arabic, which he tied again to the notion of authenticity, asking them to search out their own "Arabo-Islamic roots" (27).

Though language was certainly one of the important postcolonial issues that Algerians faced immediately after the war, others should be mentioned here as well. By independence in July 1962, political rivalries within the Algerian nationalist movement triggered thousands of assassinations and murders, coupled with vicious reprisals against those Algerians suspected of collaborating with French forces during decolonization. Hence, while Algerian politicians trumpeted the nation as a unified and cohesive national sphere and as a would-be showpiece of Third World emancipation, it had become clear to many observers that Algeria's unity was more illusion than reality and that the revolution had been hijacked by the external military wing of the FLN (the Armée des Frontières). In the famous words of Ferhat Abbas, Algeria would be left with "confiscated independence" in the decades to follow.[25]

The FLN, backed by the Armée des Frontières, did in fact confiscate the revolution on the eve of independence and immediately rendered any real transition to a democratic republic improbable. In claiming to be the only legitimate political entity after independence—the guarantor and therefore the inheritor of political legitimacy—the FLN turned Algeria into a one-party state and outlawed rival parties for more than thirty years. The subsequent centralization of authority by the FLN during the war by brutal, repressive means (a process many French intellectuals such as Sartre and de Beauvoir condoned) became concrete during the first months of Ahmed

Ben Bella's presidency (1962–65), which was subsequently overthrown by Houari Boumediene in a coup d'état in 1965; it continued under the power-hungry leadership of Houari Boumediene (1965–78), and was capped off by Chadli Bendjedid's regime (1979–89).

At the same time, FLN leaders and spokesmen—eager to claim their own version of Third World "authenticity" articulated by anticolonial theorists during the revolution—had begun to work with Islamists from the beginning of the revolutionary period. After independence, the import of this uneasy alliance between a secular, socialist state and religious, Islamic backers became clearer with the passing of the Algerian constitution of 1976, establishing Islam as the religion of the state.

Led, ironically, by the staunch secular socialist Boumediene, the FLN presented the National Charter of 1976 as a means to unify the nation, basing it on the centrist notion that ethnic, linguistic, and religious differences would divide the country—if they were addressed at all. Under Ben Bella and Boumediene, Algeria also began to institute its controversial Arabization program, a process that took many years to move through the state's primary, secondary, and university education system. When Chadli Bendjedid assumed power after Boumediene's premature death in December 1979, the government continued to centralize authority, move against a linguistic openness that would include the Berbers and other ethnic groups, and by 1997 did away with bilingualism altogether—jettisoning French and making Arabic the official language. Most importantly, the Algerian state continued to flirt with Islamists. Unfortunately, according to Benjamin Stora, "[t]he state nationalized Islam without wishing to modify it."[26]

As many observers have remarked, women's rights were unquestionably one of the clearest casualties of the growing power of Islam in Algeria after decolonization. The final blow to the women's movement came under pressure from Islamic reformers when the FLN passed the Family Code in 1984. Under the Family Code, women were rendered legally subservient to their husbands and their husband's family, forbidden to travel without the direct supervision of a male family member, could not apply for a divorce, and could not apply for marriage contracts unless approved of by a male adult family member.[27]

Two years after the Algerian Family Code became law, Simone de Beauvoir, a longtime supporter of women's rights and an intellectual very much associated with the Algerian nationalist cause, died in Paris at the age of seventy-eight. Neither she nor Sartre could have forecasted such catastrophic postcolonial political outcomes in Algeria. However, as a supporter of the FLN during decolonization, she had certainly inspired countless Algerian feminists and nationalists during and after decolonization.

Khalida [Messaoudi] Toumi, one of Algeria's best-known feminist activists, who was inspired by de Beauvoir's feminist politics and who deserves considerable attention here, put Chadli's decision to adopt the Family Code this way in her conversations with Elizabeth Schemla, published in *Unbowed: An Algerian Woman Confronts Islamic Fundamentalism* (1995): "Chadli, in contrast to Boumediene, was not a strong man who seized power himself. He was the pawn of a clan, a certain current of the FLN and the army: namely, the Islamo-baasist camp." [28] As a result, the "Islamo-baasists"—those who favored Arabization and the creation of an Islamic state in the spirit of the Baath party in Iraq—got their way and Algerian women were denied the right to travel without being accompanied by a man. Eventually, Toumi explains, the Family Code allowed women to exist "henceforth only as 'daughters of,' 'mothers of,' or 'wives of' " (52).

Toumi acted against the FLN's position on women beginning on March 8, 1980—International Women's Day. As a student, she helped organize a successful protest in defense of women's rights, forcing the government to back down momentarily (49). However, Chadli remained under pressure from Islamic hardliners and continued to push forward with the Code. The women's movement could not withstand the pressure of the regime and was defeated by the government. Khalida Toumi's actions led to her arrest in 1981, but, after her release, she went on to teach mathematics in a lycée in Algiers in the mid-1980s. As a math teacher, she witnessed another phenomenon associated with the problem of authenticity that she found disturbing: Arabization. According to her, it had disastrous effects on Algerian children, who were being handicapped, especially in the sciences, by Algeria's policy, because it cut off Algeria's important linguistic and cultural ties to Western nations, including France. [29]

Toumi is not alone here. Assia Djebar, another well-known Algerian writer and an important feminist, believes that Arabization programs created unnecessary problems in Algeria. Hence, rather than having French serve as a unique advantage for Algerians, the Algerian state's educational reforms (directed by men like Ahmed Taleb Ibrahimi) were caught up in absurd identity politics after decolonization. As Djebar put it in her reflections on contemporary Algeria, *Algeria White*, which she first published in 1995:

Today it is Arabic again, modern Arabic as it is called, which is taught to the young under the pompous guise of our "national language."

The institutionalized mediocrity of the educational system since 1962—despite a clear effort toward making the population literate: literacy has almost tripled in thirty years—was practiced on two levels: promoting the "national language" by officially restricting the living space of the other languages; then, in addition to this sterilizing monolingualism, the diglossia peculiar to Arabic (the structure's vertical variability that can give the child who is being educated a precious agility of mind) was handled badly by comparison with other Arab countries, by banishing a dialect that was vivid in its regional iridescence, subtle in the strength of its challenges and its dream.

Thus, the denial of an entire population's genius went hand in hand with the mistrust of a minority of French-language writers whose production, in spite of the lack of anything better, continued in exile.

Jacques Berque, declaring in 1992 that "Islamism thinks of itself as a material modernity, as it wholly refuses any intellectual bases," comes to Algeria and its linguistic choices: "Here is a situation," he says, "that exists in none of the other twenty Arab countries" also confronted with diglossia and the presence of one or two other languages. "One may say," he concludes, "that Algeria has shown a talent for creating a major problem out of something that began as an advantage!"[30]

The issue of Arabic aside, Khalida Toumi became increasingly active in the women's movement. In 1985 she became the founding president of the Association pour l'Égalité des Droits entre les Femmes et les Hommes; in 1989 she became the founding president of the Association Indépendante pour le Triomphe du Droit des Femmes, one of the organizations acknowledged by the FLN. Also in 1989, in an inevitable and important sign of democratic reform, the FLN recognized the Front Islamique du Salut (FIS).

As it turned out, this effort by the FLN to liberalize the election process and allow for alternative political parties had enormous consequences for Algerian politics; as Benjamin Stora has pointed out, between 1989 and 1990 over forty new parties came into existence in Algeria (198). By far, the most important of these was the FIS, led by Abassi Madani and Ali Benhadji, which aspired to create a theocratic, Islamic republic. According to Stora, the sudden liberalization of Algerian politics by the FLN under Chadli was a case of too much, too late. The sudden reform was, in Stora's words,

> too great an innovation: for the *first time*, an Arab and Muslim country authorized a party that had Islam as its foundation, and the instillation of an 'Islamic republic' as its openly announced goal. The army chiefs thought that the legalization of an Islamist party was a mistake in a country where religion played such a strong role and constituted one of the levers of national cohesion. Others, like Chadli Bendjedid and his prime minister, Mouloud Hamrouche, felt that institutional guarantees were enough to ward off any subversive threat. (203)

However "subversive" the FIS turned out to be, it was not the only political party that enjoyed a relative burst of democratic freedom in Algeria. In fact, in the early 1990s, Khalida Toumi became vice president of the Mouvement pour la République, which was founded by Said Sadi.[31] Sadi was then a member of the Rassemblement pour la Culture et la Démocratie (RCD) and also remained a member until May 2001. As a movement that grew out of the Berber opposition, the RCD campaigned on a secularist platform, separating Islam from state politics in Algeria, though Toumi eventually broke with the RCD on ideological grounds.

Khalida Toumi, who had been harassed and intimidated by the FLN since 1981, received national attention on March 22, 1990, when she confronted Abassi Madani (the coleader of the FIS) in a political debate on Algerian national television. The following month, over one hundred thousand supporters of the FIS gathered in Algiers and demanded the application of *shair'a* (Islamic law) along with an end to Algeria's bilingualism. Soon thereafter, on June 12, the FIS won the municipal elections, taking most of the large cities throughout Algeria. Toumi noted the irony of the FIS's sweeping electoral victories: "I viewed it as one of the injustices of history. We paid very dearly in the precious fight for democracy we'd been waging for more than a decade, and it was the 'Barbus' ['Bearded Ones'] who were reaping the benefits" (97–98). The tragic and ironic part of this was that the FIS party made it perfectly clear that once it won the first-ever national democratic elections in Algeria's history, it would henceforth cancel the election process and institute *shair'a*.

When the First Gulf War started at the beginning of 1991, the Islamist movement in Algeria watched in shame and awe at the Saudia Arabian government's decision to side with the Americans in the war against Iraq, despite the Algerian Islamists' distaste for the secularism of Saddam Hussein. As Stora records it, the FIS Islamists' abhorrence of the collaboration of the Saudi regime with the United States produced statements like this from Algerian extremists: "Let us brandish the torch of Islam. Let us brandish the jihad. Down with the servants of colonialism! No to Iraqi intervention in Kuwait, no to the intervention of unbelievers in Saudi Arabia, no to the governments that have compromised with the West" (208). In other words, in connections that have become all too apparent after September 11, 2001, there were increasingly important links between the militant Islamic groups such as the Group Islamique Armée (GIA) in Algeria in the 1990s and growing worldwide terrorist networks such as Al Qaeda. The Islamists in Algeria took the Saudis' decision to comply with the American request for airbases during the First Gulf War as their cue to seek the expulsion of the Western infidels (including Jews) from the Islamic Holy Lands. This reaction would ripple through radical Islamic groups elsewhere, including Osama bin Laden and those in Afghanistan's Taliban.

Less than six months after the First Gulf War started, the FIS called for a general strike in Algeria in an effort to cripple the government. In retaliation, two weeks later, on June 30, both Abassi Madani and Ali Benhadj were arrested and imprisoned. (They were sentenced to twelve-year terms and were only released in 2003. They are currently banned from all political and public activity by the Algerian government, and, as a result, journalists can neither interview nor cite them.) Finally, despite President Chadli's efforts to stop the Islamic movement in Algeria with the arrest of the leaders of the FIS, on December 26, 1991, the FIS won in the first round of national legislative elections. About three weeks later, on January 11, 1992, Chadli was forced by the military to step down from office. Within a day, the military nullified the previous elections (showing the FIS victory) and dissolved the Algerian National Assembly. That same month, a new military-backed political body, known as the High State Committee (HSC) and initially directed by Mohamed Boudiaf—a hero of the war of liberation who was assassinated, just six months later—filled the void left by the FLN's sudden demise.

In March 1992 the FIS was outlawed, with their leaders being sent to concentration camps in the south or "disappeared" (a technique learned from the French) by the Algerian military in its own brutal repression of Islamic movements. As evidenced here, Algeria's lightening-speed political liberalization had led directly into one of the most severe political crises in recent history. By the time of Boudiaf's murder, Algeria was well on its way to full-scale civil war from which it has yet to recover. Liamine Zéroual was appointed president by the military clans in January 1994. Nevertheless, several armed Islamic guerrilla movements (including the GIA) continued throughout the 1990s to clash with the military-backed state. The result, according to William Quandt, was that between 1992 and 1998 an average of about two hundred Algerians died per week. [32] In 1999 elections were held again, and Abdelaziz Bouteflika, with the support of the omnipresent military, became the new Algerian president.

Throughout these political shifts, Khalida Toumi continued to agitate for democracy and women's rights in Algeria as the civil conflict raged. Already afraid of an assassination attempt on her life, she was formally condemned to death by the FIS in 1993 and subsequently went on to survive at least three confirmed Islamists' attempts to kill her, including one in 1994 that wounded her and killed a bodyguard and another person. Yet she continued to serve in the Algerian parliament.

In 2002, especially after its massacres of unarmed civilians in Kabylia in 2001, the government knew that if it was going to continue to receive international assistance (in particular from the U.S. government) in its battle against Islamic militancy and compete for foreign investment, it would have to reform its image and make real progressive efforts to reform Algerian domestic politics. The prime minister, Ali Benflis (FLN), called for a bold restructuring of the ministries in June 2002. Five feminists were appointed to top governmental posts, including Mouredine Salah, Rachid Harraoubia, and Khalida Toumi. Khalida Toumi was named Algeria's first woman minister of communications and culture and the official spokesperson for the Algerian government. She accepted the post, as she says, in order to place women on the agenda of the Algerian government, and this includes working toward the repeal of the repressive Family Code. As she stated in a March 2003 interview with Cédric Morin: "It's up to elected women, me in this case, to make their voices heard where we are. It's a matter of persuading as many ministers as possible, to call their attention, at every occasion, to the condition of women." [33]

Ghost of the Past

In the first edition of Uncivil War I cited a play written by Khalida Toumi's brother, Alek Toumi, originally published under his pen name (Alek Baylee) and entitled Madah-Sartre (which was published in France in 1998). After

Uncivil War was published in 2001, with the help of a colleague I was able to find Alek Toumi and ask him about his work. During my first interview with him, I learned that his sister was Khalida Toumi, and I also learned that long before Alek Toumi could ever dream of seeing his sister become a minister in the Algerian government, the escalating civil war in Algeria in the early 1990s had had a profound impact on him and other Algerian intellectuals in exile.

With his sister condemned to death by fundamentalists and persecuted by the government for her unflinching criticism of its treatment of women, Alek Toumi feared the worst for his family in Algeria during the 1990s. But, as he told me, he and his family were no strangers to adversity. [34] Literally a child of the Algerian revolution, Alek was born on October 2, 1955, in a small village in Kabylia. Too young to recall many of the events except for hearing gunfire outside the home, he does remember the unusual diversity within his village, in which he lived among other Kabyles, Arabs, *pieds noirs*, and Jews. However, during the war, his father, who was both a mayoral advisor and sympathetic toward the FLN, was arrested by the French, tortured, and put in a concentration camp—euphemistically called a "relocation camp" by the French—for six months. In 1965, at the age of nine and a half, his father sent the young Toumi to study at Les Pères-Blancs, an all-boys Catholic boarding school in Algiers. The language at the school was French, the orientation Cartesian rationalism. But before Toumi left for boarding school, his father was arrested a second time—this time by the FLN for being an original member of the Front des Forces Socialistes (FFS), which was created by Hocine Aït Ahmed in September 1963 in order to oppose Ben Bella's regime. Ben Bella ordered the army to put down the opposition in Kabylia in October 1963, and the elder Toumi was blacklisted after his release from the FLN's political prison.

The young Toumi was old enough to remember the arrest of his father by the FLN and especially the cruelty of the neighborhood kids who ridiculed him and his family (interview). Perhaps even more traumatic, the FLN labeled the FFS as a separatist movement in 1963. Hence his earlier nom de plume, Alek Baylee, pronounced as one word: "Alekbaylee," or "the Kabyle." He received his baccalaureate in 1974 and in 1976 moved to the United States to study at the University of Wisconsin–Madison. After returning to Algeria in 1982, he again left in 1984 to pursue a PhD at the University of Wisconsin and has remained in the United States.

Alek Toumi received his PhD in French in 1993 and, as is the case with many in the Algerian diaspora, paid critical attention to the political developments at home and kept in frequent contact with his family. In particular, Toumi followed the course of events leading to Algeria's "glasnost" along with his sister's dangerous political career. He was especially concerned with the gruesome displays of violence and spectacular acts of continuing terrorism perpetrated against Algerian intellectuals. [35]

One of the most prominent assassinations was that of Tahar Djaout. By January 1993, Djaout was one of Algeria's leading intellectual voices. At the time he was a thirty-nine-year-old novelist and journalist for *Algérie-Actualité* and had cofounded *Ruptures*—a respected magazine critical of both the Islamists and the state. Djaout's position on intellectual freedom in the context of the civil war was legendary, and he refused to remain silent. Tragically, he was shot in the head by Islamists on May 26, 1993, and died a week later. The wave of assassinations of prominent Algerian intellectuals continued, including those of Abdelkader Alloula, Mahfoud Boucebci, M'Hamed Boukhobza, Saïd Mekbel, and Youssef Sebti.

From the United States Toumi followed the news of attacks on Algeria's intelligentsia. In Toumi's words: "I was terrified about what they were going to do to my sister and to my parents. They killed Djaout, then they started killing [other] intellectuals. Then, in 1994 they [the FIS] had initiated the *marriages de jouissances*, which had never appeared before, where they would kidnap these girls—sometimes as young as twelve—and they gang rape them, then they decapitate them, and so on" (interview). For Toumi, Algeria had become a nightmare that had to be lived, on the outside, where he was helpless to defend his family and his friends and where he began to think of how best to channel his anxiety. As with many other exiled intellectuals throughout history, Toumi's decision to write flowed from this predicament.

Alek Toumi began to pen his first play in 1993 and was particularly interested in revisiting Sartre and de Beauvoir. It was this first play that originally attracted my attention due to his clever reincarnation of the characters of Sartre and de Beauvoir and their insertion into the middle of Algeria's civil war. As Toumi put it to me: "I imagined that Sartre went to Djaout's funeral and got kidnapped. But if Sartre comes back, logically you can't have Sartre without de Beauvoir. They always go together, and from a theatrical point of view, you don't need to present Sartre; he's intellectual with a capital I. And de Beauvoir's the mother of feminism." Toumi also noted that Sartre and de Beauvoir had supported the FLN during the revolution and commented that Sartre would be of special interest because "today he would be caught between a rock and a hard place," between his former support for the FLN, which he could seemingly no longer maintain, and the FIS, "which he would reject" (interview).

Madah-Sartre's story is that of two Algerias and, indirectly, one of two siblings, an exiled writer and his activist sister. It is a story in which two protagonists, the ghosts of Sartre and de Beauvoir, square off against the antagonists of a FIS-GIA terrorist cell led by Madah (short for Mad-d-Allah, a cocktail-like word symbolizing religious extremism). Finally, it is a powerful comment on the intellectuals of the Algerian diaspora, for Madah also represents the fictionalization of Anouar Haddam, an exiled FIS leader with whom Toumi was uncomfortably sharing the space of the Algerian diaspora within the United States (interview). [36]

Inspired by the play *Marat-Sade*, written by Peter Weiss, *Madah-Sartre* starts in the heavens with Simone de Beauvoir asking Sartre if he is certain he wants to attend the funeral of Djaout. Soon after Sartre and de Beauvoir descend to earth, they are stopped and kidnapped by the GIA. They are immediately separated, in Toumi's spoof of Sartre's *No Exit*, with de Beauvoir being taken by women captors and Sartre by men. In reading the play, it becomes immediately clear why Toumi published *Madah-Sartre* under a pen name. Knowing that the model for his central fictional antagonist was living only a few states away, Toumi's fears were understandable—especially given Toumi's penchant for stridently lampooning Islamic extremists. For example, in an early scene in which Sartre talks to an artist who has also been kidnapped, Sartre asks why the GIA carried out the abduction, and the artist replies: "They are convinced that they are the 'Soldiers of God.' But . . . they are only thugs, opportunists, sadistic and psychotic men who use God" (18). The artist continues later: "They loot in the name of God. They kill in the name of God. They rape in the name of God" (19).

Madah-Sartre is more than an attack on Algerian Islamists; it is also an unequivocal critique of Le Pouvoir, the military extremists who have terrorized the entire Algerian population. *Madah-Sartre* is, however, part of a much wider literary corpus devoted to multipronged criticism of contemporary Algerian politics. For example, Tahar Djaout's last novel, *Le Dernier été de la raison*—first published in 1999 and then published in English as *The Last Summer of Reason* (2001)—which Djaout was writing when he was murdered, has a similar and equally devastating critique of both Le Pouvoir and the religious terrorists. What makes Toumi's writings stand out is the way in which he carefully crafted his unflinching attack around the theme of intellectuals and the legacy of the French-Algerian War.

Fed up with the Islamists' policy of killing intellectuals, Toumi ridicules the terrorists for their murderous impiety. In deriding Islamists, he simultaneously celebrates the intellectuals' role in society. "For the last ten years," as he stated in his interview with me, "especially since '93, it has been extremely dangerous to be an intellectual because you have to be openly critical of the fundamentalists, who have been against intellectuals since the early 1980s, but also of the corrupt, FLN-backed generals, who are a mafia of corrupt people that created the FIS. When you do that [criticize these people], you risk not only your own life but also the lives of your immediate family. Being an intellectual means that the right of dissent is sacred. If you take that away I don't think you can have intellectuals. That's something nonnegotiable" (interview).

Toumi's defense of the intellectual's right of dissent is perhaps best illustrated in act 3, "Intellectuals are Jews." Here Sartre meets Madah, the leader of the terrorist cell. Madah, a fanatical Islamist, explains to Sartre that it was his defense of Algerians during the war of liberation that "redeem[ed]" him and rendered his soul worth saving. When Sartre questions why he was taken, Madah replies that Sartre had encouraged "critics and critical thinking," but that his worst sin of all was also his raison d'être: being an intellectual (22). Madah explains that, as the "prototype" of an intellectual, it was Sartre who convinced others to question authority.

Thirty years after independence, Madah reminds Sartre's ghost that he had endorsed extreme violence in Algeria as a means to refashion postcolonial authenticity. The important difference being, Madah states, that whereas Sartre had acted in a universe without God and had erred in supporting women's rights, these actions remained unpardonable crimes for Madah: "A society without God and governed by women is doomed to failure" (24). Admitting to some of his own errors over the years, Sartre counters by comparing the discourse of the FIS with that of Jean-Marie Le Pen's National Front: "Your discourse is the same as the French extreme right, based on exclusion. Jean-Marie with a turban would look very much like you."

As counterintuitive as it may seem, Toumi does have a point in stressing this connection between Jean-Marie Le Pen and the FIS. Le Pen had stated publicly that his (albeit xenophobic) movement was interested in working with the FIS before they were disbanded—despite his virulent anti-

immigration, anti-Arab position—because the FIS would not encourage
Muslim immigration and had, in fact, pledged to Le Pen that it would work
to repatriate Algerian immigrants living in France. Hence Madah's Pétain-
like reaction to Sartre: "We [the FIS and the FN] have the same enemies:
Jews, feminists and secular intellectuals, those who are against God. 'God,
country, and family' " (25).

After another heated exchange between Sartre and Madah, Toumi moves
to the issue of alterity, a critical dimension of the play, of Sartrian philosophy, and a central concern of Uncivil War. "You have an obsession," Sartre
continues, with "the Other. Eliminate others who are different" (26). Toumi
parlays alterity into a discussion of democratic pluralism in contemporary
Algeria. For Toumi, this is a conflict in which there remain only two incompatible solutions: adoption of full democratization of society or the imposition of theocracy. The ghost of Sartre, and Toumi himself, remain committed to democracy. In Toumi's view, "the concept of an Islamic republic is a
completely ludicrous idea" (interview).

Throughout Madah-Sartre, Sartre stays true to his secular ideals and refuses to convert to Islam, though Madah refuses to give up hope. But the Algerian Islamists ("fascislamists," to use Toumi's word for them) in Madah-
Sartre want to do more than purify Algeria of infidels. Algeria must, they
say, free itself of feminists. For this reason, Sartre is encouraged by Madah
to sacrifice de Beauvoir, to shed her blood to save his soul. Admitting his
frustration, Sartre asks a simple question of Madah. "Have you ever wondered WHY you have this hate in you?" (35). To which Madah replies in ex-
asperation, "Who gave you the right to speak for the third world? . . . Why
should we adopt your values?" (36). To which Sartre retorts: "Democracy
and freedom are not Western luxuries, but rather a right for everyone . . .
All Others who are different I accept . . . That's called tolerance. But you,
Madah, you hate difference, you fight it. You claim responsibility for the
killing of secular and Muslim intellectuals, poets, and actors" (37).

At a key point in this exchange between Sartre and his captor, Madah
holds up an image of the playwright's sister, Khalida (though not identified
by her full name, Khalida Toumi) during her famous debate on Algerian
national television with Abbasi Madani, the FIS leader, and states: "Look
at her. She came in front of the cameras without a veil: that's forbidden. She
wore tight pants: forbidden. She wore makeup: forbidden. She went to the
hair salon and curled her red hair: forbidden. She spoke French: forbidden.
She looked at him in the eye: sacrilegious. She came to challenge our values

and (furious) . . . broke . . . seven rules! Seven! She is the sister of Satan. If Khalida thinks she is flouting us, she'll pay for it one day" (37).

The playwright's decision to insert his sister here is powerfully effective. Understanding the connection between Khalida and Alek Toumi also helps us understand why Toumi devotes considerable attention to feminism throughout the play. In fact one of the most heated exchanges between Sartre and Madah concerns the issue of women's rights. As Madah explains to Sartre: "Women are the devil, Satan, temptation. . . . And your Simone with her theories has only corrupted our girls" (38).

While the play has a number of very serious points, such as the discussion of the raping of women and children, there are also a number of lighthearted moments. One of the most humorous occurs during act 5, or the "Third Attempt at Conversion." Here we find Sartre and Madah engaged in a discussion about heaven. Madah confidently asserts that he has nothing to fear after death, and Sartre—hardly a candidate to fall from heaven to discuss the virtues of the afterlife with an Islamic extremist—banters with Madah about the mysteries of God's identity. Near the end of the play, Sartre does let Madah in on a secret: that God is a woman. Madah accuses Sartre of heresy, and Sartre continues: "But it is Satan who is a man . . . The devil is a guy, macho, bearded, sexist and misogynist. The antithesis of God" (92).

After several attempts by the Islamists to convert Sartre, Toumi reintroduces de Beauvoir. The scenes involving her focus mostly on women attempting to get her to wear a chador and convert to Islam. In one effort to have de Beauvoir don a veil, the "First Chadorette" smiles at her and says. "Your name . . . Simone de 'Beau-voir' means 'beautiful-to-see.' Wear it and become Simone de Beau-veil" (57). De Beauvoir remains steadfast in her disapproval of the veil and refuses to entertain the notion of wearing one. She responds to these efforts by borrowing the criticisms of Khalida Toumi: "They [Islamists] have fabricated a new Other . . . the woman. They force you to wear this chador. This fundamentalist veil, the chador is your yellow star" (61).[37] To which the "Chief Chador" replies, again recalling Khalida Toumi: "Feminist propaganda. That is the work of Kahina. Not only has she read your books, but now, it is you who read hers . . . Unbowed! She did escape twice . . . next time, she'll pay for it" (61).

In fact, it is in Unbowed that Khalida Toumi outlines the reasons for the Islamists' hatred for women's sexuality and why the veil was suddenly being imposed on women. According to her, the Islamists—building, in Algeria's case, upon the preexisting biases of the Mediterranean patriarchal system and the enfeeblement done to women during the colonial era—were simply following their totalitarian urge to control women and hide overt signs of sexual differences. The women who refuse to submit to this gendered manipulation of themselves and their bodies simply become alien and therefore dangerous to the hegemony the Islamists seek to impose with the veil. The result, Khalida Toumi explains, is clear: Those women "become perfect targets because they embody the Other that fundamentalists need to mobilize and rally people to their cause" (109).

As it turns out, though, *Madah-Sartre* is not just the story of the miraculous return of deceased intellectuals. One of the most important characters, indeed, perhaps the most important, is the poor taxi driver, who becomes the principal protagonist in the sequel to *Madah-Sartre, Taxieur* (2001). The taxi driver is trapped in both plays in the dangerous no-man's-land of Algeria's quasi–civil war. Sadly, like most of his compatriots, he cannot escape from the violence and is consequently caught in the deadly vice between the wrath of the Islamists and state-sponsored terrorism. Hence, when the taxi driver is stopped twice in the play by "police officers," he is asked to identify which side he is on: that of Le Pouvoir or that of the FIS/GIA. Unable to appease either "policeman," the taxi driver has his face slashed by each man, and he appears in various scenes throughout the play in a desperate attempt to find someone able to suture his gaping cheeks.

Taxieur, which features the various characters seen in the 1996 play, including the taxi driver and Sartre, pushes debates over the civil war in Algeria still further. In *Taxieur*, we discover that Madah has been killed in a shootout with the Algerian authorities, and we again find Sartre in dialogue with Algerians in the midst of a civil war. In several exchanges, Sartre converses with a character by the name of Maréchalissime—an old FLN militant from the war of independence now retired from politics. Maréchalissime, who clearly represents the Algerian state's interest, explains the ins and outs of the contemporary conflict to Sartre. Maréchalissime outlines how the Islamic terrorist groups have evolved during the past several years, pushing the situation in Algeria from bad to worse. Different Islamic movements such as the GIA and the Armée Islamique (AIS) are killing each other as clans, each carrying on its own war against both the state and innocent civilians. At one point, Sartre hints at the allegations that the massacres of innocents were being perpetrated not only by the Islamists but also by the Algerian military itself and states that he knows this through his recent conversations in heaven with new arrivals from the Algerian killing fields (50).

Toward the end of the play, Sartre, being Sartre, asks for a press conference after it is revealed that he and de Beauvoir were "alive" and well in Algiers. They escaped from the terrorists by the same method that Sartre had used earlier in the play, after tiring of arguing with his captors, by simply walking through the wall. In other words, Sartre and de Beauvoir had slipped through the GIA's hands by simply walking through the walls and onto the streets of Algiers. Several journalists line up in a flurry of questions: How were the conditions of captivity? Did they talk to the terrorists? Was Sartre now a *dialoguiste*, a person trying to compromise with the terrorists or an *éradicateur*, a person who refuses negotiations and is in favor of annihilating the fundamentalists? As the press conference concludes, before Sartre is once again driven away by the taxi driver, he is asked if there is a solution. Sartre confesses that the Algerian situation is extremely complex and it was now "up to the Algerians to make their own *chorba* [soup]" (70). At the conclusion of *Taxieur*, after he drops off Sartre at the airport, the taxi driver reenters Algiers and listens to the news on the radio that there have been more massacres and another bombing in Bab El Oued. At the same time, the DJ plays a song by Matoub Lounés, who was assassinated by Islamists in Kabylia on June 25, 1998, and one of the people to whom Toumi dedicated his play.

Given the recent testimony of former Algerian officers such as Habib Souaïdia in *La sale guerre* (Dirty War), in which Souaïdia has recently accused the Algerian military of torturing and killing innocent civilians, Toumi's work is a distressing reminder of the perils of contemporary Algeria.[38] His decision to write *Madah-Sartre* and *Taxieur* in one of Algeria's most dangerous moments is itself an affirmation of the power of art and a reminder that writing can be a mighty weapon in the fight against the powerlessness of exile. Far away from his homeland, Toumi was able to address the crippling effects that violence has had on Algeria since the 1980s and especially since the cancellation of the 1992 elections. But the decision to write did not come easily. One of the first obstacles to overcome was the feeling of guilt. As Toumi states: "Exile makes you in the beginning feel guilty because here you're very safe" (interview).

However, safe or not, Toumi felt as though he had to write because he believed in the call of the intellectual to work for tolerance. First *Madah-Sartre* and then *Taxieur* present, despite their comedic effects, a powerful meditation on the degree to which Algeria has succeeded in turning the postcolonial page and on Algeria's very real problems—especially the failure to develop genuine political and religious tolerance in the postcolonial era. As Toumi puts it: "For the fundamentalists, they are convinced that they are authentic. . . . Authenticity is a notion that is very hard to define and has led to a blood bath. . . . The fundamentalists want to establish what I call a fascislamist state. One way to avoid the conflict again is to accept diversity" (interview). The acceptance of diversity, according to Toumi, is Algeria's only chance for a dignified recovery from the abuses of state power since independence.

In his newest plays, *Albert Camus: Entre la mère et l'injustice, Ben M'hidi,* and *De beauvoir à beau voile,* Toumi returns to the history of the war and its legacy today.[39] In *De beauvoir à beau voile,* Toumi addresses the recent debates in France regarding secularism, the schools, the headscarf, and rape by returning once again to Simone de Beauvoir. In *Ben M'hidi* he presents an imagined last three days of Ben M'hidi's life before he was murdered by Aussaresses. Throughout the play, Ben M'hidi converses with the fictionalized character of Marcel-Maurice Bigeard (Colonel Gee), the colonel who allegedly guarded Ben M'hidi before he was hanged by Aussaresses (Commandant O). Inspired by Ausseresses's confessions and the debate it provoked, *Ben M'hidi* is a fiercely imaginative examination of the nature of terrorism and the odd mutual respect that these two combatants held for each other, whereas *Albert Camus* is a compelling reconsideration of the paradoxes of Camus's life as he tried to work though the colonial issues. In particular, as Toumi used Sartre's play *No Exit* to address the contemporary themes found in *Madah-Sartre,* he used the moral dilemma posed in Camus's volume of short stories, *L'Exil et le royaume* (*Exile and the Kingdom,* 1957), to address the issues left by the question of Camus after his Stockholm address. As Daru, the hero of Camus's powerful and evocative short story "L'Hôte," the only work written in Camus's lifetime that touches on the Algerian War, states in Toumi's brilliant rewriting for his play: "When I speak, people twist what I say. When I say nothing, people reproach me for silence. The first would like me to lend them my voice and the second would like me to echo them. France forgets that I am Algerian and the Arabs forget that I'm pied noir" (32).

September 11 and After

On September 25, 2001, French president Jacques Chirac took a provocative step by organizing the "Journée nationale d'hommage aux harkis." This public honoring of the Algerian *harkis*—those Algerians who fought with the French military against Algerian nationalists and who number approximately thirty thousand in France today, not counting their families and descendants—outraged many Algerians. In honoring the very people whom most Algerians considered traitors, many of whom were massacred in Algeria after the war concluded, Chirac stated that France owed these Algerians a special "moral debt" because of their "sacrifice and dignity."[40] Then a year later, on November 6, 2002, Dominique de Villepin—the former French minister of foreign affairs who became the nemesis of the Bush administration during the Second Gulf War and now prime minister—gave a speech in Paris announcing the opening of "Algerian Year" in France. As he explained it, " 'Djazaïr: An Algerian Year in France' " would be "no ordinary encounter."[41]

With the looming discussions of the possibility of an impending war in Iraq in mind, de Villepin celebrated this sudden need for France and Algeria to reconnect and seek reconciliation. This is a "courageous move. Courageous because our world is living in a time of every possible danger." Rather than fall into "aggressive or warlike identities," de Villepin suggested that Algeria Year would "fly in the face of these temptations." It would establish a "dialogue" between "peoples." This dialogue would not be easy, he warned, because of the "memories of trials and sorrows. I am thinking of the Algerians, of those who returned to France after the war of independence, and of the harkis, Algerians who fought with the French in that war. Of all those who suffered." De Villepin went on to celebrate the rich cultural links between Algeria and France and called for a newfound openness and tolerance in France that would now, he hoped, embrace diversity. Following on this speech, in December 2002, de Villepin flew to Algeria and conducted diplomatic talks with the Algerian president, Abdelaziz Bouteflika, in preparation for Chirac's historic visit to Algeria.

Chirac's visit was even more interesting. Perhaps realizing that his and de Villepin's comments on the harkis (which drew universal condemnation in the Algerian press) were offensive to Algerians, he made an equally provocative move in Algeria by laying a wreath on the monument for Algerian soldiers who died during the French-Algerian War. At the same time, he received an oddly warm welcome by thousands of Algerians calling for more visas to France, and whom the New York Times correspondent covering the visit recorded as chanting "Visa à la France," a play on the wartime motto "Vive la France."[42] Chirac arrived with an entourage of French business leaders, including representatives of oil firms, who were preparing to invest in Algerian oil production contracts. When Chirac addressed the Algerian

Parliament, he made no further references to the harkis but rather to the need for an alternative solution to the Iraq crisis.

Before the visit, the Algerians (and other North Africans) were unwilling to support France's position in the UN Security Council regarding the war on Iraq. As the *International Herald Tribune* reported, part of the reason Algeria and other North African states were reluctant to take France's side was that Algeria was becoming more dependent on U.S. assistance to fight against terrorism at home.[43] Meanwhile France had continued to observe the strict arms embargo placed on Algeria, even after the 1995 bombings on the French Metro and elsewhere in Paris and despite the Islamists' claims to the contrary. Hence, knowing that the North African countries were not eager to side with France in the struggles at the United Nations for fear of a negative American reaction, Chirac made his own appeal for the Algerians and French to unite in the war against international terrorism. "Algeria and France are determined to pool their efforts to fight international terrorism." By 2003, on the eve of the Iraq conflict, France looked for a formal association with the Algerian government. As he put it in his address to the Algerian Parliament, "We must unite too in order to prepare our future. France and Algeria are part of the same Mediterranean area. We want the Mediterranean once again to become a link between peoples."

What was the reaction to this state visit by Chirac? President Bouteflika declared that President Chirac should be awarded the Nobel Peace Prize if he could prevent the planned U.S. attack on Iraq. Meanwhile, while Bouteflika praised Chirac for rethinking the need for war in Iraq and for his decision to visit Algeria as the first sitting French president since independence, human rights groups took a different approach to Chirac's visit. In a February 21, 2003, open letter to President Chirac, Human Rights Watch called on Chirac to bring up the issue of the forced "disappearances" of over seven thousand persons during the 1990s by the Algerian government. Human Rights Watch specifically urged Chirac to demand the identity of persons found in mass graves in Algeria and to insist that the Algerian government account for the thousands of abductions. Echoing calls from the era of decolonization, the letter also asked the French to put pressure on Algeria to "establish a commission to investigate 'disappearances' that has independence, authority, and integrity to obtain information in the possession of state agencies."

Set against the strange and surreal backdrop of contemporary France and Algeria, the theatrical absurdities of events like the "Second Coming" of

Sartre and de Beauvoir seem almost as believable as history itself. Almost. Nevertheless, set against the bizarre history of Franco-Algerian relations, Toumi's imagination becomes as poignant as it is useful. His artistic re-presentation and re-situation of historical actors within the hellish conditions of one of the most complicated civil wars of the contemporary era allow for the highlighting of the all-too-real perils within Algeria today. Toumi's writing is thus perfectly balanced between the make-believe world of artistic license and Algeria's real-life terrors during and after its war of independence. Toumi's plays afford unique insights into the connections between the phantoms of an Algeria past and the identity crisis of an Algeria present. This is so because, in many ways, the essence of Toumi's theatrical work corresponds to the essence of Algeria's Hamlet-like dilemma: to be or not to be . . . a militarized, Arabo-Islamic, or secular-pluralistic society. And for Toumi, who is by no means shy to attack both sides, it comes down to a simple question: Will the moral and cultural bankruptcy of Le Pouvoir (the military clans who have ruled the Algerian state with an iron fist after the suspension of the democratic process in 1992) or the jihad of religious extremists be enough to impose a Taliban-like silence on the Algerian populous, especially on Algerian intellectuals? As we shall see, the story of and behind Toumi's representation of the conflict begins well before the first act of his first play, *Madah-Sartre*.

As for France, it is not likely fully to overcome the legacy of the war. This would be, perhaps, too much to ask; however, the fact that Jean-Marie Le Pen—who most observers believed had disappeared from the political spectrum—could win 18 percent of the national vote in the 2002 election run-off against Jacques Chirac, campaigning on an extremely vitriolic anti-immigration platform (targeting Muslim North Africans in particular) is itself telling of the problems remaining just under the surface in France. France has a long way to go in overcoming the trauma of decolonization, but the recent spate of publications regarding the use of torture and the debates they sparked indicate that there have been significant developments. The dialogue with the past had continued for many years, but somehow September 11 changed the course of the conversation in unpredictable ways. And there has been a growing realization that we need to better understand decolonization's relationship to our own time, but this understanding has become at once more complex and more apt.

One salient example of the legacy's complexity is represented in the August 2004 kidnapping of the two French journalists, Christian Chesnot (Radio France Internationale) and Georges Malbrunot (of *Le Figaro*), by the Islamic Army of Iraq. According to the Arabic news network Al Jazeera, Chesnot and Malbrunot were taken hostage by these radical Islamists out of protest against the parliamentary law passed in March 2004, banning the wearing of headscarves (by Muslim girls) that was scheduled to take effect in France at the beginning of the 2004 academic year. (They were eventually released in December 2004.) President Chirac, no doubt hoping to immunize France's domestic Muslims regarding this ban, which was already in the form of proposed legislation, claimed during his trip to Algeria in March 2003 that he indeed understood how the war in Iraq might change things. He stated to a group of Algerian students that "war would simply 'reinforce the camp of hatred.' " [44] The kidnapping illustrates that the French government had not immunized the French public by its anti–Iraq War stance and the domestic discrimination in public schools had not gone unnoticed among Muslims outside of France. As Ayad Allawi, Iraq's interim prime minister, stated: "Neutrality doesn't exist, as the kidnapping of the French journalists has shown. . . . The French are deluding themselves if they think that they can remain out of this." [45]

But in France there was universal public outrage against the kidnapping, and in an unusual turn of events, even those Muslim leaders most vociferous in their criticism of the French headscarf ban united behind Chirac's government, condemned the kidnapping, and stated publicly that efforts to remove the ban would have to be done through domestic legal channels.

In concluding, it is important to bear in mind that today's urgency in understanding history requires even more vigilance in order not to repeat yesterday's lessons. Or, in borrowing a line from Shakespeare's *Macbeth*, what should be avoided is a situation in which "Fair is foul, and foul is fair." We must remain on guard against the effects that confessions of torture and the temptation to misuse these confessions may have on events today. This is why, I believe, ghost walking in Algiers can be good exercise for us all. We need not go to a cauldron, as did Macbeth, to conjure up phantoms. Contemporary writers such as Toumi have helped us a great deal in confronting that necessity. Yet the question remains. Are societies, in France and Algeria, and now elsewhere throughout the world, able to hear these new voices of dissent, or will they succumb to the temptation to make foulness fair by forming heroes out of the clay of yesterday's villains?

CONCLUSION
The Politics of Identity

In place of imposing one's vision of things on the Other, we would be better off accepting the Other's difference.

ALEK BAYLEE (TOUMI), 1996

The French-Algerian War represents one of the most critical moments in modern French history since the French Revolution. During the period between 1954 and 1962 the politics of identity permeated French intellectual life, just as the war and decolonization percolated through nearly all aspects of everyday life. The war forced intellectuals to rethink their notions of selfhood and nationalism, which until then had been bound to notions of universalism. This rethinking in turn called into question the foundational ideas of modern France: liberty, equality, fraternity. The issue of Franco-Muslim reconciliation was a key factor in advancing this crisis, and the related identity politics factored into French and Algerian efforts to redefine themselves during decolonization. French intellectuals' efforts at self-definition and their compulsion to represent Algerian identity had important political consequences for their own day-to-day lives as well as the lives of the Algerian people.

However we have also seen that the Algerians' eventual rejection of Franco-Muslim reconciliation once again forced French and Algerian intellectuals to reassess the status of contemporary identity politics. Contrary to what we may have expected at the outset, it took many years for intellectuals—French and Algerians alike—to reach the point where the differences between the French and Algerian peoples were considered irreconcilable. Various factors account for this gradual progression from reconciliation to rupture, but there should be no doubt that the dissolution of what was called Franco-Muslim reconciliation can be attributed to the problem of violence and a host of issues associated with the politics of representing Algerian and French identity.

It should also be clear that, regardless of what came to be seen as the impending doom of reconciliation, the idea remained an extremely powerful narcotic, if not an illusion, for many well-intended French liberals, leftists, and Algerians sympathetic to France. The introduction of Algerian nationalists' criticisms of the French efforts to revivify reconciliation showed how critical Algerian intellectuals were of French representations of Algerians, especially that of Algerian nationalists. French intellectuals were often unaware of, if not impervious to, Algerian intellectuals' opposition both to reconciliation and to French attempts to represent Algerian identity. This was seen most clearly in Algerian criticisms of the liberal and conservative French intellectuals' depictions of Algerian nationalists as fanatical, "Oriental," and "backward-looking terrorists."

To see the factors that led the French to ignore what the Algerians were really saying, it was first necessary to underscore the ambiguities within the anticolonialist community in relation to the issues of reconciliation and self-representation. Although many French intellectuals were able to work through the politics of decolonization with admirable energy, they often stumbled when it came to determining the limits of decolonization itself. In other words, many French intellectuals, particularly the Marxists, though willing to grant Algerian nationalists the right of independence, remained hostile to the idea of a radical break between the two nations. Most French intellectuals—and some Algerian ones as well—fully believed that such an Algeria would be worse off economically, politically, and, most important, culturally. This desire to keep Algeria even nominally tied to France was critically related to the inability of French (and some Algerian) intellectuals to accept the idea that French culture and civilization could no longer be considered universal.

It would be incorrect, then, to assume that most French intellectuals believed it immediately necessary to break the bonds between the French and the Algerian people. It would be even more incorrect to suppose that French intellectuals as a block argued that France had to abandon Algeria completely. Indeed, during the first years of the war (from 1954 to 1957), there was a remarkably high degree of ambivalence toward the idea of the complete independence of Algeria, even within the anticolonialist movement in France. In many ways, this was related to the peculiar elements of the French left, which were quick to denounce the suppression of freedom in North Africa but still unwilling to rush to condemnation over the Soviet Union's imperialism in Hungary as well as other satellite states.

After all, French and Algerian ambivalence toward the concept of absolute separation was conditioned by intellectuals' ambivalence toward themselves. We have seen that the question of intellectual legitimacy served as an approximate compass in the debates over decolonization, meaning that the debates among the French over the construction and ownership of intellectual legitimacy flushed out some of the more complex issues relating to the politics of representation and self-definition. Most important, we have seen how intellectual legitimacy—the self-representation of the intellectual—was bound to the issue of Franco-Muslim reconciliation and how, in turn, the representation of Algerian identity was woven into the tapestry of French politics and conceptions of Otherness.

But the theoretical damage had been done. After the Algerian revolution took place, those Algerian leaders who had taken power used the same arguments Fanon and Sartre had made about identity in general, and authenticity in particular. Many Algerian leaders and intellectuals spoke of a new postcolonial identity and the necessity of finding the "authentic" Algerian. In many ways, the Algerians had come to believe some of the arguments put forth by Sartre and by Fanon especially, whom they mistook for one of their own. Hence, in the immediate postcolonial period, Algeria attempted to structure itself politically along the socialist lines spelled out by Fanon and Sartre. Neglecting other dimensions that could not be purged, the country was able to operate in the illusion that Fanon's prophecy had come true, believing that they were indeed able to create something close to Fanon's authentic new man.

It took many years to discover how harmful the effects of this mythology truly were. Now, over forty years after liberation, the calls for authenticity continue, ironically, to haunt the very people who were able to benefit from their dissemination. It is not surprising, then, that contemporary actors now speak of the "Second Algerian War." What is surprising is that the leaders who had suffered the agony of torture at the hands of a desperate France now practice many of the same "antiterrorist" tactics against the very forces that had been so blindly overlooked in the formulation of the "new man." It is clear now, as soldiers guard the Arc de Triomphe, the Eiffel Tower, and schools throughout Algeria, that the repercussions of the legacy of colonialism and the failure of identity politics can still be felt.

Unfortunately, as Algerians have seen all too clearly, the quest to establish authentic identity through violence never ends. The Algerian state fell into the temptation of fabricating a national identity by limiting democratic freedoms and by persecuting its internal opponents, first during decolonization and then long after the end of the revolution. The longer this went on after independence, the more impossible it became for the state to exit from this dangerous game. Unwilling to compromise its supreme place after the revolution, the FLN quickly developed into a totalitarian regime and continued to hammer away at an identity politics that ultimately sacrificed the very ideals of the revolution itself. Eventually the secular nationalists were beaten at their own game and found themselves increasingly outflanked by a growing conservative Islamic movement that also used the question of religious authenticity to discredit the secular government.

In order to appease this movement, in 1984 the Algerian government stripped women of political equality with the punitive Family Code. A few years later, the FLN fell from power, and Algerian Islamists, with the backing of conservative Islamic states such as Saudi Arabia, stood ready to reap the rewards of its national electoral success and impose shair'a on the population. This process was then halted by a sudden but predictable military coup in 1992 that catapulted the country into a catastrophic civil war. By the mid-1990s, in the middle of this civil war, outside Islamic movements (some with ties to Al Qaeda) realized what was at stake in Algeria and sent armed Islamic guerrillas, who again brought with them their own notion of authenticity. Caught off guard, many local Islamic movements suddenly found themselves outflanked by even more extreme forces that followed the long-established pattern of using the notion of authenticity in Algeria to justify violence. The civil war in the 1990s thus demonstrated just how easy it was to recycle this form of identity politics in a country that had been unable to lay to rest this notion of authenticity after independence.

There are other ironies. French intellectuals returned to Algeria in the 1990s to assess the current crisis. Jules Roy and Francis Jeanson, to name two important writers, have noted how different Algeria is now and that a sadness has descended over the young nation. But while Roy and Jeanson returned in the flesh to reassess the problems of identity, Sartre and de Beavoir have traveled there in spirit and in the imagination of the Algerian writer Alek Baylee Toumi. In his 1996 play *Madah-Sartre*, Toumi has the ghosts of Sartre and Beauvoir revisit the Algeria of today. In Algeria, the two deceased writers are kidnapped during a taxi ride by the radical wing of the FIS, the GIA. Their intention is that Sartre and Beauvoir confess their wrongs and convert to Islam. During Sartre's interrogation by GIA member Madah, he refuses to convert, and Madah asks, "Why do you want to burn in hell with the Others? Why make this horrible choice?" (34). After being told that Beauvoir will be killed again, Sartre responds, "Hate is not something innate. Hate is a sentiment that one learns from one's parents, in the family, from one's friends, in one's town. It is above all the fear of the Other, fear mixed with a lot of ignorance" (35). Madah then declares his desire to rid Algeria of non-Islamic influences by eliminating the Berbers and their language. Sartre, seeing now how his philosophy has been used first by the FLN and now the Islamists, replies: "You want to exterminate culture because it is impure. It is self-hatred. How can you hate yourselves so? Hell is yourselves; it is not Others!" (41). Thus the imaginary Sartre is confronted with the so-called authentic postcolonial man—the very type of person Camus and Daniel had warned would be produced by violence and the quest for illusory authenticity.

Ironically, in act 7 of the play, Sartre praises his old friend, Albert Camus. Madah asserts, "Yesterday you condemned Camus. Today you defend him." "I can assure you," Sartre replies, "that today Camus is against what you are doing. Camus was for a diverse Algeria, free and democratic. Certainly, he was against independence because he thought that an Algeria uniquely Arab or Arab-Islamist would end in self-destruction. History has not proven him wrong. Your project of a totalitarian Islamic society is a negation of citizenship and the purging of identity. It is nihilism" (81). And so the Sartre who once preached that killing Europeans and killing the colonial system could be done with the same stone finds himself confronted with the very type of hatred his philosophy helped nourish and the very people he helped liberate.

Finally, one of the greatest French ironies of all has only just appeared on the eve of the publication of this second edition of *Uncivil War* and, perhaps not ironically, involves the historian's craft and the French state's efforts to revive its claims of colonial benevolence. On February 23, 2005—no doubt in response to continued historical scrutiny and domestic and international criticism of the conduct of the French state in the colonial world—the French National Assembly passed Law 2005–158. In large part the result of a coalition of pressure groups comprised of ex-colonials, veterans, and Algerian *harkis* now living in France, this new law states that "the Nation expresses its gratitude" to the men and women who "participated in the work accomplished by France" in its former colonial territories—especially in Algeria, Morocco, Tunisia, and Indochina. [1] Coming as it does at a time when historians have begun to uncover the harsh realities of French colonial history, the statute, as Claude Liauzu (French historian and one of the many French intellectuals who publicly condemned the state's actions) has pointed out in his recent article in *Le Monde diplomatique*, represents an affront to historical inquiry and is an unapologetic effort to silence historians. Nowhere is this more glaring than in article 4, which states the following:

University research programs accord to the French presence overseas, especially in North Africa, its rightful place [la place qu'elle mérite]. Academic programs recognize in particular the positive role of the French presence overseas, especially in North Africa, and accord to history and to the sacrifices the French army coming from these territories the eminent place they deserve.

By taking this formal position, the French state has decided to sacrifice historical inquiry for the sake of political exigency. This is most certainly because the French National Assembly fears that the reputation of the French state has been sullied by its conduct in the colonial world and especially during the era of decolonization. "This law," as Liauzu points out, "is an attempt to settle important debates: the relationship between memory and history and the relations between historians and power [le pouvoir]." Can you imagine, he continues, a class where one teaches exclusively the "positive role" of the French oeuvre?

Contemporary French historians cannot imagine such a course, nor, it is fair to say, could the readers of this book. And it is quite clear why. However difficult and painful it is for politicians to separate history from memory in the present political climates of France and Algeria, it is obvious that the narrative of the French-Algerian War continues to reverberate throughout Algeria and France and in the memories and the imaginations of French and Algerians alike. Perhaps it will be a never-ending story. We have learned all too well over the past forty years that colonialism persists long after the colonizers leave. At the very least, colonialism's legacy still exists in the collective memories of the peoples on both sides of the Mediterranean; it can be read in novels, newspapers, history books, political speeches, and philosophical works. In the end, is this not what the postcolonial world is made of—threads from the past woven into the fabric of the present and future? If the French and Algerian peoples are not willing to wear the multicolored fabric of their full identity (past and present), if they cannot embrace an honest retelling of history and a forthright acknowledgment of past misdeeds, then it is clear that the story will continue to fester. If their governments succeed in dictating what historians may teach, as the French state would have it, then there can be no hope of ever overcoming the terrible legacy of this most painful aspect of each nation's history.

NOTES

Introduction

1. I use the term "French-Algerian War" throughout this work to refer to the Algerian war of liberation from France. I have intentionally abstained from the more conventional "Algerian war" because I believe the term is Franco-centric. Algeria has fought many wars without France. Hence, leaving aside the question of whether an undeclared colonial war can be called anything other than a civil war, I have settled on the more specific and neutral name French-Algerian War. I wish to thank John Ruedy for this insight.

2. I am not attempting to write a history of the war or of intellectuals during the era of decolonization; much has already been written on these subjects, and I do not aspire to replicate these efforts here. For general histories of the French-Algerian War see Yves Courrière's masterful multivolume *La Guerre d'Algérie*, John Talbott's *The War Without a Name: France in Algeria, 1954–1962*, Paul Henissart, *Wolves in the City: The Death of French Algeria*, Alistair Horne's, *A Savage War of Peace, Algeria 1954–1962*, and John Ruedy's excellent *Modern Algeria: The Origins and Development of a Nation*. For a comprehensive history see Bernard Droz and Evelyne Lever, *Histoire de la guerre d'Algérie (1954–1962)*; for the FLN see Martha Crenshaw Hutchinson, *Revolutionary Terrorism: The F.L.N. in Algeria, 1954–1962*; for FLN activities in France see Ali Haroun's important *La 7ᵉ Wilaya: La Guerre du FLN en France, 1954–1962*; for French intellectuals' collaboration with Algerian nationalists see Hervé Hamon and Patrick Rotman, *Les Porteurs de valises: La résistance française à la guerre d'Algérie*; for the most thorough history of French intellectuals during the war see Paul Clay Sorum, *Intellectuals and Decolonization in France*, Jean-Pierre Rioux and Jean-François Sirinelli, *La Guerre d'Algérie et les intellectuels français*, David L. Schalk's seminal *War and the Ivory Tower: Algeria and Vietnam*, Geoffrey Adams, *The Call of Conscience: French Protestant Responses to the Algerian War, 1954–1962*, and Philip Dine, *Images of the Algerian War: French Fiction and Film, 1954–1992*. For the period preceding the era of decolonization see David Prochaska, *Making Algeria French: Colonialism in Bône, 1870–1920*, Patricia M. E. Lorcin, *Imperial Identities: Stereotyping, Prejudice, and Race in Colonial Algeria*, Raymond Betts's groundbreaking *Assimilation and Association in French Colonial Theory, 1890–1914* and *France and Decolonization, 1900–1960*, and Alice L. Conklin, *A Mission to Civilize: The Republican Idea of Empire in France and West Africa, 1895–1930*. For more recent reassessments of the war see Pierre Vidal-Naquet, *Face à la raison d'état: Un historien dans la guerre d'Algérie*, Benjamin Stora, *La*

329

Gangrène et l'oubli: La mémoire de la guerre d'Algérie, and Osman Benchérif, *The Image of Algeria in Anglo-American Writings, 1785–1962*. For the history of Islam in Algeria see Ricardo René Laremont, *Islam and the Politics of Resistance in Algeria, 1783–1992* and Julia A. Clancy Smith's superb *Rebel and Saint: Muslim Notables, Populist Protest, Colonial Encounters (Algeria and Tunisia, 1800–1904)*.

On the bibliographical level, my focus is at odds with Sorum's *Intellectuals and Decolonization in France*, the most comprehensive study of French intellectuals and the French-Algerian War. I do not assume, as Sorum does, "that in the debate over decolonization the writings of intellectuals can be studied without a great deal of attention to their biographies" (xi). To ignore the importance of biography would be to miss the relationship between intellectuals, their personal trajectories throughout the conflict, and the mutations the war forces within the careers of many. We should not deny that for some the major determinants of positions were intellectual, but I agree with Judt that the Algerian crisis helped ease the change from "universalist projections of a certain idea of France" (287). For many, ideological, political, or religious questions outweighed considerations of intellectual legitimacy. Albert Camus and Jacques Soustelle are good examples.

3. Ory and Sirinelli, *Les Intellectuels en France de l'affaire Dreyfus à nos jours*, 9. For purposes of simplicity I am accepting Ory's and Sirinelli's definition of intellectual as "a person of culture, creator or mediator, placed in the situation of a politician, producer or consumer of an ideology."

4. Judt, *Past Imperfect*, and François Furet, *Passing of an Illusion*. In my many conversations with Furet before his untimely death, he continually stressed the importance of the French-Algerian War for French intellectuals. He even noted that during this era he had been committed to the French left and the decolonization of Algeria. Decolonization was in his opinion a critical factor in post–World War II intellectual life.

5. See Stora, *La Gangrène et l'oubli*; see also Wood, *Vectors of Memory*.

6. Ory and Sirinelli also argue that this analogy is important (199). Many French intellectuals, especially the young historian Pierre Vidal-Naquet, consciously evoked Dreyfus as the battle cry of protest against the army's use of torture and brutality from the mid-1950s to the early 1960s (see chapter 6). Raymond Aron also used the analogy: "When the question of France comes up, there is no such thing as an impartial spectator. At the end of the last century Dreyfusards and anti-Dreyfusards were to be found all over the world (there were fewer anti-Dreyfusards abroad than at home)." Aron, *France Steadfast and Changing*, 2.

7. Soustelle lived through an assassination attempt during the war. A long-

time Gaullist, he eventually was forced to break with de Gaulle only after it became clear that de Gaulle was willing to let Algeria go. Soustelle remained pro–Algérie française and became one of the central leaders of the reborn Conseil National de la Résistance (CNR), the political group that came into existence after the defeat of the OAS. He always maintained that the OAS and CNR were two entirely different organizations. For an extended discussion of Soustelle's career after the French-Algerian War see James D. Le Sueur, "Before the Jackal: The International Uproar over *Assassination!*"

8. Interview with Paul Ricoeur, October 20, 1993.

9. This was acknowledged at the time by Aron, Maurice Merleau-Ponty, and Georges Gurvitch.

10. Ory and Sirinelli point out that since the official French government comprised the socialist left, it was also necessary for the intellectual left to distance itself from the political left in France.

11. Interview with Madeleine Rebérioux, October 5, 1993. The tensions within this position will become apparent as the study progresses.

12. Morin, *Autocritique*, 11. There was a similar identity crisis within the Algerian community. One important example was Ferhat Abbas, who had argued before the revolution that Algeria had lost its identity. Because of this he was thought to be too "francisé" by the hard-line Algerian nationalists who decided that only violence could lead to independence.

13. See Ricoeur, *État et violence*.

14. Aron, *France Steadfast and Changing*, 1.

15. Journalists actively attacked the French state over censorship. Taking the position that intellectuals must be free to seek and speak the truth, journalists were among the first to protest state activities in both France and in Algeria. Many were spied on with wiretapping and other methods by the secret police. Interview with Gilles Martinet, March 2, 1994.

16. For Sartre's use of the Other in his phenomenology before decolonization, see *Being and Nothingness: An Essay on Phenomenological Ontology* and *Anti-Semite and Jew*.

17. See Theunissen, *The Other*, and Fabien, *Time and the Other*. See also Hegel, *Phenomenology of Mind*; Husserl, *Ideas*; and Heidegger, *Being and Time*.

18. Roth, *Knowing and History*, 2.

19. The irony of this is brought out in later chapters when I argue that the encounter with the colonial Other helped lead to the demise of communism in France and caused many intellectuals to rethink the utility of Marxist theory. The theoretical (mostly anthropological) encounter with the Other emphasized the local or culturally specific dimensions of identity that could not be

completely assimilated into the universalist aspirations of communism. This posed an immense theoretical problem for French theorists sympathetic to communism or pursuing Marxist theory.

20. Interview with Paul Ricoeur, October 4, 1993.

21. Interview with Gilles Martinet, March 2, 1994. Messali Hadj (1898–1974) is often called the "father" of Algerian nationalism. His movement, Mouvement National Algérien (MNA) was liquidated by the rival FLN during the war. For the history of Algerian nationalism see Ruedy, *Modern Algeria*; Salah El Din El Zein El Tayeb, *National Ideology of Radical Algerians*; Emanuel Sivan, "L'Étoile Nord Africaine and the Genesis of Algerian Nationalism"; and Stora, *Messali Hadj*.

22. These tactics are currently being employed by the militant Islamic fundamentalist Front Islamique du Salut (FIS) in Algeria. It is perhaps one of the greatest and cruelest ironies that the same violent methods that brought the FLN to power (claiming the lives of thousands of Algerians) are being used against moderate Algerians today by the FIS and their militant wing, the Group Islamique Armée (GIA). According to current estimates, the deaths resulting from the conflicts between Algerian governmental forces, the FIS, and moderate Algerians now total over eighty thousand. This violence is in large part the consequence of the suspension of the results of the first democratic election in 1992.

23. Interview with Mohammed Harbi, October 4, 1993.

24. The French did not create the notion Third World, but were simply appropriating it for their own political agenda.

25. See chapters 5 and 6, and especially Bourdieu's and Daniel's criticisms of Sartre and Fanon in chapter 7.

26. For an extended discussion of hybridity in Algeria, see Le Sueur's introduction to Feraoun's *Journal*.

1. History and Franco-Muslim Reconciliation

1. Answers to the question: "Que feriez-vous si vous étiez invisible?" dated June 22, 1957, are from the private papers of Germaine Tillion. In the following, I have tried to keep as close to the original texts as possible.

2. Interview with Germaine Tillion, May 23, 1994.

3. She may finally have abandoned the idea of reconciliation on March 15, 1962, the day the OAS murdered six of her friends and colleagues who were working for the Centres Sociaux in Algeria. See chapter 3.

4. The term *ultra* refers to radical right-wing, French colonials in Algeria whose pro-French position led them to reject all measures of compromise and to

support all military and political measures aimed at keeping Algeria French. Their extremist politics often put them at odds with the metropolitan French population and politicians who no longer wanted to maintain the colonial status quo.

5. By identity debates I mean both the representation of Algerian and French identity (in the news media, government publications, private correspondence, and published works) and efforts of self-definition by French and Algerian intellectuals. By intellectuals, I mean primarily people who wrote about Algeria—journalists, philosophers, social scientists, novelists, and educators—those who described the effects of the war on the French nation, Algerians, the "Occident," the "Orient," and French and Algerian identity. I translate "Occident" as "West" throughout; when appropriate I leave "Orient" as is.

6. Todorov, On Human Diversity, 1. Todorov is not the only historian to point out the importance of monogenesis and polygenesis in European intellectual history. Léon Poliakov, in Aryan Myth, also argues for the importance of these ways of viewing human identity for the development of European racism. In particular, see his chapter "The Anthropology of the Enlightenment." Also see George L. Mosse, Toward the Final Solution; George Stocking, "The Persistence of Polygenist Thought in Post-Darwinian Anthropology"; and Nancy Stepan, Idea of Race in Science.

7. Patricia Lorcin, in Imperial Identities, makes a similar distinction, as do Agnes Murry in Ideology of French Imperialism, Raoul Girardet in L'Idée coloniale, and Raymond Betts in Assimilation and Association in French Colonial Theory.

8. See also Joseph-Arthur de Gobineau, Inequality of Human Races.

9. Yet Todorov is careful not to overstep the limits of comparison: "We are both right and wrong to project recent history against an earlier history in this way: right, because we cannot overlook the practical consequences of an ideology . . . wrong because [these French theoreticians] never envisioned the extermination of the inferior races in gas chambers. . . . Without seeking to impute to nineteenth-century authors what was going to happen in the twentieth century, we have to observe that the pernicious implications of these doctrines are not entirely absent, either, from the minds of the French racialists" (161).

10. Betts, Assimilation and Association in French Colonial Theory, 12.

11. Napoleon III did have the best interest of Algerians in mind. Unlike his republican counterparts, he generally respected Algerians, in particular the emir Abdelkader, the former leader of the Algerian resistance against the

French. For a superb discussion of the "Arab Kingdom," see Lorcin's "The 'Royaume Arabe' (1860–1870)" in *Imperial Identities*, 76–95.

12. In 1919 the French created a segregated two-college electoral system in Algeria: the French and Muslim Colleges. Both would elect members to Algeria's Consultative Assembly. Only Muslims who were ex-soldiers, significant property owners, or others chosen by the French could vote in the Muslim College. In 1945 de Gaulle's provisional government increased the number of Muslims allowed to vote to about sixty thousand.

13. Betts, *Assimilation and Association*, 26.

14. Émile Sedeyn, preface to *Philosophie de la colonisation*, by Edgard Denancy, 2.

15. Conklin, *Mission to Civilize*, 1.

16. Betts, *Assimilation and Association*, 30–31.

17. Conklin, *Mission to Civilize*, 21.

18. Leroy-Beaulieu, *De la Colonisation chez les peuples modernes*, xxiv.

19. Girardet, *L'Idée coloniale en France*, 127–28.

20. Soustelle, *Algérie: Le chemin de la paix*, 17.

21. "Déclaration de Monsieur Jacques Soustelle Gouverneur Générale de l'Algérie à Radio-Algérie le 12 janvier 1956," SHAT, 1 H 2464/D 1.

22. Feraoun, *Journal*, 65–66.

23. Jean [El Mouhoub] Amrouche, "Notes pour une esquisse de l' état d'âme du colonisé," in *Un Algérien s'adresse aux Francais, ou l'histoire d'Algérie par les textes, 1943–1961*, 50.

24. Amrouche, "Quelques raisions de la révolte algérienne," 23.

25. Amrouche and Feraoun wrote about similar problems, but they did not, in the end, share the same conclusion. In fact, in his journal of the war, Feraoun criticized Amrouche for overdramatizing the interior aspect of the Algerian conflict. "There is nothing more Jesuit than the heartbreak that he simulates, nothing more false than this inferiority complex that he dares to spread out lengthwise in columns. Here is a gentleman who has denied everything to the Kabyle. He is Gallicized to the tips of his fingernails." Feraoun, *Journal*, 236.

26. Beauvoir and Halimi, *Djamila Boupacha*, 74.

27. The fact that this happened in 1960 was extremely important because after de Gaulle took power in 1958 he pledged to stop the practice of torture in Algeria. Furthermore, André Malraux, minister of culture under de Gaulle, had publicly affirmed that torture was no longer in use. See also chapter 6. For an extended discussion of torture, see James D. Le Sueur, "Torture and the Decolonization of French Algeria: Nationalism, 'Race,' and Violence

During Colonial Incarceration," and Jacqueline Guerroudj, *Des Douars et des prisons*. See also chapter 6.

28. "Déclaration d'Abdelkader Guerroudj au début du procès," 1572.

2. Imbroglios and Intellectual Legitimacy

1. Sartre delivered a lecture in 1948 to a group of North African leaders telling them that they were being oppressed by the same capitalist forces as French workers. In a rhetorical strategy that became the hallmark of his attempt to combine the proletariat's struggle against capitalist oppression with the North Africans' struggle against French colonialism, Sartre offered these words: "Someone suggested to me that I speak about liberty. I first thought about refusing. Those who struggle for their liberation know better than the oppressors what liberty is." However, he continued, "It is because our liberty is in danger that we can speak of your liberty. . . . There is an abstract France and then there is the working mass who fights for liberty against the oppressor." For a full account of Sartre's speech, see "Ceux qui vous oppriment, nous oppriment pour les mêmes raisons."

2. Interview with Jean Daniel, October 20, 1993. Daniel is referring here to around 1900 and to the anti-Semitic movement in Algeria.

3. *New York Times*, November 8, 1954, 3

4. Mendès France had been planning to bring Soustelle into his government even before the outbreak of the revolution. The prime minister's first choice had been Paul Rivet, former director of the Musée de l'Homme. Rivet refused, saying he was too occupied with his work, and suggested Soustelle, a man of "honor" and "intelligence," as the person best suited for the position. See Rivet to Mendès France, Paris, June 15, 1954, DPMF, IPMF, Algérie IV, Soustelle.

5. Equally important is his active recruitment of two of France's best known and most respected liberal intellectuals, sociologist-ethnographer Germaine Tillion and Vincent Monteil, a specialist in Arabic, to aid him with his efforts at reform in Algeria. Tillion and her attempt to create an administrative and educational network called the Centres Sociaux to foster continued Franco-Muslim cooperation in Algeria are the subjects of chapters 2 and 3. Although much could be written about Monteil's role in the creation of the Sections Administratives Specialisés (SAS), I have chosen not to concentrate on the SAS in the present work.

6. In the 1930s he had been at the heart of the leftist Comité de Vigilance des Intellectuels Antifascistes and was later named secretary general of the Ligue des Intellectuas Français, organized just after Munich to fight against

Hitler's propaganda. At the outbreak of World War II, Soustelle was conducting field research in Mexico, but returned immediately to France and enlisted. He was then sent back to America on a mission shortly before the Armistice on July 1940, after which he joined de Gaulle and the Free French in London. De Gaulle charged him with creating the Comité des Français Libres and establishing diplomatic ties with other governments, mainly Mexico, South and Central America, and the West Indies. Soustelle reentered London in 1942 and remained a leading political figure and a staunch Gaullist until de Gaulle began to make plans for France to leave Algeria.

7. Ruedy, Modern Algeria, 162.

8. For Soustelle's account of the Philippeville massacre, see his Aimée et souffrante Algérie, 121–22.

9. Ruedy, Modern Algeria, 163.

10. Soustelle, "Lettre d'un intellectuel à quelques autres," 2.

11. CONFIDENTIAL, Algiers, June 1, 1955, 3–5, IPMF, DPMF, Algérie IV, chap. 6, Soustelle.

12. Soustelle's educational reforms were in part an attempt to develop further contact with the Algerian elites to keep them from becoming future revolutionaries (see chapters 3 and 4).

13. Gouvernement Général de l'Algérie, Pour l'Algérie, pour la France: Directives aux autorités locales, (Avril 1956), 139.

14. Le Monde, September 28, 1955, 4.

15. Ruedy, Modern Algeria, 63.

16. Comité d'Action, 2. André Breton and other surrealists signed the manifesto, thus signaling the reintroduction of the surrealists into politics.

17. Morin, Autocritique, 191–97.

18. Among the several hundred names on the original manifesto were Jean Amrouche, Simone de Beauvoir, Regis Blachère, André Breton, Aimé Césaire, Jean Cocteau, Jean Daniel, Jean-Marie Domenach, Marguerite Duras, Jean Genet, Georges Gurvitch, Charles-André Julien, Henri Lefebvre, Claude Lévi-Strauss, Roger Martin du Gard, Louis Massignon, François Mauriac, Jean-Jacques Mayoux, Paul Ricoeur, Françoise Sagan, Jean-Paul Sartre, Jean Wahl, Gaston Wiet, and George Bataille. It is worth pointing out that Jean Genet's signature was highly criticized in the French press because of his well-known past.

19. Soustelle quipped that the list of names on the manifesto contained both well-known intellectuals and "unknown ones, who, without doubt, desired to leave their obscurity" and "a few demoiselles quite unqualified to treat the problems of which they knew nothing. As little as I worried about the spe-

cialists, the unknowns and the demoiselles, I attached greater importance to the opinions of writers and professors [*universitaires*] whom I respected and among whom I counted friends. That is why I decided to respond." *Aimée et souffrante Algérie*, 170. Among the so-called "demoiselles" to whom he was referring were de Beauvoir, Duras, and Sagan. Camus took an equally sexist approach toward anticolonial French intellectuals who in his opinion talked about but knew nothing of Algeria. He referred to them, regardless of gender, as the "female left wing." See Todd, *Albert Camus*, 333.

20. At the outbreak of the French-Algerian War Soustelle was director of studies at the École Pratique des Hautes Études, but was formally detached on February 1, 1955, for the duration of his functions as governor general of Algeria. He was reinstated on March 20, 1956.

21. Soustelle, "Lettre d'un intellectuel," 1.

22. Parisian dailies like *Le Monde* and *Le Figaro* constantly referred to the Algerians as rebels, bandits, and outlaws. Indeed, one of the first assaults of the anticolonialist French intellectuals was against the French press for using these terms to describe the Algerian nationalists. See Colette and Francis Jeanson, *L'Algérie hors la loi*. See also Robert Barrat, "Chez les hors-la-loi."

23. Soustelle, "Lettre d'un intellectuel," 3.

24. Soustelle to Rivet, March 30, 1956, Correspondance Soustelle, Bibliothéque du Musée de l'Homme, Paris. It is important to add that Soustelle and Rivet, along with other French conservative elites, signed their names to a pro–Algérie française manifesto, "Un Appel pour le salut et le renouveau de l'Algérie Française," in April 1956. Both Soustelle and Rivet defended Algérie française before the United Nations in New York in 1957. Rivet went even further in a *Combat* interview, in July 1956, stating that he was in favor of French Algeria, thus provoking even more debate.

25. Comité d'Action, "Réponse au Gouverneur Général de l'Algérie," 2.

26. For an expanded version of this argument see Bourdet, "Votre Gestapo d'Algerie," 6–7.

27. This theme returns throughout the war and resurfaces in 1987 in Jacques Vergès's comments during the Klaus Barbie trial.

28. Letter from Jacques Soustelle to Comité, December 23, 1955, reprinted in "Réponse au Gouverneur Général de l'Algérie," 6.

29. "Réponse du Comité, January 10, 1956," in "Réponse au Gouverneur Général de l'Algérie," 6.

30. Amrouche, "Quelques raisons du maquisard," 22. For more on Amrouche, see Jean Giono, *Entretiens avec Jean Amrouche et Taos Amrouche* and François Mauriac, *Souvenirs retrouvés*.

31. In 1945 ("La France d'Europe, la France d'Afrique," *Le Figaro*; reprinted in *Un Algérien*), Amrouche had begun to treat the two-France theme, arguing that in Algerian France racism is "more than a doctrine." It is "an instinct, a rooted conviction" (8).

32. Césaire, "Le Temps du régime colonial est passé," 50.

33. For an interesting analysis of the importance of the Bandung Conference for the "Afro-Asiatic" peoples, see Malek Bennabi, *L'Afro-Asiatisme*.

34. Mayoux, "En un moment historique," 5.

35. Mascolo, "Pour l'abolition du colonialisme," 10.

36. Diop, "Pour l'amitié des peuples," 41.

37. Sartre, "Colonialisme est un système," 25.

38. A French Catholic, he had moved to Algeria following Liberation and had since 1950 attempted to prepare the French in Algeria for what he saw as inescapable changes. In 1950, he founded the journal *Consciences algériennes*, which lasted only a brief time and was revived in 1954 as *Consciences maghribines*. For his own reflections on his involvement with Algerian nationalism, see his *Mémoires d'outre-siècle*, vol. 1, *D'une Résistance à l'autre*.

39. Mandouze, "Reconnaitre ce qui est," 44.

40. After the December 2, 1955, dissolution of the French National Assembly and the January 2, 1956, electoral victory of the Republican Front, there was hope for a peaceful end to the war. But on January 26 Guy Mollet was selected to form a new government, putting an end to hopes of the progressivists. Mendès France was named minister of state *sans portefeuille*. Christian Pineau became minister of foreign affairs, François Mitterrand minister of justice, and Maurice Bourgès-Maunoury minister of war. Regardless, Mandouze met with Mendès France to bring messages from the FLN leaders.

41. Both Morin and Guérin attested to Sartre's objectivity concerning the treatment of the two rival Algerian factions.

42. Guérin, "Aux Membres du Comité d'Action des Intellectuals contre la Poursuite de la Guerre en Afrique du Nord," 1, BDIC, Archives Guérin, 721/91/2.

43. Morin, *Autocritique*, 192.

44. According to Chérmany, this was never carried out and was the result of a small faction who were eager to see the pro-Messalist French intellectuals leave. Chérmany conceded that he was a longtime friend of Messali Hadj and had worked with him in the past. Interview with Robert Chérmany, February 24, 1994.

45. In 1998 Morin once again expressed his commitment to an accurate historical account of the MNA through his decision to publish Chems Ed Din's *L'Affaire Bellounis* with his preface.

46. Morin, preface to *L'Affaire Bellounis*, by Chems Ed Din, 7.
47. Guérin, "Aux Membres du Comité d'Action," 2; Dresch, "Les Francais d'Algérie."
48. It is also the only speech not reprinted in the bulletin recording the speeches of this meeting.
49. Guérin's January 27 speech was titled "L'Algérie n'a jamais été la France" in *Guerre d'Algérie et colonialisme*.
50. Régis Blachère to Guérin, Paris, February 6, 1956, BDIC, Archives Guérin, 721/91/3.
51. Guérin to François Mauriac, December 13, 1954, BDIC, Archives Guérin, 721/91/2.
52. Guérin to Habib Bourguiba, February 10, 1956, BDIC, Archives Guérin, 721/91/2.
53. Comité d'Action, *Bulletin* 3 (February 18, 1956): 4.
54. Unsigned letter to the Comité, Mascolo papers.
55. Dionys Mascolo to Guérin, Paris, February 3, 1956, Mascolo papers.
56. Guérin, "L'Algérie hors la loi," 12.
57. Daniel, "Entre le chagrin et le haussement d'épaules," 11.
58. Interview with Francis Jeanson, December 11, 1993.
59. Jeanson to Daniel, January 16, 1956, 1, BDIC, Archives Guérin, 721/91/4.
60. This particular stance set the precedent for what would happen in Algeria for the remaining six years. The French government in Paris would never fully recover its ability to govern with authority in Algeria.
61. When Lacoste took over in Algeria, the post he occupied was officially changed from governor general to resident minister as a result of administrative conflicts Soustelle had had with the French government in Paris. Soustelle claimed that his ability to govern effectively in Algeria had been prevented by his obligation to report to the minister of the interior. As a result, Lacoste was able to bypass many of the obstacles Soustelle criticized. Ironically, as seen in the next two chapters, this allowed Lacoste to virtually hand over much of his newly acquired power to the French military.
62. Comité d'Action, *Bulletin* 4 (May 1956): 1.
63. The Comité repeatedly published political tracts from both the FLN and the MNA along with its own publications.
64. "Lettre des ethnologues," IMEC, Fonds Esprit, 1, ESP EI–02-02.
65. "L'Opinion des universitaires arabisants," 7. This group was composed of Arnaldez, Cahen Dresch, Gaulmier, Julien, Lombard, Massignon, Rodinson, Wiet, and even Blachère.
66. A similar dilemma faced pro-Communist intellectuals in 1939 with the Nazi-

Soviet pact, and as in 1939, communist failure to criticize the Soviet Union led to political Paralysis in France.

67. Aimé Césaire to Maurice Thorez, in *Oeuvre historique et politique*, 3:470.

68. "Contre l'intervention," *France observateur*, November 8, 1956; reprinted in Jean-François Sirinelli, *Intellectuels et passions françaises*, 177–78. According to Martinet, after the *France observateur* criticized Soviet intervention, subscribers increased substantially (interview with Giles Martinet, March 2, 1994). On November 29, 1956, an open letter by Soviet writers was published in *France observateur* along with a rebuttal by Colette Audry, Simone de Beauvoir, Janine Bouissounouse, Jean Cau, Claude Lanzman, Michel Leiris, Claude Morgan, Marcel Péju, Henri Pichette, Gérard Philippe, Promidès, J.-F. Rolland, Claude Roy, Jean Paul Sartre, Tristan Tzara, and Louis de Villefosse. The Soviets defended the Hungarian suppression on the grounds that the "uprising" was motivated by fascists and anti-revolutionaries. The same French intellectuals who had condemned Soviet actions in Budapest had not shown equal force in condemning recent French aggression against Suez.

69. Tony Judt's criticism of Sartre. See Judt, *Past Imperfect*, 156, 184–86.

70. Sartre, "Après Budapest," 15.

71. Comité d'Action des Intellectuels to its members, Paris, November 21, 1956, IMEC, Fonds L'Esprit, ESP2.EI–02-02.

72. Jean-Marie Domenach to Comité d'Action, IMEC, Fonds L'Esprit, ESP2.EOI–02-02.

73. Guérin, *Ci-gît le colonialisme*, 95.

74. When he met Francis Jeanson on his way to Éditions du Seuil, Sartre offered the petition condemning the invasion to Jeanson for his signature. Reading the names, which Sartre had just begun to collect, Jeanson saw that they were all ex-Communists, i.e., anti-Communists, and to Sartre's surprise Jeanson said: "We'll talk about it tomorrow." It was never discussed further. In other words, although Jeanson was not a member of the PCF, he did not want to align himself with others on Sartre's list known to be extreme anti-Communists. Interview with Francis Jeanson, December 11, 1993.

75. Morin, *Autocritique*, 197.

76. Interview with Edgar Morin, December 4, 1993.

77. Notes of Dionys Mascolo, Mascolo papers. Mascola was referring to Jean Dresch.

78. Interview with Dionys Mascolo, February 16, 1994.

79. Dionys Mascolo to the Comité, November 19, 1956, Mascolo papers.

3. Educational Reform and the Problem of Reconciliation

1. Aimard (French) was inspector and chief of the Bureau of Studies; Basset (French), inspector and chief of personnel training; Max Marchand (French), inspector of the academy, and a respected writer, director of the Centres Sociaux; Ali Hammoutene (Algerian) and Salah Ould Aoudia (Algerian), inspectors for Algiers; Mouloud Feraoun (Algerian), celebrated writer and adjunct to the director.

2. Very little has been written about the Centres Sociaux. See Nelly Forget, "Le Service des Centres Sociaux en Algérie," Jean-Philippe Ould Aoudia, L'Assassinat de Château-Royal, and Serge Jouin and Jean-Philippe Ould Aoudia, "Les Centres Sociaux Éducatifs en Algérie." For an excellent history of education in Algeria before decolonization, see Fanny Colonna, Instituteurs algériens.

3. Harrison, Challenging De Gaulle, 116. The "barbouzes" were French agents who went undercover to fight the OAS.

4. In the interwar period about 10 percent of the Algerian administration's budget went to education; of that, only about 10 percent went to the education of Muslims. In 1944, about 111,000 Muslim children were enrolled in primary schools, not even 9 percent of the population. Ruedy, Modern Algeria, 126.

5. I am using the term Franco-Muslim as it was frequently employed during the war. I am aware that the term was biased because it usually implied the integration of Muslims into French society and not the reverse. Europeans (including a small Jewish population) totaled about 10 percent, Muslims (Arabs and Berbers) 90 percent. The term is extremely important because it came to represent an influential and usually liberal line of thought throughout the war. In order to facilitate discussion, I have separated the two principal communities into "French" (meaning the population of European origin) and "Algerians" (the population of non-European origin). Further distinction, as in the case of Berbers such as the Kabyles, is noted as required.

6. Comité Algérien pour l'Éducation de Base, "Appel," Algiers, January 1951, Tillion papers.

7. Soustelle, "Discours à l'Assemblée Algérienne, February 23, 1955," in Pour une politique de paix et de progrès en Algérie, 3.

8. A month after he created the Centres Sociaux, on November 22, 1955, Soustelle wrote a governmental note to police and other Algerian administrators outlining his views for winning the Algerians over. See "Attitude à observer à l'égard des populations musulmanes dans la lutte contre le terrorisme," BDIC, Q pièce 508 rés.

9. "Discours," 4.

10. Soustelle, "Interview de l'information," March 21, 1955, in *Pour une politique,* 8.

11. "Discours," 6.

12. An anthropologist, she had spent many years in the Algerian countryside during the 1930s and had made lasting friendships with many important tribal and communal leaders (for an account, see Tillion, *Il était une fois l'ethnographie*). Moreover, a survivor of the Ravensbrook concentration camp and an important figure in the French Resistance, she had become an important figure in the French postwar intellectual community.

13. At the request of Louis Massignon, the Islamic scholar at the Collège de France, she was asked to verify reports that the French military was bombing the civilian (Muslim) population in Algeria. According to Tillion, Massignon had been infuriated by these reports, and because she was one of the French intellectuals most familiar with Algerian society, he asked her to return to the regions she had studied as an ethnographer from 1930 to 1940. Tillion accepted the request and arrived in Algeria in January 1955. For Tillion's autobiographical account of her experiences in Algeria see Tillion, *France and Algeria*.

14. Germaine Tillion to Louis Massignon, March 11, 1958, Massignon papers.

15. Interview with Germaine Tillion, May 23, 1994. She was referring to sterilization.

16. In one of the first educational documents published by the Centres Sociaux, the claim that Islam represented an incurable threat to Algerian demography was countered with the following footnote (Centres Sociaux, "Projet de Scolarisation totale de l'Algérie," December 1955, 6, Tillion papers):

> Contrary to what one generally believes, Islam does not constitute an obstacle for the control of births (it is in this domain infinitely more liberal than Catholicism) but on the family level, all the mental attitudes of the Algerian peasant are pre-Islamic, which is to say, sometimes in absolute contradiction with the spirit of the letter of the Qur'an. When one measures the small chance of survival in the society . . . the peasant society in Algeria is an archaic type of society where that sacred character is very strongly marked—and normally confused with a religious character (therefore Qur'anic)—when it is always pre-Qur'anic and often anti-Qur'anic.
>
> Above all, natality is much more influenced by the economic situation than it is by religion.

17. Tillion to Massignon, March 11, 1955, Massignon papers. This is important

because Soustelle was heavily criticized for his inability to withstand the ultras' pressures (see chapter 4).

18. In a letter written just after her arrival in Algeria, Tillion noted that, while Algerian nationalists had resorted to "frightening morals" (terrorism), some French policemen had resorted to torture. Tillion to Massignon, January 23, 1955, Massignon papers. It was widely known that one of the primary forms of torture during the French-Algerian War and other wars was the use of bathtubs in order to "interrogate" prisoners. Tillion makes reference to bathtubs in the letter.

19. The Youth Movements included the Algerian Muslim Boy Scouts, Algerian Muslim Scouts, and the Association of Camps and Vacations of Muslim Girl Scouts.

20. Isabelle Raymonde Deblé, speech in homage to Charles Aguesse, Saint Brieuc, November 4, 1992, 5, Deblé papers.

21. Centres Sociaux 1 (April 1956): 3.

22. Interview with Tillion, May 23, 1994.

23. Centres Sociaux, Direction générale de l'éducation nationale en Algérie, 19.

24. "Projet de scolarisation totale de l'Algérie: Les Centres Sociaux," December 1955, Tillion papers.

25. Centres Sociaux 1 (April 1956): 6.

26. Centres Sociaux, Direction générale, 25.

27. "Projet de scolarisation totale de l'Algérie," 3.

28. "Libres propos sur l'analphabétisme," 7.

29. "La Communauté aux bombes du Milk-Bar et de Diar es-Saâda," 8: "the people implicated do not appear, it seems, to belong to any existing organization. They acted as individuals or in small groups with common affinities and through common relations. These affinities were later skillfully exploited by the FLN through the intermediaries of 'special' agents."

30. Bromberger, "PAR AMITIÉ."

31. At the Frenchwoman's request, I am withholding her name.

32. Bromberger, "PAR AMITIÉ," 12.

33. Private papers of the Frenchwoman.

34. Letter of support, May 30, 1957, private papers of the Frenchwoman.

35. Letter of support, June 1, 1957, private papers of the Frenchwoman.

36. Charles Aguesse, July 17, 1957, private papers of the Frenchwoman.

37. "Réflexions d'un prêtre sur le terrorisme."

38. Poirot-Delpech, "Des Piens modérées sont requisés contre la plupart des inculpés."

39. Poirot-Delpech, "Le Tribunal se refuse à confondre l'esprit de charité et l'action nationaliste."

40. Following the trial results, Coudre's lawyer acknowledged that his defendant's actions resulted from a desire to keep an open dialogue between the two communities.

41. Bromberger, "Plusieurs des inculpés ont été les dupes du F.L.N."

42. "Voici le verdict des juges militaires."

43. Duval, "Une Déclaration de Mr. Duval," 6. For more of Duval's comments on the French-Algerian War, see his *Messages de paix*.

44. Duval, "Une Déclaration de S. Exc. Mgr. Duval archevêque d'Alger."

45. "Des Esprits faux" (editorial).

46. Michelet, "Le Procès des Chrétiens d'Algérie."

47. Gonnet, "L'Affaire des libéraux d'Alger."

48. Feraoun, *Journal*, 220–21.

49. In the correspondence and notes of Aguesse kept by Isabelle Deblé, I found no references to the progressivist trial or how he intended to neutralize its effects on the Centres.

50. Aguesse, "Editorial," *Centres Sociaux* 8.

51. "L'Enquête sociologique."

52. Aguesse, "Editorial," *Centres Sociaux* 9.

53. Beauvoir, *Force of Circumstance*, 388.

54. Since leaving his position as governor general, Soustelle had moved further and further to the right.

55. Lacoste, like Soustelle before him, had proved to be unable to resist the pressures and the influences of the French ultras who wanted the French government to do everything in its powers to keep Algeria French.

56. Comité de Salut Public de l'Éducation Nationale to Colleagues, Algiers, May 30, 1958, Tillion papers. This note was signed by Lombard and Fourestier, the latter a representative of the Centres Sociaux. At the bottom of the form, Centres employees were asked to either condone or condemn the events of May 13: "I approve of the position of the C.S.P. of National Education on the subject of the role of the Centres Sociaux" or "I have the following reservations."

57. Comité de Salut Public de l'Éducation Nationale to Comité de Salut Public du Quartier de ——, June 1, 1959, Tillion papers.

58. Letter to Monsieur le Recteur, June 10, 1958, Tillion papers.

59. In concluding their comments to the rector, the Service members wrote:

> It is up to you to tell us if the papers to be signed have been transmitted by regular means and accompanied by cover letters which

would call into doubt the patriotism of a part of Centre Sociaux' personnel.

They [the members] want to make their anxiety and bitterness known by having a general suspicion thrown on them, since December 1955, in attempting an "integration of the hearts."

60. "Projet et note de Service, addressé le 18/8/58 au recteur," Deblé papers.

61. According to French educational statistics, the number of Muslims compared to Europeans in traditional, European-style education in Algeria was negligible, but there was some progress. For example, in 1957 the ratio of Muslims to non-Muslims being educated in maternal care classes at the primary school level was 346,008 to 123,248. By 1959, that had climbed to 616,474 Muslims to 129,207 non-Muslims. In *enseignement du second degré* the numbers were much worse: 6,806 to 30,663 in 1957, rising in 1959 to 10,238 to 34,413. In 1959 there were 163 Muslim to 1,206 non-Muslim students at the Écoles Normales and 11,753 to 9,336 in the technical and professional schools. And, at the level of *enseignement supérieur* in the university faculties, there were 421 Muslim to 4,394 non-Muslim students in 1957 and 814 to 5,739 in 1959. See Capdecomme, "Éducation nationale en Algérie," 27.

62. "Ordonnance du 20 août 1958 sur la Scolarisation accelerée de l'Algérie pendant 8 ans," Ministre de l'Éducation Nationale, Académic d'Alger, 1, Deblé papers.

63. Capdecomme, "La Scolarisation accelerée de l'Algérie," 1, Deblé papers.

64. In Tillion's writings (discussed later), this tension between her vision of Europe (which represented hope and modernity) and Islam (which represented "archaic society") makes clear how deeply ingrained this division between European and Islamic civilizations was in the French imagination. It was precisely this dichotomy that made intellectuals such as Tillion certain that Algeria's only chance for survival in the modern world was in French educational and social reform.

65. Quiriconi, "Un Reseau FLN."

66. Note on the arrests kept by the Centres Sociaux, Deblé papers.

67. The reasons for the arrests were often feeble. For example, the twenty-year-old Muslim monitor was arrested, as she put it, "because I love a *fellagha* to whom I write and who is right now in Tunis." After stating that she had been the only woman among twenty-five military men, one of whom tried to make advances on her, she wrote to Deblé: "save me. . . . I am a wreck. . . . I am not afraid of the basement or the rats who visit me. They are not nasty. . . . I beg you, take pity on me." With the aid of Deblé and others, she was released

345

on June 9, 1959. Letter to Isabelle Deblé, Deblé papers. On Deblé's request, I am not reproducing the sender's identity.

68. "Les Centres Sociaux d'Alger était noyauté par le FLN."

69. See Tricot, *Mémoires*, and his very important *Les Sentiers de la paix*.

70. "Audience de M. Lepetre avec M. Tricot, Attaché à la Présidence de la République, Paris—27 July 1959 à 3 p.m.," Deblé papers.

71. "Noyautage communiste des Centres Sociaux d'Algérie."

72. "Tentatives de subversion dans les Centres Sociaux?"

73. "Note sur les Centres Sociaux Éducatifs en Algérie, Algiers, October 20, 1959," 1–2, Lesne papers.

74. "Note . . . October 20, 1959," 5–6, Lesne papers. Before concluding, Lesne wrote that Aguesse's intellectual qualities and the "purity of [his] intentions" were never in question.

75. Hammoutene, *Réflexion*, 70.

76. Feraoun, *Journal*, 121–22. He noted this because he had just attended an official reception with French authorities.

77. Feraoun to Emmanuel Roblès, *Lettres à ses amis*, 181–82. Also cited in Le Sueur, introduction to Feraoun, *Journal*, xxxviii.

78. Feraoun to Paul Flamand, August 6, 1961, *Lettres à ses amis*, 187. Also cited in Le Sueur, introduction to Feraoun *Journal*, xxxviii.

79. Hammoutene, *Réflexions*, 35.

80. Feraoun, *Journal*, 153.

81. Hammoutene, *Réflexions*, 53.

82. Horne, *Savage War of Peace*, 364.

83. "Address by President Charles de Gaulle on Algerian Policy Broadcast over French Radio and Television on January 29, 1960," in de Gaulle, *Major Addresses, Statements, and Press Conferences*, 71.

84. Saive, "Graves révélations du colonel Gardes: Les 'centres Sociaux' étaient noyautés par le FLN."

85. Le Recteur to Monsieur le Ministre de l'Éducation National, December 14, 1960, Lesne papers.

86. "Un Communiqué du Rectorat d'Alger."

87. "M. Capdecomme défend les Centres Sociaux."

88. Theolleye, "Le Colonel Godard." This claim seems to be indicative of the problem. Many of the staff were Muslim, and the army saw this as proof that the Service was sympathetic to the FLN.

89. Marcel Lesne to Monsieur le Délégué Général en Algérie, February 20, 1961, Lesne papers.

90. Feraoun, *Journal*, 304.

91. Hammoutene, *Réflexions*, 136.

92. In his October 19, 1961, journal entry he noted that an SAS commander had asked one of his colleagues in another Centre to act as an "information agent" for the military. See Hammoutene, *Réflexions*, 139.

93. Feraoun wrote on November 2, 1956, that Roblès was "more than just a friend or a Frenchman. I cannot connect him to any motherland because he is from everywhere, and that is exactly where I come from." See Feraoun, *Journal*, 147.

94. Feraoun to Roblès, February 17, 1962, in *Lettres*, 198.

95. Feraoun, *Journal*, 314.

96. Forestier, "Crime contre la culture."

97. Feraoun did not die immediately but four hours later in the hospital.

98. Tillion, "La Bêtise qui froidement assassine."

99. Tillion received several personal letters commending her for her very public attack against the dangerous OAS. For example, Vincent Monteil, her former colleague and co-member of Soustelle's cabinet, the Islamic scholar responsible for creating the SAS, noted that he understood and agreed with Tillion's rage at this odious crime of the OAS. Vincent Monteil to Germaine Tillion, Dakar, March 28, 1962, Tillion papers. Likewise, a director of a French lycée wrote of the possible utility of the martyrs for Algeria's future. "The death of our martyrs is, distressing, cruel, and painful, but it will not be useless." The acts of "murdering imbeciles" will come to good if they mark the end of the "seven years of imbecilic murdering." Letter from S. Bouberet to Germaine Tillion, March 19, 1962, Tillion papers.

100. "Obsèques des six dirigeants des Centres Sociaux assassinés à El Biar," 7.

101. Interviews with Marcel Gast, Isabelle Deblé, and Germaine Tillion.

4. The Unbearable Solitude of Being

1. I am using the word *question* much as Ernst Cassirer did in *Question of Jean-Jacques Rousseau*. In other words, not only are Camus's actions to be investigated here but also what Camus meant to public debates during the decolonization of Algeria and how his reputation influenced others in their ongoing struggles either to merge or separate anticolonialism and intellectual legitimacy.

2. Camus's term for *political correctness* was *conformity*.

3. Bourdet, "Camus ou les mains propres," 18.

4. Beauvoir, *Force of Circumstance*, 383–84.

5. Camus, unlike many other intellectuals, used *Arab*, not *Muslim*, to depict Algeria's non-European population.

6. See Jean Sénac's criticisms of Camus regarding his comments at Stockholm.

7. Neither Daniel nor Roy shared Camus's belief that at all costs Algeria should remain French. While Camus was alive, Roy did not openly criticize him, but he did issue a postmortem corrective to Camus's political shortcomings after his death. Daniel, although against violence, did not agree with Camus that Algeria should remain French no matter what the price. See chapter 2; see also Todd, *Albert Camus*.

8. It is useful to keep in mind that Camus's understanding of Algeria was mitigated by his affiliation with the PCA. Interview with Benjamin Stora, June 15, 1998.

9. Camus, "L'Enseignement," in "Misere de la Kabylie," *Essais*, 919. It is unclear why Camus focused only on the Kabyles. Some historians and Algerians have suggested that it may reflect the well-known tendency to perpetrate the policy of divide and rule.

10. Camus was also aware that both metropolitan France and the French in Algeria would deny responsibility for the fiscal costs of reforms. According to him, it was exactly this game—which on one hand affirmed that Algeria was indeed France, and on the other denied France's obligations to all people in Algeria—that was the source of most contradictions in Algerian politics. See *Essais*, 935.

11. Camus always claimed later that his writings on Algeria caused his expulsion from North Africa. This has been contested by biographers who indicate that there is no evidence of Camus's expulsion. When he left Algeria, the Frontist newspaper for which he worked had already been ordered to cease publication because of violations of wartime censorship.

12. Camus, "Letters to a German Friend: First Letter," in *Resistance*, 9.

13. Abbas (1899–1985) was one of Algeria's most controversial nationalist leaders. After unsuccessfully trying to mediate between the FLN and the French, he formally joined the FLN in 1956. Two years later he was made president of the Gouvernement Provisoire de la République Algérienne (GPRA). (The GPRA was created in Cairo in September 1958 as a reaction to de Gaulle's leadership. Using the prestige of leaders such as Abbas, the FLN saw the GPRA as a means to draw international attention to the movement. (It was the GPRA that terminated the Evian Accords in 1962.) Later, in August 1961, Abbas was supplanted by Ben Youssef Ben Khedda, setting a more radical tone for Algerian politics. In autumn 1962, Abbas returned to politics as the president of Algeria's newly formed National Constituent Assembly. But his faithfulness to liberalism quickly marginalized him among Algeria's revolutionary elite, and he resigned in August 1963.

14. Ruedy, *Modern Algeria*, 145–46. One of the most important Algerian nationalists, PPA founder Messali Hadj, was currently serving sixteen years of forced labor. His party had been banned in 1939.

15. Camus, "Crise en Algérie," in *Essais*, 941.

16. Camus, "Le Malaise politique," in *Essais*, 951.

17. Camus, "Le Parti du manifeste," in *Essais*, 957.

18. Members included Robert Barrat, Régis Blachére, Claude Bourdet, Yves Dechezelles, Jean Marie Domenach, Daniel Guérin, Charles André Julien, Louis Massignon, Maurice Merleau-Ponty, Paul Rivet, Jean-Paul Sartre, Jean Wahl, and others.

19. By this time Camus had already amassed a significant body of work: *Noces* (1941) *L'Étranger* (1942), *Le Mythe de Sisyphe* (1942),*Caligula* (1944), *Le Malentendu* (1944), *Prométhée aux enters* (1947), *La Peste* (1947), *L'État de siége* (1948), *L'Éxile d'Héléne* (1948),*Actuelles I* (1950). For an excellent discussion of Camus's fiction vis-à-vis the Algerian question see Saïd, "Camus and the French Imperial Experience," in *Culture and Imperialism*, 169–85.

20. Camus, "Les Justes," in *Théâtre, récites, nouvelles*, 339–40.

21. In an interview with me, Jeanson confessed that he has often regretted starting this polemic. Interview with Francis Jeanson, December 11, 1993.

22. Mouloud Feraoun to Albert Camus, May 27, 1951, in *Lettres à ses amis*, 203.

23. Camus's joining the staff added prestige to the journal, which already housed Nobel laureate François Mauriac's *Bloc-notes*. See Todd's discussion of Camus's relationship with L'Express in *Albert Camus*.

24. Almost immediately after joining the staff at *L'Express*, Camus fell into a polemic with Gilles Martinet and Claude Bourdet at *France observateur* over their publication of a confidential letter from Camus in an attempt to demonstrate that he was not a good journalist. In this polemic, the journalistic style of Françoise Giroud, also at *L'Express*, was pitted against Camus's. See Camus's response: "Le Vrai déba," *L'Express*, June 4, 1955; reprinted in *Essais*.

25. Camus, "Terrorisme et repression."

26. It is impossible to overemphasize this point. For Camus it was essential to prevent the French from seeing the FLN as the only representative body of Algeria's Arabs. By 1958 it had successfully wiped out the Messalists and cowed all other currents. But in 1955–56 it could not be considered the sole interlocutor of the French government in Algeria.

27. Camus, "L'Avenir algérien," 6.

28. Borrowing from Edward Said's classic *Orientalism*, one might detect a hint of Orientalism in Camus's writings; I have shied away from the term because it

does not fully explain Camus's views, which are far more nuanced than the common understanding of Orientalist discourse.

29. Camus, "La Vraie démission," in *Essais*, 976.

30. Camus, "Letter to an Algerian Militant," in *Resistance*, 127–28.

31. Camus, "Les Raisons de l'adversaire," in *Essais*, 978. One can only imagine Camus's reaction if someone had suggested he accept Étain's similar pleas for the French Resistance to stop using terrorism against the Nazi occupants.

32. Camus, "Trêve pour les civils." See also "Appeal for a Civilian Truce in Algeria," in *Resistance*, 37–42.

33. The Muslim sponsors (unknown to Camus at the time, all clandestine FLN members) were Mouloud Amrane, Mohamed Lebjaoui, Boualem Moussaoui, and Amar Ouzegane. The French Algerians were Jean de Maisonseul, Louis Miquel, Mauria Perrin, Charles Poncet, Emmanuel Roblès, and Roland Simounet. See Lottman, *Albert Camus*, 588–601.

34. Camus, "Trêve pour les civils."

35. Le Comité pour une Trêve Civile to Monsieur le Président du Conseil (n.d.), Paris, Institut Pierre Mendès France, Algérie VI.

36. Lottman, *Albert Camus*, 600.

37. Camus, "Appeal for a Civilian Truce in Algeria," in *Resistance*, 134.

38. Their commitment to the revolution surfaced when one of the participating Muslims said to Camus: "Only the men who do battle have the right to address that subject [civil truce]." See Roblès, *Albert Camus et la trêve civile*, 7.

39. Feraoun, *Journal*, 71.

40. Monsieur Bret to Albert Camus, Strasbourg, January 10, 1956, IMEC, Fonds Camus, Courrier Express, 1955–1956, A4.

41. Albert Camus to Monsieur Bret, Paris, January 23, 1956, IMEC, Fonds Camus, Courrier Express, 1955–1956, A4.

42. Camus made a clear ideological distinction between what he considered the positive attributes of colonialism and the Soviet's appetite for the political domination of Eastern Europe.

43. "POETS, WRITERS, SCHOLARS OF THE ENTIRE WORLD. HUNGARIAN WRITERS ARE ADDRESSING YOU. LISTEN TO OUR CALL. WE ARE FIGHTING AT THE BARRICADES FOR LIBERTY OF OUR COUNTRY, FOR THAT OF EUROPE AND FOR HUMAN DIGNITY. WE ARE DYING. BUT OUR SACRIFICE SHOULD NOT BE IN VAIN. AT THIS SUPREME HOUR, IN THE NAME OF A MASSACRED NATION, WE ADDRESS OURSELVES TO YOU, CAMUS, MALRAUX, MAURIAC, RUSSEL, JASPERS . . . AND MANY OTHER FIGHTERS OF THE MIND. THE HOUR HAS SOUNDED AND THE TIME FOR

SPEECHES IS OVER. ACTS ARE NECESSARY. DO SOMETHING. ACT. THROW OFF THE HORRIBLE INERTIA OF THE OCCIDENT. ACT. ACT. ACT." Telegram from Hungarian insurgents, n.d., IMEC, Fonds Camus, B4 (10) Politique I.

44. Camus to François Fejtö, October 31, 1956, IMEC, Fonds Camus, B4 (10) Politique I.

45. For a fuller description of the failures of the French left concerning the Hungarian tragedy, see Judt, *Past Imperfect*, 128–29.

46. Camus, "Réponse à un appel," in *Essais*, 1780.

47. Roger Martin du Gard to Camus, November 10, 1956, IMEC, Fonds Camus, B4 (10) Politique I.

48. Jacques Rodier to Camus, Paris, November 10, 1956, IMEC, Fonds Camus, B4 (10) Politique I.

49. Camus to Rodier, December 7, 1956, IMEC, Fonds Camus, B4 (10) Politique I

50. Camus, "Discours de la Salle Wagram," in *Essais*, 1783.

51. Camus, "Reflections on the Guillotine," in *Resistance*.

52. Minister of Justice, Direction of Criminal Affairs and Pardons, Legislative Service, "RAPPORT À MONSIEUR LE PRÉSIDENT DU CONSEIL, Decret No. Fixant en Algérie le mode d'exécution des condamnés à mort," IPMF, P. Soudet, Études Algérie.

53. Le Sous-Directeur des Affairs Criminelles et de Grâce to [Monsieur le Directeur du Cabinet a l'attention de Monsieur Aubouin, Chargé en mission], June 13, 1956, IPMF, P. Soudet, Études Algérie, 3.

54. Mauriac, *Bloc-notes*, 1:477.

55. Yves Dechezelles to Camus, Paris, July 26, 1957, IMEC, Fonds Camus, B3 (4) Algérie I.

56. Giséle Halimi to Camus, Paris, July 28, 1957, IMEC, Fonds Camus, B3 (4) Algérie I.

57. Dechezelles to Camus, Paris, September 21, 1957, IMEC, Fonds Camus, B3 (4) Algérie I.

58. Camus to Monsieur le Président de la République, Paris, September 26, 1957, IMEC, Fonds Camus, B3 (4) Algérie I. Guy Mollet was president of the council and prime minister of France at the time.

59. Camus to Monsieur le Président de la République, Paris, October 28, 1957, IMEC, Fonds Camus, B3 (4) Algérie I.

60. Guy Mollet to Camus, Paris, November 22, 1957, IMEC, Fonds Camus, B3 (4) Algérie I.

61. Stibbe had been informed through a mutual friend of Camus's position on

Ben Sadok, distaste for the FLN, and antipathy for the politics of the new left. Angrily, Stibbe fired off a rebuke to Camus. Pierre Stibbe to Camus, November 30, 1957, IMEC, Fonds Camus, B3 (4) Algérie I. Sartre testified on behalf of Ben Sadok on December 10, 1957, even comparing him to Charlotte Corday. See Le Monde, December 12, 1957, 20.

62. Camus to Monsieur le Président de la Cour d'Assises de la Seine, Paris, December 1957, IMEC, Fonds Camus, B3 (4) Algérie I.

63. Camus to Stibbe, Paris, December 4, 1957, IMEC, Fonds Camus, B3(4) Algérie I.

64. I agree with Tony Judt that "Camus was an unpolitical man," but only if one defines "nonpolitical" as "unaffiliated" in the strictest political sense. See Judt, Burden of Responsibility, 104. Camus's position on France's right to remain in Algeria can hardly be called nonpolitical in the broader sense of the word. Indeed, it is this unhealthy combination of the dual meanings of "nonpolitical" that makes the question of Camus so provocative.

65. This was also the case for other Algerian writers (Feraoun, Mammeri, Chraïbi, and Dib) who, according to Camus, were part of the "European" civilization.

66. Camus, "The Wager of Our Generation," interviewed in Demain, in Resistance, 243.

67. Daniel, "Albert Camus, 'l'algérien,' " 13.

68. Feraoun to Camus, Algiers, November 30, 1957, in Lettres à ses amis, 205. In the same letter, Feraoun described the situation in Algeria in a more depressing tone: "That which affects you, affects us all and we all know it. But we live in very difficult times, when the temptation is great to renounce friendship in order to hate."

69. Camus, "Discours du 10 décembre 1957," in Essais, 1071.

70. Camus, "Create Dangerously," lecture, University of Uppsala, December 14, 1957, in Resistance, 249.

71. "Déclarations de Stockholm," Le Monde, December 14, 1957, in Essais, 1881.

72. Camus to Monsieur le Directeur, Le Monde, Paris, December 17, 1957, in Essais, 1883.

73. Schalk, War and the Ivory Tower, 66.

74. L'Association des Algériens en Suéde, Stockholm, to Albert Camus, December 17, 1957, in Essais, 1883.

75. Jean Sénac (1926–73), born of French and Spanish descent in Algeria, became an FLN sympathizer during the Algerian revolution. His poetry celebrated Algeria's future independence. He is best remembered for his collec-

tions entitled *Poésie* and *Matinale de mon peuple*. He was murdered in Algiers in 1973.

76. Jean Sénac to Camus, December 18, 1957, IMEC, Fonds Camus, B3 (4) Algérie I, V Lettres françaises d'Algérie.

77. Sénac, "Camus au secours de Lacoste?" 3 (manuscript copy), IMEC, Fonds Camus, B3 (4) Algérie I, V Lettres françaises d'Algérie.

78. Camus to Sénac, Paris, December 19, 1957, IMEC, Fonds Camus, B3 (4) Algérie I, V Lettres françaises d'Algérie. Camus's mother was deaf.

79. Kateb Yacine to Camus, reprinted in Corpet and Dichy, eds., *Kateb Yacine, éclats de mémoire*, 33.

80. Martinet, "Qu'Albert Camus prenne enfin position," 15.

81. Discours d'Albert Camus communiqué par M. Bernfeld, president des Amitiés Méditerranien, January 22, 1958, 2, IMEC, Fonds Camus, B4 (11).

82. Camus, "Algeria 1958," in *Resistance*, 144.

83. Camus to Jeanne Sicard, Directeur, El Biar, May 24, 1957, IMEC, Fonds Camus, B3 (4) Algérie I, V Lettres françaises d'Algérie.

84. Camus, "Avant-propos," to *Chroniques algériennes*, in *Essais*, 891.

85. Feraoun, "La Source de nos communs malheurs," *Preuves* 91 (September 1958), in *L'Anniversaire*, 36.

86. Ahmed Taleb [Ibrahimi], "Lettre ouverte à Albert Camus," August 26, 1959, in *Lettres de prison*. Alleg brought torture in Algeria to the international stage with his devastating book, *La Question* (see chapter 6). See also Schalk, *War and the Ivory Tower*, 67.

87. Tillion, "Albert Camus et l'Algérie," 71. Tillion's comment here supports Tony Judt's observation that Camus's conception of Algeria "had been formed in the thirties," when the notion of an integrated community in Algeria was the dominant paradigm of many Algerians and Europeans alike. See Judt, *Burden of Responsibility*, 118. The same claim could be made for Tillion, who lived as an ethnographer in Algeria from 1934 to 1940. See Tillion, *La Traversée du mal*.

88. Sartre, "Albert Camus," 17.

89. Bourdet, "Camus on les mains propres," 18.

90. Daniel, "Albert Camus," 27.

91. Feraoun, "Le Dernier message" (January 27, 1960), *Preuves* 110 (April 1960); in *L'Anniversaire*, 45.

92. Roy, "Pourquoi j'ai écrit: 'La Guerre d'Algerie,'" interview, *Vérité-Liberté* (October 1960); reprinted as the preface to *La Guerre d'Algérie*, 17. See also Philip Dines's excellent discussion of Roy in *Images of the Algerian War*, 82–88.

93. "Un Entretien avec Jules Roy sur la guerre d'Algérie," 55.

94. Roy, *La Guerre d'Algérie*, 21.

95. When I interviewed Jules Roy in Paris, I was struck by his unqualified commitment to his friend Camus. As Roy said to me, Camus was "the master." Interview with Jules Roy, Paris, October 21, 1993. Roy went to Algeria and published his thoughts on the Algerian question out of profound respect for Camus because he firmly believed that Camus would eventually have changed his mind and broken his silence.

96. Alain Jacob, " 'La Guerre d'Algérie' de Jules Roy," *Le Monde* (November 9–10, 1960); in *La Guerre d'Algérie*, 233.

97. Patrick Kessel, "Jules Roy et la guerre d'Algérie," *France observateur* (October 6, 1960); in *La Guerre d'Algérie*, 233–45.

98. Claude Roy, "Jules Roy et la guerre d'Algérie," *Libération* (October 5, 1960); in *La Guerre d'Algérie*, 247–54.

99. Charles de Gaulle, "Lettre à Jules Roy, écrivain," in *Lettres, notes, et carnets*, 411.

100. André Benichou to Monsieur le Directeur de *L'Express* [Jean Daniel], Paris, n.d., Daniel papers.

101. Jean Daniel to André Benichou, Paris, August 8, 1960, Daniel papers. In a letter to Daniel, Benichou attacked Daniel for his sympathy for the FLN. Benichou went on to argue that Camus's name had been unfairly cited in connection with the possible negotiation with the FLN and stated that it was obvious that his letters of protest would never be published because they were censored on reception. They would never be published, moreover, because "the so-called progressivist-liberal-socialists were ardent enemies of freedom of expression," Daniel Papers.

102. René Char to Jean Daniel, September 4, 1960, Daniel papers.

103. See Wood, "Colonial Nostalgia and *Le Premier homme*," *Vectors of Memory*, 143–65. For a comparison of Camus's First Man to Feraoun's Journal, see Roger Kaplan's review of *Journal*, as "The First Man" *The New Republic*, November 6, 2000, 31–38.

104. See Daniel, "Un Intellectuel contre l'Histoire," 8.

105. Chelfi, "Les Beignets de la rue Bab-Azoun."

106. Milosz, "Un Homme déchiré comme moi-même." See also Milosz, *Captive Mind*.

107. Kovac, "Camus aurait milité pour l'embargo," 27.

108. See Mimouni, "Camus et l'Algérie intégriste," 14.

5. Shifting Views of Reconciliation

1. Not all intellectuals held this position; many continued to hope for reconciliation until the cease-fire on March 19, 1962.

2. Aron later lamented that his criticism of the left in *Opium* nearly cost him his long-awaited appointment. It was his "most glaring error," he said, to allow the book to be published three weeks before the election of the new holder of the Sorbonne chair of sociology. See Aron, *Committed Observer*, 161.

3. Aron, *Opium of the Intellectuals*, 312.

4. Aron, "Bandoeng conférence de l' équivoque," 1.

5. Aron, "La France joue sa dernière chance en Afrique," 18.

6. Aron, *La Tragédie algérienne*, iii.

7. Aron's vision of the West, for which he used the term *Occident*, included Western Europe and the United States; by non-Occidental countries he meant Asia, the Middle East, North Africa, and the Soviet Union. It is important to remember that Aron pictured the East-West (Orient-Occident) conflict as primarily involving a confrontation between the Americans and Soviets.

8. This was especially true, Aron claimed, since neither had been willing to grant internal autonomy to Tunisia and Morocco until terrorism forced the issue.

9. Aron's claim is absurd. According to French figures cited by John Ruedy (which Ruedy admits could be incorrect), in 1948 only 3 percent of male Muslims in Algeria had more than one wife. These statistics show a rapid decline in polygamy: in 1886 the French recorded that 16 percent of male Algerians had more than one wife. In this case, Aron's arguments tell us more about his own stereotypes of Algerians than about the Algerian people. See Ruedy, *Modern Algeria*, 128–29.

10. This is also how Germaine Tillion had referred to France's obligations in Algeria.

11. Aron did not think very highly of the Algerians who would assume leadership after the French departure: "The Algerians want the French to recognize their right to self-government. The fact is, in every way you look at it, that we have before us, in Algeria, the National Front (the FLN) and not the Neo-Destour and no civilian leader comparable to Mr. Bourguiba, no religious leader comparable to the Sultan [of Morocco]" (65).

12. See Benda, *Treason of the Intellectuals*.

13. Aron made several references to correspondence between him and Camus; oddly, no trace of these letters can be found in either Camus's or Aron's papers.

14. Roger Duchet to Raymond Aron, Paris, June 20, 1957, CRPRA, Fonds Raymond Aron, Algérie Lettres. See Duchet's collection of editorials for *France Indépendante* published as *Pour le salut publique*. In his article of July 29, 1957, "Pas de nouveau 'Genève,'" Duchet attacked Mohamed Yazid (a prominent

FLN leader who represented Algeria in the United States) for his intransigence on the issue of independence for Algeria and argued that the French leftist intellectuals had become just as dangerous to France as the FLN: "The political men such as Daniel Meyer, François Mitterrand, and Mendès France (we saw their collusion with the Communists in the famous night of special powers), the journals such as L'Express, L'Observateur, and Témoignage chrétien, the intellectuals such as François Mauriac, Maurice Duverger, and even, Alas! Raymond Aron, used the same arguments and defend the same thesis [as the FLN]. They sow doubt. Now a country that doubts is a country which abandons itself" (104).

15. Aron to Duchet, Paris, June 22, 1957, CRPRA, Fonds Aron, Algérie Lettres.

16. Duchet to Aron, Paris, June 23, 1957, CRPRA, Fonds Aron, Algérie Lettres. Duchet, along with others like Georges Bidault, Bachaga Boualem, and Jacques Soustelle were active participants in the extreme right-wing organization Rassemblement pour l'Algérie Française.

17. Jean Bommant to Aron, n.p., n.d., CRPRA, Fonds Aron, Algérie Lettres.

18. Claude Monflier to Aron, Colomb-Béchar, November 20, 1957, CRPRA, Fonds Aron, Algérie Lettres.

19. Robert Brassy to Aron, Paris, July 26, 1957, CRPRA, Fonds Aron, Algérie Lettres.

20. Robert Lacoste to Aron, Algiers, June 21, 1957, CRPRA, Fonds Aron, Algérie Lettres.

21. Jean Fabiani to Aron, June 19, 1957, CRPRA, Fonds Aron, Algérie Lettres.

22. H. Légier Dergranges to Aron, Paris, July 3, 1957, CRPRA, Fonds Aron, Algérie Lettres.

23. In the letter, Amrouche spoke of a recent attack made on Aron by Maurice Schumann during a gathering of intellectuals. Schumann was one of Aron's fiercest critics. See Schumann, Le Vrai malaise des intellectuels de gauche.

24. Jean Amrouche to Aron, Paris, December 3, 1957, CRPRA, Fonds Aron, Algrie Lettres.

25. Soustelle, Le Drame algérien et la décadence française, 1.

26. Soustelle may very well have been thinking of Camus in writing this.

27. Charles de Gaulle to Jacques Soustelle, August 19, 1957, private papers of Madame de la Croix.

28. This point is extremely important because Soustelle always maintained that he had been duped by de Gaulle, meaning that de Gaulle, not Soustelle, was the one who changed his position on Algeria. See Soustelle, Vingt-huit ans de gaullisme and L'Espérance trahie, for his account of De Gaulle's "betrayal" of French Algeria. See also James D. Le Sueur, "Before the Jackal: The Interna-

tional Uproar over Assassination!" historical essay to Ben Abro, Assassination! July 14, 183–254.

29. Daniel, "Des Vacances algériennes . . . ," 4.

30. Interview with Germaine Tillion, Paris, May 17, 1994.

31. Tillion, Algeria: The Realities, vi.

32. When Soustelle attacked Aron for his analysis of the Algerian drama in 1957, Soustelle pointed to Tillion's Algérie en 1957 as proof of the mission that remained for France in Algeria.

33. She continued by arguing that the reverse was also true: "And the other way round. In other words, when it comes to the religious attitudes, a Breton shepherd has more in common with a shepherd of the Ouarsenis than either of them has with compatriots who have university degrees." In my interviews and conversations with Tillion she often stressed the differences between contemporary Algerians and the French, thus indicating how estranged the two communities had become as a result of the increased influence of Islam in Algeria.

34. The actual number of Algerian workers in France during the war was closer to two hundred thousand.

35. By responsibilities, Tillion meant France's obligation to be involved in Algerian politics and society.

36. See Conklin, Mission to Civilize.

37. In 1955 Servan-Schreiber wrote to Soustelle, asking that he not misinterpret the L'Express writings as attacks on his administration.

38. Servan-Schreiber, "Un Rappelé parle," 15.

39. Servan-Schreiber, Lieutenant in Algeria, 46.

40. The term bicot, the closest English translation of which is "gook," was a highly derogatory word commonly used to denote Algerian Muslims. Its original meaning is related to "sheepskin."

41. Mouloud Feraoun also lamented the totalitarian character of the French state and the potential for the FLN to act in an authoritarian way. See Feraoun, Journal.

42. Serge Hurtig to Pierre Mendès France, Paris, March 27, 1957, IPMF, DPMF, Algérie XIV, A.F.N.

43. Mendès France to Hurtig, April 2, 1957 IPMF, DPMF, Algérie XIV, A.F.N.

44. Peyrega, "Le Doyen de la Faculté de Droit d'Alger écrit à M. Bourgès-Maunoury," 4. It appeared later in other publications such as L'Express. See also Jacques Peyrega to Monsieur le Ministre de la défense nationale," Algiers, March 18, 1957, IPMF, DPMF, Algérie XIV, A.F.N.

45. Very soon after de Bollardière's house arrest, several supporters, including

Christian Pineau, François Mitterrand, and Gaston Defferre, defended him. Even former Resistance hero Vercors sent his Legion of Honor back to President Coty in protest against the government's treatment of the general. As a result, in the Assembly, Guy Mollet publicly distanced himself from General Massu's paratroopers. See Horne, *Savage War of Peace*, 233.

46. Comité de Résistance Spirituelle, *Des Rappelés témoignent*, 5.

47. "Mélée, decembre 56 . . ." in *Des Rappelés témoignent*, 77.

48. "Il faut absolument que je fasse partager à quelqu'un ma culpabilité," in *Des Rappelés témoignent*, 76.

49. Capitant, "Le Miracle français."

50. *Le Dossier Jean Muller: De la pacification à la repression.*

51. Mauriac, *Bloc-notes*, 1:445.

52. Sartre, "Vous êtes formidables," reprinted in *Situations V* (Paris: 1964), 57.

53. In his argument, Sartre pointed to Mollet's April creation of the Commission de Sauvegarde des Droits et des Libertés en Algérie. Lacoste had asked Camus to take part in this commission, but Camus refused.

54. Simon, *Contre la torture*, 11–12.

55. "Le Complot," *Le Monde* (April 17, 1957), in *Contre la torture*, 133.

56. "Où le FLN se trompe," *Le Monde* (April 19, 1957), in *Contre la torture*, 137

57. Message des Forces Armées, *Morale de la guerre et morale de l'armée* (no. 21), April 1957, SHAT, I H2579/3.

6. Visions of Reconciliation, Visions of Rupture

1. The sources vary on the number killed, from 301 to 303.

2. "Un Allocution du président René Coty," 1. Coty was speaking specifically to countries such as the United States, which had an FLN "ambassador" in Washington DC.

3. Bellounis himself was later killed on July 23, 1958.

4. I thank William Cohen for this information. For an excellent analysis of the extent of FLN propaganda concerning violence as it relates to Mélouza, see Ihaddeden, "La Propaganda du FLN," 184, 190.

5. "Note de renseignements," P.R.G. de Médéa, n. 2909, Médéa, June 24, 1957, SHAT, I H1685/DI.

6. Mélouza has been written about by several historians. Alistair Horne attributed the massacre to the FLN on the basis of statements later made by Yacef and documents taken from the body of Amirouche, the Wilaya 3 leader. Horne and others have long agreed that responsibility for Mélouza can definitely be imputed to the FLN. Historians such as John Ruedy, Yves Courriére, and Mohammed Harbi also support this claim.

7. The Mélouza massacre was more commonly mentioned than the Wagram massacre.

8. It is difficult to know whether Fanon actually thought the French had carried out the massacre or whether he was trying to minimize the moral damage it had caused to the revolution. Since at this writing Fanon's personal papers remain inaccessible, it is impossible to know whether there is any evidence that would support or contradict his claims made in the name of the FLN.

9. Fanon, "Disappointments and Illusions of French Colonialism," El Moudjahid 10 (September 1957), in Toward the African Revolution, 59.

10. The harkis were Algerians who fought on the French side during the war. In 1957–58, the estimated total number of harkis collaborating with French authorities reached about sixty thousand. Clayton, Wars of French Decolonization, 139.

11. "Aprés le drame de Mélouza, Enquéte de l'ONU," 1.

12. Moreau, "Assez de sang et d'horreurs!" 1.

13. "Mélouza était un village FLN," 1.

14. Note to le Colonel Chef du Bureau Psychologique de la 10ring R. M., Algiers, July 4, 1957, SHAT, 1 H2464/D2.

15. Bachir Hadj Ali, "Lettre à nos amis français," Algiers, June 9, 1957, SHAT, 1 H2464/D2. Hadj Ali's letter was also published in France observateur under the heading, "Mélouza and the Algerian Communists" (June 20, 1957): 20.

16. Ben Smaïl, "Un Journaliste tunisien revient de Mélouza," 10.

17. Daniel, "L'Algérie: l'indignation est justifiée," 3.

18. Folliet, "Non à l'atroce!" Folliet had written several articles on the progressivist trials. He had also criticized the French government's handling of the issue of torture and the French army; see "Se taire ou dire vrai?"

19. "Communiqué du Bureau politique de la Nouvelle Gauche," 4.

20. Bourdet, "Mélouza, crime et faute," 4.

21. Domenach, "Les Enchéres de la terreur," 104.

22. Feraoun, Journal, 212.

23. Cited in Horne, Savage War of Peace, 246.

24. I saw these photographs in Germaine Tillion's private papers and was told they were sent to other politicians and advisers. Tillion was part of a five-member group called the Commission Internationale contre le Régime Concentrationnaire that visited Algeria's "relocation camps" and also the Mélouza site. See Tillion, La Traverses du mal, 108–9.

25. L'Opinion mondiale juge les sanglants "libérateurs" de Mélouza et de Wagram, 1.

26. Signed by Robert Barrat, Claude Bourdet, René Capitant, Jean Daniel, Gilles Martinet, Jean Nantet, André Philip, Jean Rous, Pierre-Henri Simon, Pierre

Stibbe, and George Suffert, the text was published in *France observateur* on June 6, 1957, reprinted in the pamphlet.

27. Ministre de l'Algérie, Cabinet du Minister, *Aspects véritables de la rébellion algérienne*. It is not clear whether the French distributed the book in the United States in the same manner as in France.

28. *True Aspects of the Algerian Rebellion*, 6.

29. Louis Marin to Monsieur Gorlin, November 15, 1957, CAOM, Lacoste 234.

30. Louis Papy to Gorlin, November 13, 1957, CAOM, Lacoste 234.

31. Charles Brunold to Monsieur le Conseiller, November 15, 1957, CAOM, Lacoste 234.

32. Faculté des Sciences de Lille, Cabinet du Doyen [name illegible] to Gorlin, Lille, November 14, 1957, CAOM, Lacoste 234.

33. F. Charles-Roux to Michel Gorlin, November 27, 1957, CAOM, Lacoste 234.

34. Paul Vienney to Robert Lacoste, Paris, November 17, 1957, CAOM, Lacoste 234.

35. Domenach, "Les Enchères," 104.

36. Gorlin to Jean-Marie Domenach, Algiers, March 29, 1958, IMEC, Fonds Esprit, ESP2 C3-01-01.

37. Casamayor, "Lettre à un ultra," 276; see also, *Le Bras séculier*.

38. Though not Algerian by birth, Fanon was one of the major contributors to El Moudjahid. I refer to him as an Algerian nationalist only in his capacity as a spokesman for the FLN.

39. Fanon, *Black Skin, White Masks*.

40. Fanon, "Letter to a Frenchman," in *Toward the African Revolution*, 48.

41. Fanon, "Letter to the Resident Minister" in *Toward the African Revolution*, 53.

42. Fanon, "Algeria Face to Face with French Torturers," in *Toward the African Revolution*. Fanon was expelled from Algeria for participating in a strike of doctors sympathetic to the FLN.

43. Fanon, "French Intellectuals and Democrats and the Algerian Revolution," in *Toward the African Revolution*, 76.

44. Fanon called this "active pseudo-solidarity."

45. Recall that the Comité d'Action des Intellectuels dissolved precisely over this issue.

46. Fanon is clearly referring to Tillion's and Soustelle's arguments.

47. Mauriac did not mention here that Ferhat Abbas had also converted to the FLN, thus destroying hopes for Algerian moderation.

48. Mauriac, "Bloc-notes," *L'Express* (January 9, 1958): 32; in *Bloc-notes*, 2:14–15. The *loi-cadre* was a series of moderate reforms Lacoste intended to implement; they were never enacted because of the ultras' resistance.

49. Martinet, "Réponse au F.L.N.," 4.
50. Domenach, "Une Mauvaise philosophic," 247.
51. Mauriac, "Le FLN et nous," 32.
52. Amrouche was a Kabyle Christian. Mauriac then reproduced Amrouche's letter attacking Mauriac's recent L'Express article on the FLN:

> We [Algerian nationalists] do give the impression that we are merely giving our opinions on the heartbreaking truth for all Algerians: the frightening historical void, the feeling of not existing in one's own eyes but only in the conscience of the Other [dans la conscience d'autrui], the feeling of not being in the world. To ask the FLN to renounce the claim of Algerian nationality . . . is to ask them to sign, if not forever, then at least for many years, the official death certificate of the Algerian people. Algeria must first be Algeria, it must simply be [qu'elle soit tout simplement], it must be recognized as foreign to France, it must pull itself out of the political nothingness where the conquest and the colonial enterprise has taken it. . . . This will be the end of an illusory friendship, but also the beginning of a new relationship where friendship can be reestablished between strangers, on the basis of new equality, and no longer on the relationship between a master and a slave or a master and a student.

53. Amrouche, "Pour un dialogue entre Algériens et Français, 12.
54. Martinet, "L'Indépendance, condition nécessaire mais non suffisante," 12.
55. Daniel, "Un Français d'Algérie," 26.
56. Daniel, "Jean-Paul Sartre," unedited interview, January 13, 1958, in Le Temps qui reste, 251–55.
57. In Force of Circumstance Simone de Beauvoir wrote, "In Algeria there was only one choice, Fascism or the F.L.N. In France we thought it was different. It seemed to us that the Left had nothing to teach the Algerians, and that El Moudjahid was quite right to put them in their place. But we still believed that it was possible to work for their independence by legal means" (370).
58. Daniel, "Le Destin algérien, la France, et l'Occident," 27.
59. In an interview with Pierre Vidal-Naquet about the origins of his concern for Maurice Audin, he told me that his primary concern has been the protection of the institutions of the French Republic. Having lost both of his parents in a Nazi concentration camp, he stated that as a Jew he had wanted to do everything in his power to keep an analogous fascism from creeping into France through the French-Algerian War. Interview with Pierre Vidal-Naquet.

60. Mauriac, Bloc-notes, 1:499.
61. Vidal-Naquet, L'Affaire Audin, 30.
62. Vidal-Naquet went further and claimed that racism with regard to a *sans nom patronymique* such as Mohammed might prevent the French from getting active in the efforts to end the war. Hence, because Audin was "French," the French would be more inclined to express outrage at his treatment. The expression "sans nom patronymique" referred to people without traditional French names.
63. Duclos, "L'Allocution de Jacques Duclos."
64. In 1961 the members of the Bureau of the Comité Maurice Audin were Laurent Schwartz, president; Jean Dresh and Henri Marrou, vice-presidents; Michel Crouzet, Jacques Panijel, Madeleine Rebérioux, and Pierre Vidal-Naquet, secretaries. In an interview Vidal-Naquet stated that, as the Comité continued its efforts to discover the truth concerning Audin's case, one of the greatest obstacles was the PCF. According to Vidal-Naquet, the PCF tried to make sure that every time Audin's name was mentioned it was done with reference to it. Tensions grew so strong between the Comite, the Audin family (Audin's wife was a strong PCF supporter), and the PCF that Vidal-Naquet and other members of the Comité were nearly forced to resign. Interview with Pierre Vidal-Naquet, Paris, May 25, 1994.
65. Schwartz, preface to L'Affaire Audin by Pierre Vidal-Naquet, 53.
66. With L'Affaire Audin, Vidal-Naquet demonstrated that the army's claim that Audin had not been shot but escaped was contradicted by the evidence.
67. Bouvard, "La Sorbonne rend hommage à Maurice Audin," 4.
68. La Question was published in Paris by Éditions de Minuit on February 17, 1958. Minuit had become famous for its clandestine publishing activity during the Nazi occupation.
69. Alleg, The Question, with an introduction by Jean-Paul Sartre, 39.
70. "Une Victoire" was first published in L'Express on March 6, 1958, but was immediately suppressed by the French government. It later became the introduction to Alleg's work when La Question was republished in March 1958, and was again confiscated and destroyed by the government. Sections of the essay were then republished in L'Observateur on March 8 and in Le Canard enchainé on March 12. Another edition of La Question was published with Sartre's essay in Switzerland by La Cité on April 11, 1958.
71. Sartre, "A Victory," introduction to The Question by Henri Alleg, 14–15. It is worth noting that the Algerian Muslims who were tortured were also French citizens, just not "French stock."
72. Mauriac, Bloc-notes, 2:36.

73. Mauriac, *Lettres d'une vie*, 340.

74. Denise Barrat was later one of the anticolonialist intellectuals arrested for signing the Manifesto of 121.

75. Domenach, "La Seconde victoire," 6.

76. "Note d'information à propos du livre de Henri Alleg intitulé 'La Question,'" SHAT, I H2464/D2, 3.

77. Reprinted in *The Question*, 123. It is somewhat ironic that when he assumed his post as minister of culture under de Gaulle, Malraux was criticized by Algerians in much the same way as he criticized the government for Alleg's treatment.

78. Sartre, "Le Peuple ne doit compter que sur lui-même," Comité de Défence des Libertés Républicaines du VIᴱ Arrondisement, BDIC, O pièce 362 rés.

79. Sartre, *Témoignages et documents sur la guerre en Algérie*, 3. Other anti-Gaullist intellectuals created a short-lived publication called *Le 14 juillet* in response to de Gaulle's "illegitimate" ascension to power at the hands of the *colons*. Among those contributing were Mormand Babel, Jean-Louis Bedouin, Maurice Blanchot, André Breton, Marguriete Duras, Jean Duvignaud, Louis René des Forêts, Daniel Guérin, Claude Lefort, Gérard Legrand, Dionys Mascolo, Edgar Morin, Maurice Nadeau, Brice Parain, Marcel Péju, Benjamin Péret, Jean Pouillon, Jean François Revel, Jean Schuster, Gérard Spitzer, and Elio Vittorini. See *Le 14 Juillet* 1 (July 14, 1958); 2 (October 25, 1958).

80. Sartre, "Le Peuple ne doit compter sur lui-même."

81. Bouhired remained in prison throughout the war. She was released afterward, and Vergès eventually married her. In a 1998 interview, Vergès told me that he much admired her during the war because she was in fact a revolutionary and was not claiming to be entirely innocent, unlike Djamila Boupacha. Interview with Jacques Vergès, Paris, June 20, 1998.

82. Cited in *The Gangrene*, 12.

83. See Beauvoir and Halimi, *Djamila Boupacha*, 203–46.

84. Jeanson claimed that it was important for him to go into hiding and that he was actually asked to do so by the FLN leader because he had "in his hands" all the information concerning FLN activities in France. Interview with Francis Jeanson, December 11, 1993.

85. Jeanson, "Cette Algérie, conquise et pacificiée . . . I," 613.

86. See Jeanson's introduction and afterword to Fanon's *Peau noire, masques blancs*.

87. For the most complete history of the development of the Jeanson network see Hervé Hamon and Patrick Rotman's *Les Porteurs de valises*. See also Marie-Pierre Ulloa's superbly researched thesis, *Francis Jeanson*.

88. Sartre's letter read at the opening of the Jeanson trial (actually written by Claude Lanzmann, cited in de Beauvoir's *Force of Circumstance*, 545–46) stated of Jeanson:

> [T]his practical solidarity with the Algerian fighters was not dictated to him solely by the nobility of his principles or by his general wish to combat oppression wherever manifested; it sprang too from a political analysis of the situation in France itself. The independence of Algeria has in fact been won. . . .
>
> This independence, therefore, I repeat is a certain fact. What is not certain is the future of democracy in France. For the war in Algeria has made this country rotten. The increasing restriction of liberties, the disappearance of political life, the general acceptance of the use of torture, the permanent opposition of the military to the civil powers, are all marks of a development that one can without exaggeration qualify as Fascist. In the face of this development, the Left is powerless, and it will remain so as long as it refuses to unite its efforts with those of the only force which today is truly fighting the common enemy of Algerian and French liberties. And that force is the FLN.
>
> This was the conclusion reached by Francis Jeanson, it is the conclusion I have reached myself. . . . those French people who are helping the FLN are not animated simply by noble sentiments with regard to an oppressed people, nor are they putting themselves at the service of a foreign cause; they are working for themselves, for their own freedom and for their future.

89. Jeanson, "Lettre à Jean-Paul Sartre," 1535.
90. "La Gauche française et le FLN."
91. Daniel, "Socialisme et anti-colonialisme," 809.
92. "Réponse à Jean Daniel."
93. Dionys Mascolo, one of the original founders of the Comité d'Action, was one of the principal motivators for the Manifesto of 121.
94. Cohen-Solal, *Sartre*, 420.
95. White, *Genet*, 411. See also Sartre, *Saint Genet*, for a fascinating discussion of Genet's "Otherness."
96. Cited in White, *Genet*, 411.
97. Morin, "Les Intellectuels et l'Algérie," 5.
98. Mascolo, "Lettre," 3.
99. Jeanson, *Notre Guerre*, 14–15.

7. The Politics of Othering

1. By Franco-Algerian or Franco-Muslim reconciliation I mean attempts to find a Political or social solution to the war. Whereas for procolonialist intellectuals reconciliation meant the continued existence of France in Algeria, for anticolonialist intellectuals (at least during the first years of the war), it meant something much more vague, best described as continued cultural and intellectual cooperation between the two sovereign states of France and Algeria.

2. For Sartre's uses of the concept see *Being and Nothingness* and *Anti-Semite and Jew*; for Fanon's see *Black Skin, White Masks*.

3. Jean-François Lyotard, the French intellectual credited with coining the term *postmodern*, was extremely active in the struggle against the colonial regime in Algeria during decolonization. See Lyotard's contributions to the journal *Socialisme et barbarie*.

4. See Schalk, *War and the Ivory Tower*, 104, 302n48. After amnesty Maschino was allowed to return to France, where he consciously attempted to take on an Algerian identity (under his adopted Arabic name Tarik, following his marriage to Fadéla M'Rabet). He later became a lycée professor of philosophy and turned extremely conservative. In 1984 he published *Voulez-vous vraiment des enfants idiots?*, in which he attacked the youth of his time for intellectual laziness. He continues to write on French educational issues.

5. Maschino, "Pour les français l'algérien lui-même," 6.

6. Jacques Berque, "Étude pour un nouvelle méthode politique de la France au Maroc" (rédigée à Rabat le 1er mars 1947), 8, Fondation Nationale des Sciences Politiques, SC7, Dr 4.

7. Berque, *Arabies*, 175.

8. Berque, "Leçon inaugurale," 6, faite le samedi, 1 décembre 1956, Collége de France, Chair d'Histoire Sociale de l'Islam Contemporain, Bibliothéque de le Musée de l'Homme. The importance of this lecture is also noted by Albert Hourani in his essay, "In Search of a New Andalusia: Jacques Berque and the Arab," in *Islam in European Thought*, 129–35.

9. Fanon made a similar argument about the power of the radio during the Algerian revolution.

10. Berque, "L'Inquiétude Arabe des temps modernes."

11. Berque, "The North of Africa," 18–19. Here Berque is referring to Sartre's *Anti-Semite and Jew*; he also comments on Camus's contribution.

12. Louis Massignon, "Colloque universitaire du 2 juin 1957 sur le 'problème algérien,'" in *Opera Minora*, 3:668.

13. Jacques Berque and Louis Massignon, "Dialogue sur 'les Arabes.'"

14. Bourdieu, *Algerians*. The revised edition of *La Sociologie de l'Algérie* (1970) included an important additional chapter, "The Revolution within the Revolution," first published as "Révolution dans la révolution" in the October 1961 issue of *Esprit*.

15. Methodologically, these terms were significant to Bourdieu's account of Algerian identity because they combined structuralism and phenomenology.

16. Tillion, *France and Algeria*, 56.

17. The first half of *France and Algeria* was devoted to a discussion of the relationships between Algerian and French patriots; the second half focused on the clear divisions created by the radicalization of the revolution. The divisions, she claimed, represented "Volume One" and "Volume Two" of human history.

18. "The war, following inflexible laws, though every day intensifying the practical mixture of the two populations and their anxious curiosity about each other, has seemed to divide them further and further. Between them stretches the smooth, fragile, but continually renewed partition that isolates two elements: air, water—autonomous universes. Nothing was more alarming than to listen to the echoes of two worlds so close and so distant, and to lean over mute Algeria, when the chatter of fraternization still vibrated in our memory" (172).

19. Merleau-Ponty, *Adventures of the Dialectic*, 189.

20. Sartre, *Critique of Dialectical Reason*, vol. 1, *Theory of Practical Ensembles*. For a comprehensive analysis see McBride, *Sartre's Political Theory*, and Laing and Cooper, *Reason and Violence*.

21. Sartre was not only attacking anthropology in *Critique*. He claimed that both "sociology" and "economism" had to be "dissolved in history" (716). More specifically, he criticized the "contemporary work of sociology" (Tillion) that used the term "pauperization" to explain the relationship between "backward" and industrial societies. In fact, he went as far as to claim that "the term 'pauperization' and the pseudo-concept which underlies it become utterly useless" because "they are both designed to take us modestly back to the *process*."

22. In an interview, Lévi-Strauss told me that as an anthropologist he did not feel qualified to offer his opinions on decolonization in Algeria. Indeed, one of the problems during the French-Algerian War, according to him, was that too many unqualified intellectuals were entering the debates without sufficient expertise on the subject. He also expressed regret that so many French intellectuals had been for Algerian independence, since it was clear

that Algeria's leaders had been unable to lead the nation properly. Interview with Claude Lévi-Strauss, May 28, 1994.

23. Lévi-Strauss, *Savage Mind*, 245. It is important to note that Lévi-Strauss dedicated *Savage Mind* to Merleau-Ponty.

24. Aron, *History and the Dialectic of Violence*.

25. In *Savage Mind* Lévi-Strauss did admit that "in both our cases Marx is the point of departure of our thought" (246).

26. Levinas, *Totality and Infinity*, 21.

27. There are important similarities between Levinas's and Louis Massignon's use of "hospitality." Both use the term to describe ethical relations between individuals.

28. Berque, *French North Africa*, 331.

29. "For the European, who, or rather, what was the 'native'? A menace, an uncertain quality, something to be made use of or at best to be taken care of" (388).

30. Sartre, review of Albert Memmi, *Portrait du colonisé, précédé du Portrait du colonisateur*.

31. Sartre, introduction *The Colonizer and the Colonized* by Albert Memmi, xxii.

32. Laing and Cooper, *Reason and Violence*, give a very good explanation of Sartre's obsession with this issue.

33. Memmi, *The Colonizer and the Colonized*, 9.

34. It is pretty clear here that Memmi was warning against the excessive use of force by organizations such as the FLN and MNA.

35. In an interview, Memmi told me that part of the reason he decided to write *Dependence* (the follow-up to *The Colonizer and the Colonized*) was his desire to avoid unnecessary violence and move beyond strict binary categories. Interview with Albert Memmi, Paris, October 6, 1993.

36. Fanon, *Dying Colonialism*, 24.

37. Fanon, "Pourquoi nous employons la violence." Fanon was appointed ambassador for Algeria's provisional government in Accra in 1960.

38. According to Simone de Beauvoir, it was Fanon who asked Sartre to write the preface to *The Wretched of the Earth*. See Beauvoir, *Force of Circumstance*, 591.

39. The Melun Conference, held June 25–29, 1960, was the first important step in arriving at the cease-fire that would be secured by the Evian Accords. It was announced on June 14 when de Gaulle stated publicly that France was willing to negotiate with the "insurrection'"s leaders, the GPRA. Because de Gaulle demanded a conditional cease-fire before talks could begin, the conference was quickly abandoned by the FLN.

40. Sartre, preface to Fanon's *Wretched of the Earth*, 24.

41. Fanon, *Wretched of the Earth*, 36.

42. Others such as Feraoun and Camus did understand that the violence of the French-Algerian War would not simply disappear after independence. Camus warned against this throughout the war, and Feraoun wrote about it quite extensively in his *Journal*. Here it must be stated that while Fanon (as a non-Algerian) helped solidify the mythology of violence, Feraoun (as an Algerian) and Camus (as a *pied noir*) understood that violence would pose a danger for Algerians because they would be unable to avoid the authoritarianism of the FLN, which relied almost uniquely on this violence.

43. Fanon went still further in borrowing Aimé Césaire's expression when defining what it would mean to educate the masses politically after independence: it would mean "to invent souls."

44. For Sartre, the question of the youth was extremely important because, according to him, "the only true men of the left in France today were found among those under twenty years old." Karol, "Un Entretien avec Jean-Paul Sartre," 2.

45. "Entretien avec Jean-Paul Sartre," 3.

46. Daniel, "Essai 'Les Damnés de la terre' par Frantz Fanon," 36.

47. Daniel, *Le Blesseur*, 65.

48. Daniel also wrote that Sartre was hypocritically attacking the "West, Europe, France, the bourgeoisie" at the same time that he denied his membership in each of these communities. It was for this reason that he looked to Fanon, in whom he found "the exemplary alienated [*l'aliéné exemplaire*]" (69).

49. Daniel did not criticize only Sartre, he also attacked Mauriac and others, though for other reasons.

50. Bourdieu, "Révolution dans la révolution." Bourdieu wrote the essay while teaching a course on Algerian culture at the University of Algiers. In publishing it he was taking dangerous chances. He had already been forced to go into hiding several times and was placed on the "red list"—the arrest and menace list of the French military. French colonels were present during lectures on Algerian culture, waiting to arrest him. Luckily, he managed to escape each of the attempted arrests. Interview with Pierre Bourdieu, March 30, 1994 Paris.

51. Aron, preface to Bourdieu's *Algerians*, v.

52. Bourdieu, *Algerians*, 146.

53. Bourdieu also acknowledged that Algerians were making a further distinction of the "Europeans of Algeria," which meant essentially that, as with those of Spanish origin, the Algerians refused to "ascribe" to them the "qualities of the true Frenchmen" (152).

54. Bourdieu was undoubtedly relying on a phenomenological method to explain some of the cultural aspects of colonial society. For instance, he made several references to how the "looks" and "critical eyes of Europeans" altered Algerians' behavior, one of the most salient examples being clothing (e.g., the veil) which according to him represented the symbolic "language of refusal" (157).

55. *Speculative* is Bourdieu's word for Fanonian writing. In discussing his distrust for Fanon's analysis, which was representative of many other writers, Bourdieu claimed: "But above all I wanted to get away from speculation—at the time, the works of Frantz Fanon, especially *Wretched of the Earth*, were the latest fashion, and they struck me as being both false and dangerous." See "Field Work in Philosophy," an interview with Axel Honneth, H. Kocyba, and B. Schwibs, reprinted in Bourdieu, *In Other Words*, 7.

56. Interview with Pierre Bourdieu, March 30, 1994, Paris.

57. Ricardo René Laremont has also made this claim in *Islam and the Politics of Resistance in Algeria*. In particular, Laremont points out that Houari Boumediene—who overthrew Ahmed Ben Bella in 1965 in a coup d'état and instituted a firm authoritarian regime in Algeria—adopted Fanon's ideas concerning the revolutionary potential of the Algerian peasantry. Laremont argues that because Fanon did not understand the importance of Islam, Fanon's position on Islam did not have enduring consequences. However, Fanon's misguided views on the peasantry and violence did have lasting importance because Boumediene appropriated them: "Besides embracing Fanon's views on the peasantry's role in the revolution, Boumediene fully accepted Fanon's ideas about the need for violence to effect political change, and he shared Fanon's suspicion and disdain for the urban bourgeoisie" (151).

58. See Stora, "Deuxième guerre algérienne?" In particular, Stora argues that the original violence of colonization in 1830 was further compounded by the anticolonial violence from 1954 to 1962. The authoritarian postindependence Algerian state continued to compound the violence in order to ensure the status of the FLN, until, finally, the Islamists employed the same pattern of mimicry in their attempt to overthrow the corrupt and abusive FLN in the 1990s. Fanon was without question one of the intellectuals who helped ensure the perpetuation of violence in the postcolonial era. Stora also writes: "Algerians find themselves confronted by a falsified overflowing memory [*trop plein de mémoire*] that valorizes the use of force, the overthrow of society by armed struggle. The memory of the war of independence is transmitted in a magnified, legendary, heroic manner according to one theme: France was

defeated militarily, defeated by arms. This history depicts violence as good, as the decisive 'motor' [of history]." Stora, "Algérie: absence et surabondance de mémoire," 150. See also Carlier, "D'une Guerre à l'autre."

59. It goes without saying that the French right and extreme right (especially the OAS and CNR) were in very real terms far more dangerous than the left.

8. The Legacy of Violence

1. For an early warning, see Bourdieu and Sayad, Le Déracinement.
2. Roberts, Battle Field Algeria, 354. For Algerian comments on this shift during the war, see Feraoun, Journal.
3. Julliard, "La morale on question," 357.
4. Vidal-Naquet, Torture.
5. For more on the OAS, see my essay, "Before the Jackal," in Assassination!
6. See Death Squadrons: The French School, directed by Marie-Monique Robin (New York: Icarus Films, 2003).
7. Cohen, "Algerian War," 219.
8. See Le Sueur, "Torture and the Decolonization of French Algeria"; see also Branche, La Torture et l'armée, and Aussaresses, Battle for the Casbah.
9. Massu, La Vraie Bataille d'Alger, 168.
10. For a full account of this debate, see Cohen, "Algerian War," 219–39.
11. Le Monde, June 22, 2000. See also Shatz, "Torture of Algiers," 53–56.
12. "L'appel à la condamnation de la torture durant la guerre d'Algérie," L'Humanité, October 31, 2000.
13. Bigeard, J'ai mal à la France, 174.
14. Ighilahriz, L'Algérienne, 258.
15. For Jacques Massu, see Le Monde, November 22 and November 24, 2000.
16. Cited from BBC News, January 9, 2001.
17. New York Times, January 26, 2002.
18. Dershowitz, Why Terrorism Works, 152–53. Alan Dershowitz had already argued on November 8, 2001, in an opinion piece in the Los Angeles Times, for the introduction of torture warrants in the United States' fight against terrorism.
19. It is worth pointing out that crevette, the French word for shrimp, sounds like the verb crever—to die painfully.
20. Alleg, Retour sur "La Question," 22.
21. Le Monde, October 28, 2002.
22. "Le nouvel appel des 12," L'Humanité, May 13, 2004. This petition was again signed by eleven of the original twelve. Laurent Schwart had died in July 2002.
23. Stora, Algeria, 1839–2000, 181–82.

24. Taleb Ibrahimi, *De la décolonisation à la révolution culturelle*, 16.
25. See Abbas, *L'indépendance confisquée*.
26. Stora, *Algeria 1839–2000*, 191.
27. Larzeg, *Eloquence of Silence*, 155. For a full discussion of the Family Code, see Larzeg's description on pp. 150–57.
28. Messaoudi, *Unbowed*, 48. Khalida Messaoudi has since retaken her maiden name and now goes by Khalida Toumi.
29. Messaoudi, *Unbowed*, 72–74.
30. Djebar, *Algeria White*, 228–29.
31. Germaine-Robin, *Femmes rebelles d'Algérie*, 79.
32. Quandt, *Between Ballots and Bullets*, 66.
33. "Être femme en Algérie," *Lien Social* 656 (March 2003).
34. Interview with Alek Toumi, January 15, 2002. Hereafter referred to as "interview" in the text.
35. See Mouffok, *Être journaliste en Algérie*.
36. In 1991, Anouar Haddam was elected to the Algerian National Assembly from Tlemcen as a member of the FIS party. After the government canceled the second round of the elections in January 1992, he fled the country. In April 1993 Haddam filed for asylum with the Chicago Asylum Office in the United States. Haddam took up residence in Washington DC, as the leader of the FIS in exile. At the same time, according to Rachid Boudjedra, Haddam also helped recruit young Algerians to fight in Afghanistan on behalf of the CIA; see Boudjedra, *Lettres algériennes*, 205. In December 1996, Haddam's asylum request was denied and he was taken into custody by the United States government. At the same time, charges were brought against him by U.S.-based human rights organizations citing terrorist campaigns waged by the FIS and GIA of the kind which had targeted Toumi's sister. Haddam later was held by the U.S. Justice Department, on order of Attorney General Janet Reno, on "secret evidence" charges in November 1997. He remained in custody until February 2002. While in an American jail in 1997, he was condemned to death in absentia by the Algerian government, and the U.S. government has refused to extradite him to Algeria because it believes his life is still in danger there.
37. See Messaoudi, "Le voile, c'est notre étoile jaune," *Le Nouvel Observateur* 22–28 (September 1994): 11–12.
38. See Souaïdia, *La sale guerre*. See also Souaïdia, *Le procès de la sale guerre*.
39. *De beauvoir à beau voile* and *Ben M'hidi* are not yet published.
40. "Discours de Monsieur Jacques Chirac président de la république a l'occasion de la journée d'hommage national aux harkis," *Interpress Service*, Octo-

ber 1, 2001, http://www.elysee.fr/elysee/francais/interventions/discours_et_
declarations/2001/septembre/discours_de_m_jacques_chirac_president_
de_la_republique_a_l_occ . . .

41. Dominique de Villepin, "Algeria Year" and "Opening Speech by Mr. Do-
minique de Villepin, Minister of Foreign Affairs," Paris, November 6, 2002,
France-diplomatie. See also Dominque de Villepin, *Toward a New World* (New
York: Melville House, 2004).

42. Elaine Sciolino, "Algerians Give Chirac a Warm Welcome," *New York Times*,
March 3, 2003.

43. Barry James, "Chirac's Trip to Algeria Seen as a Balancing Act," *International
Herald Tribune*, February 27, 2003.

44. Elizabeth Bryant, "Chirac Softens Tone on Baghdad," *United Press International*, March 4, 2003.

45. Elaine Sciolino, "Hostages Urge France to Repeal Head Scarf Ban," *New York
Times*, August 31, 2004. After this manuscript went to press, these journalists
were released in December 2004, after four months of captivity.

Conclusion

1. As cited in Claude Liauzu, "Une loi contre l'histoire," *Le Monde diplomatique*
52, no. 613 (April 2005): 28.

SELECTED SOURCES AND BIBLIOGRAPHY

Archives

The archival sources used in this study fall into three categories: French National Archives, archives of private foundations, and private papers held by individuals or families.

National Archives

Archives d'Histoire Contemporaine, Fondation Nationale de Recherche Politique, Paris SV7

Archives du Ministre de l'Éducation National, Paris 770508/28; 770508/38

Archives Nationales, Paris AJ 78 30; AJ 78 31

Bibliothèque de Documentation Internationale Contemporaine, Nanterre (BDIC) Archives Daniel Guérin: F Rès. 688/18/1 (1); F Rès. 688/19/1; F 721/18/3; F 721/81/2; F 721/89/4; F 721/90/2; F 721/91/1; F 721/91/2; F 721/91/4; Q pièce 362, rès.; Q pièce 508, rès.

Centre des Archives d'Outre-Mer, Aix-en-Provence (CAOM) Cabinet Morin 3 Soustelle 77; Soustelle 16; Soustelle 29; Lacoste 214; Lacoste 234 1 K 569 Cabinet Salan 7

Collège de France, Paris Fonds du Collège de France

Institut Mémoire de l'Édition Contemporaine, Paris (IMEC) Fonds Albert Camus: Courrière Express; Politique I; Algérie I Fonds Esprit: ESP2 C3–01-01

Institut Pierre Mendès France, Paris (IPMF)

Documents Pierre Mendès France (DPMF): Algérie I; Algérie II; Algérie III; Algérie IV; Algérie V; Algérie VI; Algérie VII; Algérie XI; Algérie XIV; P. Soudet, Études Algériens, 3

Maison des Sciences de l'Homme, Bibliothèque du Musée de l'Homme, Paris MS 1/733; MS 1/2161; MS 1/2162; MS 1/2164; MS 1/4877; MS 1/4878; MS 1/5929

Mission des Archives Nationales auprès du Rectorat de l'Académie de Paris, Paris Archives Georges Gurvitch Carton 6

Service Historique de l'Armée de Terre, Paris (SHAT) 1 H 1158/6; 1 H 1158/7; 1 H 1159/3; 1 H 1206/1; 1 H 1680/D1; 1 H 1685/D1; 1 H 1721/1; 1 H 2088/D3; 1 H 2413/D3; 1 H 2456/D4; 1 H 2464/DI; 1 H 2464/D2; 1 H 2464/D3; 1 H 2467/D2; 1 H 2579/3

Private Foundations and Institutes

Centre de Recherche Politique Raymond Aron, Paris (CRPRA) Fonds Raymond Aron Algérie Lettres

Institut Français d'Histoire Sociale, Paris (IFHS) 14 AS 247

373

Institut d'Histoire du Temps Present, Paris (IHTP) Archives Paret Fonds Charles-André Julien

Private Papers

Madame de la Croix

Jean Daniel

Isabelle Raymonde Deblé

Daniel Massignon

Eve Paret

Germaine Tillion

Pierre Vidal-Naquet

Interviews

Henri Alleg (March 9, 1994)

Etienne Balibar (May 16, 1994)

Jacques Berque (October 2, 1993)

Robert Bonnaud (September 27, 1993)

Pierre Bourdieu (November 23, 1993; March 30, 1994)

Robert Chérmany (February 24, 1994)

Jean Daniel (November 25, 1993)

Isabelle Deblé (February 7, 1994)

Marcel Gast (May 9, 1994)

Mohammed Harbi (October 4, 1993)

Francis Jeanson (December 11, 1993)

Jean Leca (April 22, 1994)

Marcel Lesne (May 26, 1994)

André Mandouze (June 21, 1994)

Gilles Martinet (March 2, 1994)

Dionys Mascolo (February 16, 1994)

Albert Memmi (October 6, 1993)

Edgar Morin (December 4, 1993)

Claude Lévi-Strauss (March 28, 1994)

Madeleine Rebérioux (October 5, 1993)

Paul Ricoeur (October 20, 1993)

Jules Roy (October 21, 1993)

Robert Silman (April 16, 1994)

Benjamin Stora (June 15, 1998)

Germaine Tillion (February 3, May 17, May 23, 1994)

Alek Baylee Toumi (January 15, 2002)

Joseph Tubiana (February 28, 1994)

Jacques Vergès (June 20, 1998)
Pierre Vidal-Naquet (September 8, 1993; May 25, 1994)

Newspapers and Periodicals

L'Action
Alger républicain
Après-demain
Les Cahiers de la République
Centres Sociaux: Bulletin de liaison d'information et documentation
Le Canard enchainé
Combat
Confluent
Consciences algériennes
Consciences magribines
Démocratie
L'Écho d'Alger
L'Enseignement publique
L'Express
Esprit
Le Figaro
France indépendante
France observateur
Journal d'Alger
La Gauche
L'Humanité
Libération
Le Monde
El Moudjahid
New York Times
Le Nouvel observateur
The Observer
Preuves
Les Temps modernes
Le 14 Juillet
Paris-Presse
Résistance algérienne
Revue française de science politique
Rivarol
6 aux Écoutes
Sociologie

Sud-Ouest

Témoignage chrétien

Verité-Liberté

Vérités pour . . .

Primary Sources

Abbas, Ferhat. Autopsie d'une guerre. Paris: Granier, 1980.

———. Guerre et révolution d'Algérie: La nuit coloniale. Paris: Julliard, 1964.

———. L'Indépendance confisquée, 1962–1978. Paris: Flammarion, 1984.

Abro, Ben. Assassination! July 14. Historical essay by James D. Le Sueur. Lincoln: University of Nebraska Press, 2001.

Adamov, Arthur, et al. Déclaration sur le droit à l'insoumission dans la guerre d'Algérie. Paris: n.p., 1960.

Aguesse, Charles. "Éditorial." Centres Sociaux 8 (January–February 1958): 1.

———. "Éditorial." Centres Sociaux 9 (March–May 1958): 1.

Aït Ahmed, Hocine. La Guerre et l'après guerre. Paris: Minuit, 1964.

Albertini, Eugène, Georges Marçais, and Georges Yver. L'Afrique du Nord: Française dans l'histoire. Paris: Archat, 1955.

Alleg, Henri. La Question. Paris: Minuit, 1958.

———. The Question. Introduction by Jean-Paul Sartre. New York: Braziller, 1958.

Alleg, Henri. Retour sur "La Question": Entretien avec Gilles Martin. Paris: Éditions Aden, 2001.

Alleg, Henri, Jacques de Bonis, Henri J. Douzon, and others. La Guerre d'Algérie. Vol. 1, De l'Algérie des origines à l'insurrection. Paris: Temps actuels, 1984.

———. La Guerre d'Algérie. Vol. 2, Des promesses de paix à la guerre ouverte. Paris: Messidor, 1986.

———. La Guerre d'Algérie. Vol. 3, Des complots du 13 mai à l'indépendance. Paris: Éd. Messidor, 1986.

"Un Allocution du président René Coty." L'Écho d'Alger (May 31, 1957): 1.

Amrouche, Fadhma A. M. My Life Story: The Autobiography of a Berber Woman. New Brunswick NJ: Rutgers University Press, 1988.

Amrouche, Jean. Un Algérien s'adresse aux Français, ou l'histoire d'Algérie par les textes, 1943–1961. Edited by Tassadit Yacine. Paris: L'Harmattan, 1994.

———. D'une Amitié: Correspondance Jean Amrouche–Jules Roy (1937–1962). Aix-en-Provence: Édisud, 1985.

———. "La France d'Europe, la France d'Afrique." Le Figaro, 1945. Reprinted in Un Algérien s'adresse aux Français, ou l'histoire d'Algérie par les textes, 1943–1961. Edited by Tassadit Yacine. Paris: L'Harmattan, 1994.

———. "Pour un dialogue entre Algérien et Français." France observateur (January 16, 1958): 12.

————. "Quelques raisons du ma quisard." Reprinted as "Quelques raisons de la révolte algérienne" in *Un Algérien s'adresse aux Français.* Edited by Tassadit Yacine. Paris: L'Harmattan, 1994.

"Après le drame de Mélouza, Enquête de l'O.N.U." *L'Humanité* (June 3, 1957): 1.

Aron, Raymond. *L'Algérie et la République.* Paris: Plon, 1958.

————. "Bandoeng conférence de l'équivoque." *Le Figaro* (April 27, 1955): 1.

————. *The Committed Observer: Interviews with Louis Missik and Dominique Wolton.* Chicago: Regnery Gateway, 1983.

————. *Democracy and Totalitarianism: A Theory of Political Systems.* Ann Arbor: University of Michigan Press, 1990.

————. *Études Politiques.* Paris: Gallimard, 1972.

————. *Espoir et peur du siècle: Essais non partisans.* Paris: Calmann-Lévy, 1957.

————. "La France joue sa dernière chance en Afrique." *Le Figaro* (October 12, 1955).

————. *France Steadfast and Changing: The Fourth to the Fifth Republic.* Cambridge MA: Harvard University Press, 1960.

————. *Histoire et dialectique de la violence.* Paris: Gallimard, 1973.

————. *History and the Dialectic of Violence: An Analysis of Sartre's Critique de la raison dialectique.* Translated by Barry Cooper. New York: Harper and Row, 1975.

————. *Marxism and the Existentialists.* New York: Simon & Schuster, 1969.

————. *Memoirs: Fifty Years of Political Reflection.* New York: Holmes and Meier, 1990.

————. *L'Opium des intellectuels.* Paris: Calmann-Lévy, 1955.

————. *The Opium of the Intellectuals.* New York: Doubleday, 1957.

————. Preface to *The Algerians,* by Pierre Bourdieu. Boston: Beacon Press, 1962.

————. *La Tragédie algérienne.* Paris: Plon, 1957.

Aussaresses, Paul. *The Battle of the Casbah: Terror and Counter-Terrorism in Algeria, 1955–1957.* New York: Enigma Books, 2002.

Barrat, Robert. "Chez les hors-la-loi." *France observateur* 279 (September 15, 1955): 16–18.

————. "Complice, victime, ou sauveur?" *France observateur* (July 12, 1958): 6.

————. "Le Fait national algérien phenomène irréversible." In *Le Guerre d'Algérie et colonisme: Textes des interventions et messages prononcés au cours du meeting du 27 janvier 1956,* 12–17. Paris: Comité d'Action des Intellectuels contra la Poursuite de la Guerre en Afrique du Nord, 1956.

————. *Justice pour le Maroc.* Paris: Seuil, 1953.

Barthes, Roland. "Écrivains et écrivants." *Arguments* 4, no. 20 (1960): 41–44.

Baylee, Alek. "Madah-Sartre: Sartre et Beauvoir aux mains du GIA." *Algérie littérature/Action* 6 (December 1996): 5–96.

Beauvoir, Simone de. *Force of Circumstance.* Translated by Richard Howard. New York: Putnam, 1963.

———. *Les Forces des choses.* Paris: Gallimard, 1963.

———. *The Mandarins.* New York: Morton, 1991.

Beauvoir, Simone de, and Gisèle Halimi. *Djamila Boupacha.* Paris: Gallimard, 1962.

———. *Djamila Boupacha: The Story of the Torture of a Young Algerian Girl Which Shocked Liberal French Opinion.* Translated by Peter Green. New York: Macmillan, 1962.

Benabdallah, Abdessamad. *Défense politique.* Paris: Maspero, 1961.

Benda, Julien. *La Trahison des clercs.* Paris: Bernard Grasset, 1927.

———. *The Treason of the Intellectuals.* New York: Norton, 1969.

Benhabiles, Cherif. *L'Algérie française vue par un indigène.* Alger: Orientale Fontana Frères, 1914.

Benmohamed, Mouloud. *Algérie: Mensonges et vérités sur "La sale guerre."* Algiers: n.p., 2001.

Bennabi, Malek. *L'Afro-Asiatisme: Conclusions sur la Conférence de Bandoeng.* Cairo: Société d'Édition et de Communication, 1956.

———. *Islam in History and Society.* Islamabad: Islamic Research Institute, 1988.

Benrabah, Mohamed et al. *Les Violences en Algérie.* Paris: Odile Jacob, 1998.

Ben Smaïl, Mohamed. "Un Journaliste tunisien revient de Mélouza." *France observateur* (June 13, 1957): 10.

Berque, Jacques. *Andalousies: Leçon de cloture au Collège de France.* Paris: Sindbad, 1981.

———. *Arabies: Entretiens avec Mirèse Akar.* Paris: Stock, 1980.

———. *The Arabs: Their History and Future.* New York: Praeger, 1964.

———. *Bibliographie de la culture arabe contemporaine.* Paris: Sindbad, Les Presses de UNESCO, 1981.

———. *Une Cause jamais perdue: Pour une Méditerranée plurielle: Écrits politiques, 1956–1996.* Paris: A. Michel, 1998.

———. "Cent vingt-cinq ans de sociologie maghrébine." *Annales* 11, no. 3 (July–September 1956): 296–324.

———. *Dépossession du monde.* Paris: Seuil, 1964.

———. *French North Africa: The Maghrib between Two World Wars.* New York: Praeger, 1967.

———. "L'Inquiétude Arabe des temps modernes." *Revue des études islamiques* 1 (1958): 1505–19.

———. *Il reste un avenir: Entretiens avec Jean Sur.* Paris: Arléa, 1993.

———. *L'Islam au défi.* Paris: Gallimard, 1980.

—. *Leçon inaugurale faite le samedi 1 décembre 1956.* Nogent-le-Rotrou: Daupeley Gouverneur, 1957.

—. *Le Magreb entre deux guerres.* Paris: Seuil, 1962.

—. *Mémoires des deux rives.* Paris: Seuil, 1989.

—. *New Minority Groups in the Citadel of Europe: Multidisciplinary Conference on the Educational and Cultural Aspects of Community Relations.* Strasbourg, December 5–7, 1989. Strasbourg: Council of Europe, 1991.

—. "The North of Africa." In *Research on Racial Relations: Articles Reprinted from the International Social Sciences Journal,* 11–31. New York: UNESCO, 1966.

—. *L'Orient second.* Paris: Gallimard, 1970.

—. *Structures sociales du Haut-Atlas.* Paris: Presses Universitaires de France, 1955.

Berque, Jacques, and Louis Massignon. "Dialogue sur 'les Arabes.'" *Esprit* 288 (October 1960): 1505–19.

Bidault, Georges. *Algérie: L'oiseau aux ailes coupées.* Paris: La Table Ronde, 1958.

Bigeard, Marcel-Maurice. *J'ai mal à la France.* Paris: Éditions du Polygone, 2001.

Blachère, Régis. *Analecta.* Damascus: Institut Français de Damas, 1975.

Bodin, Louis. *Les Intellectuels.* Paris: Presses Universitaires de France, 1962.

Bodin, Louis, and Jean Touchard. "Les Intellectuels dans la société française contemporaine: Définitions, statistiques et problèmes." *Revue française de science politique* 9 (December 1959): 835–59.

Bonnet, Yves. *Lettre à une algérienne.* Paris: La Boite à Documents, 1998.

Boualam, Saïd (Bachaga). *Les Harkis au service de la France.* Paris: France-Empire, 1963.

—. *Mon pays . . . la France!* Paris: France-Empire, 1962.

Boudjedra, Rachid. *Fis de la haine.* Paris: Denoël, 1992.

—. *Lettres algériennes.* Paris: Grasset, 1995.

—. *The Repudiation.* Translated by Gold Lambrova. Colorado Springs CO: Three Continents, 1995.

Boudiaf, Mohamed. *Où va l'Algérie?* Algiers: Rahma, 1992.

—. *La Préparation du 1 novembre: Suivi d'une lettre ouverte aux algériens.* Paris: El Jarida, 1976.

Bouhali, Larbi. *La Guerre de libération et la lutte pour la paix.* N.p., 1960.

Bourdet, Claude. "Alger, Oran, c'est notre affaire!" *France observateur* (May 10, 1962): 28.

—. "L'Algérie de demain et nous." *France observateur* (June 28, 1962): 6.

—. "L'Algérie est indépendante." *France observateur* (April 25, 1957): 3.

—. "Des Attentats pas si aveugles." *France observateur* (May 18, 1961): 4.

—. "Calculs pour un massacre." *France observateur* (March 29, 1962): 7.

————. "Camus ou les mains propres." *France observateur* (January 7, 1960): 18.

————. "De Gaulle dans le système d'Alger." *France observateur* (June 12, 1958): 4.

————. "Et maintenant, la paix!" *France observateur* (April 27, 1961): 4.

————. " 'La France qui donna les droits de l'homme à l'Europe . . . ' " *France observateur* (August 6, 1959): 24.

————. "Le Glissement de la démocratie." *France observateur* (July 25, 1957): 5.

————. "La Guerre contre le monde arabe." *France observateur* (November 1, 1956): 4.

————. "L'Incorrigible paternalisme persiste en Afrique du Nord." *France observateur* (July 7, 1955): 6–7.

————. "Une Loi rapiécée, une Algérie déchirée." *France observateur* (September 26, 1957): 3.

————. "Mélouza, crime et faute." *France observateur* (June 6, 1957).

————. "Ne pas gacher les idées." *France observateur* (February 9, 1961): 2.

————. "La Police complice des fascistes?" *France observateur* (April 26, 1956): 4.

————. "Pour empêcher la négotiation on enlève les négociateurs." *France observateur* (October 25, 1956): 4.

————. "La Répression et ses 'Yalu.' " *France observateur* (June 16, 1960): 6.

————. "Second échec pour les ultras." *France observateur* (August 30, 1956): 3.

————. "Le Silence est de sang." *France observateur* (April 11, 1957): 3.

————. "De la Torture au coup d'état." *France observateur* (May 15, 1958): 3.

————. "Tortures en Oranie? Robert Lacoste, souvenez-vous!" *France observateur* (September 27, 1956): 4.

————. "Vers la guerre d'Algérie." *France observateur* (May 26, 1955): 7–8.

————. "Votre Gestapo d'Algérie." *France observateur* (January 13, 1955): 6–7.

————. "Le 'Vrai débat' de Camus." *France observateur* (June 9, 1957): 6–7.

Bourdieu, Pierre. *Algeria 1960: Essais.* Translated by Richard Nice. Cambridge: Cambridge University Press, 1979.

————. *The Algerians.* Translated by Alan C. M. Ross. Preface by Raymond Aron. Boston: Beacon Press, 1962.

————. "The Attitude of the Algerian Peasant toward Time." In *Mediterranean Country-men: Essays in the Social Anthropology of the Mediterranean.* Edited by Julian Pitt-Rivers. Paris: Mouton, 1963.

————. "La Hantise du chômage chez l'ouvrier algérien: Proléteriat et système colonial." *Sociologie du travail* 4, no. 4 (1962): 313–31.

————. *Homo academicus.* Translated by Peter Collier. Palo Alto CA: Stanford University Press, 1988.

————. *The Inheritors: French Students and Their Relation to Culture.* Chicago: University of Chicago Press, 1979.

————. *In Other Words: Essays towards a Reflexive Sociology.* Translated by Matthew Adamson. Palo Alto CA: Stanford University Press, 1990.

————. *Leçon inaugurale: Faite le vendredi 23 avril 1982.* Paris: Collège de France, 1982.

————. *The Logic of Practice.* Translated by Richard Nice. Palo Alto CA: Stanford University Press, 1990.

————. "Making the Economic Habitus: Algerian Workers Revisited." *Ethnography* 1, no. 1 (July 2001): 17–42.

————. *Outline of a Theory of Practice.* Translated by Richard Nice. New York: Cambridge University Press, 1990.

————. *Pascalian Mediations.* Translated by Richard Nice. Palo Alto CA: Stanford University Press, 2000.

————. *Questions de sociologie.* Paris: Minuit, 1982.

————. "Les Relations entre les sexes dans la société paysanne." *Les Temps modernes* 195 (1962): 307–31.

————. "Révolution dans la révolution." *Esprit* 291 (January 1961): 27–40.

————. *Sociologie de l'Algérie.* Rev. ed. Paris: Presses Universitaires de France, 1970.

————. "Les Sous-prolétaires algériens." *Les Temps modernes* 199 (1962): 1031–51.

Bourdieu, Pierre, Alain Darbel, Jean-Paul Rivet, and Claude Seibel. *Travail et travailleurs en Algérie.* Paris: Mouton, 1963.

Bourdieu, Pierre, and Abelmalek Sayad. *Le Déracinement: La crise de l'agriculture traditionnelle en Algérie.* Paris: Minuit, 1964.

Bourdieu, Pierre, and Loïc J. D. Wacquant. *An Invitation to Reflexive Sociology.* Chicago: University of Chicago Press, 1992.

Bourguiba, Habib. "L'Algérie est une nation." *France observateur* (February 9, 1956): 4.

Bouvard, Georges. "Homage de la Sorbonne à Maurice Audin." *L'Humanité* (December 3, 1957): 1, 4.

Bouzaher, Hocine. *Des Voix dans la casbah: Théâtre algérien militant.* Algiers: Entreprise Nationale du Livre, 1986.

Bromberger, Serge. "PAR AMITÉ, IMPRUDENCE, OU PASSION: Des progressivistes chrétiens en sont venu à aider et à cacher des terroristes." *Le Figaro* (March 26, 1957): 12.

————. "Plusieurs des inculpés ont été les dupes du FLN." *Le Figaro* (July 23, 1957): 4.

———. *Les Rebelles algériens*. Paris: Plon, 1958.

Brunschwig, Henri. "Colonial Imperialism." *Confluent* 4 (July 1955): 217–28.

———. "Colonisation-décolonisation: Essai sur le vocabulaire usuel de la politique coloniale." *Cahiers d'études africaines* 1, no. 1 (January 1960): 44–54.

———. *Mythes et réalités de l'impérialisme colonial français, 1789–1914*. Paris: Colin, 1960. Camus, Albert. "L'Avenir algérien." *L'Express* (July 23, 1955): 6.

———. *Essais*. Paris: Gallimard, 1965.

———. *First Man*. Translated by David Hapgood. New York: Knopf, 1995.

———. "La Preuve à faire." *L'Express* (January 3, 1956): 20.

———. *The Rebel*. Translated by Anthony Bower. New York: Vintage, 1956.

———. *Resistance, Rebellion, and Death*. Translated by Justin O'Brien. New York: Vintage, 1974.

———. *The Stranger*. New York: Vintage, 1989.

———. "Terrorisme et repression." *L'Express* (July 9, 1955): 4.

———. *Théâtre, récits, nouvelles*. Paris: Gallimard, 1962.

———. "Trêve pour les civils." *L'Express* (January 10, 1956): 16.

Capdecomme, Laurent. "Éducation nationale en Algérie." In *Algérie d'aujourd'hui: Conférence de presse*. Délégation générale du gouvernement en Algérie service de l'information. Algiers: Baconnier, 1960.

Capitant, René. "Le Miracle français." Preface to *L'Histoire s'avance masquée*, by Louis Vallon. *L'Express* 301 (March 29, 1957): 4.

Carlier, Omar. "D'une guerre à l'autre, le redéploiement de la violence entre soi." *Confluences méditerranées* 25 (Spring 1998): 123–37.

Casamayor. *Le Bras séculier: Justice et police*. Paris: Seuil, 1960.

———. "Les Indicateurs." *Esprit* 287 (September 1960): 1345–59.

———. "Lettre à un ultra." *Esprit* 258 (February 1958): 276–86.

"Les Centres Sociaux d'Alger était noyauté par le F.L.N." *Sud-Ouest* (July 28, 1959).

Césaire, Aimé. "Le Colonialisme." *La Nouvelle critique* 51 (January 1954): 9–131.

———. "Culture et colonization." *Présence africaine* 8–10 (June–November 1956): 191–205.

———. *Discourse on Colonialism*. Translated by Joan Pinkham. New York: Monthly Review Press, 1971.

———. *Lettre à Maurice Thorez*. Paris: Présence Africaine, 1956.

———. *Oeuvres complètes*. Vol. 3, *Oeuvre historique et politique: Discours et communications*. Fort-de-France: Désormeaux, 1976.

———. *Return to My Native Land*. Translated by John Berger and Anna Bostock. Baltimore: Penguin, 1969.

———. "Le Temps du régime colonial est passé. In *Guerre d'Algérie et colonialisme: Textes des interventions et messages prononcés au cours du meeting du 27 janvier 1956*.

Paris: Comité d'Action des Intellectuals contre la Poursuite de la Guerre en Afrique du Nord, 1956.

——. *Toussaint Louverture: La révolution française et le problème colonial*. Paris: Livre Club Diderot, 1960.

Challe, Maurice. *Notre révolte*. Paris: La Cité, 1968.

Charbonnier, Georges. *Entretiens avec Lévi-Strauss*. Paris: Plon and Julliard, 1961.

Charnay, Jean-Paul, ed. *De l'Impérialisme à la décolonisation*. Paris: Minuit, 1965.

——, ed. *Normes et valeurs dans l'Islam contemporain*. Paris: Payot, 1966.

Chelfi, Mustapha. "Les Beignets de la rue Bab-Azoun." *Le Nouvel observateur* (June 9–15, 1994): 24.

Chevallier, Jacques. *Nous, Algériens . . .* Paris: Calmann-Lévy, 1958.

Cohen-Solal, Annie. *Sartre: A Life*. New York: Pantheon, 1987.

Comité d'Action des Intellectuels contre la Poursuite de la Guerre en Afrique du Nord. "Reponse au Gouverneur Général de l'Algérie." Paris, 1955.

Comité Central du Parti Communiste Algérien. *Pour une nation Algérienne: Libre, souveraine et heureuse*. N.p., n.d.

Comité Maurice Audin. *Sans commentaire*. Paris: Minuit, 1961.

Comité de Résistance Spirituelle. *Des Rappelés témoignent*. Paris: Comité de Résistance Spirituelle, 1957.

"Communiqué du Bureau politique de la Nouvelle Gauche." *France observateur* (June 6, 1957).

"Un Communiqué du Rectorat d'Alger." *Le Journal d'Alger* (December 27, 1960).

"La Communité aux bombes du Milk-Bar et du car de Diar-es-Saâda." *L'Écho d'Alger* (March 22, 1957): 8.

Crouzet, Michel. "La Bataille des intellectuels français." *La Nef* 12–13 (October–January 1963): 47–65.

Daniel, Jean. "Albert Camus, 'l'algérien.'" *Action* (October 21, 1957): 13.

——. "Albert Camus: Parlons de lui." *L'Express* (January 7, 1960): 27.

——. "L'Algérie: L'independance et la révolution." *L'Express* (March 30, 1961): 9–10.

——. "L'Algérie: L'indignation est justifiée, mais l'exploitation sans issue . . ." *L'Express* (June 7, 1957): 3.

——. *La Blessure*. Paris: Grasset, 1992.

——. "Colonialisme et bonne conscience." *Preuves* 65 (July 1956): 14–21.

——. *De Gaulle et l'Algérie*. Paris: Seuil, 1986.

——. "Le Destin algérien, la France, et l'Occident." *Revue générale Belge* (January 1958): 27–30.

——. "Entre le chagrin et le haussement d'épaules." *L'Express* (January 13, 1956): 11.

————. "Essai 'Les Damnés de la terre' par Frantz Fanon." *L'Express* (November 30, 1961): 36.

————. "Un Français d'Algérie." *Preuves* (September 1957): 25–29.

————. "Un Intellectuel contre l'Histoire." *Nouvel observateur* 1544 (June 9–15, 1994): 8.

————. "Journal d'un journaliste." *Esprit* 251 (June 1957): 982–91.

————. "La Réponse aux propositions Soustelle est attendue." *L'Express* (January 3, 1956): 4.

————. "Socialisme et anti-colonialisme." *Esprit* 284 (May 1960): 809–14.

————. *Le Temps qui reste.* Paris: Stock, 1973.

————. "Des Vacances algériennes . . ." *L'Express* (21 June 1957): 4.

Darboise, J.-M., M. Heynard, and J. Martel. *Officiers en Algérie.* Paris: Maspero, 1960.

Death Squadrons: The French School. Directed by Marie-Monique Robin. New York: Icarus Films, 2003.

Debré, Michel. *Entretiens avec le général de Gaulle, 1961–1969.* Paris: A. Michel, 1993.

"Déclaration d'Abdelkader Guerroudj au début de procès." *Les Temps modernes* 145 (March 1958): 1564–74.

Déclaration sur le droit à l'insoumission dans la guerre d'Algérie. Paris: n.p., 1960.

De Gaulle, Charles. *Lettres, notes, et carnets: Juin 1958–décembre 1960.* Paris: Plon, 1985.

————. *Major Addresses, Statements, and Press Conferences, May 19, 1958–January 31, 1964.* New York: French Embassy Press, 1964.

————. *Memoirs of Hope: Renewal 1958–1962; Endeavour 1962–.* Translated by Terrence Kilmartin. London: Weidenfeld and Nicolson, 1971.

Déjeux, Jean, ed. *Culture algérienne dans les textes.* Paris: Publisud, 1995.

Denancy, (Charles) Edgard. *Philosophie de la colonisation.* Paris: Bibliothèque de la Critique, 1902.

Dershowitz, Alan M. *Why Terrorism Works: Understanding the Threat, Responding to the Challenge.* New Haven CT: Yale University Press, 2002.

De Villepin, Dominique. "Algeria Year: Opening Speech by Mr. Dominique de Villepin, Minister of Foreign Affairs." Paris, November 6, 2002, *France-diplomatie.*

————. *Toward a New World.* New York: Melville House, 2004.

Dib, Mohammed. *Who Remembers the Sea.* Boulder CO: Three Continents Press, 1985.

Diop, Alioune. "Pour l'amitié des peuples." In *Guerre d'Algérie et colonialisme: Textes des interventions et messages prononcés au cours du meeting du 27 janvier 1956.* Paris:

Comité d'Action des Intellectuals contre la Poursuite de la Guerre en Afrique du Nord, 1956.

Djebar, Assia. *Aleria White: A Narrative.* Translated by David Kelley and Marjolijn de Jager. New York: Seven Stories Press, 2000.

———. *Le Blanc de l'Algérie.* Paris: Albin Michel, 1995.

———. *So Vast the Prison.* New York: Seven Stories, 1999.

———. *Women of Algiers in Their Apartment.* Charlottesville: University of Virginia Press, 1992.

Domenach, Jean-Marie. "Algérie, propositions raisonnables." *Esprit* 249 (May 1957): 777–89.

———. "Conditions de la grandeur." *Esprit* 267 (November 1958): 715–20.

———. "Croyez-vous à la démocratie?" *L'Express* (April 30, 1959): 9–10.

———. "Les Damnés de la terre." *Esprit* 304 (March 1962): 454–63; 305 (April 1962): 634–45.

———. "Démoralisation de la Nation." *Esprit* 250 (April 1957): 577–79.

———. "Les Enchères de la terreur." *Esprit* 7–8 (July–August 1957): 104–6.

———. "Les Intellectuels et le communisme." *Espirit* 228 (July 1955): 1200–1225.

———. "Une Mauvaise philosophie." *Esprit* 258 (February 1958): 247–49.

———. "Politique et action culturelle." *Esprit* 424 (May 1973): 1116–23.

———. "Pour une reconversion du courage." *L'Express* (26 July 1957): 4.

———. "Resistances." *Esprit* 284 (May 1960): 794–808.

———. "Sauve-qui peut?" *Esprit* 283 (April 1960): 707–10.

———. "La Seconde victoire." *L'Express* (April 3, 1958): 6.

———. "S'entendre contre l'irréparable." *Esprit* 291 (January 1961): 1–6.

Le Dossier Jean Muller: De la pacification à la répression. Paris: Cahiers du Témoignage Chrétien 38, n.d.

Dresch, Jean. "L'Eurafrique." *Présence africaine* 7 (April–May 1956): 13–25.

———. "Les Français d'Algérie." In *Le Guerre d'Algérie et colonisme: Textes des interventions et messages prononcés au cours du meeting du 27 janvier 1956.* Paris: Comité d'Action des Intellectuels contra la Poursuite de la Guerre en Afrique du Nord, 1956.

Drif, Zohra. *La Mort de mes frères.* Paris: Maspero, 1960.

Duchet, Roger. *Pour le salut publique.* Paris: Plon, 1958.

Duclos, Jacques. "L'Allocution du Jacques Duclos." *L'Humanité* (December 5, 1957): 6.

"Du F.L.N. à la révolution." *Les Temps modernes* 198 (November 1962): 817–29.

Duquesne, Jacques. *L'Algérie, ou la guerre des mythes.* Paris: Desclée de Brouwer, 1958.

Duval, Léon-Etienne. "Une Déclaration de Mr. Duval." *L'Écho d'Alger* (July 31, 1957): 6.

———. "Une Déclaration de S. Exc. Mgr. Duval archevêque d'Alger." *Témoignage chrétien* (August 9,1957): 100.

———. *Messages de paix, 1955–1962.* Paris: Desclée de Brouwer, 1962.

Duverger, Maurice. "Absence française." *Le Monde* (March 16, 1957).

———. "Les Deux trahisons." *Le Monde* (April 7, 1956).

Ed Din, Chems. *L'Affaire Bellounis: Histoire d'un générale fellagha: Précédé de Retour sur la guerre d'Algérie de Edgar Morin.* Paris: L'Aube, 1998.

"L'Enquête sociologique." *Centres Sociaux* 8 (January–February 1958): 17.

"Entretien avec Jean-Paul Sartre." *La Voie communiste* 20 (February 1961): 3.

"Des Esprits faux." Éditorial, *L'Écho d'Alger* (August 2, 1957): 1.

"Être femme en Algérie." *Lien Social* 656 (March 2003).

Fanon, Frantz. *L'An cinq de la révolution algérienne.* Paris: Maspero, 1959.

———. *Black Skin, White Masks.* Translated by Charles Lam Markmann. New York: Grove, 1968.

———. *Damnés de la terre.* Paris: Maspero, 1961.

———. *A Dying Colonialism.* Translated by Haakon Chevalier. New York: Grove, 1967.

———. *Peau noire, masques blancs.* Introduction by Francis Jeanson. Paris: Seuil, 1952.

———. *Pour la révolution africaine: Écrits politiques.* Paris: Maspero, 1964.

———. "Pourquoi nous employons la violence." *Vérité-Liberté* 1 (May 1960): 4, 9.

———. *Toward the African Revolution: Political Essays.* Translated by Haakon Chevalier. New York: Grove, 1969.

———. *The Wretched of the Earth.* Introduction by Jean-Paul Sartre. Translated by Constance Farrington. New York: Grove, 1963.

Feraoun, Mouloud. *L'Anniversaire.* Paris: Seuil, 1972.

———. *Les Chemins qui montent: Roman.* Paris: Seuil, 1957.

———. *Le Fils du pauvre.* Paris: Seuil, 1954.

———. *Journal, 1955–1962: Reflections on the French-Algerian War.* Edited and with an introduction by James D. Le Sueur. Translated by Mary Ellen Wolf and Claude Fouillade. Lincoln: University of Nebraska Press, 2000.

———. *Jours de Kabylie.* Algiers: Bouchène, 1990.

———. *Lettres à ses amis.* Paris: Seuil, 1969.

———. *The Poor Man's Son: Menrad, Kabyle Schoolteacher.* Translated by Lucy Mc-Nair. Introduction by James D. Le Sueur. Charlottesville: University Press of Virginia, 2005.

———. *La Terre et le sang: Roman.* Paris: Seuil, 1953.

Folliet, Joseph. "Non à l'atroce!" *Témoignage chrétien* 674 (June 7, 1957): 1.

———. "Se taire ou dire vrai?" *Témoignage chrétien* 670 (May 10, 1957): 20.

Forestier, Denis. "Crime contre la culture." *L'Enseignement publique* 26 (March 23, 1962): 1209.

Fromentin, Eugène. *Between Sea and Sahara: An Algerian Journal.* Athens: Ohio University Press, 1999.

La Gangrène. Paris: Minuit, 1959.

The Gangrene. Translated by Robert Silvers. New York: Lyle Stuart, 1960.

Gautier, E.-F. *L'Algérie et la métropole.* Paris: Payot, 1920.

Giono, Jean. *Entretiens avec Jean Amrouche et Taos Amrouche.* Edited by Henri Godard. Paris: Gallimard, 1990.

Gobineau, Arthur de. *The Inequality of Human Races.* 1915. Reprint, New York: Fertig, 1999.

Gonnet, Jean. "L'Affaire des libéraux d'Alger." *Le Monde* (June 6, 1957).

Gouvernement Général de l'Algérie. *Pour l'Algérie, pour la France: Directives aux autorités locales (Avril 1956).* Algiers, 1956.

Guérin, Daniel. *L'Algérie caporalisée?* Paris: CSE, 1965.

———. "L'Algérie hors la loie." *France observateur* (January 26, 1956): 12.

———. "L'Algérie n'a jamais été la France." In *Guerre d'Algérie et colonialisme: Textes des interventions et messages prononcés au tours du meeting du 27 janvier 1956.* Paris: Comité d'Action des Intellectuals contre la Poursuite de la Guerre en Afrique du Nord, 1956.

———. *Ci-gît le colonialisme: Algérie, Inde, Indochine, Madagascar, Maroc, Palestine, Polynésie, Tunisie-Témoignage militant.* Paris: Mouton, 1973.

———. *Pitié pour le Maghreb.* Paris: Chantenay, 1953.

———. *Quand l'Algérie s'insurgeait, 1954–1962: Un anticolonialiste témoigne.* Claix: Pensée Sauvage, 1979.

———. *La Révolution française et nous.* Brussels: Taupe, 1969.

Guerre d'Algérie et colonialisme: Textes des interventions et messages prononcés au cours du meeting du 27 janvier 1956. Paris: Comité d'Action des Intellectuals contre la Poursuite de la Guerre en Afrique du Nord, 1956.

Guerroudj, Jacqueline. *Des Douars et des prisons.* Algiers: Bouchène, 1993.

Hadj, Messali. *Les Mémoires de Messali Hadj, 1898–1939.* Edited by Renaud de Rochebrun. Paris: Lattès, 1982.

Halimi, Gisèle. "La Défense hors la loi." *Les Temps modernes* 167–68 (February–March 1960): 1185–91.

———. "D'Henri Alleg à Djamila Boupacha." *Les Temps modernes* 171 (June 1960): 1822–27.

———. "Prisonnière des parachutistes." *France observateur* (June 12, 1958): 5.

Hammoutene, Ali. *Réflexions sur la guerre d'Algérie*. Paris: Publisud, 1982.

Hegel, G. W. F. *The Phenomenology of Mind*. New York: Harper, 1967.

———. *Philosophy of Right*. New York: Oxford University Press, 1972.

Heidegger, Martin. *Basic Writings*. New York: Harper, 1977.

———. *Being and Time*. New York: Harper, 1962.

———. *An Introduction to Metaphysics*. New Haven CT: Yale University Press, 1987.

Husserl, Edmund. *Ideas: General Introduction to Pure Phenomenology*. New York: Collier, 1962.

Hyppolite, Jean. *Études sur Marx et Hegel*. Paris: M. Rivière, 1955.

———. *Genèse et structure de la Phénoménologie de l'esprit de Hegel*. Paris: Aubier, 1946.

———. *Introduction to Hegel's Philosophy of History*. Gainesville: University of Florida Press, 1996.

———. *Sens et existence dans la philosophie de Maurice Merleau-Ponty*. Oxford: Clarendon Press, 1963.

Ighilahriz, Louisette. *Algérienne*. Paris: Fayard Calmann-Lévy, 2003.

Ihadden, Zahir. "La Propaganda du FLN pendant la guerre de libération nationale." In *La Guerre d'Algérie et les Algériens 1954–1962: Actes de la table ronde organisée à Paris, 26–27 mars 1996*, edited by Charles-Robert Ageron, 180–95. Paris: Colin, 1997.

Jeanson, Colette, and Francis Jeanson. *L'Algérie hors la loi*. Paris: Seuil, 1955.

Jeanson, Francis. *L'Algérie: De retour en retour*. Paris: Seuil, 1991.

———. "Cette Algérie, conquise et pacifiée . . . I." *Esprit* 4 (April 1950): 613–34.

———. "Cette Algérie, conquise et pacifiée . . . II." *Esprit* 5 (May 1950): 841–61.

———. *La Foi d'un incroyant*. Paris: Seuil, 1963.

———. Introduction to *Peau noire, masques blancs*, by Frantz Fanon. Paris: Seuil, 1952.

———. "Lettre à Jean-Paul Sartre." *Les Temps modernes* 169–70 (April–May 1960): 1535–49.

———. *Notre guerre*. Paris: Minuit, 1960.

———. *Le Procès du réseau Jeanson*. Paris: Maspero, 1961.

———. *Sartre, par lui-même*. Paris: Seuil, 1955.

———. *La Révolution algérienne: Problèmes et perspectives*. Milan: Feltrinelli, 1962.

Julien, Charles-André. *L'Afrique du Nord en marche*. Paris: Julliard, 1952.

Julliard, Jacques. "La morale on question." *Esprit* (October 1962).

Karol, K. S. "Un Entretien avec Jean-Paul Sartre: Jeunesse et Guerre d'Algérie." *Vérité-Liberté* 3 (July–August 1960): 2.

Kateb, Yacine. *Abdelkader et l'indépendance algérienne*. Algiers: SNED, 1983.

———. *Le Cercle des represailles: Théâtre*. Paris: Seuil, 1959.

———. *Nedjma*. Charlottesville: University of Virginia Press, 1991.

———. *Le Polygone étoilé*, 1929–1989. Paris: Seuil, 1966.

Khrushchev, Nikita. *Khrushchev Remembers: The Last Testament*. Translated by Strobe Talbott. Boston: Little Brown, 1970.

Kojéve, Alexandre. *Introduction à la lecture de Hegel: Leçons sur la Phénoménologie de l'esprit*. Paris: Gallimard, 1947.

———. *Introduction to the Reading of Hegel: Lectures on the Phenomenology of Spirit*. Edited by Allan Bloom. Translated by James H. Nichols Jr. Ithaca NY: Cornell University Press, 1969.

Kovac, Nikola. "Camus aurait milité pour l'embargo." *Le Nouvel observateur* (June 9–15, 1994): 27.

Lacheraf, Mostefa. *L'Algérie: Nation et société*. Paris: Maspero, 1965.

———. *Algérie et Tiers-monde: Agressions, resistances et solidarités intercontinentales*. Algiers: Bouchène, 1989.

———. *La Culture algérienne contemporaine: Essai de définitions et perspectives: Communication faite par l'auteur au 1ᴱᴿ colloque national algèrien de la culture, Alger, 29 mai–5 juin 1969*. Algiers: Services Culturels du Parti, 1968.

———. *Littératures de combat: Essais d'introduction, étude et préfaces*. Algiers: Bouchène, 1991.

———. *Des Noms et des lieux: Mémoires d'une Algérie oubliée*. Algiers: Casbah Éditions, 1998.

Laparre, R. P. E. *Journal d'un prêtre en Algérie, Oran 1961–1962*. Paris: Fuseau, 1964.

Lartérguy, Jean. *The Centurions*. London: Hutchinson, 1961.

Le Pen, Jean-Marie. *Le Pen 91: Analyses et propositions*. Maule: Éditions de Présent, 1992.

Leroy-Beaulieu, Paul. *De la Colonisation chez les peuples modernes*. 6th ed. Paris: Féx Alcan, 1908.

Leulliette, Pierre. *St. Michael and the Dragon: A Paratrooper in the Algerian War*. London: Heinemann, 1964.

Lévi-Strauss, Claude. "Réponse à quelques questions." *Esprit* 31, no. 322 (July–December 1963): 628–52.

———. *La Pensée sauvage*. Paris: Plon, 1962.

———. *The Savage Mind*. Chicago: University of Chicago Press, 1966.

———. *The Scope of Anthropology*. Translated by Sherry Ortner Paul and Robert A. Paul. London: Jonathan Cape, 1967.

———. *Structural Anthropology*. Translated by Claire Jacobson and Brooke Grundfest Schoepf. New York: Basic Books, 1963.

———. *Tristes tropiques*. New York: Penguin, 1975.

Lévi-Strauss, Claude, and Didier Eribon. *Conversations with Claude Lévi-Strauss*. Translated by Paula Wissing. Chicago: University of Chicago Press, 1988.

Levinas, Emmanuel. *Entre Nous: On Thinking-of-the Other*. New York: Columbia University Press, 1998.

———. *Ethics and Infinity: Conversations with Philippe Nemo*. Pittsburgh: Duquesne University Press, 1982.

———. *Totalité et infini: Essai sur l'extériorité*. The Hague: Nijhoff, 1961.

———. *Thinking of the Other*. New York: Columbia University Press, 1998.

———. *Totality and Infinity: An Essay on Exteriority*. Pittsburgh: Duquesne University Press, 1988.

"Libres propos sur l'analphabétisme." *Centres Sociaux* 7 (December 1956–January 1957): 7.

Lyotard, Jean François. *Phenomenology*. Albany NY: SUNY Press, 1991.

———. *Political Writings*. Minneapolis: University of Minnesota Press, 1993.

———. *The Postmodern Condition: A Report on Knowledge*. Minneapolis: University of Minnesota Press, 1989.

"M. Capdecomme défend les centres sociaux." *Le Monde* (January 15–16, 1961): 3.

Mandouze, André. *Mémoires d'outre-siècle*. Vol. 1, *D'une Résistance à l'autre*. Paris: Viviane Hamy, 1998.

———. "Reconnaitre ce qui est." In *Guerre d'Algérie et colonialisme: Textes des interventions et messages prononcés au cours du meeting du 27 janvier 1956*. Paris: Comité d'Action des Intellectuals contre la Poursuite de la Guerre en Afrique du Nord, 1956.

Mannoni, Octavo. *Prospero and Caliban: The Psychology of Colonization*. New York: Praeger, 1964.

———. "Psychologie de la révolte Malgache." *Esprit* 4, no. 166 (April 1950): 581–95.

Martinet, Gilles. "Une Année ordinaire?" *France observateur* (December 27, 1962): 24.

———. "L'Anti-France." *France observateur* (June 18, 1959): 3.

———. "Comment agir avec les communistes." *France observateur* (May 16, 1957): 3.

———. "Comment sortir du chaos?" *France observateur* (May 10, 1962): 6.

———. "Les Crises du monde communiste." *France observateur* (December 6, 1962): 32.

———. "Les Déserteurs." *France observateur* (April 21, 1960): 2.

———. "Une Dévaluation honteuse." *France observateur* (August 15, 1957): 3.

————. "La Distance entre de Gaulle et le F.L.N." *France observateur* (October 7, 1959): 3.

————. "Les Frères ennemis." *France observateur* (July 5, 1962): 6.

————. "La Gauche et ses divisions." *France observateur* (April 27, 1961): 6.

————. "L'Indépendance, condition nécessaire mais non suffisante." *France observateur* (January 16, 1958): 12.

————. "La Leçon de Budapest." *France observateur* (November 8, 1956).

————. "Leur capitulation et notre combat." *France observateur* (May 29, 1958): 4.

————. "De la Lutte antiterroriste à l'étouffement de la gauche." *France observateur* (September 18, 1958): 3.

————. "La Négociation reprendra-t-elle?" *France observateur* (June 15, 1961): 3.

————. "Non jamais!" *France observateur* (May 29, 1958): 30.

————. "Pas de combat sur deux fronts." *France observateur* (January 11, 1962): 6.

————. "Qu'Albert Camus prenne enfin position." *France observateur* (December 26, 1957): 15.

————. "Qui sont les traîtres?" *France observateur* (April 28, 1960): 2.

————. "Réponse au F.L.N." *France observateur* (January 2, 1958): 4.

————. "Le Réveil de la gauche." *France Observateur* (October 5, 1961): 5.

————. "Révolution et décolonisation." *France observateur* (September 6, 1962): 8–10.

————. "Savoir terminer une guerre." *France observateur* (May 25, 1961): 3.

————. "Traditions révolutionnaires. Esprit 257 (December 1957): 771–78.

————. "Vieilles et nouvelles gauches." *France observateur* (November 15, 1956): 4.

Maschino, Maurice T. "Le Dossier des réfractaires." *Le Temps modernes* 169–70 (April–May 1960): 1550–62.

————. *L'Engagement (le dossier des réfractaires)*. Paris: Maspero, 1961.

————. "Lettre." *Esprit* 206 (July–August 1960): 1343–44.

————. "Pour les français l'algérien lui-même, en tant qu'homme, est contestable." *Résistance algérienne* (June 10–20, 1957): 6.

————. *Le Refus*. Paris: Maspero, 1960.

————. *Voulez-vous vraiment des enfants idiots?* Paris: Hachette, 1984.

Mascolo, Dionys. *Le Communisme: Révolution et communication, ou la dialectique des valeurs et de besoins*. Paris: Gallimard, 1993.

————. "Lettre." *France observateur* (October 13, 1960): 3.

————. "Pour l'abolition du colonialisme." In *Guerre d'Algérie et colonialisme: Textes des interventions et messages prononcés au cours du meeting du 27 janvier 1956*. Paris:

Comité d'Action des Intellectuals contre la Poursuite de la Guerre en Afrique du Nord, 1956.

———. À la Recherche d'un communisme de pensée: Entêtements. Paris: Fourbis, 1993.

Massignon, Louis. Opéra minora: Textes recueilles, classés, et présentés avec une bibliographie par Y. Moubarac. 3 vols. Paris: Presses Universitairés de France, 1969.

———. Parole donnée. Paris: Julliard, 1962.

Massu, Jacques. Baden 68: Souvenirs d'une fidélité gaulliste. Paris: Plon, 1983.

———. Le Torrent et la digne. Paris: Plon, 1972.

———. La Vraie Bataille d'Alger. Monaco: Éditions du Rocher, 1971.

Mauriac, François. Bloc-notes. 5 vols. Paris: Seuil, 1993.

———. De Gaulle. Garden City NY: Doubleday, 1966.

———. "Le FLN et nous." L'Express 297 (March 1, 1957): 32.

———. Lettres d'une vie, 1904–1869. Edited by Caroline Mauriac. Paris: Grasset, 1981.

———. Souvenirs retrouvés: Entretiens avec Jean Amrouche. Paris: Fayard, 1981.

Maurienne, pseud. Le Déserteur. Paris: Minuit, 1960.

Mayoux, Jean-Jacques. "En un moment historique." In Guerre d'Algérie et colonialisme: Textes des interventions et messages prononcés au cours du meeting du 27 janvier 1956. Paris: Comité d'Action des Intellectuals contre la Poursuite de la Guerre en Afrique du Nord, 1956.

Mazouni, Abdallah. Culture et enseignement en Algérie et au Maghreb. Paris: Maspero, 1969.

"Mélouza était un village F.L.N." L'Humanité (June 3, 1957): 1.

Memmi, Albert. The Colonizer and the Colonized. Translated by Howard Greenfield. Boston: Beacon Press, 1967.

———. Portrait du colonisé précédé du Portrait du colonisateur. 1957. Reprint, Paris: Gallimard, 1985.

Merleau-Ponty, Maurice. Adventures of the Dialectic. Translated by Joseph Bien. Evanston IL: Northwestern University Press, 1973.

———. Les Aventures de la dialectique. Paris: Gallimard, 1955.

———. Humanism and Terror: An Essay on the Communist Problem. Translated by John O'Neill. Boston: Beacon Press, 1969.

———. In Praise of Philosophy and Other Essays. Translated by John Wild and James M. Edie. Evanston IL: Northwestern University Press, 1988.

———. Sense and Non-Sense. Translated by Hubert Dreyfus and Patricia Allen Dreyfus. Evanston IL: Northwestern University Press, 1964.

———. Sens et non-sens. Paris: Nagel, 1948.

———. Signs. Translated by Richard McCleary. Evanston IL: Northwestern University Press, 1964.

———. *Texts and Dialogues.* Translated by Michael B. Smith et al. Atlantic Highlands NJ: Humanities Press, 1992.

———. *Themes from the Lectures at the Collège de France.* Translated by John O'Neill. Evanston IL: Northwestern University Press, 1970.

Messaoudi, Khalida. "Le voile, c'est notre étoile jaune." *Le Nouvel observateur* (22–28 September 1994): 11–12.

Michelet, Edmond. "Le Procès des Chrétiens d'Algérie." *Témoignage chrétien* (July 19, 1957): 5.

Milosz, Czeslaw. *The Captive Mind.* New York: Knopf, 1953.

———. "Un Homme déchiré comme moi-même." *Le Nouvel observateur* (June 9–15, 1994): 26.

Mimouni, Rachid. "Camus et l'Algérie intégriste." *Le Nouvel observateur* (June 9–15, 1994): 14.

Ministre de l'Algérie, Cabinet du Ministre. *Aspects véritables de la rebellion algérienne.* Algiers: Société Anonyme de l'Imprimerie Générale, [1957?].

———. *The True Aspects of the Algerian Rebellion.* N.p., n.d.

Mitterrand, François. *Politique, I. Oeuvres complètes, 1933–1977.* Paris: Rencontre, 1977.

Montefiore, Alan, ed. *Philosophy in France Today.* New York: Cambridge University Press, 1983.

Moreau, Yves. "Assez de sang et d'horreurs!" *L'Humanité* (June 3, 1957): 1.

Morin, Edgar. *Autocritique.* Paris: Seuil, 1970.

———. "L'Heure zéro des intellectuels du parti communiste français." *France observateur* (October 25, 1956): 18–19.

———. "Intellectuels: Critique du mythe et mythe de la critique." *Arguments* 4, no. 20 (1960): 35–40.

———. "Les Intellectuels et l'Algérie." *France observateur* (September 29, 1960): 5.

———. "Retour sur la guerre d'Algérie." Preface to *L'Affaire Bellounis,* by Chems Ed Din. Germenos: L'Aube, 1998.

———. "De la Torture." *France observateur* (July 9, 1959): 24.

Mouffok, Ghania. *Eircumflextre journaliste en Algérie, 1988–1995.* Paris: Reporters sans frontières, 1996.

Nizan, Paul. *Aden, Arabie.* New York: Monthly Review Press, 1968.

Nous devons rester en Algérie parce que nous y sommes: Témoignage d'un instituteur du "Bled." Paris: Rivarol, 1956.

"Noyautage communiste des centres sociaux d'Algérie." *6 aux Écoutes* (October 30, 1959): 1.

OAS parle. Paris: Julliard, 1964.

"Obsèques des six dirigeants des centres sociaux assassiné à El Biar." *Le Figaro* (March 19, 1962): 7.

"L'Opinion des universitaires arabisants." *Comité d'Action Bulletin* 5 (1956): 7.

L'Opinion mondiale juge les sanglants "libérateurs" de Mélouza et de Wagram. Paris, 1957.

Ortiz, Joseph. *Mes combats: Carnets de route, 1954–1962.* Paris: Pensée Moderne, 1964.

Péju, Marcel. "De l'Affaire des avocats' au 'réseau des intellectuels.'" *Les Temps modernes* 167–68 (February–March 1960): 1435–40.

————. "La Gauche française et le FLN." *Les Temps modernes* 167–68 (February–March 1960): 1512–29.

————. "Une Gauche respectueuse." *Les Temps modernes* 169–70 (April–May 1960): 1512–29.

————. "Mourir pour de Gaulle?" *Les Temps modernes* 175–76 (October–November 1960): 481–502.

Pélégri, Jean. *Ma Mère l'Algérie.* Algiers: Laphomic, 1989.

Peroncel-Hugoz, Jean-Pierre. *Assassinat d'un poète.* Marseille: Quai, 1983.

Peyrega, Jacques. "Le Doyen de la Faculté de Droit d'Alger écrit à M Bourgès-Maunoury." *France observateur* (April 4, 1957): 4.

Philip, André. *André Philip par lui-même; ou Les voies de la liberté.* Paris: Bubier Montaigne, 1971.

Poirot-Delpech, Bertrand. "Des Piens modérées sont requisés contre la plupart des inculpés." *Le Monde* (July 24, 1957): 3.

————. "Le Tribunal se refuse à confondre l'esprit de charité et l'action nationaliste." *Le Monde* (July 25, 1957): 1.

Pour la France: Programme du Front National. Paris: Albatros, 1985.

Quiriconi, Robert-Yves. "Un Reseau F.L.N. dirigé de la métropole est détruit par Alger-Salel." *L'Écho de Alger* (July 10, 1959): 3, 10.

"Réponse à Jean Daniel." *Les Temps modernes,* 169–70 (April–May): 1530–34.

Research on Racial Relations: Articles Reprinted from the International Social Sciences Journal. New York: UNESCO, 1966.

Rey, Benoist. *Les Égorgeurs.* Paris: Minuit, 1961.

Ricoeur, Paul. "Civilisation universelle et cultures nationales." *Esprit* 299 (October 1961): 439–53.

————. *État et violence.* Geneva: Foyer John Knox, 1957.

————. "L'Insoumission." *Esprit* 288 (October 1960): 1600–1604.

Rivet, Paul. "Indépendance et liberté." *Le Monde* (February 1, 1957).

Roy, Jules. *Adieu ma mère, adieu mon coeur.* Paris: Albin Michel, 1996.

————. "Un Entretien avec Jules Roy sur la guerre d'Algérie. *Cahiers de la république* 28 (November–December 1960): 53–58.

——. *La Guerre d'Algérie*. Paris: Julliard, 1960.

——. *J'accuse le général Massu*. Paris: Seuil, 1972.

——. *Journal*. Vol. 1, *Les Années déchirement: Journal 1925–1965*. Paris: A. Michel, 1988.

——. *À Propos d'Alger de Camus et du hassard*. Paris: Le Haut Quartier, 1982.

——. *The War in Algeria*. Westport CT: Greenwood Press, 1975.

Saadi, Yacef. *Souvenirs de la Bataille d'Alger, décembre 1956–septembre 1957*. Paris: R. Julliard, 1962.

Saive, René. "Graves révélations du colonel Gardes: Les 'centres sociaux' étaient noyautés par le F.L.N." *L'Écho d'Alger* (December 13, 1960): 3.

Sarroubl, Karim. *À l'ombre de soi*. Paris: Mercure de France, 1998.

Sartre, Jean-Paul. "Albert Camus." *France observateur* (January 7, 1960): 17.

——. "L'Alibi." Interview. *Le Nouvel observateur* (November 19, 1964): 1–5.

——. *Anti-Semite and Jew*. Translated by George J. Becker. New York: Schocken, 1948.

——. "Après Budapest." *L'Express* (November 9, 1956): 15.

——. *Being and Nothingness: An Essay on Phenomenological Ontology*. Translated by Hazel E. Barnes. New York: Philosophical Library, 1945.

——. *Between Existentialism and Marxism: Sartre on Philosophy, Politics, Psychology, and the Arts*. Translated by John Mathews. New York: Pantheon, 1974.

——. *Black Orpheus*. Translated by S. W. Allen. Paris: Présence Africaine, [1963?].

——. "Ceux qui vous oppriment, nous oppriment pour les mêmes raisons." *La Gauche: Journal du rassemblement démocratique révolutionnaire* (November 15, 1948): 1–3.

——. "Colonialisme est un système." In *Guerre d'Algérie et colonialisme*. Reprinted in *Situations, V: Colonialisme et néo-colonialisme*. Paris: Gallimard, 1964.

——. "Comment faire face au terrorisme." *France observateur* (May 18, 1961): 14–15.

——. *The Communists and Peace with a Reply to Claude Lafort*. New York: Braziller, 1968.

——. "La Consienza dei francesi." *Il Contemporaneo* (July 31, 1954).

——. "Le Crime." *Le Nouvel observateur* (November 30, 1966): 12–14.

——. *Critique de la raison dialectique, précédé de Question de méthode*. Vol. 1, *Théorie des ensembles pratiques*; vol. 2, *L'intelligibilité de l'histoire*. Paris: Gallimard, 1960.

——. *The Critique of Dialectical Reason*. Vol. 1, *The Theory of Practical Ensembles*. London: Verso, 1991.

——. *The Critique of Dialectical Reason*. Vol. 2 (unfinished), *The Intelligibility of History*. New York: Verso, 1991.

————. *Essays in Existentalism*. Secaucus NJ: Citadel, 1965.

————. Foreword to *Aden, Arabie* by Paul Nizan. New York: Monthly Review Press, 1968.

————. *The Ghost of Stalin*. New York: Braziller, 1968.

————. Introduction to *Colonizer and the Colonized* by Albert Memmi. Boston: Beacon Press, 1967.

————. *Life/Situations: Essays Written and Spoken*. Translated by Paul Auster and Lydia Davis. New York: Pantheon, 1977.

————. *Le Peuple ne doit compter que sur lui-même*. Comité de Défense des libertés républicaines du VIᴱ Arrondissement. Paris: n.p., n.d.

————. *Plaidoyer pour les intellectuels*. Paris: Gallimard, 1972.

————. Preface to *The Wretched of the Earth*, by Frantz Fanon. New York: Grove, 1968.

————. Review of Albert Memmi, *Portrait du colonisé, précédé du Portrait du colonisateur*. *Les Temps modernes* 137–38 (July–August 1957): 289–92.

————. *Saint Genet, Actor and Martyr*. New York: New American Library, 1964.

————. *Sartre on Cuba*. Westport CT: Greenwood Press, 1974.

————. *Search for a Method*. Translated by Hazel E. Barnes. New York: Vintage, 1967.

————. *Les Séquestrés d'Altona*. Paris: Gallimard, 1960.

————. *Situations, V: Colonialisme et néo-colonialisme*. Paris: Gallimard, 1964.

————. *Situations, VI et VII: Problèmes du marxisme*. Paris: Gallimard, 1965.

————. *Situations, X: Politique et autobiographie*. Paris: Gallimard, 1976.

————. *Témoignages et documents sur la guerre en Algérie: Compte rendu de la conférence de presse du vendredi 30 mai 1958, sur les violations des droits de l'homme en Algérie (n. 5), juin 1958*. Clichy, 1958.

————. "Une Victoire." *L'Express* (March 6, 1958); Introduction to *La Question*, by Henri Alleg.

————. "A Victory." Introduction to *The Question* by Henri Alleg. New York: Braziller, 1958.

————. *The Words*. Translated by Bernard Frechtman. Greenwich CT: Fawcett, 1964.

Savary, Alain. *Pour le nouveau parti socialiste*. Paris: Seuil, 1970.

Schumann, Maurice. *Le Vrai malaise des intellectuels de gauche*. Paris: Plon, 1957.

Schwartz, Laurent. Preface to *L'Affaire Audin (1957–1978)*, by Pierre Vidal-Naquet. Paris: Minuit, 1989.

Secrétariat Social d'Alger. *La Cohabitation en Algérie*. Algiers: Éditions du Secrétariat Social d'Alger, 1955.

Sedeyn, Émile. Preface to *Philosophie de la colonisation*, by Edgard Denancy. Paris: Bibliothèque de la Critique, 1902.

Sénac, Jean. *Dérisions et vertige: Trouvures*. Le Paradou, France: Actes Sud, 1983.

———. *Journal Alger, janvier-juillet 1954: Suivi de Les leçons d'Edgard*. Pezanas: Le Haut Quartier, 1983.

———. *Matinale de mon peuple: Poèmes*. Rodes: Subervie, 1961.

———. *Oeuvres poétiques*. Arles: Actus Sud, 1999.

———. *Poésie*. Paris: M. Boucher, 1962.

———. *Le Soleil sous les armes: Éléments d'une poésie de la résistance algérienne*. Rodez: Subervie, 1957.

Servan-Schreiber, Jean-Jacques. "L'Appel." *L'Express* (October 6, 1960): 7–8.

———. "Avec nos soldats." *L'Express* (September 22, 1960): 5–6.

———. "Le Bilan." *L'Express* (December 15, 1960): 7–8.

———. *La Guerre d'Algérie*. Paris: Paris Match, 1982.

———. L'Indépendance." *L'Express* (August 28, 1958): 3.

———. "Une Lettre d'un non-déserteur." *L'Express* (September 13, 1958): 5–6.

———. *Lieutenant en Algérie*. Paris: Julliard, 1957.

———. *Lieutenant in Algeria*. New York: Knopf, 1957.

———. "Que veut Mendès France?" *L'Express* (May 25, 1956): 3.

———. "Un Rappelé parle." *L'Express* (March 8, 1957): 15.

———. "Rappelés pour quoi?" *L'Express* (September 10, 1955): 3.

———. "Rendez-vous au retour!" *L'Express* (July 13, 1956): 3.

———. "Le Sang qui coule." *L'Express* (September 18, 1958): 3.

———. "Le Scalpel." *L'Express* (October 13, 1960): 7.

———. "Au Service de qui?" *L'Express* (April 13, 1956): 3.

Le Service des Centres Sociaux. *Direction général de l'éducation nationale en Algérie*. Algiers, n.d.

Simon, Pierre-Henri. *Contre la torture*. Paris: Seuil, 1957.

———. "Opération bonne conscience." *Esprit* 253 (September 1957): 244–46.

———. "Le Pion et les pionniers." *France observateur* (April 4, 1957): 3.

———. *Présence du Camus*. Paris: Nizet, 1961.

Souaïdia, Habib. *La sale guerre*. Paris: Gallimard, 2001.

———. *Le procès de la sale guerre: Algérie, le général-major Khaled Nezzar contre le lieutenant Habib Souaïdia*. Paris: Découverte, 2002.

Soustelle, Jacques. *Aimée et souffrante Algérie*. Paris: Plon, 1956.

———. *Algérie: Le chemin de la paix*. Paris: Centre d'Information pour les Problèmes de l'Algérie et du Sahara, 1960.

———. *L'Anthropologie française et les civilisations autochthones de l'Amérique*. Oxford: Clarendon Press, 1989.

———. *Discours de réception de M. Jacques Soutelle à l'Académie française et réponse de M. Jean Dutourd*. Paris: Flammarion, 1984.

———. *Le Drame algérien et la décadence française: Réponse à Raymond Aron*. Paris: Plon, 1957.

———. *Envers et contre tout: Souvenirs et documents sur la France libre*. Paris: Laffont, 1947.

———. *L'Espérance trahie, 1958–1961*. Paris: Table Ronde, 1962.

———. *Jacques Soustelle vous parle*. Paris: Conférences des Ambassadeurs, 1967.

———. "Lettre d'un intellectuel à quelques autres." Paris: n.p., n.d.

———. *Lettre ouverte aux victimes de la décolonisation*. Paris: A. Michel, 1973.

———. *La Longue marche d'Israël*. Paris: J'ai Lu, 1972.

———. *A New Road for France*. New York: Speller, 1965.

———. *L'Orient, foyer de guerre*. Paris: Conférences des Ambassadeurs, 1956.

———. *La Page n'est pas tournée*. Paris: La Table Ronde, 1965.

———. *Pour une politique de paix et de progrès en Algérie: Extraits des déclarations faites par Jacques Soustelle*. Lyon: n.p., n.d.

———. *Progrès et liberté: Discours prononcé à Lyon le 12 avril 1970*. Paris: La Table Ronde, 1970.

———. *Que faire en Algérie? Conférence prononcée le 21 mars, 1956*. Paris: n.p., 1956.

———. *Que faire en Méditerranée?* Paris: Conférences des Ambassadeurs, 1970.

———. *Vingt-huit ans de gaullisme*. Paris: J'ai Lu, 1971.

———. *The Wealth of the Sahara*. New York: Council on Foreign Relations, 1959.

Stibbe, Pierre. "Jean Amrouche, vous voilà." *France observateur* (June 12, 1958): 5.

———. "Négocier et non plus réprimer." In *Le Guerre d'Algérie et colonisme: Textes des interventions et messages prononcés au cours du meeting du 27 janvier 1956*, 33–36. Paris: Comité d'Action des Intellectuels contra la Poursuite de la Guerre en Afrique du Nord, 1956.

Taleb Ibrahimi, Ahmed. *De la Décolonisation à la révolution culturelle (1962–1972)*. Algiers: Société Nationale d'Édition et de Diffusion, 1981.

———. *Discours du ministre de l'éducation nationale*. Blida: INA, 1970.

———. *Lettres de prison (1957–1961)*. Algiers: Société Nationale d'Édition et de Diffusion, 1977.

"Tentatives de subversion dans les centres sociaux?" *L'Écho d'Alger* (November 1–2, 1959): 14.

Theolley, Jean-Marc. "Le Colonel Godard, convoqué de nouveau, affirme qu'il a vu tirer le 24 janvier un fusil mitrailleur survi par les gendarmes." *Le Monde* (February 5–6, 1961): 4.

Tillion, Germaine. *L'Afrique bascule vers l'avenir: L'Algérie en 1957 et autres textes*. Paris: Minuit, 1960.

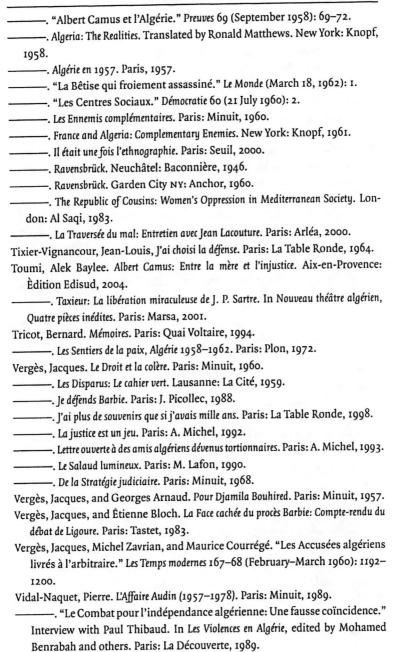

———. "Albert Camus et l'Algérie." *Preuves* 69 (September 1958): 69–72.

———. *Algeria: The Realities*. Translated by Ronald Matthews. New York: Knopf, 1958.

———. *Algérie en 1957*. Paris, 1957.

———. "La Bêtise qui froiement assassiné." *Le Monde* (March 18, 1962): 1.

———. "Les Centres Sociaux." *Démocratie 60* (21 July 1960): 2.

———. *Les Ennemis complémentaires*. Paris: Minuit, 1960.

———. *France and Algeria: Complementary Enemies*. New York: Knopf, 1961.

———. *Il était une fois l'ethnographie*. Paris: Seuil, 2000.

———. *Ravensbrück*. Neuchâtel: Baconnière, 1946.

———. *Ravensbrück*. Garden City NY: Anchor, 1960.

———. *The Republic of Cousins: Women's Oppression in Mediterranean Society*. London: Al Saqi, 1983.

———. *La Traversée du mal: Entretien avec Jean Lacouture*. Paris: Arléa, 2000.

Tixier-Vignancour, Jean-Louis, *J'ai choisi la défense*. Paris: La Table Ronde, 1964.

Toumi, Alek Baylee. *Albert Camus: Entre la mère et l'injustice*. Aix-en-Provence: Èdition Edisud, 2004.

———. *Taxieur: La libération miraculeuse de J. P. Sartre*. In *Nouveau théâtre algérien, Quatre pièces inédites*. Paris: Marsa, 2001.

Tricot, Bernard. *Mémoires*. Paris: Quai Voltaire, 1994.

———. *Les Sentiers de la paix, Algérie 1958–1962*. Paris: Plon, 1972.

Vergès, Jacques. *Le Droit et la colère*. Paris: Minuit, 1960.

———. *Les Disparus: Le cahier vert*. Lausanne: La Cité, 1959.

———. *Je défends Barbie*. Paris: J. Picollec, 1988.

———. *J'ai plus de souvenirs que si j'avais mille ans*. Paris: La Table Ronde, 1998.

———. *La justice est un jeu*. Paris: A. Michel, 1992.

———. *Lettre ouverte à des amis algériens dévenus tortionnaires*. Paris: A. Michel, 1993.

———. *Le Salaud lumineux*. Paris: M. Lafon, 1990.

———. *De la Stratégie judiciaire*. Paris: Minuit, 1968.

Vergès, Jacques, and Georges Arnaud. *Pour Djamila Bouhired*. Paris: Minuit, 1957.

Vergès, Jacques, and Étienne Bloch. *La Face cachée du procès Barbie: Compte-rendu du débat de Ligoure*. Paris: Tastet, 1983.

Vergès, Jacques, Michel Zavrian, and Maurice Courrégé. "Les Accusées algériens livrés à l'arbitraire." *Les Temps modernes* 167–68 (February–March 1960): 1192–1200.

Vidal-Naquet, Pierre. *L'Affaire Audin (1957–1978)*. Paris: Minuit, 1989.

———. "Le Combat pour l'indépendance algérienne: Une fausse coïncidence." Interview with Paul Thibaud. In *Les Violences en Algérie*, edited by Mohamed Benrabah and others. Paris: La Découverte, 1989.

———. *Face à la raison d'état: Un historien dans la guerre d'Algérie.* Paris: La Découverte, 1989.

———. *Mémoires.* 2 vols. Paris: La Découverte, 1998.

———. "Robert Bonnaud." *France observateur* 583 (6 July 1961): 4.

———. *Torture: Cancer of Democracy, France and Algeria, 1954–1962.* Translated by Barry Richard. New York: Penguin, 1963.

Vittori, Jean-Pierre. *Confessions d'un professionnel de la torture: La guerre d'Algérie.* Paris: Ramsay, 1980.

"Voici le verdict des juges militaires." *Dernière heure* (July 25, 1957): 1.

Wahl, Jean. *Introduction à la pensée de Heidegger: Cours donné en Sorbonne de janvier à juin 1946.* Paris: Librarie Générale Française, 1998.

———. *Le Malheur de la conscience dans la philosophic de Hegel.* Paris: Rieder, 1929.

Weiss, Pierre. *The Persecution and Assassination of Jean-Paul Marat as Performed by the Inmates of the Asylum of Charenton under the Direction of the Marquis de Sade.* English version by Geoffrey Skelton. Verse adaptation by Adrian Mitchell. New York: Atheneum, 1983.

Wurmser, André. "Maurice Auden et l'union pour la vérité." *Humanité-Dimanche* (December 8, 1957): 3.

Secondary Sources

Abun-Nasr, Jamil M. *A History of the Maghrib in the Islamic Period.* New York: Cambridge University Press, 1987.

Ageron, Charles-Robert. *L'Algérie Algérienne: De Napoléon III à de Gaulle.* Paris: Sindbad, 1980.

———. *Les Algériens musulmans et la France (1871–1919).* 2 vols. Paris: Presses Universitaires de France, 1968.

———. *L'Anticolonialisme en France de 1871 à 1914.* Paris: Presses Universitaires de France, 1973.

———. *France colonial ou parti colonial?* Paris: Presses Universitaires de France, 1978.

———, ed. *La Guerre d'Algérie et les algériens, 1945–1962: Actes de la table ronde organisée à Paris, 26–27 mars 1996.* Paris: Colin/Masson, 1997.

———. *Histoire de l'Algérie contemporaine.* 2 vols. Paris: Presses Universitaires de France, 1979.

———. *Modern Algeria: A History from 1830 to the Present.* Translated by Michael Brett. London: Hurst, 1990.

Adams, Geoffrey. *The Call of Conscience: French Protestant Responses to the Algerian War, 1954–1962.* Waterloo, Ontario: Wilfrid Laurier, 1998.

Agulhon, Maurice. *The French Republic, 1872–1992.* Cambridge MA: Blackwell, 1990.

Aldrich, Robert. *Greater France: A History of French Overseas Expansion.* New York: St. Martin's Press, 1996.

Algazy, Joseph. *La Tentation néo-fasciste en France de 1944 à 1965.* Paris: Fayard, 1984.

Amin, Samir. *Eurocentrism.* New York: Monthly Review Press, 1989.

————. *The Maghreb in the Modern World: Algeria, Tunisia, Morocco.* Harmondsworth: Penguin, 1970.

Amin, Samir et al. *Le Tiers monde et la gauche.* Paris: Seuil, 1979.

Anderson, Benedict. *Imagined Communities: Reflections on the Origin and Spread of Nationalism.* London: Verso, 1991.

Arendt, Hannah. *On Violence.* New York: Harcourt Brace, 1970.

Arnaud, Jacqueline. *La Littérature maghrébine de la langue française.* Vol. 1, *Origines et perspectives.* Paris: Publisud, 1986.

Arnaud, Jacqueline, Jean Déjeux, and Arlette Roth, eds. *Anthologie des écrivains maghrébins d'expression française.* Paris: Présence Africaine, 1985.

Ashcroft, Bill, Gareth Griffiths, and Helen Tiffin, eds. *The Empire Writes Back: Theory and Practice in Post-Colonial Literatures.* New York: Routledge, 1989.

Balibar, Étienne, and Immanuel Wallerstein. *Race, Nation, Class: Ambiguous Identities.* New York: Verso, 1991.

Bédarida, François, and Étienne Fouilloux, eds. *La Guerre d'Algérie et les chrétiens.* Paris: Institut d'Histoire du Temps Présent, 1988.

Benchérif, Osman. *The Image of Algeria in Anglo-American Writings, 1785–1962.* Lanham MD: University Press of America, 1997.

Ben Jelloun, Tahar. *French Hospitality: Racism and North African Immigrants.* New York: Columbia University Press, 1999.

Benrabah, Mohamed et al. *Les Violences en Algérie.* Paris: Odile Jacob, 1999.

Bensemmane, M'Hamed. "Mouloud Mammeri's *Le Sommeil du juste* as a Counter-Vision of Colonial Humanism. *Journal of Algerian Studies* 3 (1998): 71–77.

Betts, Raymond. *Assimilation and Association in French Colonial Theory, 1890–1914.* New York: Columbia University Press, 1961.

————. *Decolonization.* New York: Routledge, 1998.

————. *France and Decolonization, 1900–1960.* New York: St. Martin's Press, 1991.

Bhabha, Homi K. *The Location of Culture.* New York: Routledge, 1994.

————. "Remembering Fanon: Self, Psyche, and the Colonial Condition." Foreword to *Black Skin, White Masks,* by Frantz Fanon. London: Pluto, 1986.

Boahen, Adu A. *African Perspectives on Colonialism.* Baltimore: Johns Hopkins University Press, 1987.

Boschetti, Anna. *The Intellectual Enterprise: Sartre and "Les Temps modernes."* Evanston IL: Northwestern University Press, 1988.

Branche, Raphaëlle. *La Torture et l'armée pendant la guerre d'Algérie, 1954–1962.* Paris: Gallimard, 2001.

Breckman, Warren. *Marx, the Young Hegelians, and the Origins of Radical Social Theory.* New York: Cambridge University Press, 1999.

Brée, Germaine. *Camus and Sartre: Crisis and Commitment.* New York: Delacorte, 1972.

Brett, Michael. "Dad's Algeria: Jacques Berque and Albert Camus on the Land of Their Fathers." *Journal of Algerian Studies* 1 (1996): 84–102.

Brown, L. Carl, and Matthew S. Gordon, eds. *Franco-Arab Encounters.* Beirut: American University of Beirut, 1996.

Bulhan, Hussein Abdilahi. *Frantz Fanon and the Psychology of the Oppressed.* New York: Plenum Press, 1985.

Burgat, François, and William Dowell. *The Islamic Movement in North Africa.* Austin: University of Texas Press, 1993.

Camus, Jean-Yves. "Political Cultures within the Front National: The Emergence of a Counter-Ideology on the French Far-Right." *Patterns of Prejudice* 26 (1992): 5–16.

Cassirer, Ernst. *The Question of Jean-Jacques Rousseau.* New Haven CT: Yale University Press, 1989.

Çelik, Zeynap. "Colonial/Postcolonial Intersections: Lieux de mémoire in Algiers." *Third Text* 49 (Winter 1999–2000): 63–72.

———. *Urban Forms and Colonial Confrontations: Algiers under French Rule.* Berkeley: University of California Press, 1997.

Chamberlain, Muriel E. *The Longman Companion to European Decolonization in the Twentieth Century.* New York: Longman, 1998.

Charef, Abed. *Algérie: Autopsie d'un massacre.* Paris: L'Aube, 1998.

Charnay, Jean-Paul. *La Vie musulmane en Algérie d'après la jurisprudence de la première moitié du XXᴱ siècle.* Paris: Presses Universitaires de France, 1991.

Chatterjee, Partha. *The Nation and Its Fragments: Colonial and Postcolonial Histories.* Princeton NJ: Princeton University Press, 1993.

———. *Nationalist Thought and the Colonial World: A Derivative Discourse.* Minneapolis: University of Minnesota Press, 1998.

Cherkaoui, Mohamed. *Les Changements du système éducatif en France, 1950–1980.* Paris: Presses Universitaires de France, 1982.

Christelow, Allan. *Muslim Law Courts and the French Colonial State in Algeria.* Princeton NJ: Princeton University Press, 1985.

Clancy-Smith, Julia A. "La Femme arabe: Women and Sexuality in France's North African Empire." In *Women, the Family, and Divorce Laws in Islamic History,* edited by Amira El Azhary Sonbol. Syracuse NY: Syracuse University Press, 1996.

————. *Rebel and Saint: Muslim Notables, Populist Protest, Colonial Encounters (Algeria and Tunisia, 1800–1904)*. Berkeley: University of California Press, 1997.

Clancy-Smith, Julia A., and Frances Gouda, eds. *Domesticating the Empire: Race, Gender, and Family Life in French and Dutch Colonialism*. Charlottesville: University of Virginia Press, 1998.

Clayton, Anthony. *The Wars of French Decolonization*. Harlow: Longman, 1994.

Cohen, William B. "The Algerian War, the French State, and Official Memory." *Historical Reflections/Reflexions Historiques*, 28, no. 2 (Summer 2002): 219–39.

————. *The French Encounter with Africans: White Response to Blacks, 1530–1880*. Foreword by James D. Le Sueur. Bloomington: Indiana University Press, 2003.

————. *Rulers of Empire: The French Colonial Service in Africa*. Stanford CA: Hoover Institution Press, 1971.

Colonna, Fanny. *Instituteurs algériens: 1883–1939*. Paris: Foundation Nationale des Sciences Politiques, 1975.

Conklin, Alice L. *A Mission to Civilize: The Republican Idea of Empire in France and West Africa, 1895–1930*. Palo Alto CA: Stanford University Press, 1997.

Connelly, Matthew. *A Diplomatic Revolution: Algeria's Fight for Independence and the Origins of the Post–Cold War Era*. New York: Oxford University Press, 2002.

————. "Taking Off the Cold War Lens: Visions of North-South Conflict During the Algerian War of Independence." *American Historical Review* 105, no. 3 (June 2000): 739–69.

Cook, Scott B. *Colonial Encounters in the Age of High Imperialism*. New York, Harper, 1996.

Cooper, Frederick. *Decolonization and African Society: The Labor Question in French and British Africa*. New York: Cambridge University Press, 1996.

Corpet, Olivier, and Albert Dichy, eds. *Kateb Yacine, éclats de mémoire*. Paris: IMEC, 1994.

Coquery-Vidrovitch, Catherine. "L'Opinion française et la décolonisation de l'Afrique noire: De la colonization à la coopération." *Itinerario* 20, no. 2 (1996): 43–50.

Courrière, Yves. *La Guerre d'Algérie (1954–1957)*. Vol. 1, *Les Fils de la toussaint*; vol. 2, *Le Temps des léopards*, 1954–1957; vol. 3, *L'Heure des colonials*; vol. 4, *Les Feux du désespoir*, 1958–1962. Paris: Fayard, 1970.

Delanty, Gerard. *Inventing Europe: Idea, Identity, Reality*. New York: St. Martin's Press, 1995.

Descombes, Vincent. *Le Même et l'autre: Quarante-cinq ans de philosophie française (1933–1978)*. Paris: Minuit, 1979.

Derrida, Jacques. "Parti pris pour l'Algérie." *Les Temps modernes* 580 (January–February 1995): 233–41.

Dine, Philip. *Images of the Algerian War: French Fiction and Film, 1954–1992.* New York: Oxford University Press, 1994.

Dreyfus, Hubert L. *Being-in-the-World: A Commentary on Heidegger's Being and Time, Division I.* Cambridge MA: MIT Press, 1991.

Droz, Bernard, and Evelyne Lever. *Histoire de la guerre d'Algérie (1954–1962).* Paris: Seuil, 1991.

Duclert, Vincent. "De l'Engagement des savants à l'intellectuel critique: Une histoire intellectuel de l'affaire Dreyfus." *Historical Reflections/Reflexions Historiques* 24, no. 1 (1998): 25–62.

Dunwoodie, Peter. *Writing French Algeria.* New York: Clarendon Press, 1998.

Easthope, Antony. "Bhabha, Hybridity, and Identity." *Textual Practice* 12, no. 2 (1998): 341–48.

El Machat, Samya. *Les États-Unis et l'Algérie: De la méconnaissance à la reconnaissance, 1945–1962.* Paris: L'Harmattan, 1996.

Entelis, John P. *Algeria: The Revolution Institutionalized.* Boulder CO: Westview Press, 1986.

———. *Islam, Democracy, and the State in North Africa.* Bloomington: Indiana University Press, 1997.

Eribon, Didier. *Michel Foucault.* Cambridge MA: Harvard University Press, 1991.

Esposito, John L. *Islam: The Straight Path.* New York: Oxford University Press, 1991.

———. *The Islamic Threat: Myth or Reality.* New York: Oxford University Press, 1995.

Evans, Martin. *The Memory of Resistance: French Opposition to the Algerian War (1954–1962).* New York: Berg, 1997.

Fabian, Johannes. *Time and the Other: How Anthropology Makes Its Object.* New York: Columbia University Press, 1983.

Feldblum, Miriam. *Reconstructing Citizenship: The Politics of Nationality Reform and Immigration in Contemporary France.* Albany NY: SUNY Press, 1999.

Ferro, Marc. *Histoire des colonisations.* Paris: Seuil, 1994.

Forget, Nelly. "Le Service des Centres Sociaux en Algérie." *Matériaux pour l'histoire de notre temps* 26 (January–March 1992): 37–47.

Fuller, Graham E. *Algeria: The Next Fundamentalist State?* Santa Monica CA: Rand, 1996.

Furet, François. *The Passing of an Illusion: The Idea of Communism in the Twentieth Century.* Chicago: University of Chicago Press, 1999.

Gadant, Monique. "Femmes alibi." *Les Temps modernes* 580 (January–February 1995): 221–32.

Gaspard, Françoise. *A Small City in France.* Cambridge MA: Harvard University Press, 1995.

Gates, Henry Louis Jr. "Critical Fanonism." *Critical Inquiry* 17 (Spring 1991): 457–70.

——, ed. *"Race," Writing, and Difference.* Chicago: University of Chicago Press, 1986.

Gellner, Ernest. *Nations and Nationalism.* Ithaca NY: Cornell University Press, 1983.

Germaine-Robin, François. *Femmes rebelles d'Algérie.* Paris: Les Éditions de l'Atelier, 1996.

Gibson, Nigel C., ed. *Rethinking Fanon: The Continuing Dialogue.* Amherst NY: Humanity Books, 1999.

Giles, Frank. *The Locust Years: The Story of the Fourth Republic, 1945–1958.* London: Secker and Warburg, 1991.

Giono, Jean. *Entretiens avec Jean Amrouche et Taos Amrouche.* Paris: Gallimard, 1990.

Girardet, Raoul. *L'Idée coloniale en France.* Paris: Table Ronde, 1972.

Gordon, Lewis R., T. Denean Sharpley-Whiting, and Renée T. White. *Fanon: A Critical Reader.* Oxford: Blackwell, 1996.

Grandguillaume, Gilbert. *Arabisation et politique linguistique au Maghreb.* Paris: Maisonneuve et Larousse, 1983.

Grew, Raymond, and Patrick J. Harrigan. *School, State, and Society: The Growth of Elementary Schooling in Nineteenth-Century France, a Quantitative Analysis.* Ann Arbor: University of Michigan Press, 1991.

Guha, Ranajit, ed. *A Subaltern Studies Reader, 1986–1995.* Minneapolis: University of Minnesota Press, 1997.

Halls, W. D. *Education, Culture, and Politics in Modern France.* New York: Pergamon, 1976.

Hamon, Hervé, and Patrick Rotman. *Les Porteurs de valises: La résistance française à la guerre d'Algérie.* Paris: A. Michel, 1982.

Harbi, Mohammed. *L'Algérie, l'état et le droit: 1979–1988.* Paris: Arcantere, 1989.

——, ed. *Les Archives de la révolution algérienne.* Paris: Jeune Afrique, 1981.

——. *Le FLN: Mirage et réalité.* Paris: Jeune Afrique, 1985.

——. *L'Islamisme dans tous ses états.* Paris: Arcantere, 1991.

——. *1954: La guerre commence en Algérie.* Brussels: Complexe, 1984.

——. *Aux Origines du Front de Libération Nationale: La scission du PPA–MTLD: Contribution à l'histoire du populisme révolutionnaire en Algérie.* Paris: C. Bourgois, 1975.

Hargreaves, Alec G. "Algerians in Contemporary France: Incorporation or Exclusion?" *Journal of Algerian Studies* 3 (1998): 31–47.

——. *Immigration and Identity in Beur Fiction: Voices from the North African Community.* New York: Berg, 1991.

————. *Immigration, "Race," and Ethnicity in Contemporary France.* New York: Routledge, 1995.

Hargreaves, Alec G., and Michael J. Heffernan, eds. *French and Algerian Identities from the Colonial Times to the Present: A Century of Interaction.* Lewiston: Edwin Mellen, 1993.

Hargreaves, Alec G., and Mark McKinney, eds. *Post-Colonial Cultures in France.* New York: Routledge, 1997.

Hargreaves, John. *Decolonization in Africa.* 2nd ed. New York: Longman, 1999.

————. "From Colonisation to Avénement: Henri Brunschwig and the History of Afrique Noire." *Journal of African History* 31 (1990): 347–52.

Harik, Elsa M., and Donald G. Schilling. *The Politics of Education in Colonial Algeria and Kenya.* Papers in International Africa Series 43. Athens: Ohio University Center for International Studies, 1984.

Haroun, Ali. *La 7ᴇ Wilaya: La guerre du FLN en France, 1954–1962.* Paris: Seuil, 1986.

Harper, Graeme, ed. *Colonial and Postcolonial Incarceration.* London: Continuum, forthcoming.

Harpigny, Guy. *Islam et christianisme selon Louis Massignon.* Louvain-la-Neuve: Université Catolique de Louvain, 1981.

Harrison, Alexander. *Challenging De Gaulle: The O.A.S. and the Counterrevolution in Algeria, 1954–1962.* New York: Columbia University Press, 1989.

Harrison, Martin. "Government and Press in France during the Algerian War." *American Political Science Review* 58, no. 2 (June 1964): 273–85.

Headrick, Daniel R. *The Tools of Empire: Technology and European Imperialism in the Nineteenth Century.* New York: Oxford University Press, 1981.

Hegel et la pensée moderne: Séminaire sur Hegel dirigé par Jean Hyppolite au Collège de France (1967–1968). Paris: Presses Universitaires de France, 1970.

Henissart, Paul. *Wolves in the City: The Death of French Algeria.* New York: Simon and Schuster, 1970.

L'Historien entre l'éthnologue et le futurologue: Actes du séminaire international organisé sous les auspices de l'Association Internationale pour la Liberté de la Culture, la Foundation Giovanni Agnelli et la Fondation Giorgio Cini, Venise, 2–9 avril 1971. Paris: Mouton, 1972.

Hitchcock, William I. *France Restored: Cold War Diplomacy and the Quest for Leadership in Europe, 1944–1954.* Chapel Hill: University of North Carolina Press, 1998.

Hoisington, William A. *Lyautey and the French Conquest of Morocco.* New York: St. Martin's Press, 1995.

Horne, Alistair. *A Savage War of Peace: Algeria, 1954–1962.* New York: Viking, 1978.

Hourani, Albert. *Islam in European Thought.* New York: Cambridge University Press, 1991.

————. *A History of the Arab Peoples*. Cambridge MA: Harvard University Press, 1991.

Hughes, H. Stuart. *Consciousness and Society: The Reorientation of European Social Thought 1890–1930*. New York: Vintage, 1977.

Humbaraci, Arslan. *Algeria: A Revolution That Failed*. New York: Praeger, 1966.

Hutchinson, Martha Crenshaw. *Revolutionary Terrorism: The F.L.N. in Algeria, 1954–1962*. Stanford CA: Hoover Institution Press, 1978.

Jauffret, Jean-Charles. "The Origins of the Algerian War: The Reaction of France and Its Army to the Two Emergencies of 8 May 1945 and 1 November 1954." *Journal of Imperial and Commonwealth History* 21, no. 3 (September 1993): 17–29.

Jinadu, L. Adele. *Fanon: In Search of the African Revolution*. London: KPI, 1986.

Joly, Danièle. *The French Communist Party and the Algerian War*. New York: St. Martin's Press, 1991.

Joffé, George. *North Africa: Nation, State, Religion*. London: Routledge, 1993.

Jouin, Serge, and Jean-Philippe Ould Aoudia. "Les Centres Sociaux Éducatifs en Algérie, 1955–1962." *Cahiers du Centre Fédéral* (December 1992): 103–40.

Judt, Tony. *The Burden of Responsibility: Blum, Camus, Aron, and the French Twentieth Century*. Chicago: University of Chicago Press, 1998.

————. "The Lost World of Albert Camus." *New York Review of Books* 16 (October 6, 1994): 3–5.

————. *Past Imperfect: French Intellectuals, 1944–1956*. Berkeley: University of California Press, 1992.

Kahler, Miles. *Decolonization in Britain and France: The Domestic Consequences of International Relations*. Princeton NJ: Princeton University Press, 1984.

Kaplan, Roger. "The First Man." *The New Republic*, November 6, 2000, 31–38. A review of Feraoun's *Journal*.

Kiernan. V. G. "Europe in the Colonial Mirror." *History of European Ideas* 1 (1980): 39–61.

Killingray, David, and David Omissi, eds. *The Guardians of Empire: The Armed Forces and the Colonial Powers c. 1700–1964*. New York: Manchester University Press, 1999.

Kramer, Jane. *Unsettling Europe*. New York: Vintage, 1981.

Lacoste-Dujardin, Camille. "Le Souci de la femme méditerranéenne: Des aurès au *Harem et les cousins*." *Esprit* 261 (February 2000): 148–54.

Lacouture, Jean. *De Gaulle: The Ruler, 1945–1970*. London: Harvill, 1991.

————. *François Mauriac*. Paris: Seuil, 1980.

Laing, R. D., and D. G. Cooper. *Reason and Violence: A Decade of Sartre's Philosophy, 1950–1960*. New York: Pantheon, 1971.

Lambert, Michael C. "From Citizenship to Négritude: 'Making a Difference' in

Elite Ideologies of Colonized Francophone West Africa." *Comparative Studies in Society and History* 35, no. 1 (1993): 239–63.

Laremont, Ricardo René. *Islam and the Politics of Resistance in Algeria, 1783–1992.* Trenton NJ: Africa World Press, 2000.

Larzeg, Marnia. *The Eloquence of Silence: Algerian Women in Question.* New York: Routledge, 1994.

———. "Feminism and Difference: The Perils of Writing as a Woman on Women in Algeria." *Feminist Studies* 14, no. 1 (Spring 1988): 81–107.

Lee, Robert D. *Overcoming Tradition and Modernity: The Search for Islamic Authenticity.* Boulder CO: Westview Press, 1997.

Lenin, Vladimir I. *Imperialism: The Highest Stage of Capitalism: A Popular Outline.* New York: International Publishers, 1985.

Le Sueur, James D. "Before the Jackal: The International Uproar over *Assassination!*" Historical essay to *Assassination! July 14,* by Ben Abro. Lincoln: University of Nebraska Press, 2001.

———. "Beyond Decolonization? The Legacy of the Algerian Conflict and the Transformation of Identity in Contemporary France." *Historical Reflections/Reflexions historiques,* 28, no. 2 (2002): 277–291.

———, ed. *The Decolonization Reader.* London: Routledge, 2003.

———. "Decolonizing French Universalism: Re-considering the Impact of the French-Algerian War on French Intellectuals." *Journal of North African Studies* 6, no. 2 (2001): 167–186.

———. Foreword to *The French Encounter with Africans: White Response to Blacks, 1530–1880,* by William B. Cohen. Bloomington: Indiana University Press, 2003.

———. "Ghost walking in Algiers? Why Alek Baylee Toumi resurrected Sartre and de Beauvoir." *Modern and Contemporary France,* 10, no. 4 (2002): 507–517.

———. Introduction to *Journal, 1955–1962: Reflections on the French-Algerian War,* by Mouloud Feraoun. Edited by James D. Le Sueur. Translated by Mary Ellen Wolf and Claude Fouillade. Lincoln: University of Nebraska Press, 2000.

———. Introduction to *The Poor Man's Son: Menrad, Kabyle Schoolteacher,* by Mouloud Feraoun. Translated by Lucy McNair. Charlottesville: University Press of Virginia, 2005.

———. Introduction to *The Question,* by Henri Alleg. Lincoln: University of Nebraska Press, 2006.

———. "Torture and the Decolonization of French Algeria: Nationalism, 'Race,' and Violence During Colonial Incarceration." In *Colonial and Postcolonial Incarceration,* edited by Graeme Harper. London: Continuum, 2002.

Le Sueur, James D., and William B. Cohen, eds. *France and Algeria: Colonial Conflicts and Postcolonial Memories*. Lincoln: University of Nebraska Press, forthcoming.

Liauzu, Claude, N. Benallegue, and S. Hamzaoui. *Les Intellectuels français au miroir algérien, mouvements sociaux maghrébins*. Nice: CMMC, 1984.

Loomba, Ania. *Colonialism/Postcolonialism: The New Critical Idiom*. London: Routledge, 1998.

Lorcin, Patricia M. E. *Imperial Identities: Stereotyping, Prejudice, and Race in Colonial Algeria*. New York: Tauris, 1995.

Lottman, Herbert R. *Albert Camus: A Biography*. New York: Doubleday, 1979.

Lucas, Philippe, and Jean-Claude Vatin. *L'Algérie des anthropologues*. Paris: Maspero, 1975.

MacMaster, Neil. *Colonial Migrants and Racism: Algerians in France, 1900–1962*. New York: St. Martin's Press, 1997.

———. "Orientalism: From Unveiling to Hyperveiling." *Journal of European Studies* 28, nos. 109–110 (March–June 1998): 121–35.

Malek, Rédha. *Tradition et révolution: L'enjeu de la modernité en Algérie et dans l'Islam*. Paris: Sindbad, 1993.

Malley, Robert. *The Call from Algeria: Third Worldism, Revolution, and the Turn to Islam*. Berkeley: University of California Press, 1996.

Mamdani, Mahmood. *Citizen and Subject: Contemporary Africa and the Legacy of Late Colonialism*. Princeton NJ: Princeton University Press, 1996.

Maougal, Mohamed Lakdar. "Recognition—the Cardinal Stake of Violence: An Essay on the Neurotic Structure of the Algerian Culture Élite." *Journal of Algerian Studies* 2 (1997): 1–26.

Maran, Rita. *Torture: The Role of Ideology in the French-Algerian War*. New York: Praeger, 1989.

Martin, Jean. *Lexique de la colonisation française*. Paris: Dalloz, 1988.

Mathy, Jean-Philippe. *Extrême-Occident: French Intellectuals and America*. Chicago: University of Chicago Press, 1993.

Mazouni, Abdallah. *Culture et enseignement en Algérie et au maghreb*. Paris: Maspero, 1969.

McBride, William L. *Sartre's Political Theory*. Bloomington: Indiana University Press, 1991.

McClintock, Anne, Adamir Mufti, and Ella Shohat. *Dangerous Liaisons: Gender, Nation, and Postcolonial Perspectives*. Minneapolis: University of Minnesota Press, 1997.

McLynn, Frank. *Hearts of Darkness: The European Exploration of Africa*. London: Pimlico, 1992.

Melasuo, Tuomo. "The Islamism in Algeria." *Hemispheres* 8 (1993): 11–20.

"Mélouza était un village FLN." L'Humanité (June 4, 1957): 1.

Messaoudi, Khalida. "La Nouvelle Inquisition." Les Temps modernes 580 (January–February 1995): 213–20.

———. Unbowed: An Algerian Woman Confronts Islamic Fundamentalism: Interviews with Elisabeth Schemla. Translated by Anne Vila. Philadelphia: University of Pennsylvania Press, 1995.

Mimouni, Rachid. De la Barbarie en général et de l'intégrisme en particulier. Belfound: Le Pré aux Clercs, 1992.

Mitchell, Timothy. Colonizing Egypt. Berkeley: University of California Press, 1991.

Moore-Gilbert, Bart. Postcolonial Theory: Contexts, Practices, Politics. London: Verso, 1997.

Morris-Jones, W. H., and Georges Fischer, eds. Decolonisation and After: The British and French Experiences. London: Cass, 1980.

Morton, Patricia A. Hybrid Modernities: Architecture and Representation at the 1931 Colonial Exposition, Paris. Cambridge MA: MIT Press, 2000.

Mosse, George L. Toward the Final Solution: A History of European Racism. Madison: University of Wisconsin Press, 1985.

Mouffok, Chania. Ecircumflextre journaliste en Algérie. Paris: Reporteurs sans Frontières, 1996.

Moxon-Browne, Edward, ed. European Terrorism. New York: G. K. Hall, 1994.

Murphy, Agnes. The Ideology of French Imperialism, 1871–1881. New York: Catholic University of America Press, 1948.

Nacib, Yousset. Mouloud Feraoun. Algiers: Entreprise Nationale du Livre, 1986.

Neumann, Iver R., and Jennifer M. Welsh. "The Other in European Self-Definition: An Addendum to the Literature on International Society." Review of International Studies 17 (1991): 327–48.

Norindr, Panivong. Phantasmatic Indochina: French Colonial Ideology in Architecture, Film, and Literature. Durham NC: Duke University Press, 1996.

O'Ballance, Edgar. The Algerian Insurrection, 1954–1962. London: Faber, 1967.

Ory, Pascal, and Jean-François Sirinelli. Les Intellectuels en France, de l'Affaire Dreyfus à nos jours. Paris: Colin, 1986.

Ould Aoudia, Jean-Philippe. L'Assassinat de Château-Royal: Alger, 15 Mars 1962. Paris: Tirésias–M. Reynaud, 1992.

———. "L'Attentat contre les Centres Sociaux Éducatifs." Matériaux pour l'histoire de notre temps 26 (January–March 1992): 48–54.

———. Un Élu dans la guerre d'Algérie: Droiture et forfeiture. Paris: Tirésias, 1999.

Paret, Peter. French Revolutionary Warfare from Indochina to Algeria: The Analysis of a Political and Military Doctrine. New York: Praeger, 1964.

Parket, Emmett. *Albert Camus: The Artist in the Arena*. Madison: University of Wisconsin Press, 1966.

Paxton, Robert O. *Vichy France: Old Guard and New Order, 1940–1944*. New York: Columbia University Press, 1972.

Péju, Marcel, ed. *Le Procès du réseau Jeanson*. Paris: Maspero, 1961.

Pervillé, Guy. *De l'Empire français à la décolonisation*. Paris: Hachette, 1991.

Poliakov, Léon. *The Aryan Myth: A History of Racist and Nationalist Ideas in Europe*. New York: Basic Books, 1974.

Poster, Mark. *Existential Marxism in Postwar France: From Sartre to Althusser*. Princeton NJ: Princeton University Press, 1975.

Prakash, Gyan, ed. *After Colonialism: Imperial Histories and Postcolonial Displacements*. Princeton NJ: Princeton University Press, 1995.

Pratt, Mary Louise. *Imperial Eyes: Travel Writing and Transculturation*. New York: Routledge, 1992.

Prochaska, David. *Making Algeria French: Colonialism in Bône, 1870–1920*. New York: Cambridge University Press, 1990.

Quandt, William B. *Between Ballots and Bullets: Algeria's Transition from Authoritarianism*. Washington DC: Brookings Institution, 1998.

Rahman, Fazlur. *Islam and Modernity: Transformation of an Intellectual Tradition*. Chicago: University of Chicago Press, 1982.

———. *Islam in the Modern World*. Columbia: University of Missouri Press, 1984.

Rémond, René. "Les Intellectuels et la Politique." *Revue française de science politique* 94 (December 1959): 860–80.

Rioux, Jean-Pierre, ed. *La Guerre d'Algérie et les français: Colloque de l'Institut d'histoire du temps présent*. Paris: Fayard, 1990.

Rioux, Jean-Pierre, and Jean-François Sirinelli. *La Guerre d'Algérie et les Intellectuels français*. Brussels: Complèxe, 1991.

Roberts, Hugh. *The Battle Field Algeria, 1988–2002*. London: Verso, 2003.

———. "Ernest Gellner and the Algerian Army: The Intellectual Origins of the Problem of Algerian Studies in Britain." *Journal of Algerian Studies* 2 (1997): 27–42.

———. "The Image of the French Army in the Cinematic Representation of the Algerian War: The Revolutionary Politics of the Battle of Algiers." *Journal of Algerian Studies* 2 (1997): 90–99.

———. "The Struggle for Constitutional Rule in Algeria." *Journal of Algerian Studies* 3 (1998): 19–30.

Robinson, Cedric. "The Appropriation of Frantz Fanon." *Race and Class* 35, no. 1 (1993): 79–91.

Roblès, Emmanuel. *Albert Camus et la trêve civile*. Philadelphia: Temple University Department of French and Italian, 1988.

———. *Camus: Frère de soleil*. Paris: Seuil, 1995.

Ross, Kristin. *Fast Cars, Clean Bodies: Decolonization and the Reordering of French Culture*. Cambridge MA: MIT Press, 1996.

Roth, Michael S. *Knowing and History: Appropriations of Hegel in Twentieth-Century France*. Ithaca NY: Cornell University Press, 1988.

Ruedy, John, ed. *Islam and Secularism in North Africa*. New York: St. Martin's Press, 1994.

———. *Modern Algeria: The Origins and Development of a Nation*. Bloomington: Indiana University Press, 1992.

Said, Edward W. *Covering Islam: How the Media and the Experts Determine How We See the Rest of the World*. New York: Vintage, 1997.

———. *Culture and Imperialism*. New York: Vintage, 1994.

———. *Orientalism*. New York: Vintage, 1979.

———. *Representations of the Intellectual: The 1993 Reith Lectures*. New York: Vintage, 1994.

———. "Representing the Colonized: Anthropology's Interlocutors." *Critical Inquiry* 15 (Winter 1989): 205–25.

Schalk, David L. "Has France's Marrying Her Century Cured the Algerian Syndrome?" *Historical Reflections/Réflexions Historiques* 25, no. 1 (1999): 149–64.

———. "Reflections *d'outre-mer* on French Colonialism." *Journal of European Studies* 28, nos. 109–110 (1998): 5–23.

———. *War and the Ivory Tower: Algeria and Vietnam*. New York: Oxford University Press, 1991.

Scriven, Michael, and Peter Wagstaff, eds. *War and Society in Twentieth-Century France*. New York: Berg, 1991.

Sekyi-Out, Ato. *Fanon's Dialectic of Experience*. Cambridge MA: Harvard University Press, 1996.

Shah-Kazemi, Reza, ed. *Algeria: Revolution Revisited*. London: Islamic World Report, 1997.

Shatz, Adam. "The Torture of Algiers." *The New York Review of Books* 49, no. 18 (November 21, 2002): 53–56.

Simmons, Harvey G. *The French National Front: The Extreme Challenge to Democracy*. Boulder CO: Westview Press, 1996.

———. *French Socialists in Search of a Role, 1956–1967*. Ithaca NY: Cornell University Press, 1970.

Sirinelli, Jean-François, *Intellectuels et passions françaises: Manifestes et pétitions au XX*ᴱ *siècle*. Paris: Fayard, 1990.

Sivan, Emanuel. "Anti-Colonialism at the Age of the Popular Front: Algerian Communism 1935–1935." *Asian and African Studies* 11, no. 3 (Winter 1977): 337–74.

———. *Communisme et nationalisme en Algérie, 1920–1962.* Paris: Fondation Nationale des Sciences Politiques, 1976.

———. "Leftist Outcasts in a Colonial Situation: Algerian Communism, 1927–1935." *Asian and African Studies* 10, no. 3 (1975): 209–57.

———. "L'Étoile Nord Africaine and the Genesis of Algerian Nationalism." *Maghreb Review* 3, nos. 5–6 (January–April 1978): 17–22.

———. " 'Slave Owner Mentality' and Bolshevism: Algerian Communism, 1920–1927." *Asian and African Studies* 9, no. 2 (1974): 153–95.

Smith, Tony, ed. *The End of the European Empire: Decolonization After World War II.* Lexington MA: D. C. Heath, 1975.

Spivak, Gayatri Chakravorty. *A Critique of Postcolonial Reason: Toward a History of the Vanishing Present.* Cambridge MA: Harvard University Press, 1999.

———. *In Other Worlds: Essays in Cultural Politics.* New York: Methuen, 1987.

———. *The Post-Colonial Critic: Interviews, Strategies, Dialogues.* Edited by Sarah Harasym. New York: Routledge, 1990.

Sorum, Paul Clay. *Intellectuals and Decolonization in France.* Chapel Hill: University of North Carolina Press, 1977.

Stepan, Nancy. *The Idea of Race in Science: Great Britain, 1800–1960.* Hamden CT: Archon, 1982.

Sternhell, Zeev. *Neither Right nor Left: Fascist Ideology in France.* Princeton NJ: Princeton University Press, 1986.

Stocking, George W. Jr. "The Persistence of Polygenist Thought in Post-Darwinian Anthropology." In *Race, Culture, and Evolution: Essays in History and Anthropology,* edited by George W. Stocking Jr. Chicago: University of Chicago Press, 1982.

Stone, Martin. *The Agony of Algeria.* New York: Columbia University Press, 1997.

Stora, Benjamin. *Algeria 1839–2000: A Short History.* Foreword by William B. Quandt. New York: Columbia University Press, 2001.

———. "Algeria: The War Without a Name" *Journal of Imperial and Commonwealth History* 21, no. 3 (September 1993): 208–16.

———. "Algérie: Absence et surabondance de mémoire." In *Les Violences en Algérie.* Paris: Odile Jacob, 1998.

———. *L'Algérie en 1995: La guerre, l'histoire, la politique.* Paris: Michalon, 1995.

———. "Deuxième guerre algérienne?" *Temps modernes* 580 (January–February 1995): 242–61.

———. *La Gangrène et l'oubli: La mémoire de la guerre d'Algérie.* Paris: La Découverte, 1991.

———. Histoire de l'Algérie depuis l'indépendance. Paris: La Découverte, 1995.

———. Histoire de la guerre d'Algérie, 1954–1962. Paris: La Découverte, 1993.

———. Ils venaient d'Algérie: L'immigration algérienne en France 1912–1992. Paris: Fayard, 1992.

———. Messali Hadj: Pionnier du nationalisme algérien (1898–1974). Paris: L'Harmattan, 1986.

———. Nationalistes Algériens et révolutionnaires français au temps du front populaire. Paris: L'Harmattan, 1987.

———. Le Transfert d'une mémoire: De l'Algérie française au racisme anti-arabe. Paris: Découverte, 1999.

Talbott, John. "French Public Opinion and the Algerian War: A Research Note." French Historical Studies 9 (Fall 1975): 69–86.

———. The War Without a Name: France in Algeria, 1954–1962. New York: Knopf, 1980.

El Tayeb, Salah El Din El Zein. The National Ideology of Radical Algerians and the Formation of the FLN, 1924–1954. Durham: Center for Middle Eastern and Islamic Studies, 1987.

Taylor, Charles. Hegel. New York: Cambridge University Press, 1975.

———. Multiculturalism and the "Politics of Recognition." Princeton NJ: Princeton University Press, 1992.

———. Sources of Self: The Making of the Modern Identity. Cambridge MA: Harvard University Press, 1992.

Theunissen, Michael. The Other: Studies in the Social Ontology of Husserl, Heidegger, Sartre, and Buber. Cambridge MA: MIT Press, 1984.

Thomas, Martin. "The Dilemmas of an Ally of France: Britain's Policy Towards the Algerian Rebellion, 1954–1962." Journal of Imperial and Commonwealth History 23, no. 1 (January 1995): 129–54.

———. The French Empire at War, 1940–45. New York: Manchester University Press, 1988.

Thompson, Elizabeth. Colonial Citizens: Republican Rights, Paternal Privilege, and Gender in French Syria and Lebanon. New York: Columbia University Press, 2000.

Tocqueville, Alexis de. De la Colonie en Algérie. Paris: Complexe, 1988.

Todd, Olivier. Albert Camus: A Life. New York: Knopf, 1997.

Todorov, Tzvetan. On Human Diversity: Nationalism, Racism, and Exoticism in French Thought. Cambridge MA: Harvard University Press, 1993.

Tomlinson, Gary. Music in Renaissance Magic: Toward a Historiography of Others. Chicago: University of Chicago Press, 1994.

Toumi, Alek Baylee. Maghreb Diverse: Langue française, langues parlées, littératures et *représentations des Maghrébins, à partir d'Albert Memmi et de Kateb Yacine.* New York: Peter Lang , 2003.

Ulloa, Marie-Pierre. *Francis Jeanson, un itinéraire d'engagement (1940–1962).* Mémoire présenté pour le DEA "Histoire du XX ᴱᴹᴱ siècle." Institut d'Études Politiques de Paris Cycle Supérieur d'Histoire du XX ᴱᴹᴱ Siècle, 1997.

Ungar, Steven, and Tom Conley, eds. *Identity Papers: Contested Nationhood in Twentieth-Century France.* Minneapolis: University of Minnesota Press, 1996.

Van Dyke, Stuart Hope Jr. "French Settler Politics During the Algerian War, 1954–1958." PhD diss., University of Chicago, 1980.

Van Zanten, Agnès. "Schooling Immigrants in France in the 1990s: Success or Failure of Republican Model of Integration?" *Anthropology and Education Quarterly* 28, no. 3 (1997): 351–74.

Venner, Fiammetta. "Le Militantisme féminin d'extrême droite: Une autre manière d'être féministe"? *French Society and Politics* 11 (Spring 1993): 33–54.

Vidal-Naquet, Pierre. "La Juste et la patrie. Une française au secours de l'Algérie." *Esprit* 261 (February 2000): 140–47.

Vinen, Richard. *France, 1934–70.* New York: St. Martin's Press, 1996.

Voll, John. *Islam: Continuity and Change in the Modern World.* 2nd ed. Syracuse NY: Syracuse University Press, 1994.

Wall, Irwin M. *France, the United States, and the Algerian War.* Berkeley: University of California Press, 2001.

White, Edmund. *Genet: A Biography.* New York: Vintage, 1994.

Whiteside, Kerry H. *Merleau-Ponty and the Foundation of an Existential Politics.* Princeton NJ: Princeton University Press, 1988.

Willis, Michael. *The Islamist Challenge in Algeria: A Political History.* New York: NYU Press, 1996.

Wright, Gordon. "The Dreyfus Echo: Justice and Politics in the Fourth Republic." *Yale Review* 48, no. 3 (Spring 1957): 354–73.

Wood, Nancy. *Vectors of Memory: Legacies of Trauma in Postwar Europe.* New York: Berg, 1999.

Yansané, Aguibou. *Decolonization in West African States with French Colonial Legacy.* Cambridge: Schenkman, 1984.

Young, Ian. *The Private Life of Islam: An Algerian Diary.* London: Pimlico, 1991.

Young, Robert. *Colonial Desire: Hybridity in Theory, Culture, and Race.* New York: Routledge, 1995.

———. *White Mythologies: Writing History in the West.* London: Routledge, 1990.

Printed in the United States
117516LV00001B/247-249/A